Arata
THE LEGEND
10

WE ARE MAN, BORN OF HEAVEN AND EARTH,
MOON AND SUN AND EVERYTHING UNDER THEM.

EYES, EARS, NOSE, TONGUE, BODY, MIND...

PURITY WILL PIERCE EVIL AND
OPEN UP THE WORLD OF DARKNESS.

ALL LIFE WILL BE REBORN AND INVIGORATED.

APPEAR NOW.

D0029865

STORY & ART BY
YUU WATASE

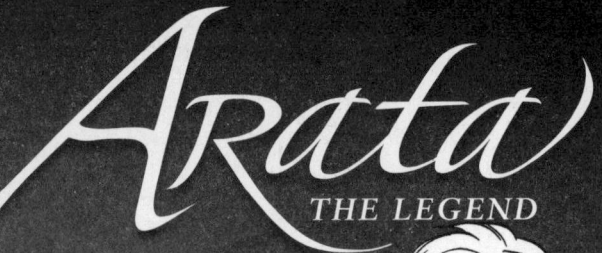

Arata THE LEGEND

CHARACTERS

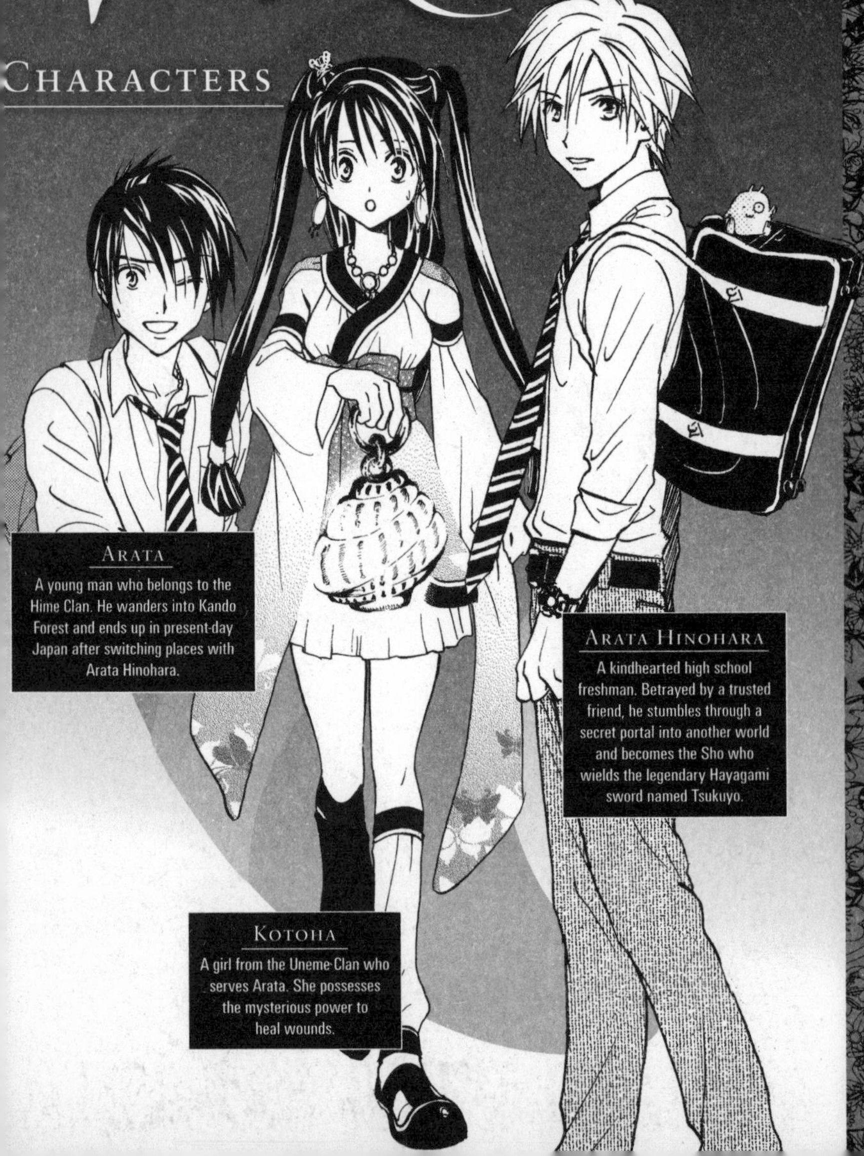

ARATA

A young man who belongs to the Hime Clan. He wanders into Kando Forest and ends up in present-day Japan after switching places with Arata Hinohara.

ARATA HINOHARA

A kindhearted high school freshman. Betrayed by a trusted friend, he stumbles through a secret portal into another world and becomes the Sho who wields the legendary Hayagami sword named Tsukuyo.

KOTOHA

A girl from the Uneme Clan who serves Arata. She possesses the mysterious power to heal wounds.

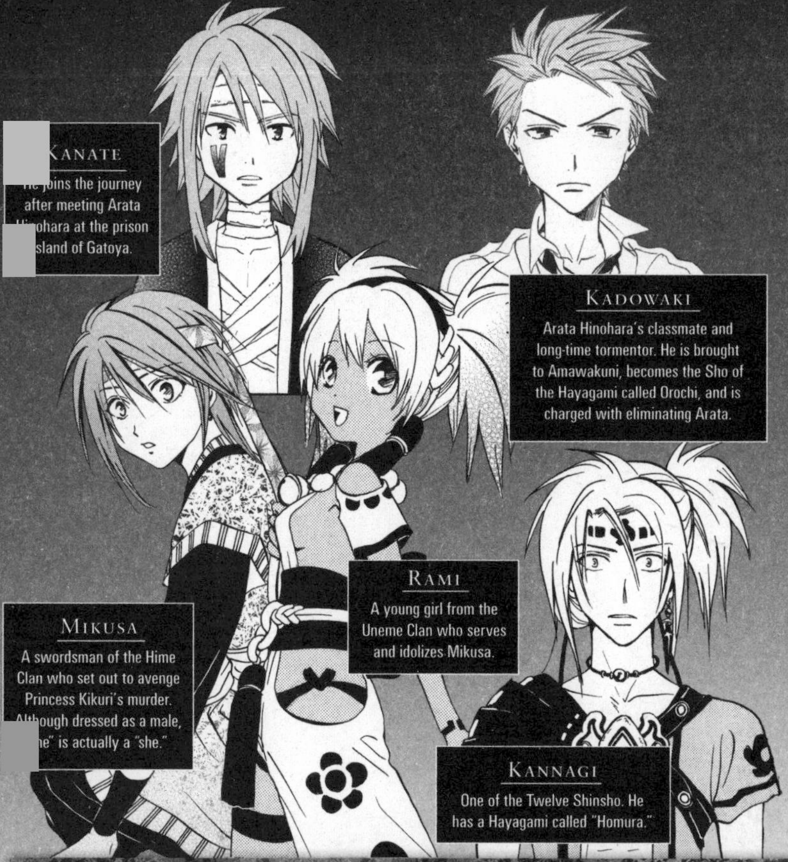
KANATE
He joins the journey after meeting Arata Hinohara at the prison island of Gatoya.
KADOWAKI
Arata Hinohara's classmate and long-time tormentor. He is brought to Amawakuni, becomes the Sho of the Hayagami called Orochi, and is charged with eliminating Arata.
RAMI
A young girl from the Uneme Clan who serves and idolizes Mikusa.
MIKUSA
A swordsman of the Hime Clan who set out to avenge Princess Kikuri's murder. Although dressed as a male, "he" is actually a "she."
KANNAGI
One of the Twelve Shinsho. He has a Hayagami called "Homura."

THE STORY THUS FAR

Betrayed by his best friend, Arata Hinohara—a high school student in present-day Japan—wanders through a portal into another world where he and his companions journey onward to deliver his Hayagami sword "Tsukuyo" to Princess Kikuri.

Hinohara infiltrates Kugura's palace and encounters Kadowaki, who has also come to raid Kugura's domain. Zokusho Eto confronts Kadowaki but is swallowed up by Kadowaki's sword, Orochi. When Kugura flies into a rage, Hinohara risks his life to protect him. Touched by Hinohara's kindness, Kugura willingly submits to him. Armed with the transformed mega-sword Tsukuyo, Hinohara uses its overwhelming power to repel Kadowaki. Witnessing this transformation, Mikusa is convinced that Hinohara is the reincarnation of the King of Hinowa and takes him to the hidden village of the Hime Clan.

10
Arata
THE LEGEND

CONTENTS

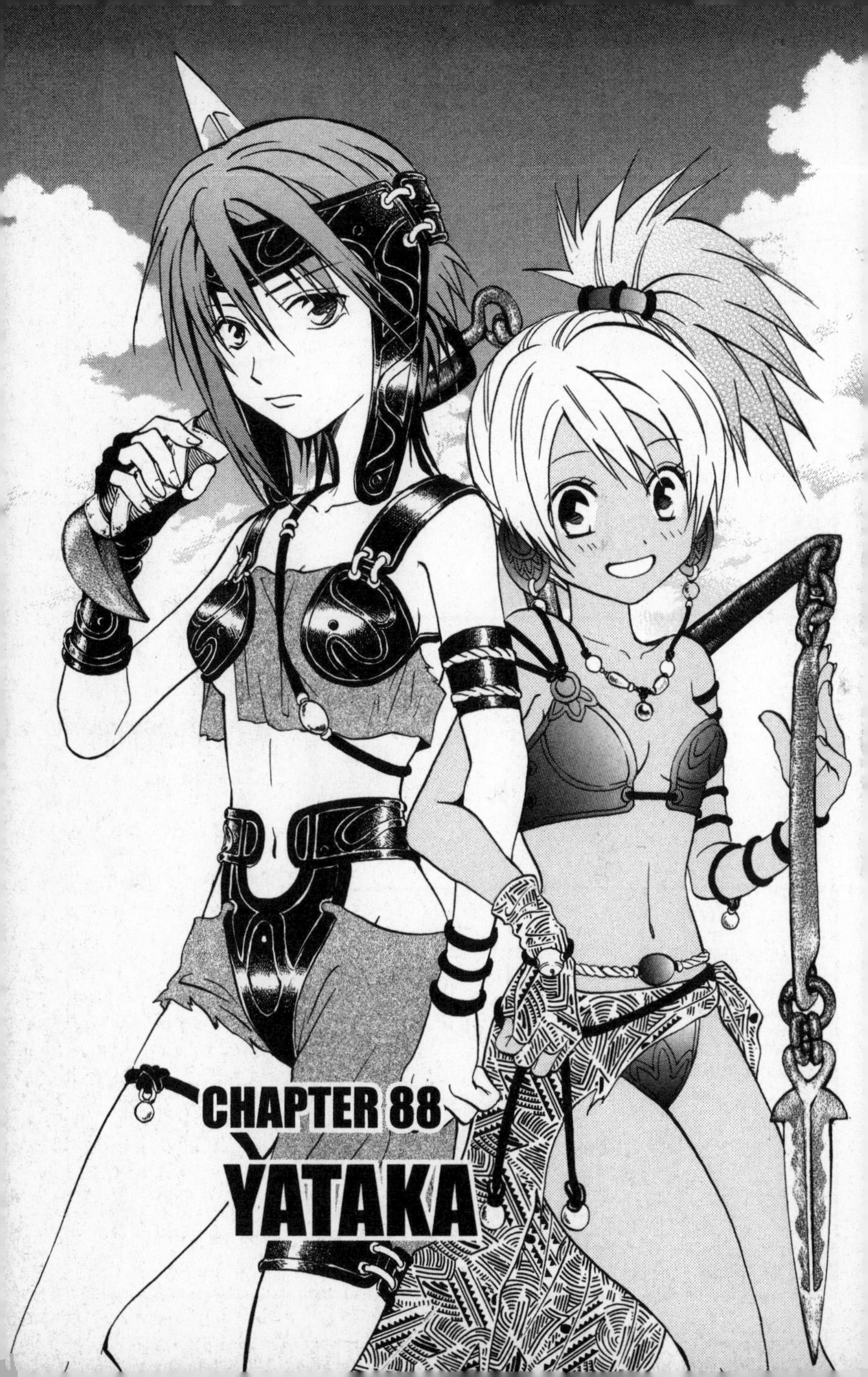
CHAPTER 88
ỲATAKA

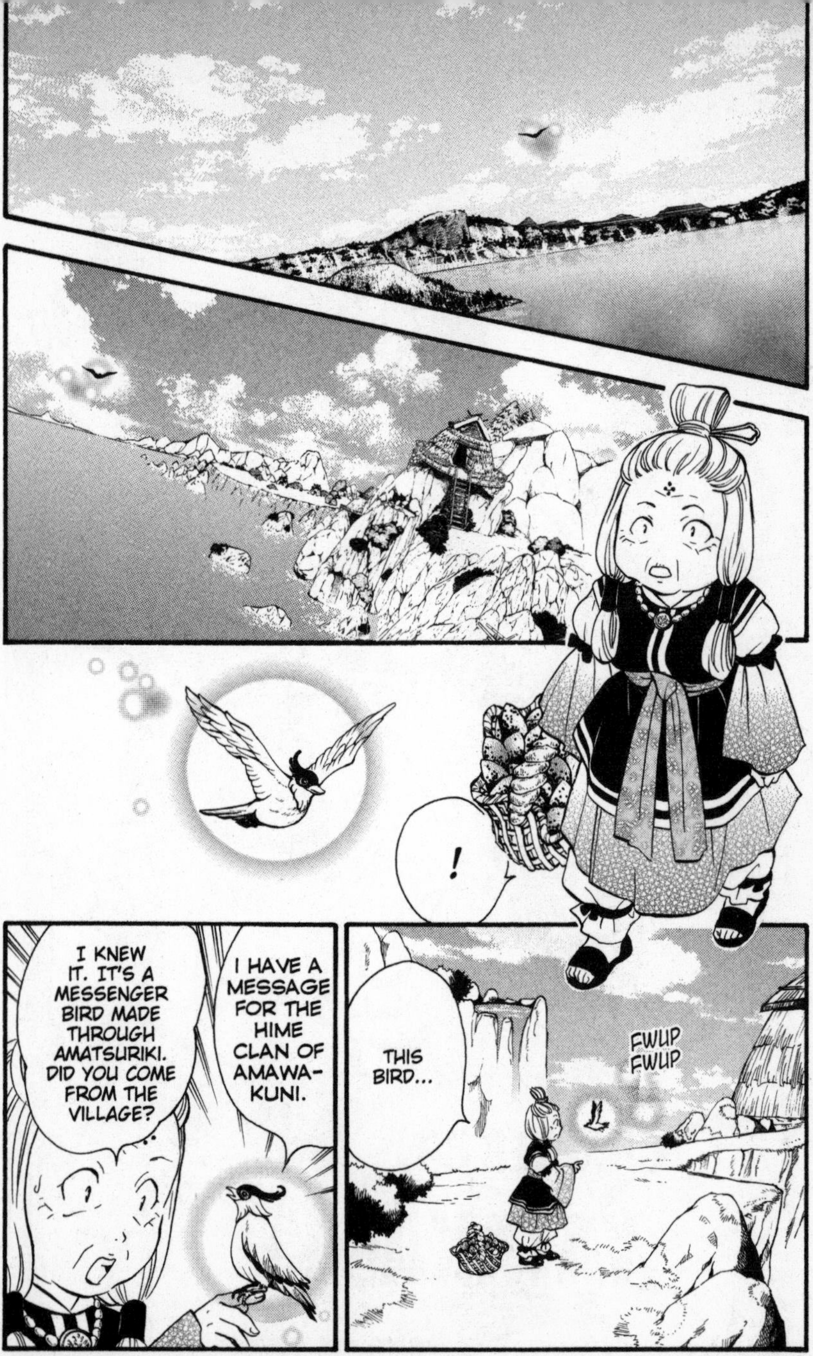
!
FWUP FWUP
THIS BIRD...
I HAVE A MESSAGE FOR THE HIME CLAN OF AMAWA-KUNI.
I KNEW IT. IT'S A MESSENGER BIRD MADE THROUGH AMATSURIKI. DID YOU COME FROM THE VILLAGE?

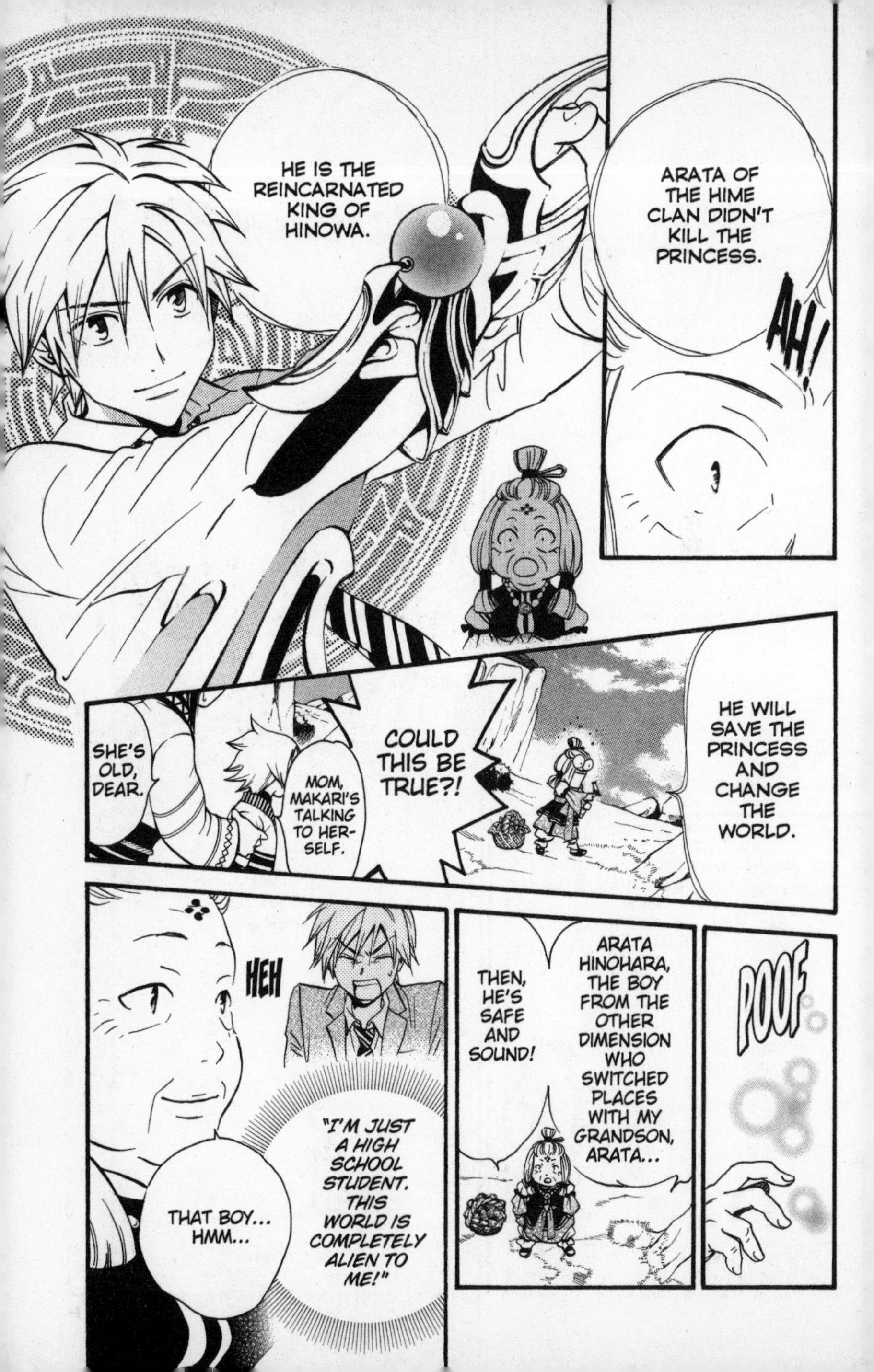
ARATA OF THE HIME CLAN DIDN'T KILL THE PRINCESS.
AH!
HE IS THE REINCARNATED KING OF HINOWA.
HE WILL SAVE THE PRINCESS AND CHANGE THE WORLD.
COULD THIS BE TRUE?!
MOM, MAKARI'S TALKING TO HER-SELF.
SHE'S OLD, DEAR.
POOF
ARATA HINOHARA, THE BOY FROM THE OTHER DIMENSION WHO SWITCHED PLACES WITH MY GRANDSON, ARATA...
THEN, HE'S SAFE AND SOUND!
HEH
"I'M JUST A HIGH SCHOOL STUDENT. THIS WORLD IS COMPLETELY ALIEN TO ME!"
THAT BOY... HMM...

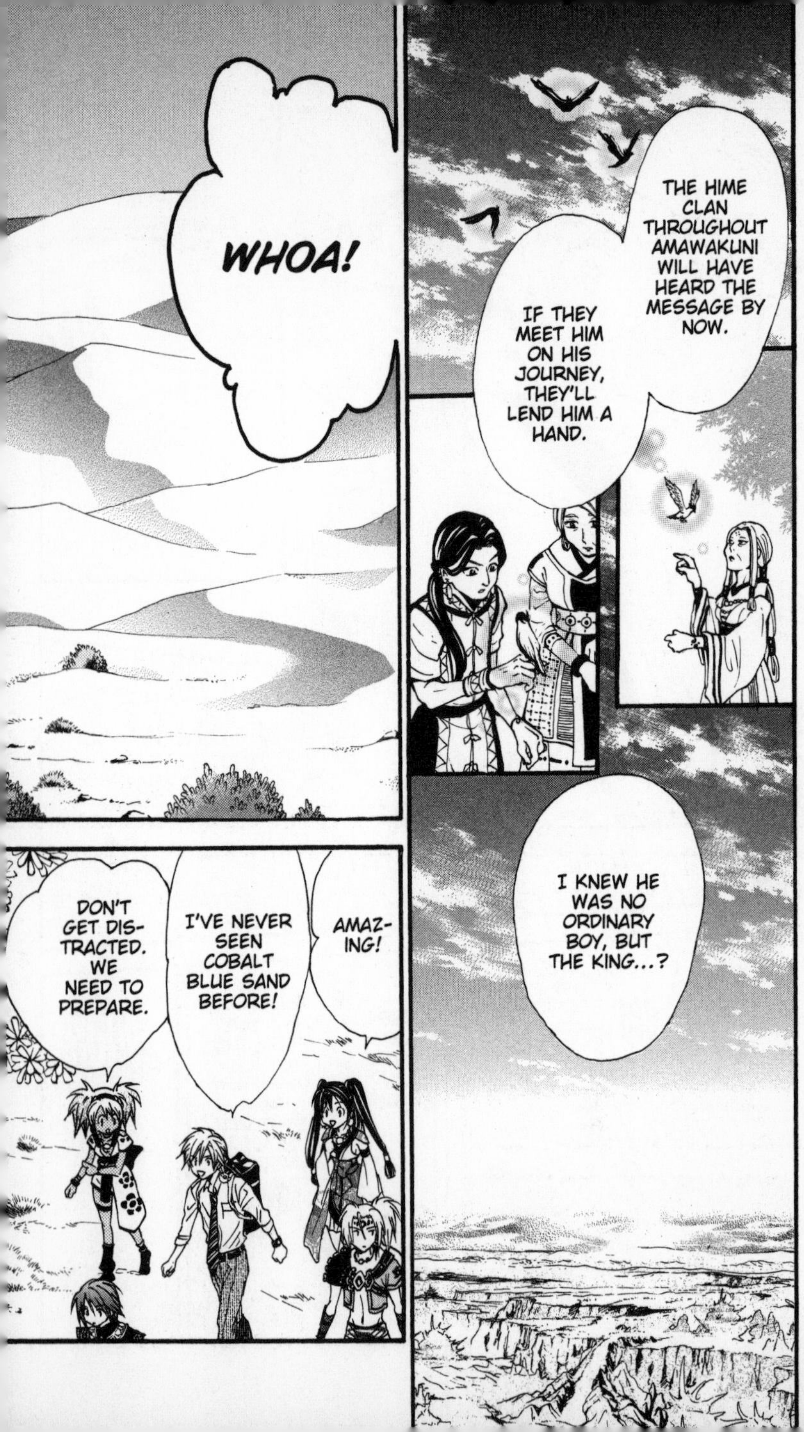
THE HIME CLAN THROUGHOUT AMAWAKUNI WILL HAVE HEARD THE MESSAGE BY NOW.
IF THEY MEET HIM ON HIS JOURNEY, THEY'LL LEND HIM A HAND.
I KNEW HE WAS NO ORDINARY BOY, BUT THE KING...?
WHOA!
AMAZ-ING!
I'VE NEVER SEEN COBALT BLUE SAND BEFORE!
DON'T GET DIS-TRACTED. WE NEED TO PREPARE.

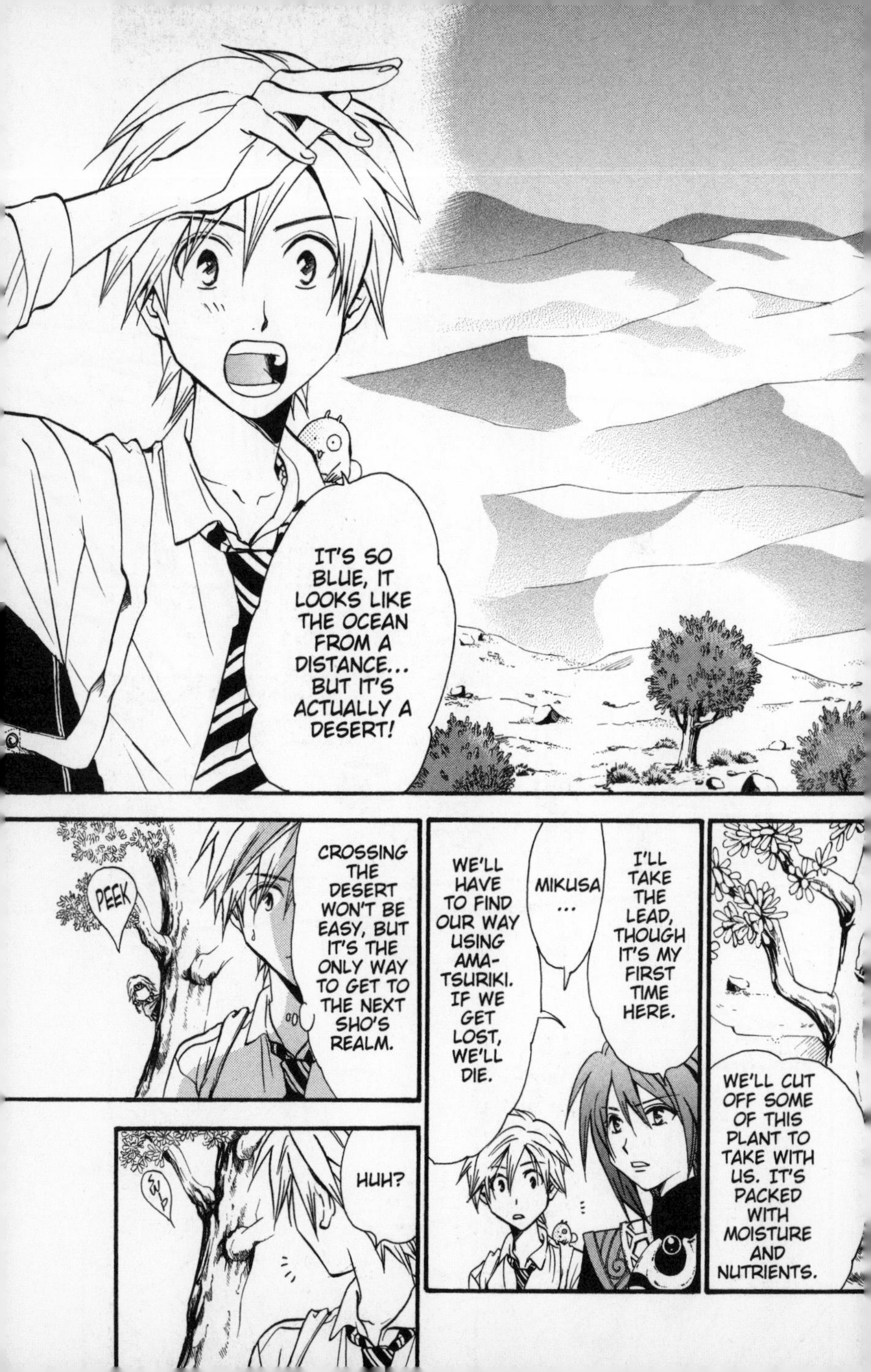
IT'S SO BLUE, IT LOOKS LIKE THE OCEAN FROM A DISTANCE... BUT IT'S ACTUALLY A DESERT!
WE'LL CUT OFF SOME OF THIS PLANT TO TAKE WITH US. IT'S PACKED WITH MOISTURE AND NUTRIENTS.
I'LL TAKE THE LEAD, THOUGH IT'S MY FIRST TIME HERE.
MIKUSA ...
WE'LL HAVE TO FIND OUR WAY USING AMA-TSURIKI. IF WE GET LOST, WE'LL DIE.
CROSSING THE DESERT WON'T BE EASY, BUT IT'S THE ONLY WAY TO GET TO THE NEXT SHO'S REALM.
PEEK
HUH?
SWIP

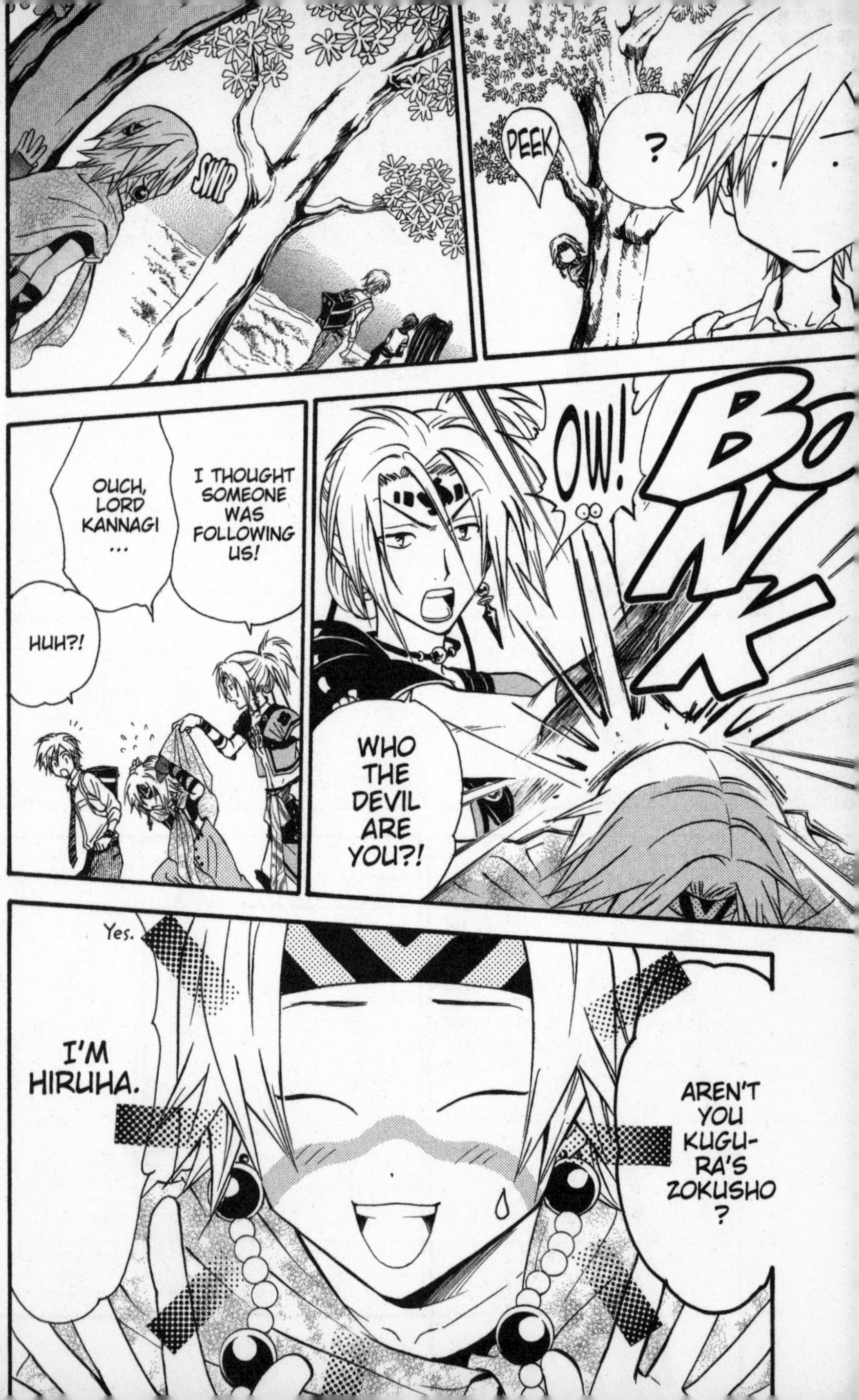
PEEK
?
SWP
BONK
OW!
WHO THE DEVIL ARE YOU?!
I THOUGHT SOMEONE WAS FOLLOWING US!
OUCH, LORD KANNAGI...
HUH?!
AREN'T YOU KUGURA'S ZOKUSHO?
Yes.
I'M HIRUHA.

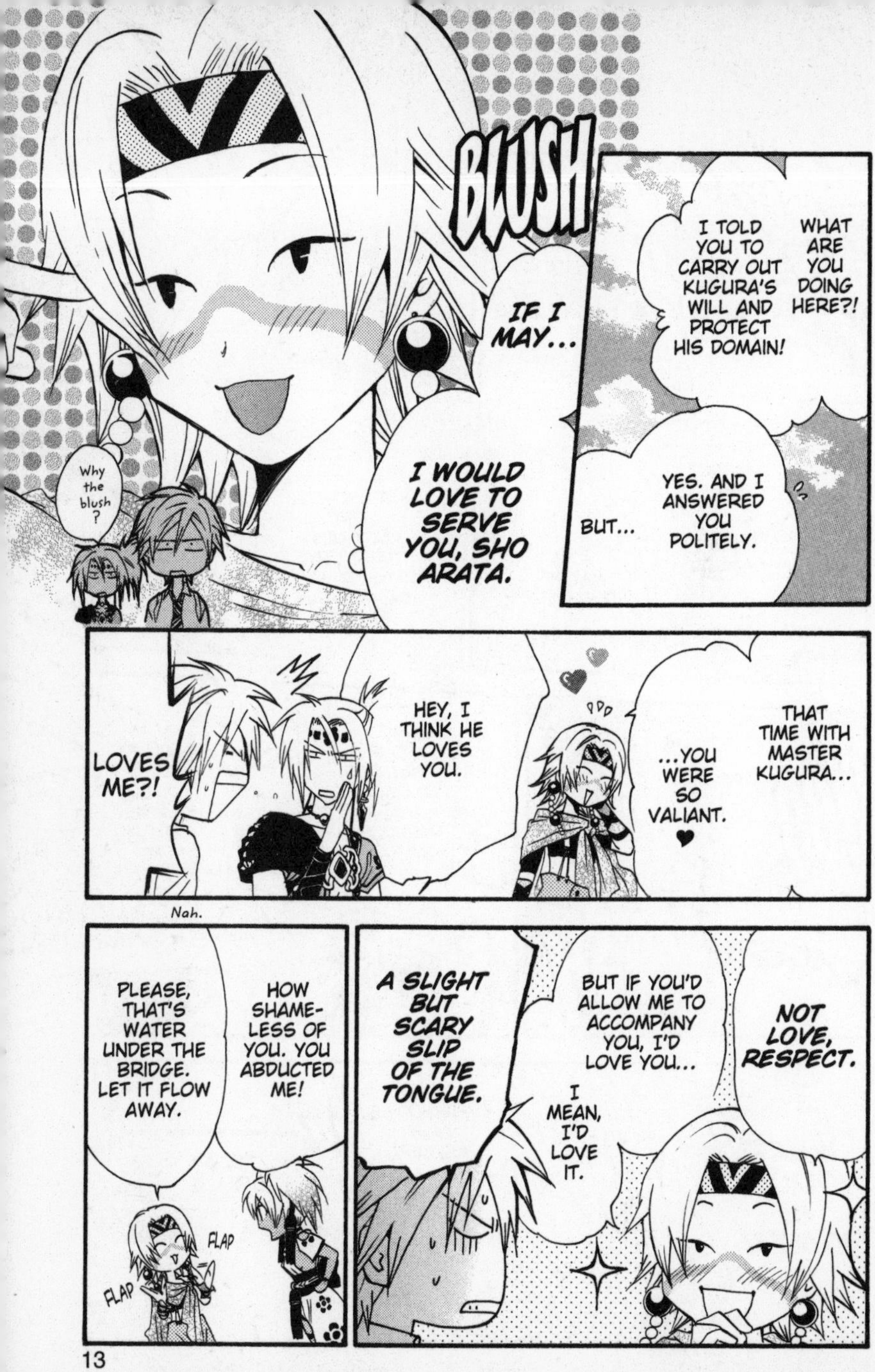
WHAT ARE YOU DOING HERE?!
I TOLD YOU TO CARRY OUT KUGURA'S WILL AND PROTECT HIS DOMAIN!
YES. AND I ANSWERED YOU POLITELY.
BUT...
BLUSH
IF I MAY...
I WOULD LOVE TO SERVE YOU, SHO ARATA.
Why the blush?
THAT TIME WITH MASTER KUGURA...
...YOU WERE SO VALIANT. ♥
HEY, I THINK HE LOVES YOU.
LOVES ME?!
Nah.
NOT LOVE, RESPECT.
BUT IF YOU'D ALLOW ME TO ACCOMPANY YOU, I'D LOVE YOU...
I MEAN, I'D LOVE IT.
A SLIGHT BUT SCARY SLIP OF THE TONGUE.
HOW SHAME-LESS OF YOU. YOU ABDUCTED ME!
PLEASE, THAT'S WATER UNDER THE BRIDGE. LET IT FLOW AWAY.
FLAP
FLAP

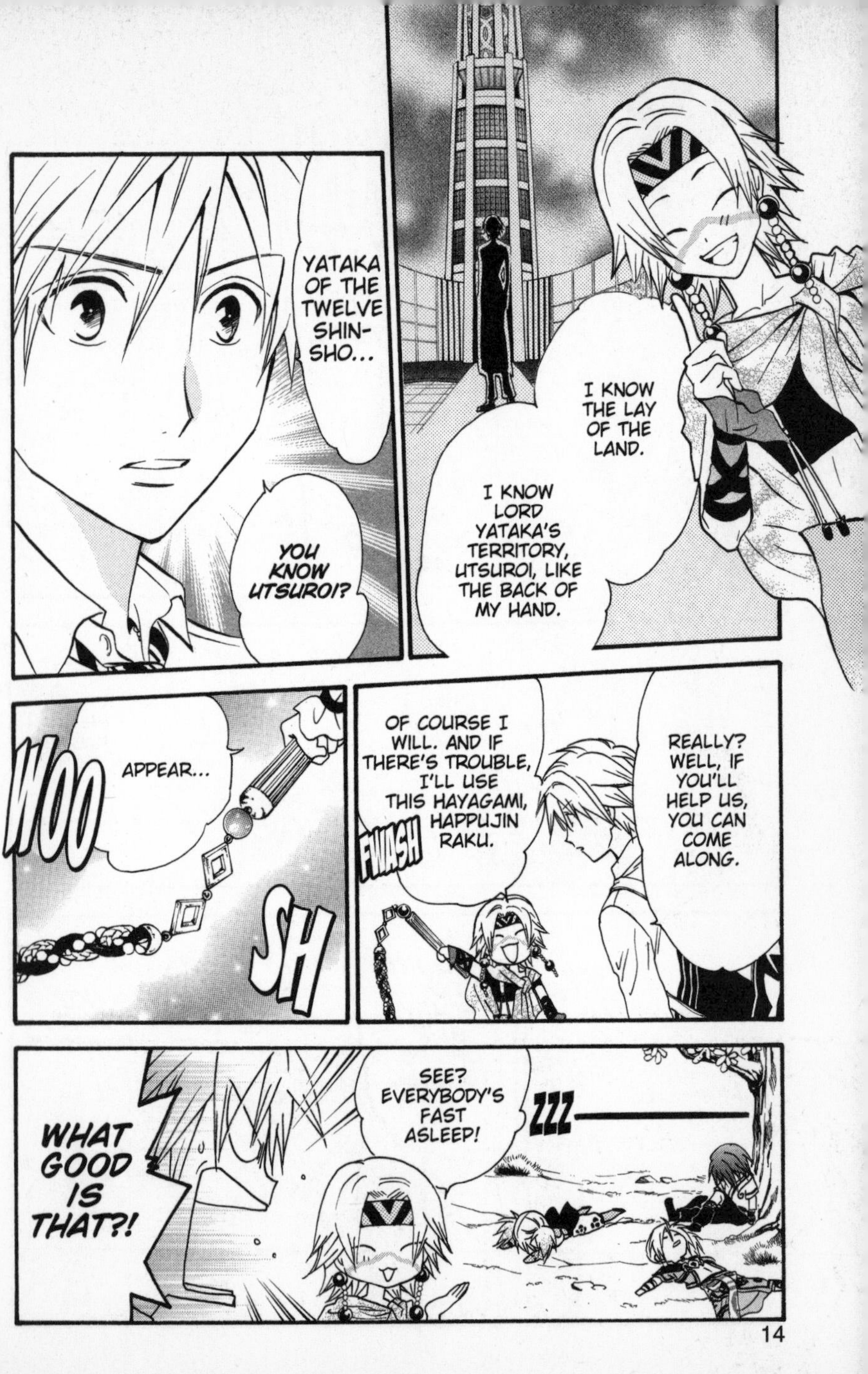
I KNOW THE LAY OF THE LAND.
I KNOW LORD YATAKA'S TERRITORY, UTSUROI, LIKE THE BACK OF MY HAND.
YATAKA OF THE TWELVE SHIN-SHO...
YOU KNOW UTSUROI?
REALLY? WELL, IF YOU'LL HELP US, YOU CAN COME ALONG.
OF COURSE I WILL. AND IF THERE'S TROUBLE, I'LL USE THIS HAYAGAMI, HAPPUJIN RAKU.
FWASH
WOOSH
APPEAR...
ZZZ—
SEE? EVERYBODY'S FAST ASLEEP!
WHAT GOOD IS THAT?!

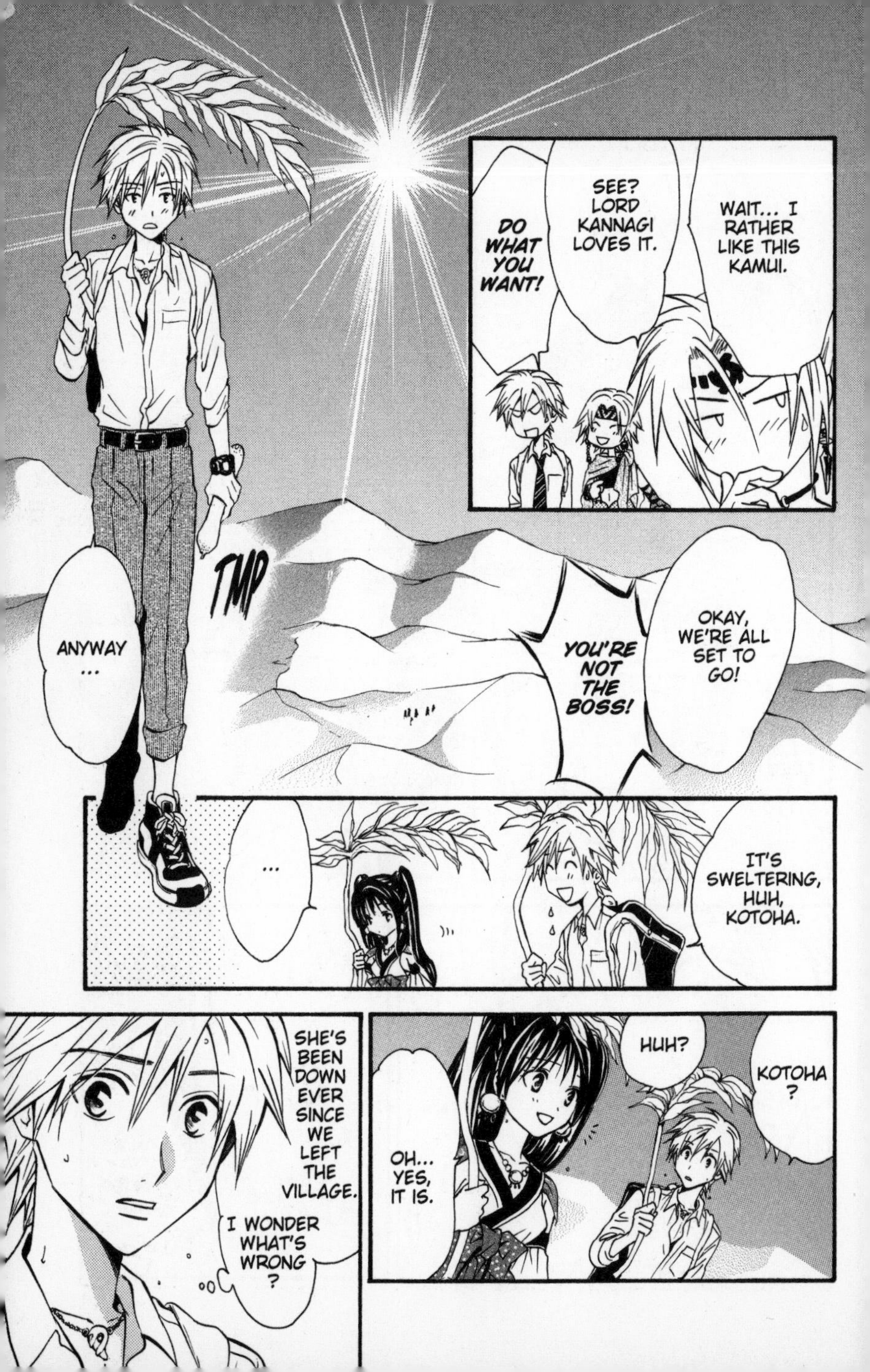
WAIT... I RATHER LIKE THIS KAMUI.
SEE? LORD KANNAGI LOVES IT.
DO WHAT YOU WANT!
OKAY, WE'RE ALL SET TO GO!
YOU'RE NOT THE BOSS!
TMP
ANYWAY...
IT'S SWELTERING, HUH, KOTOHA.
...
KOTOHA?
HUH?
OH... YES, IT IS.
SHE'S BEEN DOWN EVER SINCE WE LEFT THE VILLAGE.
I WONDER WHAT'S WRONG?

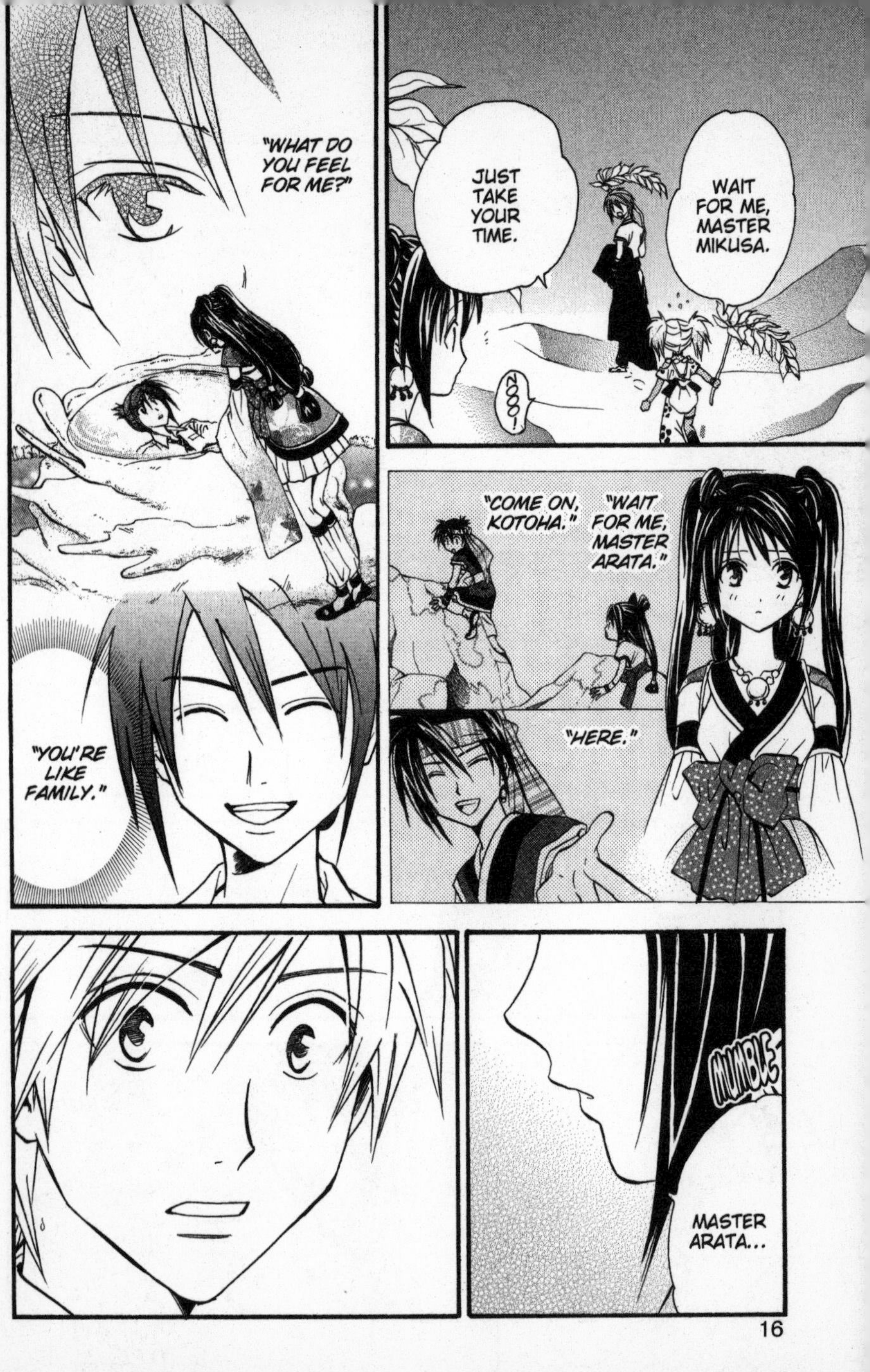
WAIT FOR ME, MASTER MIKUSA.
JUST TAKE YOUR TIME.
NOOO!
"WAIT FOR ME, MASTER ARATA."
"COME ON, KOTOHA."
"HERE."
"WHAT DO YOU FEEL FOR ME?"
"YOU'RE LIKE FAMILY."
MUMBLE
MASTER ARATA...

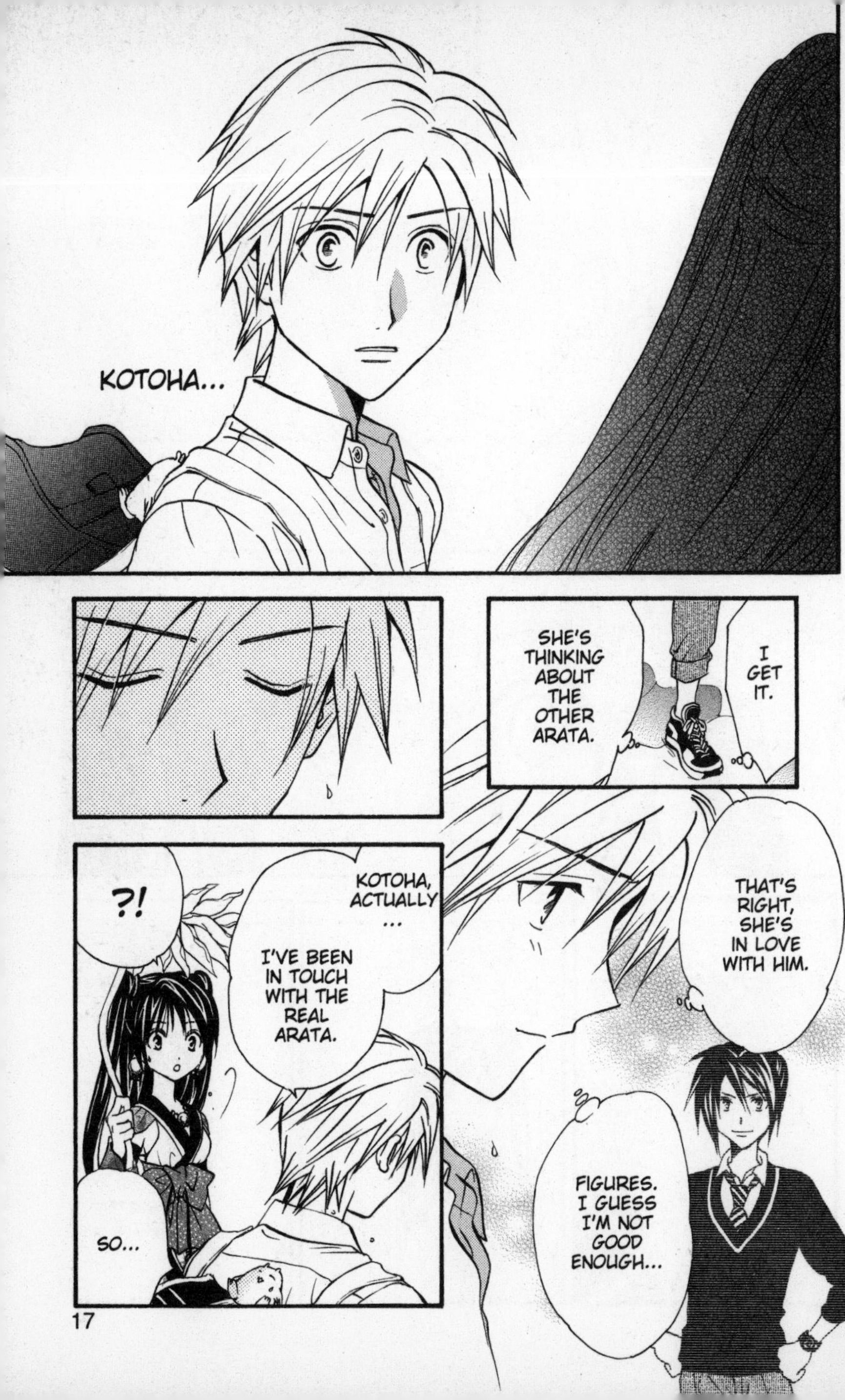
KOTOHA...
I GET IT.
SHE'S THINKING ABOUT THE OTHER ARATA.
THAT'S RIGHT, SHE'S IN LOVE WITH HIM.
FIGURES. I GUESS I'M NOT GOOD ENOUGH...
KOTOHA, ACTUALLY...
I'VE BEEN IN TOUCH WITH THE REAL ARATA.
?!
SO...

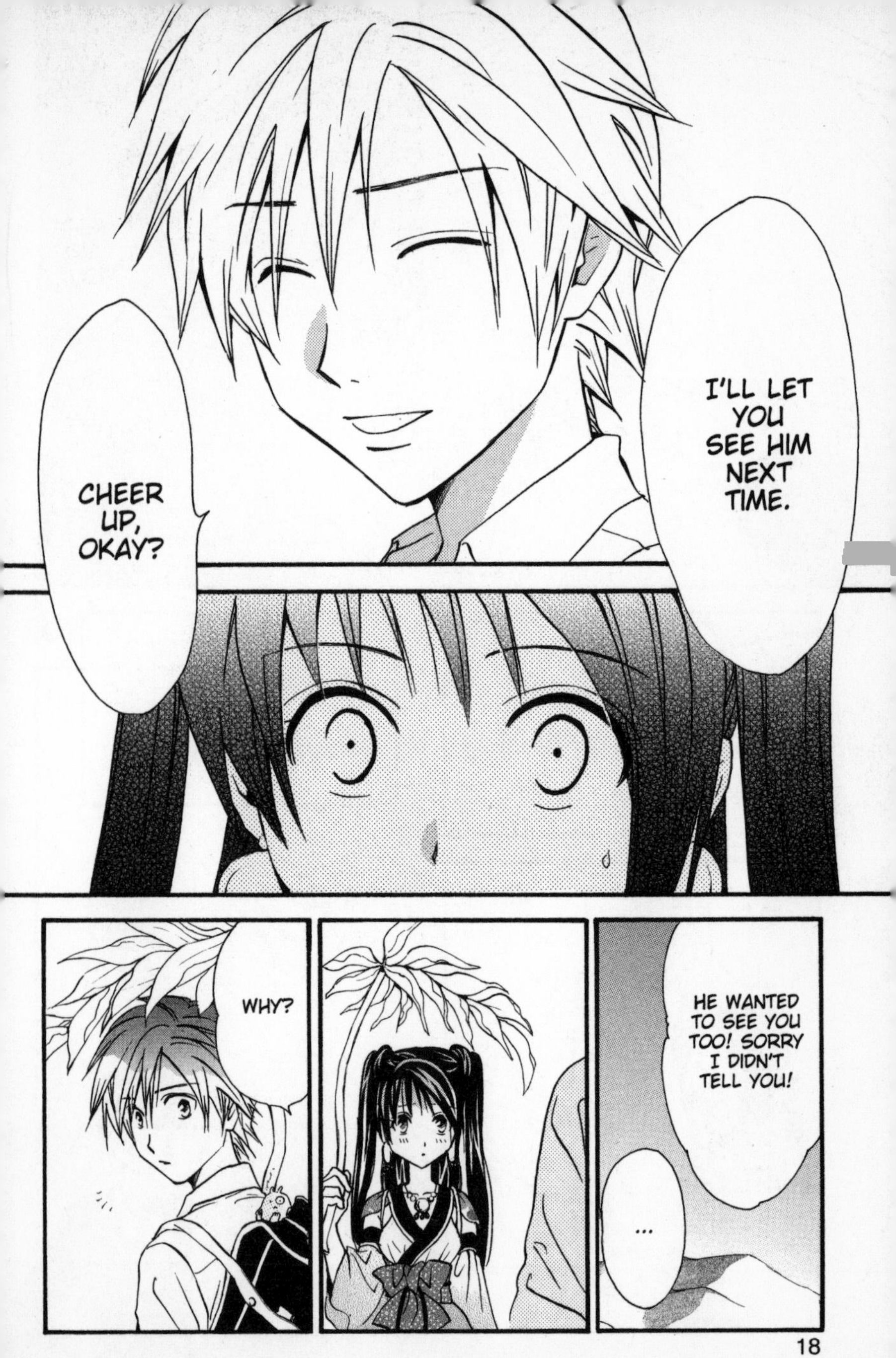
I'LL LET YOU SEE HIM NEXT TIME.
CHEER UP, OKAY?
HE WANTED TO SEE YOU TOO! SORRY I DIDN'T TELL YOU!
...
WHY?

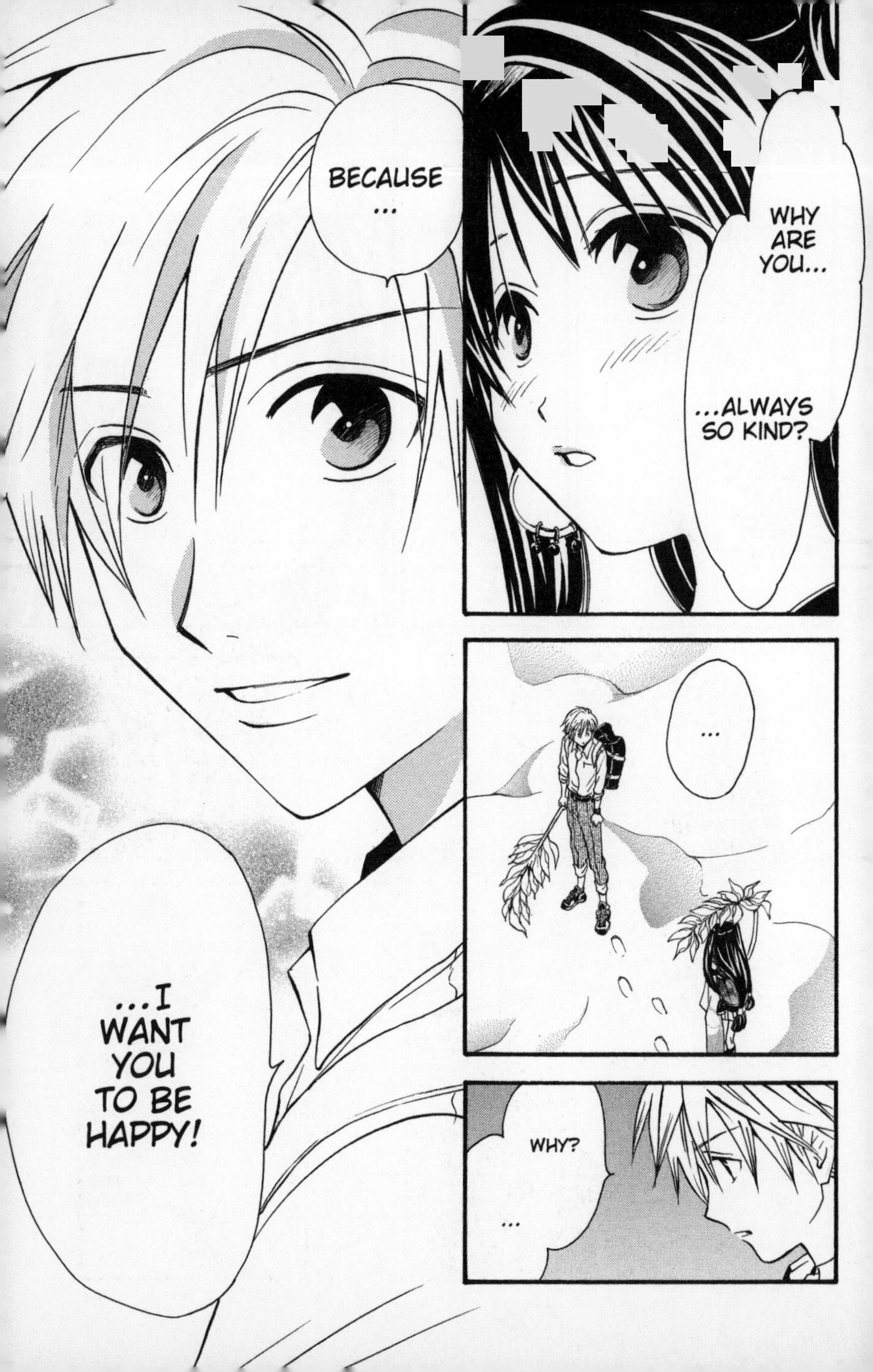
WHY ARE YOU...
...ALWAYS SO KIND?
...
WHY?
...
BECAUSE ...
...I WANT YOU TO BE HAPPY!

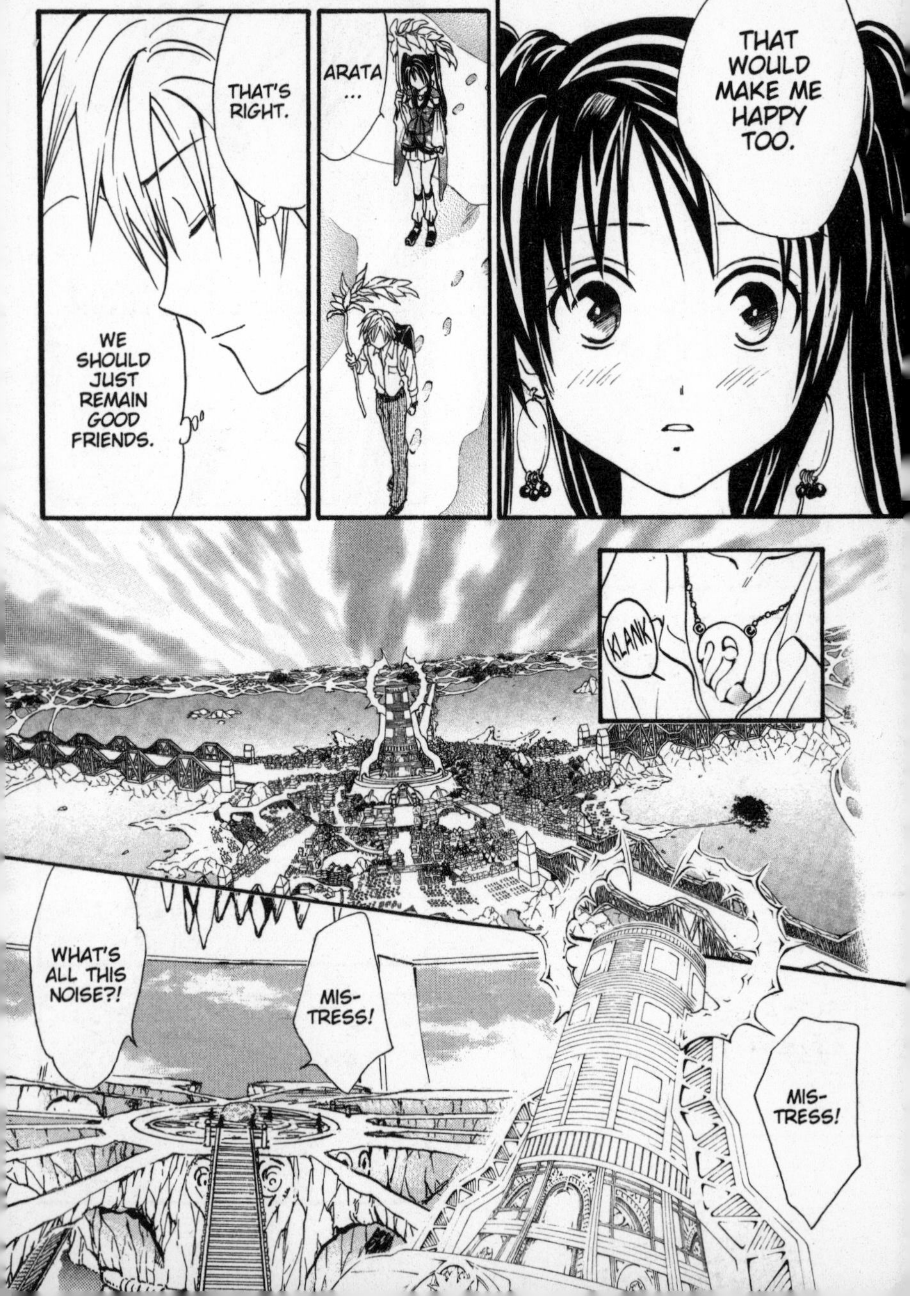
THAT WOULD MAKE ME HAPPY TOO.
ARATA ...
THAT'S RIGHT.
WE SHOULD JUST REMAIN GOOD FRIENDS.
KLANK
MIS-TRESS!
MIS-TRESS!
WHAT'S ALL THIS NOISE?!

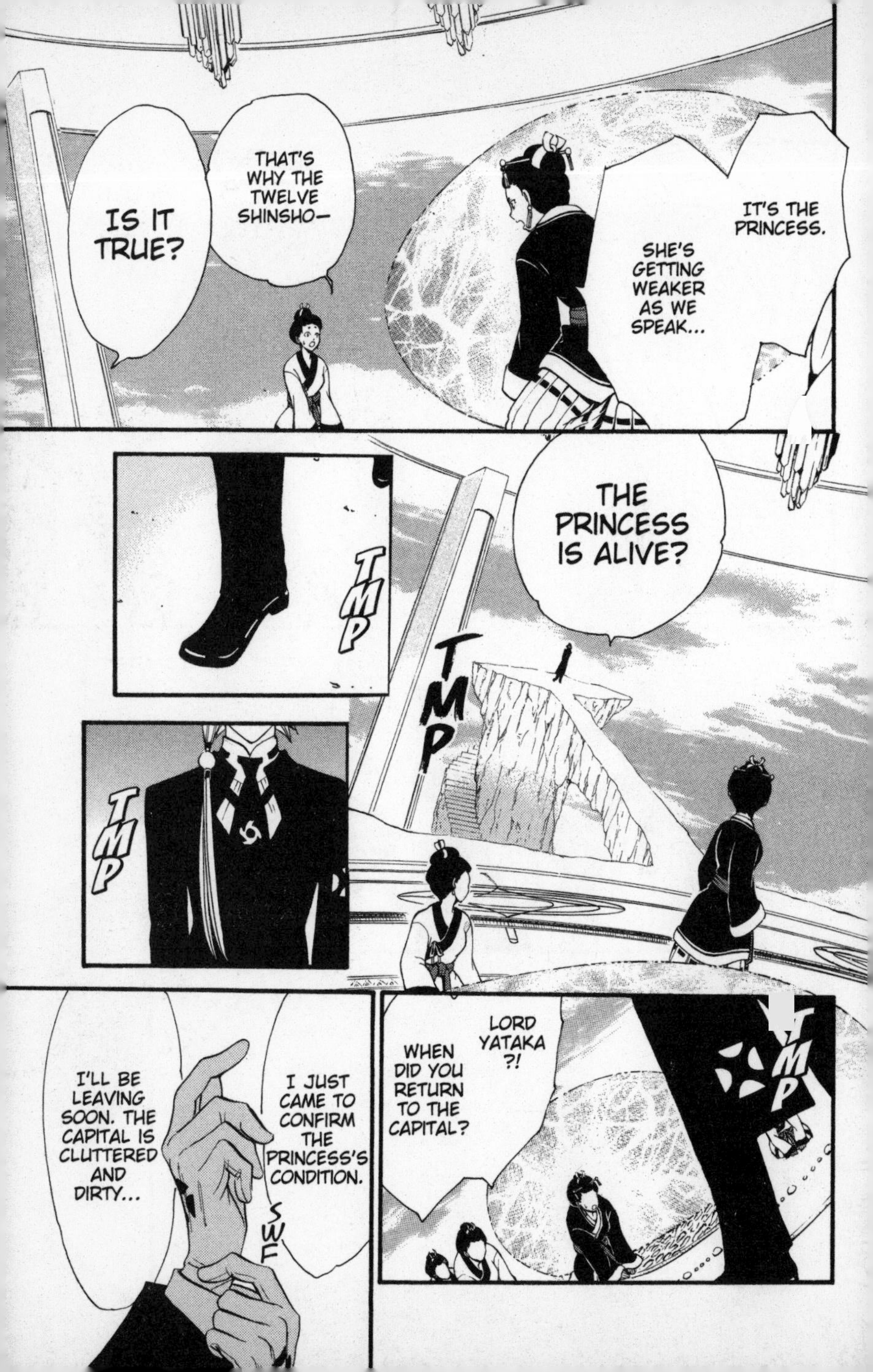
IT'S THE PRINCESS.
SHE'S GETTING WEAKER AS WE SPEAK...
THAT'S WHY THE TWELVE SHINSHO—
IS IT TRUE?
THE PRINCESS IS ALIVE?
TMP
TMP
TMP
TMP
LORD YATAKA?!
WHEN DID YOU RETURN TO THE CAPITAL?
I JUST CAME TO CONFIRM THE PRINCESS'S CONDITION.
SWF
I'LL BE LEAVING SOON. THE CAPITAL IS CLUTTERED AND DIRTY...

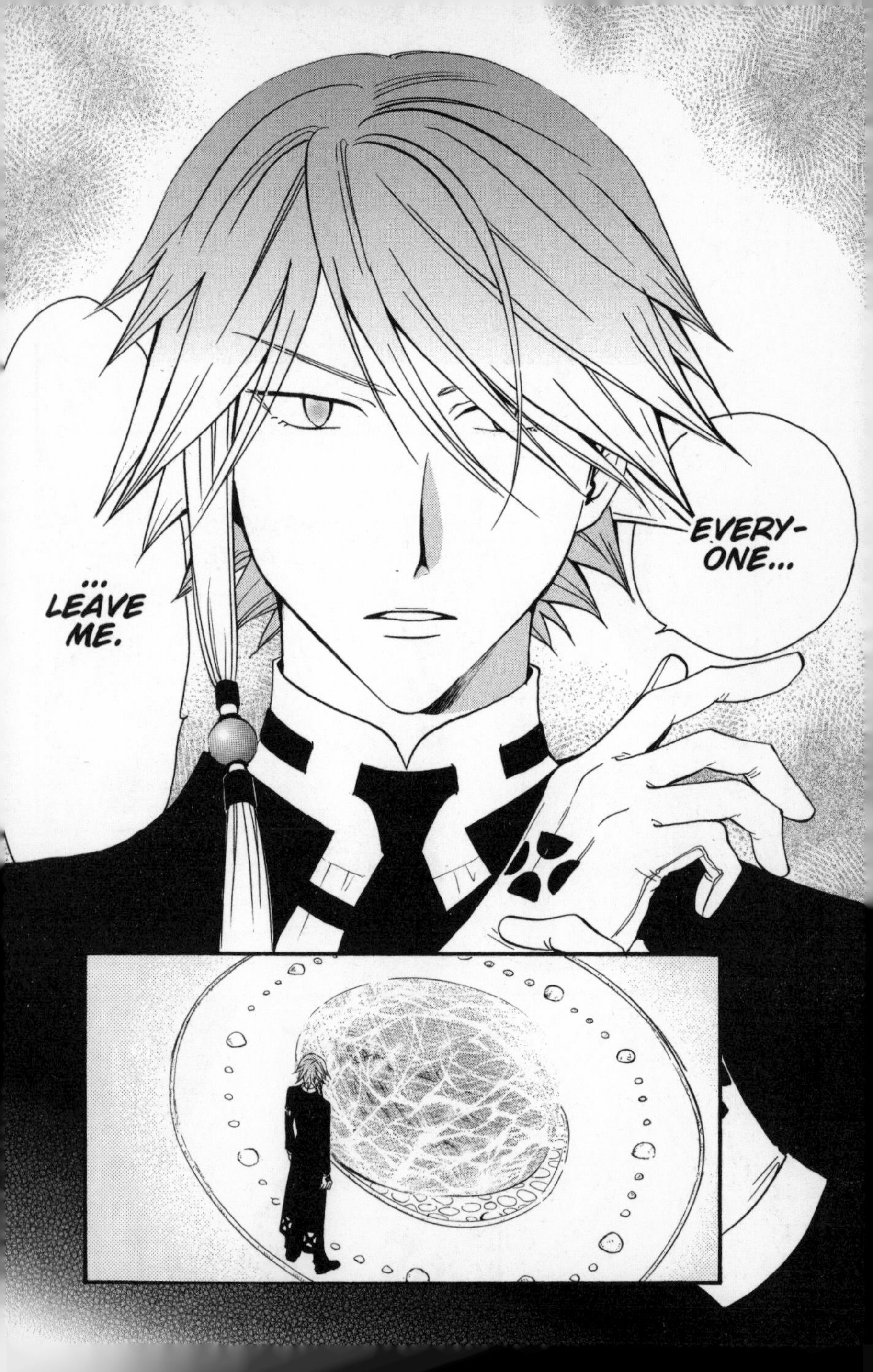
EVERY-ONE...
...LEAVE ME.

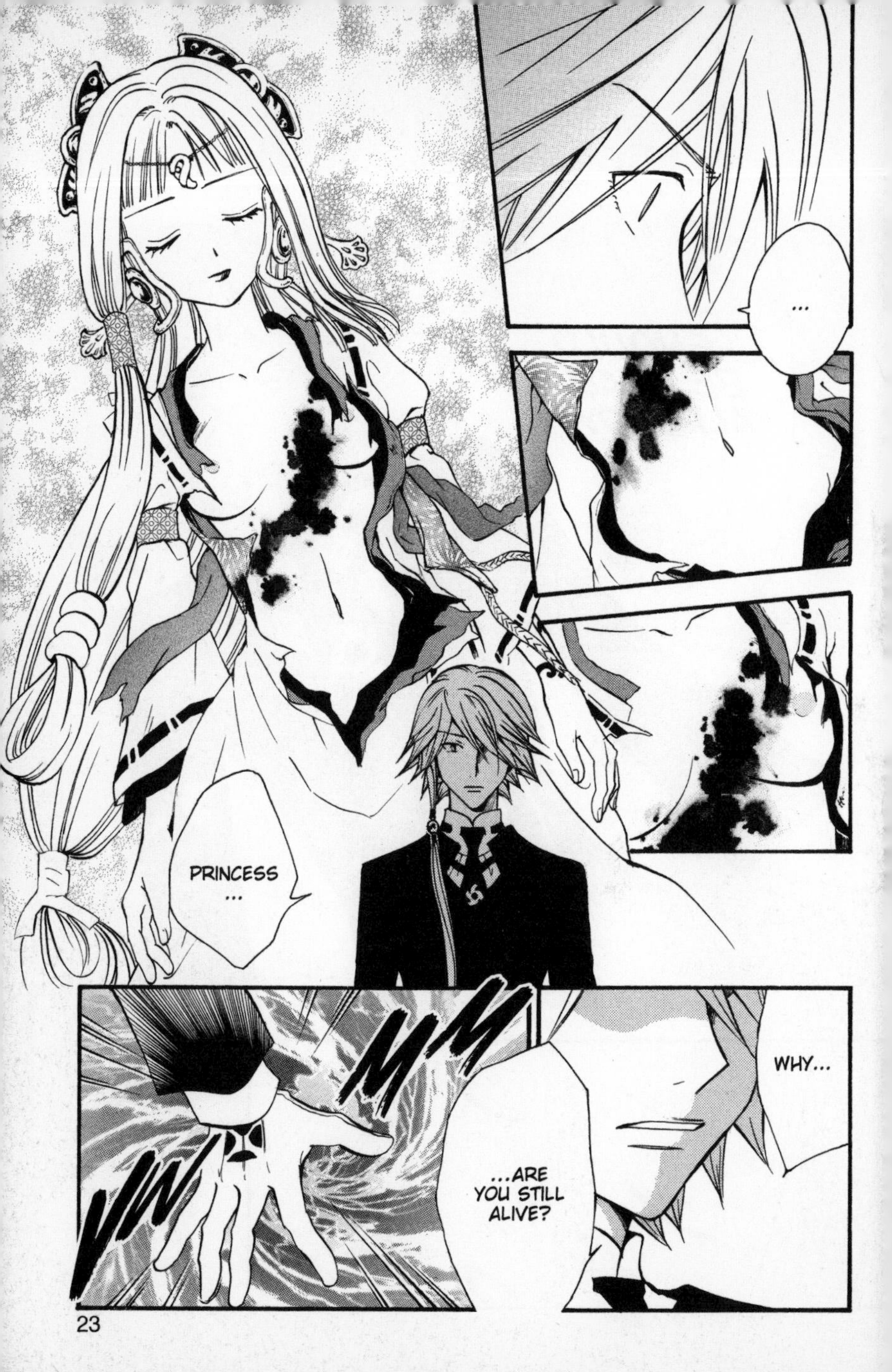
...
PRINCESS ...
WHY...
...ARE YOU STILL ALIVE?

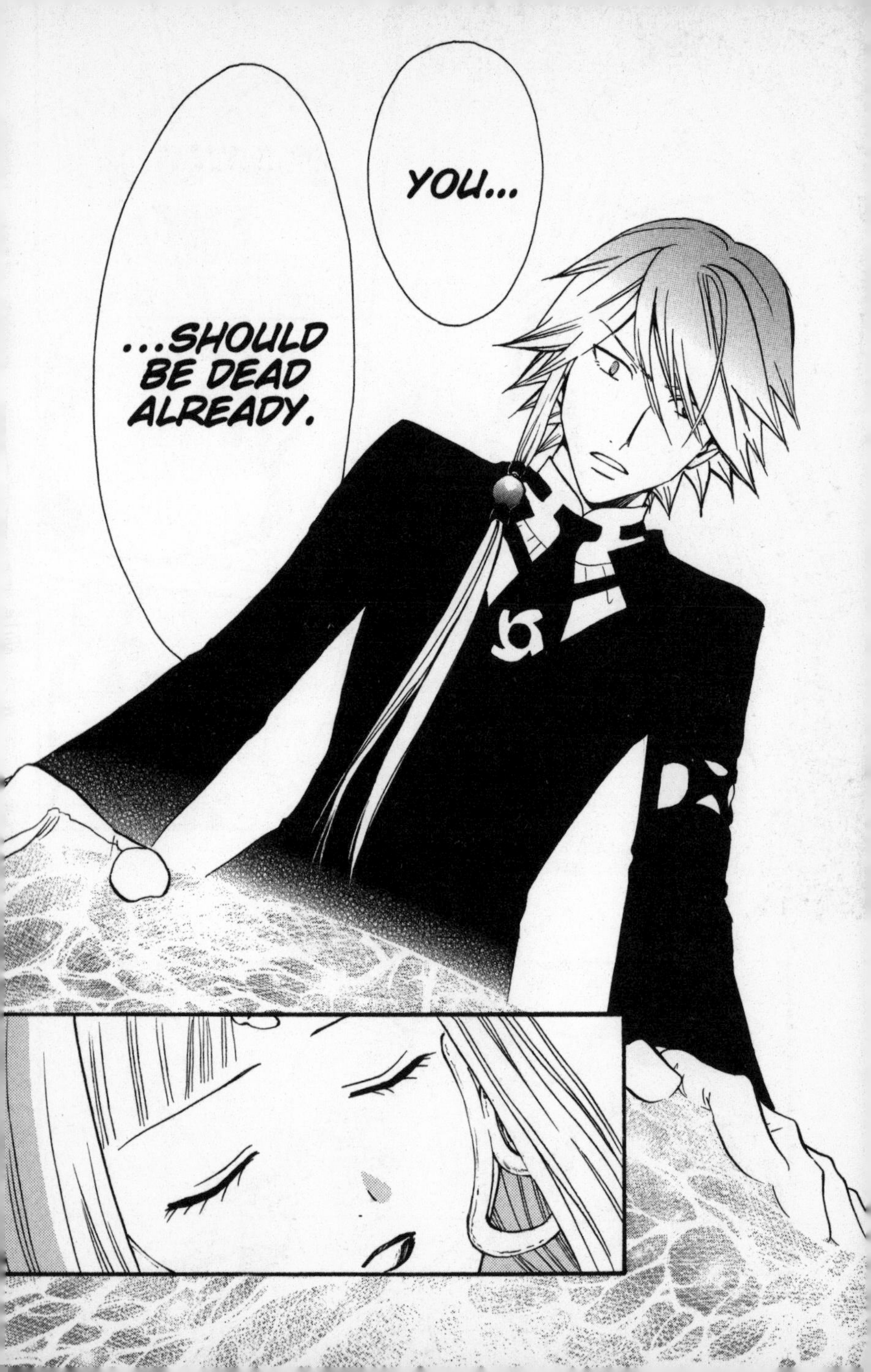
YOU...
...SHOULD BE DEAD ALREADY.

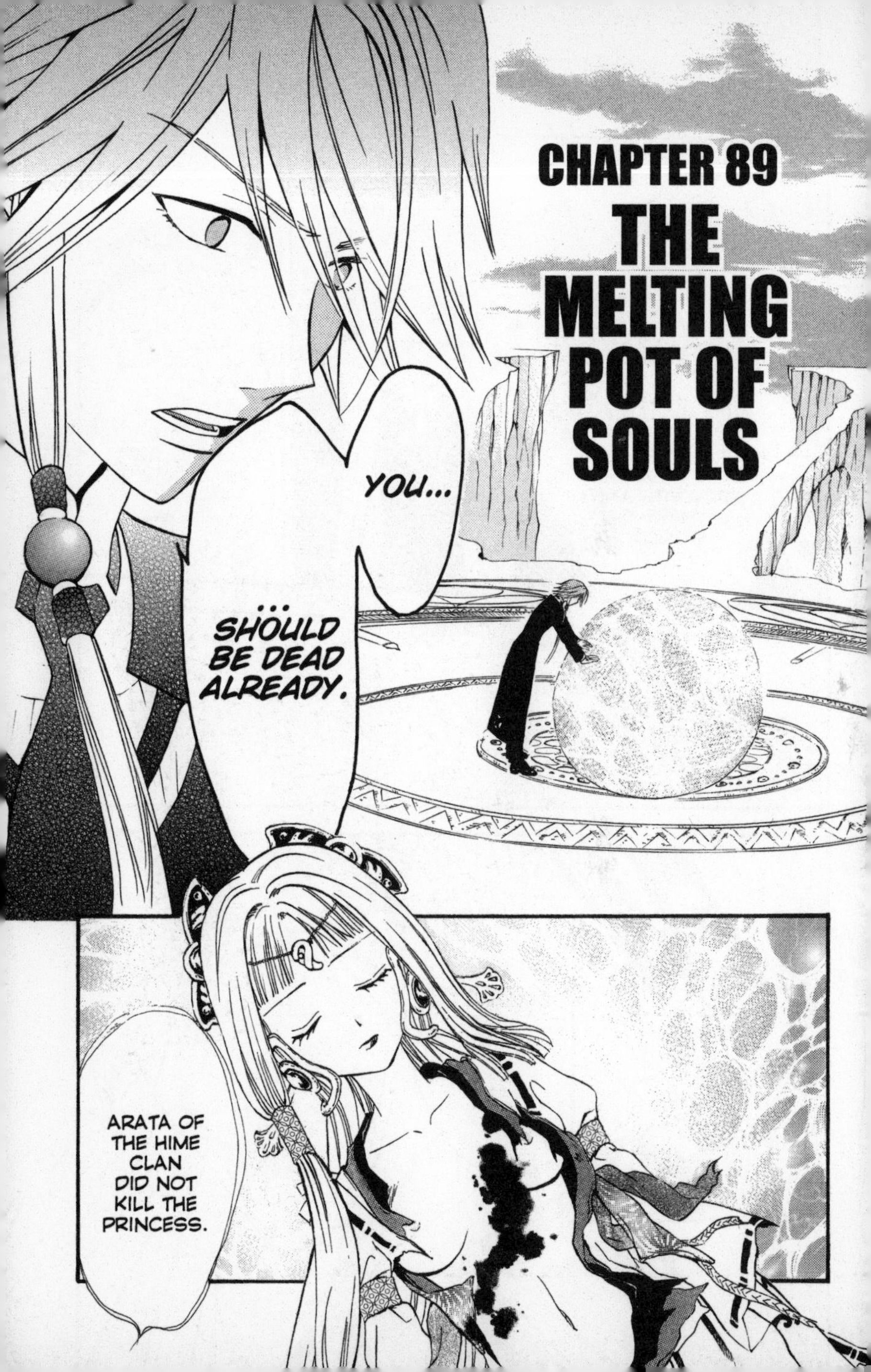
CHAPTER 89
THE MELTING POT OF SOULS
YOU...
...SHOULD BE DEAD ALREADY.
ARATA OF THE HIME CLAN DID NOT KILL THE PRINCESS.

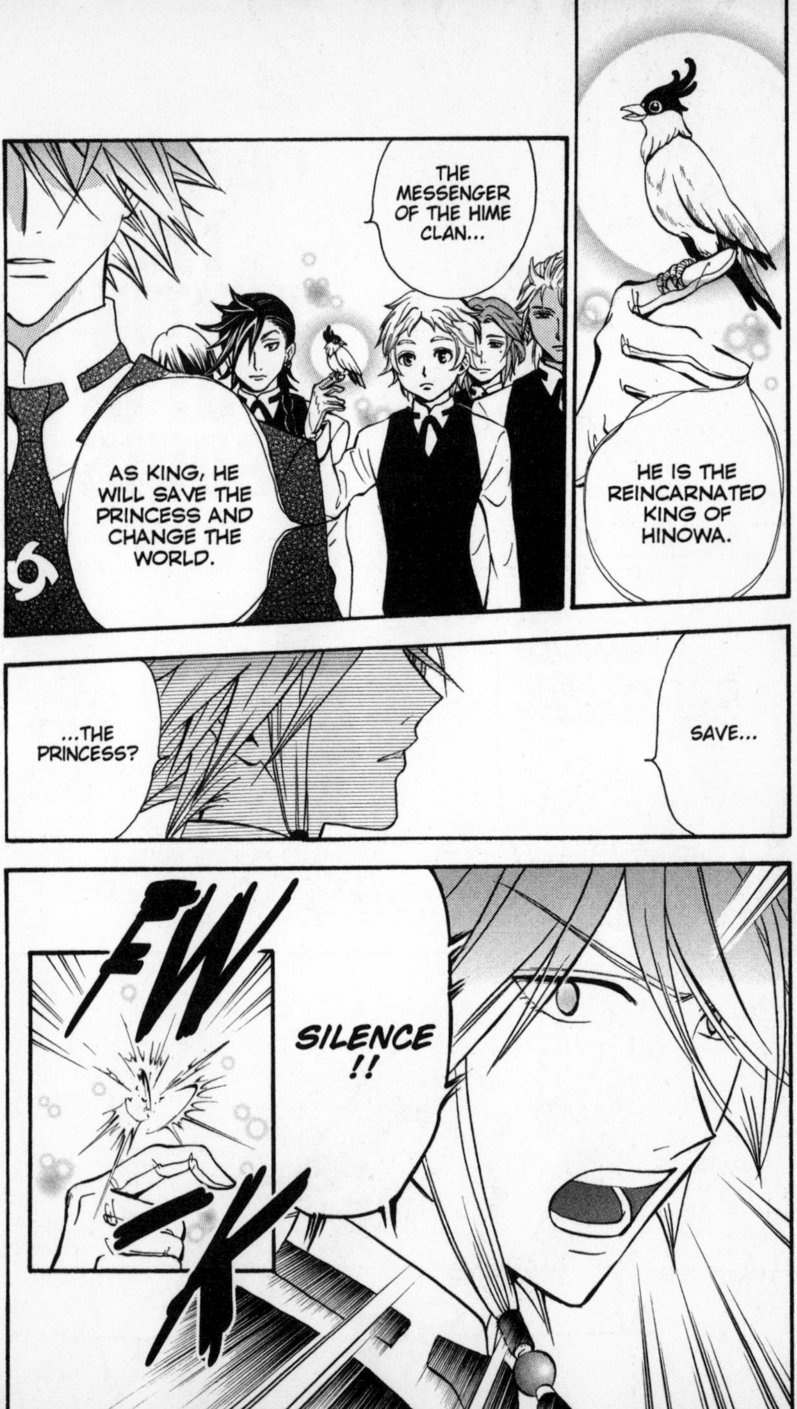
HE IS THE REINCARNATED KING OF HINOWA.
THE MESSENGER OF THE HIME CLAN...
AS KING, HE WILL SAVE THE PRINCESS AND CHANGE THE WORLD.
SAVE...
...THE PRINCESS?
SILENCE !!
FW
K

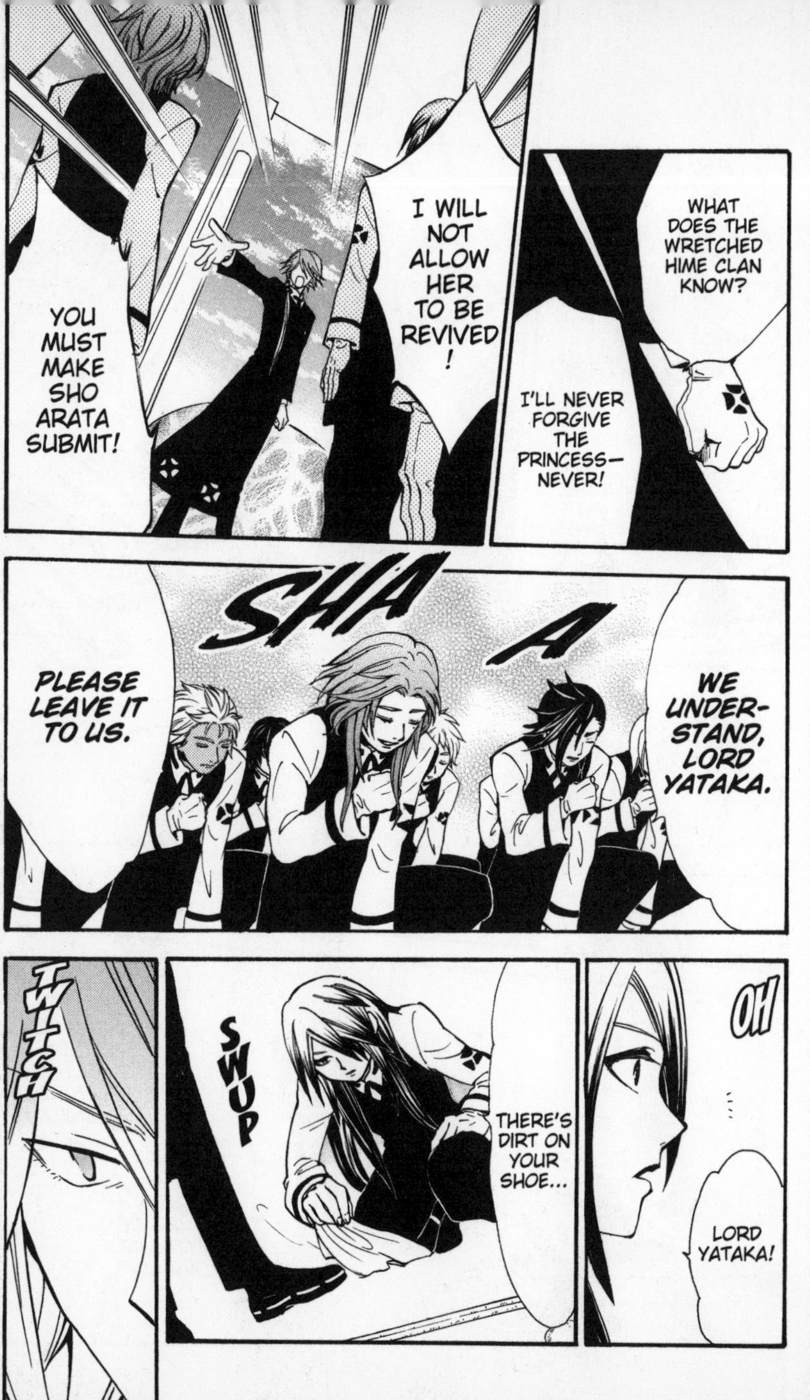
WHAT DOES THE WRETCHED HIME CLAN KNOW?
I'LL NEVER FORGIVE THE PRINCESS—NEVER!
I WILL NOT ALLOW HER TO BE REVIVED!
YOU MUST MAKE SHO ARATA SUBMIT!
SHA A
WE UNDER-STAND, LORD YATAKA.
PLEASE LEAVE IT TO US.
OH
...
LORD YATAKA!
SWUP
THERE'S DIRT ON YOUR SHOE...
TWITCH

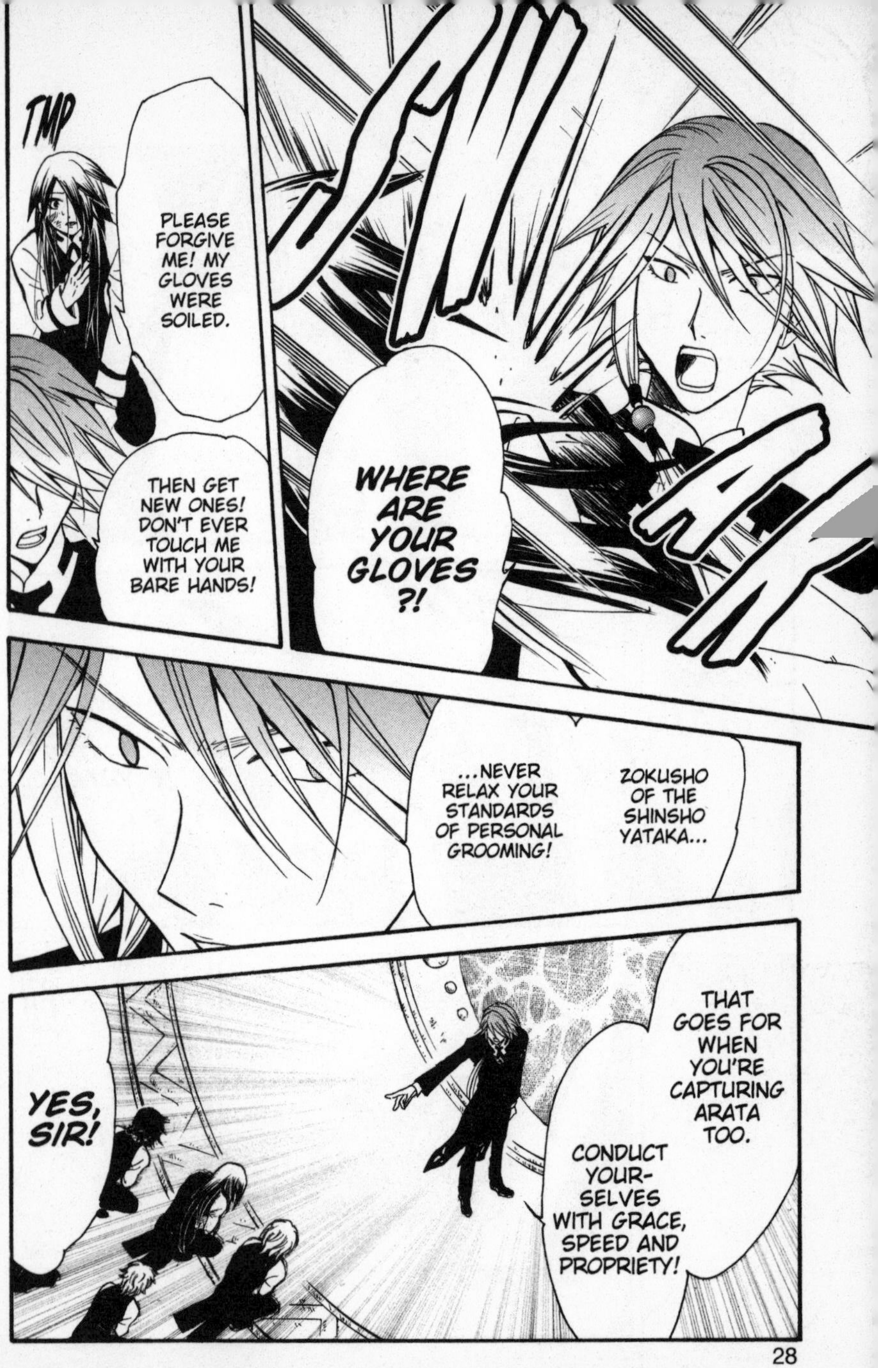
WHERE ARE YOUR GLOVES ?!
TMP
PLEASE FORGIVE ME! MY GLOVES WERE SOILED.
THEN GET NEW ONES! DON'T EVER TOUCH ME WITH YOUR BARE HANDS!
ZOKUSHO OF THE SHINSHO YATAKA...
...NEVER RELAX YOUR STANDARDS OF PERSONAL GROOMING!
THAT GOES FOR WHEN YOU'RE CAPTURING ARATA TOO.
CONDUCT YOUR-SELVES WITH GRACE, SPEED AND PROPRIETY!
YES, SIR!

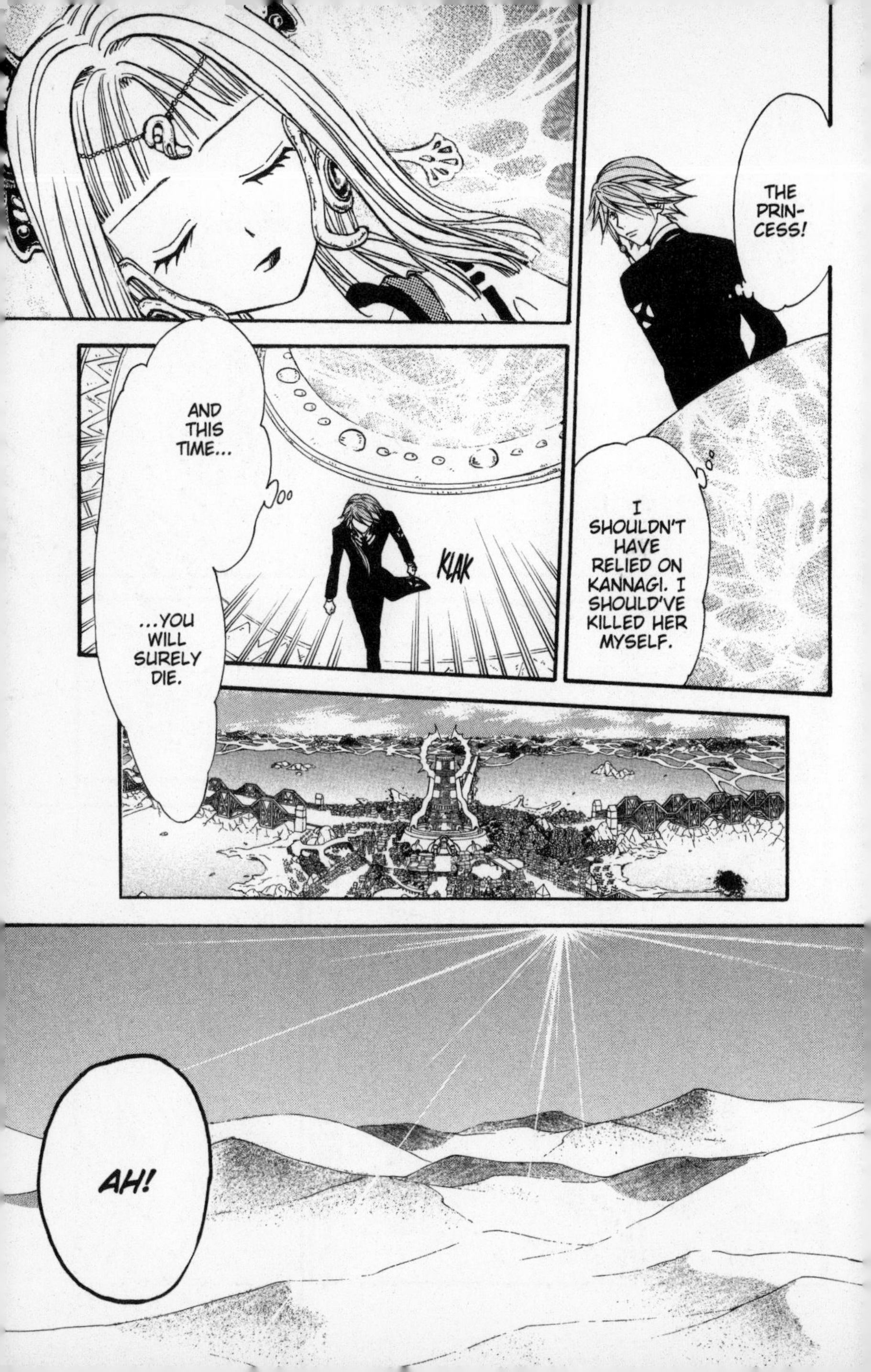
THE PRIN-CESS!
I SHOULDN'T HAVE RELIED ON KANNAGI. I SHOULD'VE KILLED HER MYSELF.
AND THIS TIME...
KLAK
...YOU WILL SURELY DIE.
AH!

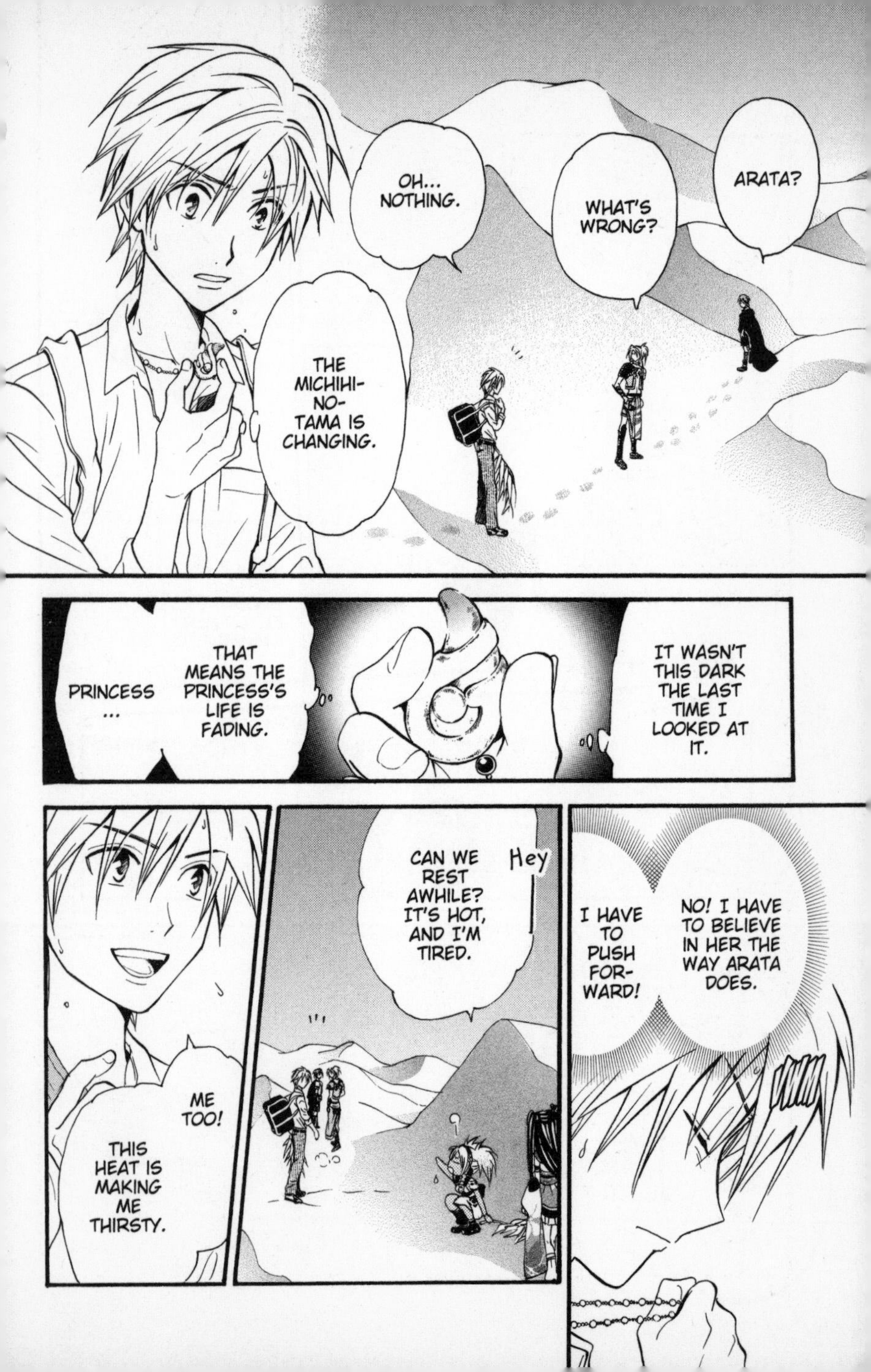
ARATA?
WHAT'S WRONG?
OH... NOTHING.
THE MICHIHI-NO-TAMA IS CHANGING.
IT WASN'T THIS DARK THE LAST TIME I LOOKED AT IT.
THAT MEANS THE PRINCESS'S LIFE IS FADING.
PRINCESS ...
NO! I HAVE TO BELIEVE IN HER THE WAY ARATA DOES.
I HAVE TO PUSH FOR-WARD!
Hey
CAN WE REST AWHILE? IT'S HOT, AND I'M TIRED.
ME TOO!
THIS HEAT IS MAKING ME THIRSTY.

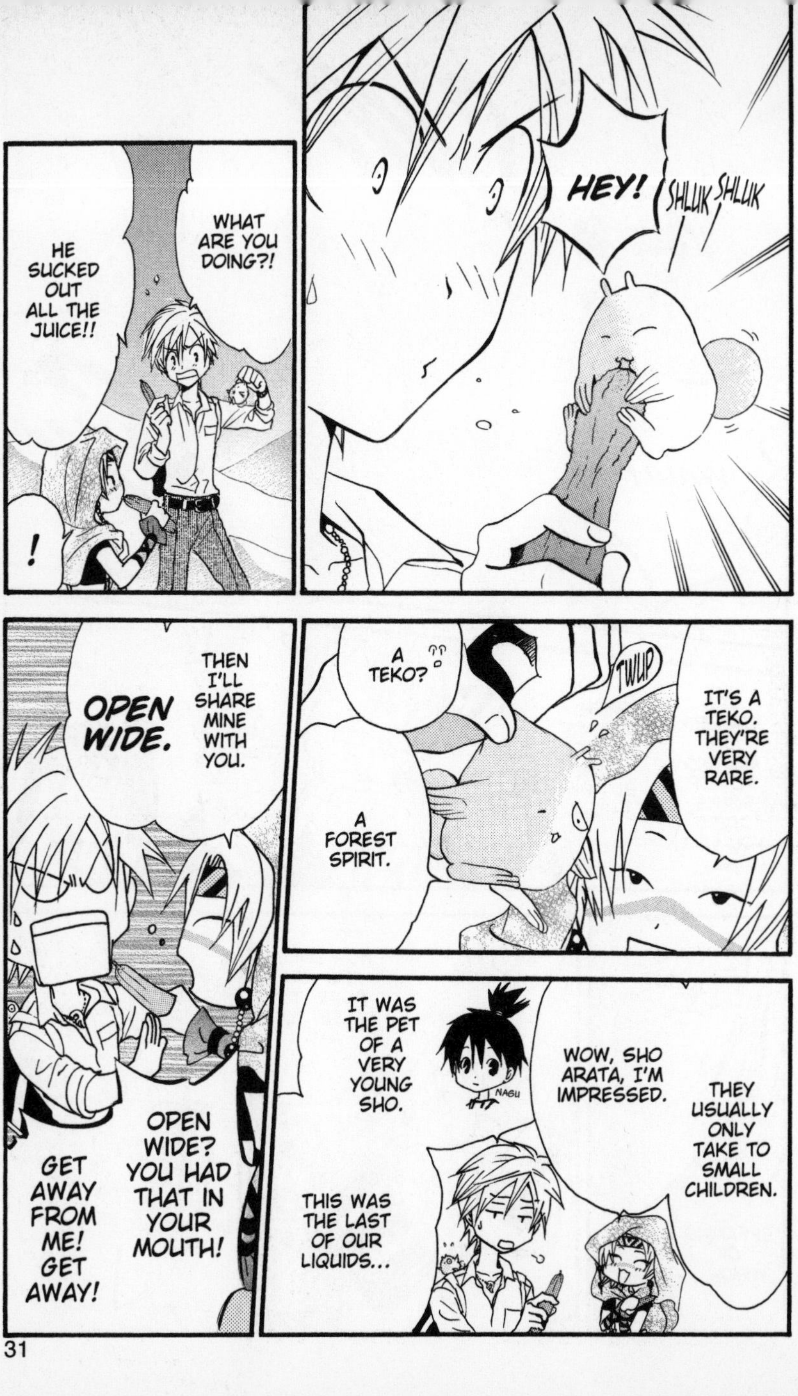
HEY!
SHLUK SHLUK
WHAT ARE YOU DOING?!
HE SUCKED OUT ALL THE JUICE!!
!
IT'S A TEKO. THEY'RE VERY RARE.
TWUP
A TEKO?
A FOREST SPIRIT.
THEY USUALLY ONLY TAKE TO SMALL CHILDREN.
WOW, SHO ARATA, I'M IMPRESSED.
IT WAS THE PET OF A VERY YOUNG SHO.
NAGU
THIS WAS THE LAST OF OUR LIQUIDS...
THEN I'LL SHARE MINE WITH YOU.
OPEN WIDE.
OPEN WIDE? YOU HAD THAT IN YOUR MOUTH!
GET AWAY FROM ME! GET AWAY!

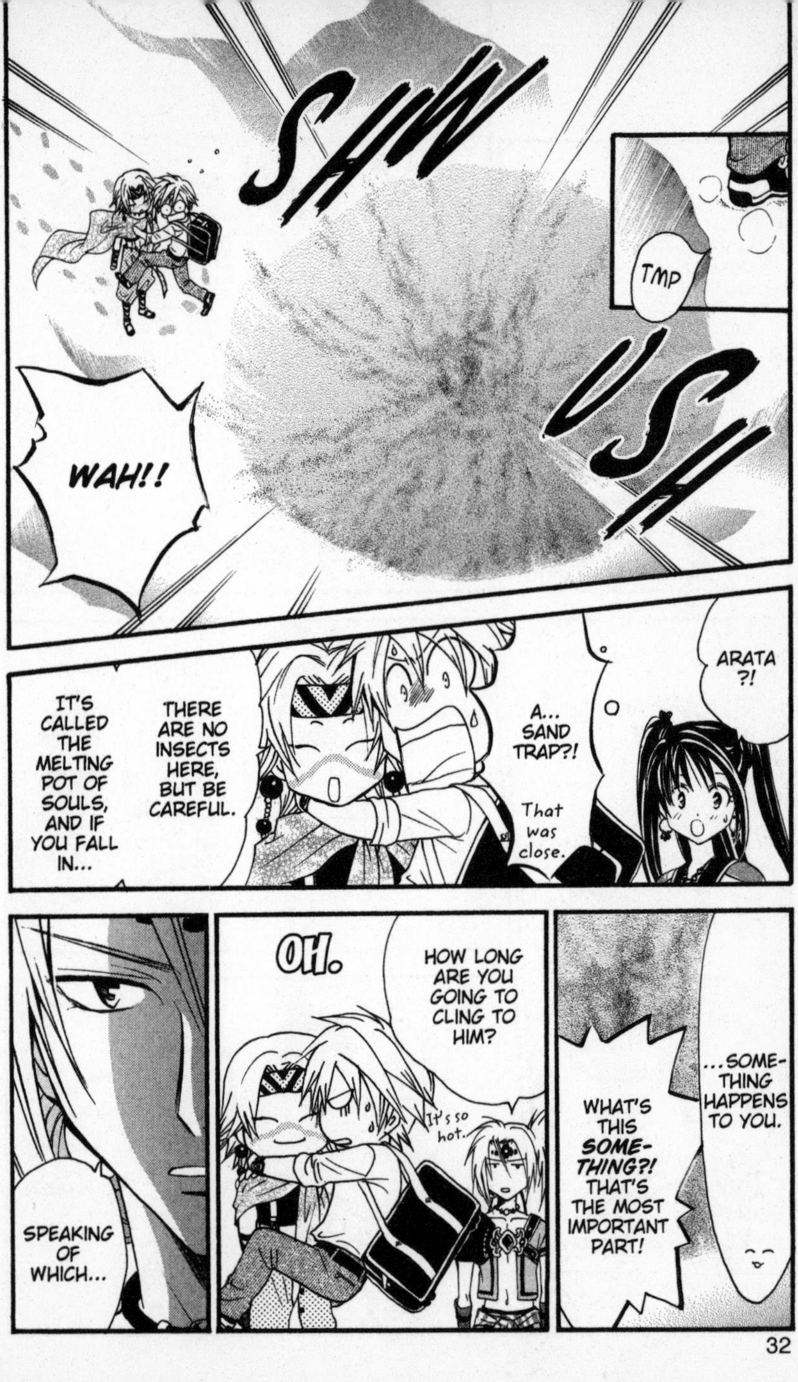
TMP
SHWUSH
WAH!!
ARATA?!
A... SAND TRAP?!
That was close.
THERE ARE NO INSECTS HERE, BUT BE CAREFUL.
IT'S CALLED THE MELTING POT OF SOULS, AND IF YOU FALL IN...
...SOME-THING HAPPENS TO YOU.
WHAT'S THIS *SOME-THING?!* THAT'S THE MOST IMPORTANT PART!
HOW LONG ARE YOU GOING TO CLING TO HIM?
OH.
It's so hot.
SPEAKING OF WHICH...

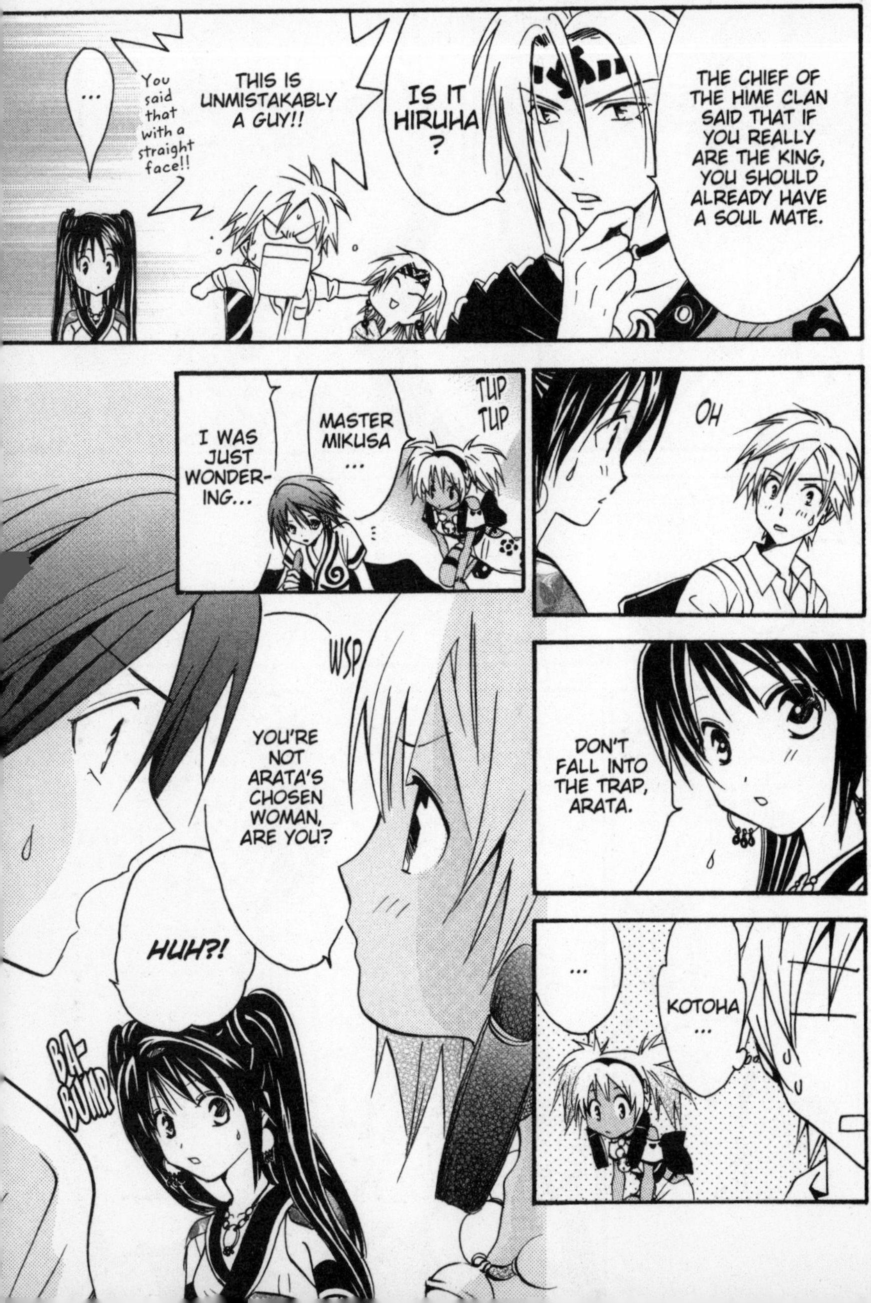
THE CHIEF OF THE HIME CLAN SAID THAT IF YOU REALLY ARE THE KING, YOU SHOULD ALREADY HAVE A SOUL MATE.
IS IT HIRUHA?
THIS IS UNMISTAKABLY A GUY!!
You said that with a straight face!!
...
OH
TUP TUP
MASTER MIKUSA ...
I WAS JUST WONDERING...
WSP
YOU'RE NOT ARATA'S CHOSEN WOMAN, ARE YOU?
HUH?!
BA-BUMP
DON'T FALL INTO THE TRAP, ARATA.
KOTOHA ...
...

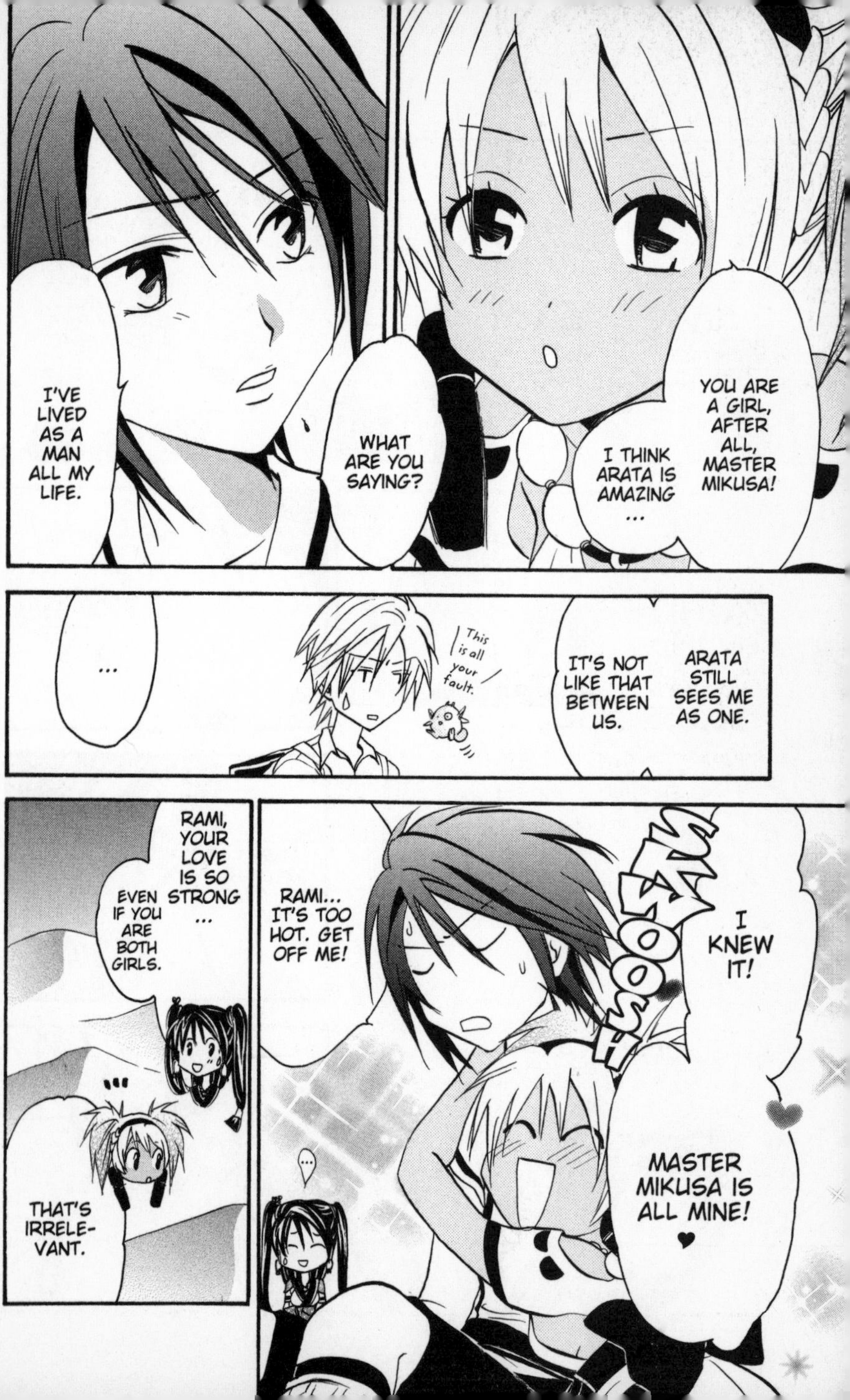
YOU ARE A GIRL, AFTER ALL, MASTER MIKUSA!
I THINK ARATA IS AMAZING ...
WHAT ARE YOU SAYING?
I'VE LIVED AS A MAN ALL MY LIFE.
ARATA STILL SEES ME AS ONE.
IT'S NOT LIKE THAT BETWEEN US.
This is all your fault.
...
SWOOSH!
I KNEW IT!
MASTER MIKUSA IS ALL MINE!
RAMI... IT'S TOO HOT. GET OFF ME!
...
RAMI, YOUR LOVE IS SO STRONG ...
EVEN IF YOU ARE BOTH GIRLS.
THAT'S IRRELEVANT.

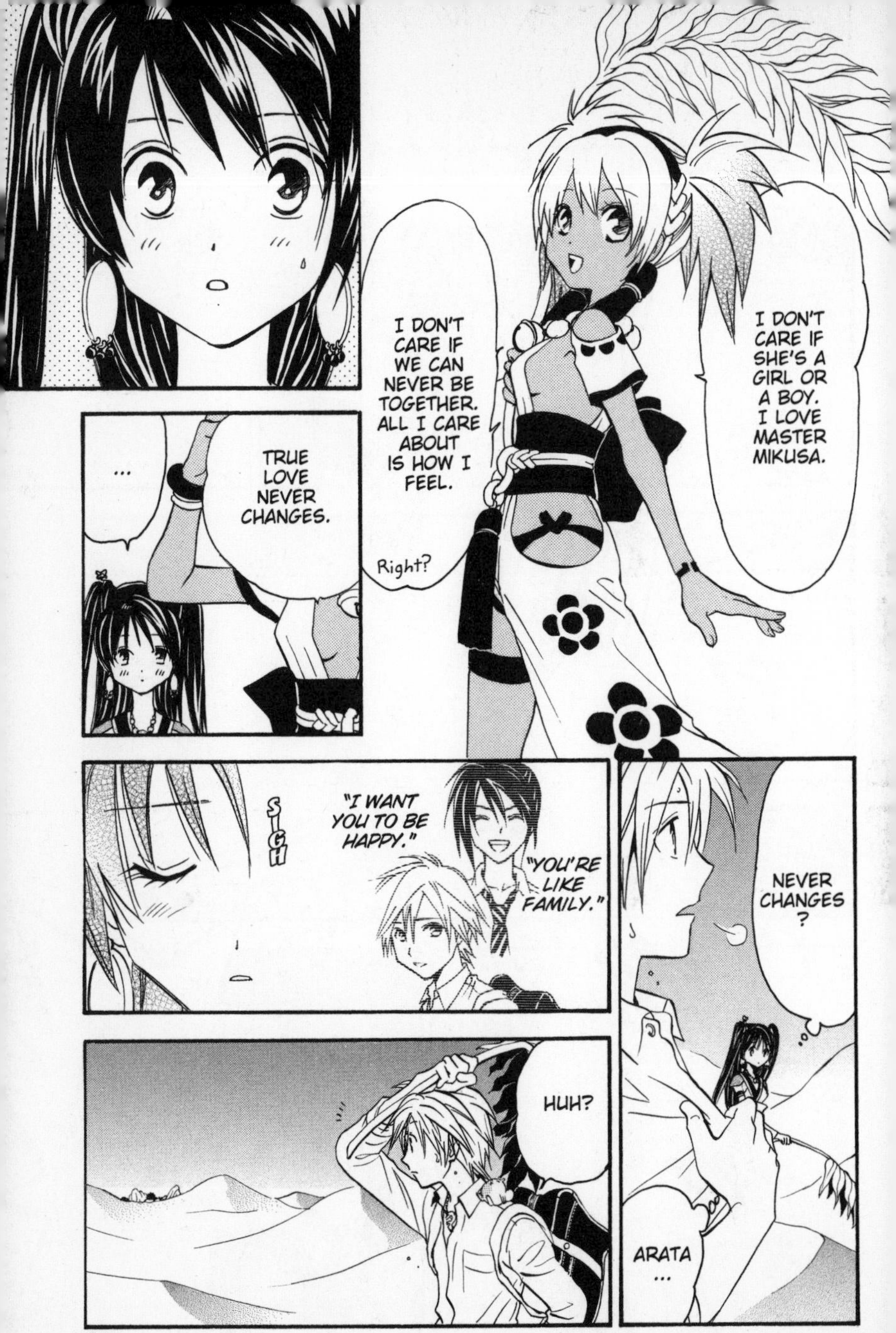
I DON'T CARE IF SHE'S A GIRL OR A BOY. I LOVE MASTER MIKUSA.
I DON'T CARE IF WE CAN NEVER BE TOGETHER. ALL I CARE ABOUT IS HOW I FEEL.
Right?
TRUE LOVE NEVER CHANGES.
...
NEVER CHANGES ?
ARATA ...
"I WANT YOU TO BE HAPPY."
"YOU'RE LIKE FAMILY."
SIGH
HUH?

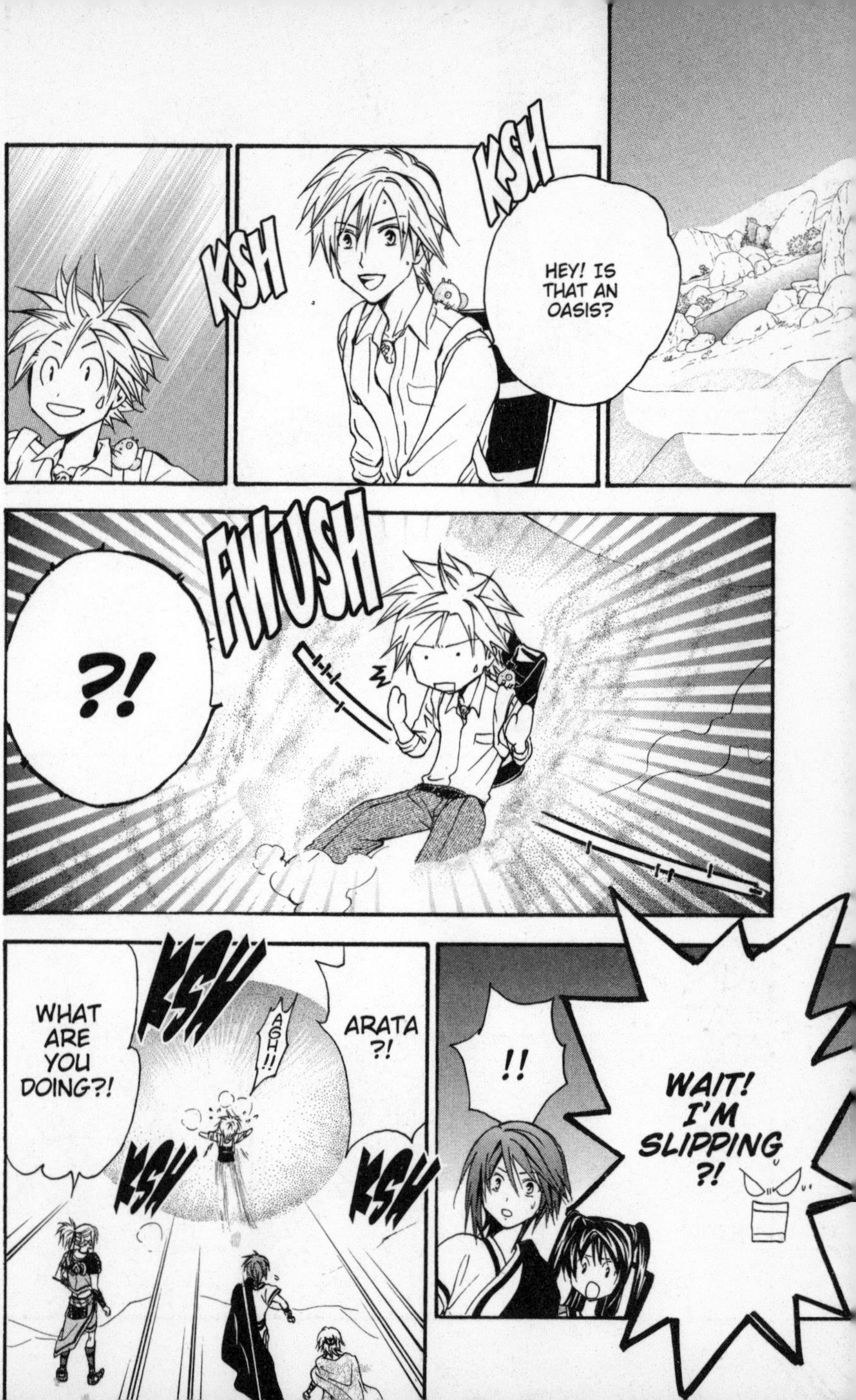
HEY! IS THAT AN OASIS?
KSH
KSH
FWUSH
?!
WAIT! I'M SLIPPING?!
!!
ARATA?!
AGH!!
WHAT ARE YOU DOING?!
KSH
KSH
KSH

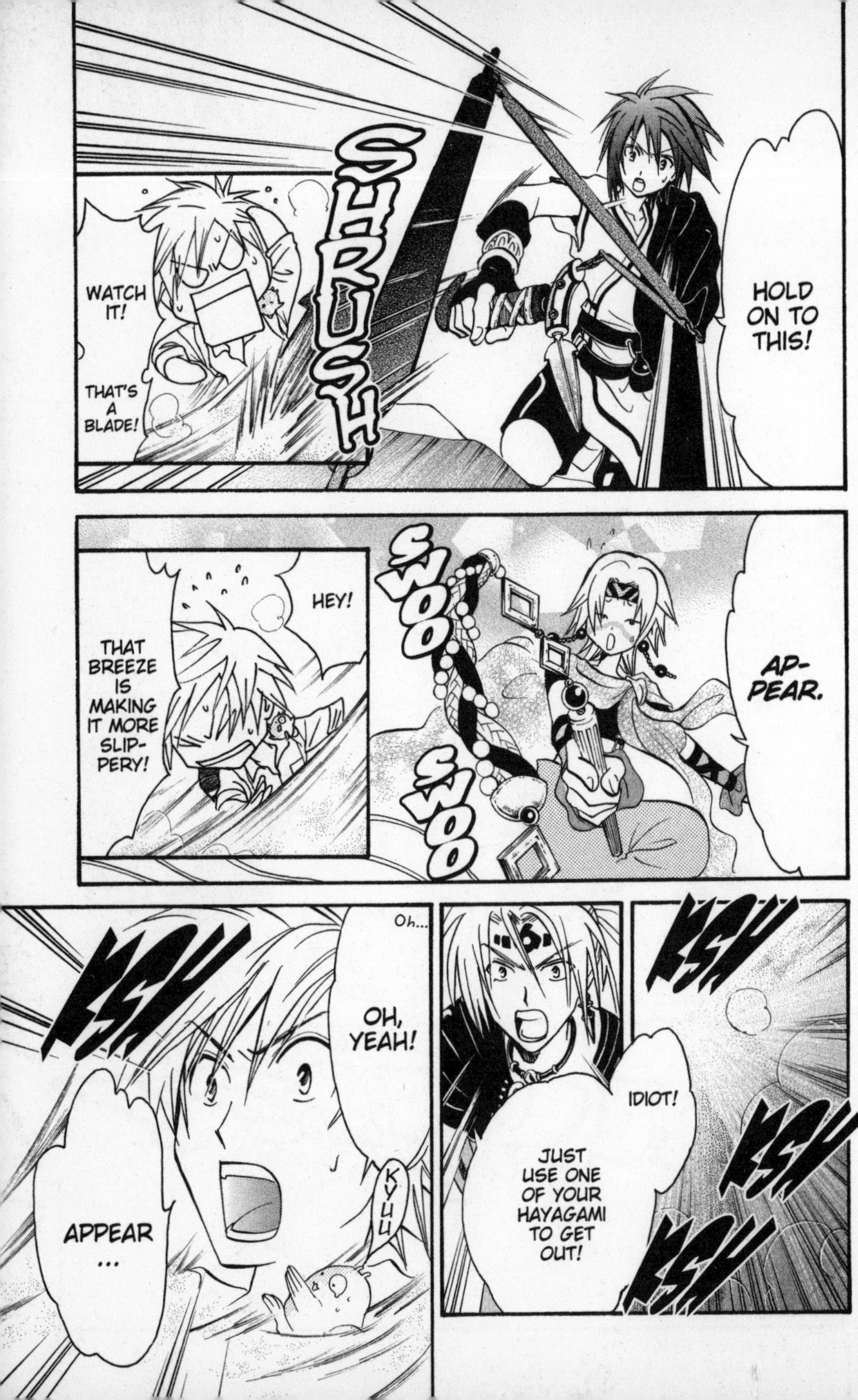
HOLD ON TO THIS!
SHRUSH
WATCH IT!
THAT'S A BLADE!
AP- PEAR.
SWOO
SWOO
HEY!
THAT BREEZE IS MAKING IT MORE SLIP- PERY!
KSH
IDIOT!
JUST USE ONE OF YOUR HAYAGAMI TO GET OUT!
KSH
KSH
Oh...
OH, YEAH!
KYUU
KSH
APPEAR ...

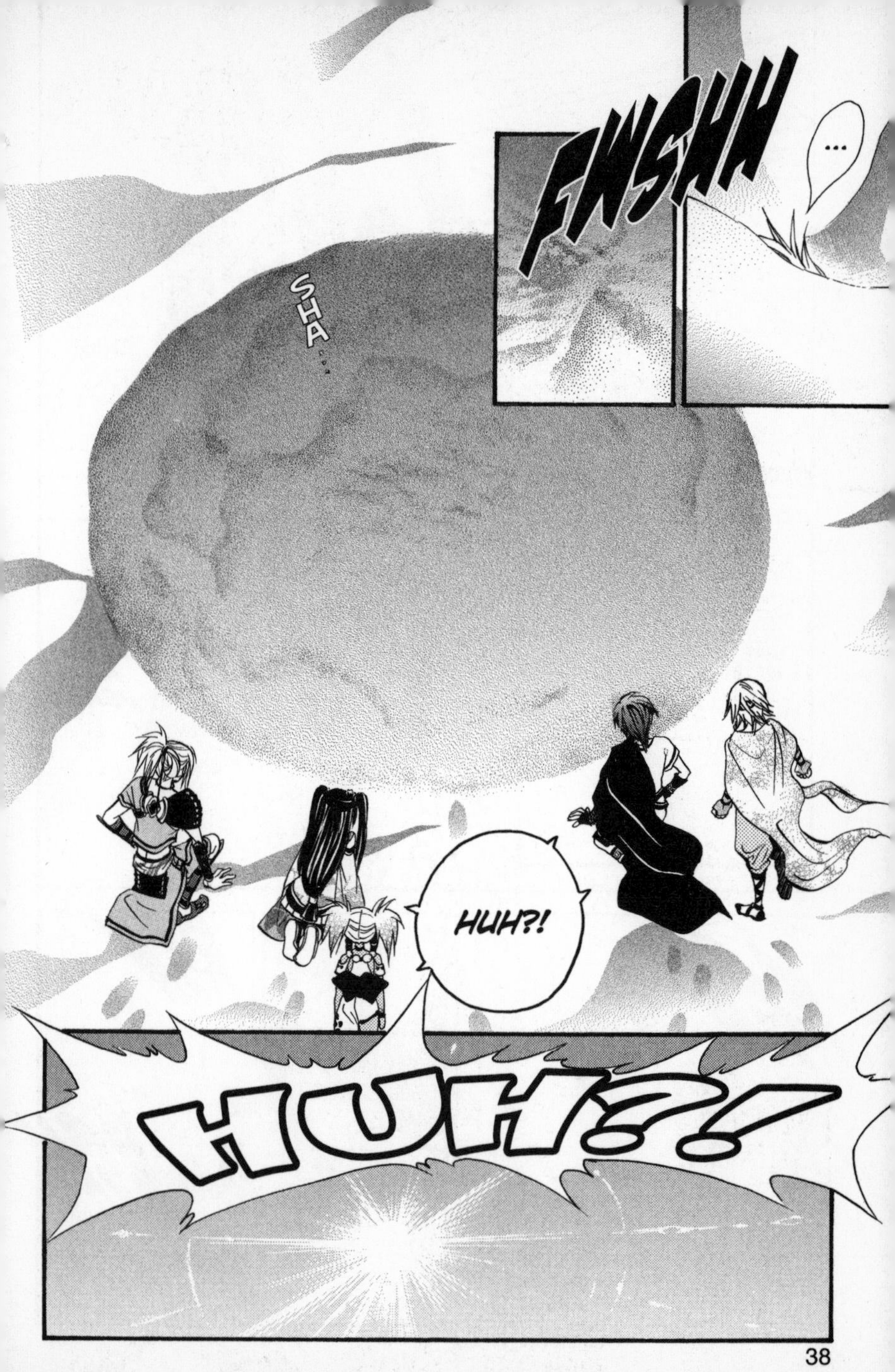
...
FWSHH
SHA...
HUH?!
HUH?!

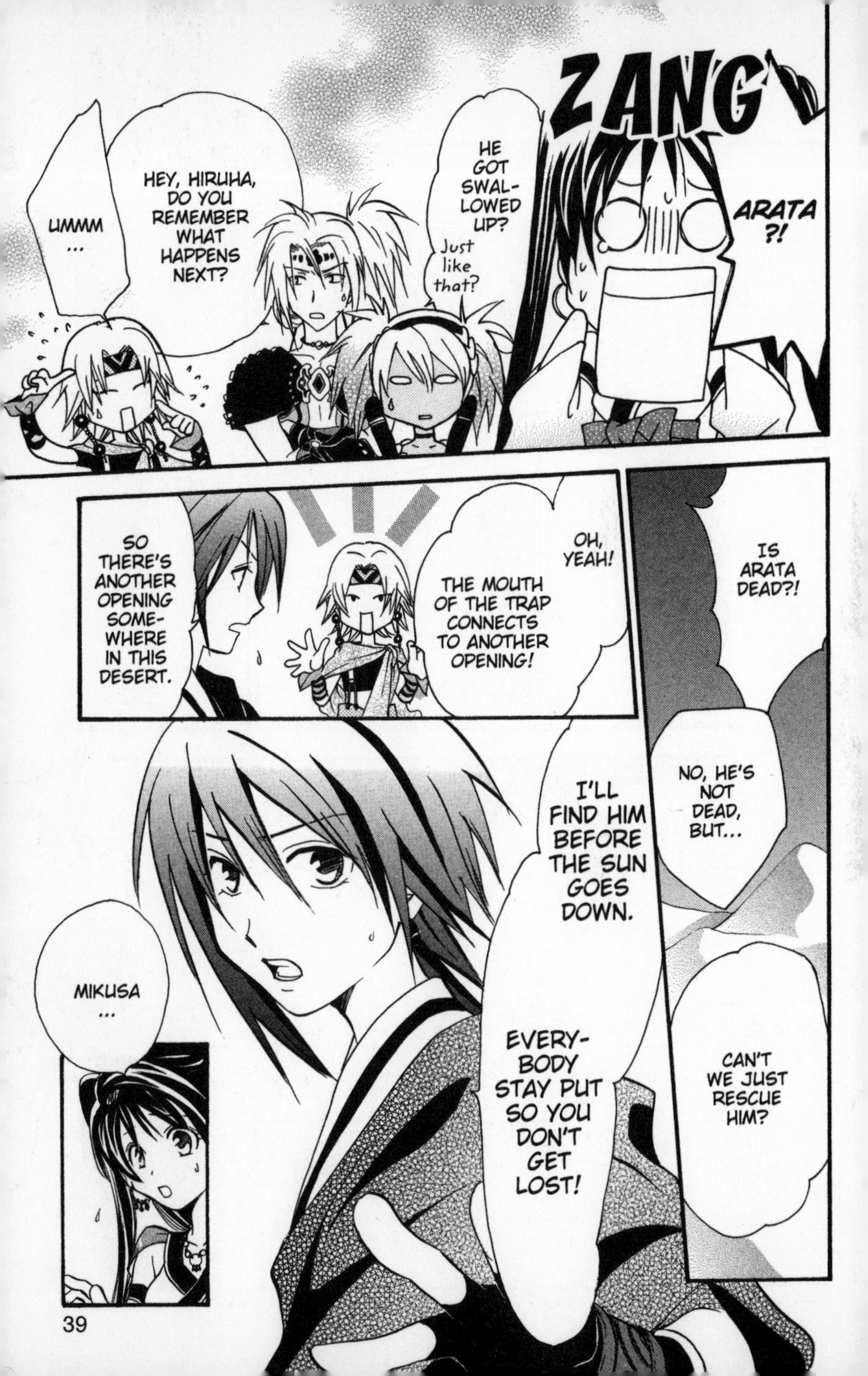
ZANG
ARATA ?!
HE GOT SWAL-LOWED UP?
Just like that?
HEY, HIRUHA, DO YOU REMEMBER WHAT HAPPENS NEXT?
UMMM ...
IS ARATA DEAD?!
NO, HE'S NOT DEAD, BUT...
CAN'T WE JUST RESCUE HIM?
OH, YEAH!
THE MOUTH OF THE TRAP CONNECTS TO ANOTHER OPENING!
SO THERE'S ANOTHER OPENING SOME-WHERE IN THIS DESERT.
I'LL FIND HIM BEFORE THE SUN GOES DOWN.
EVERY-BODY STAY PUT SO YOU DON'T GET LOST!
MIKUSA ...

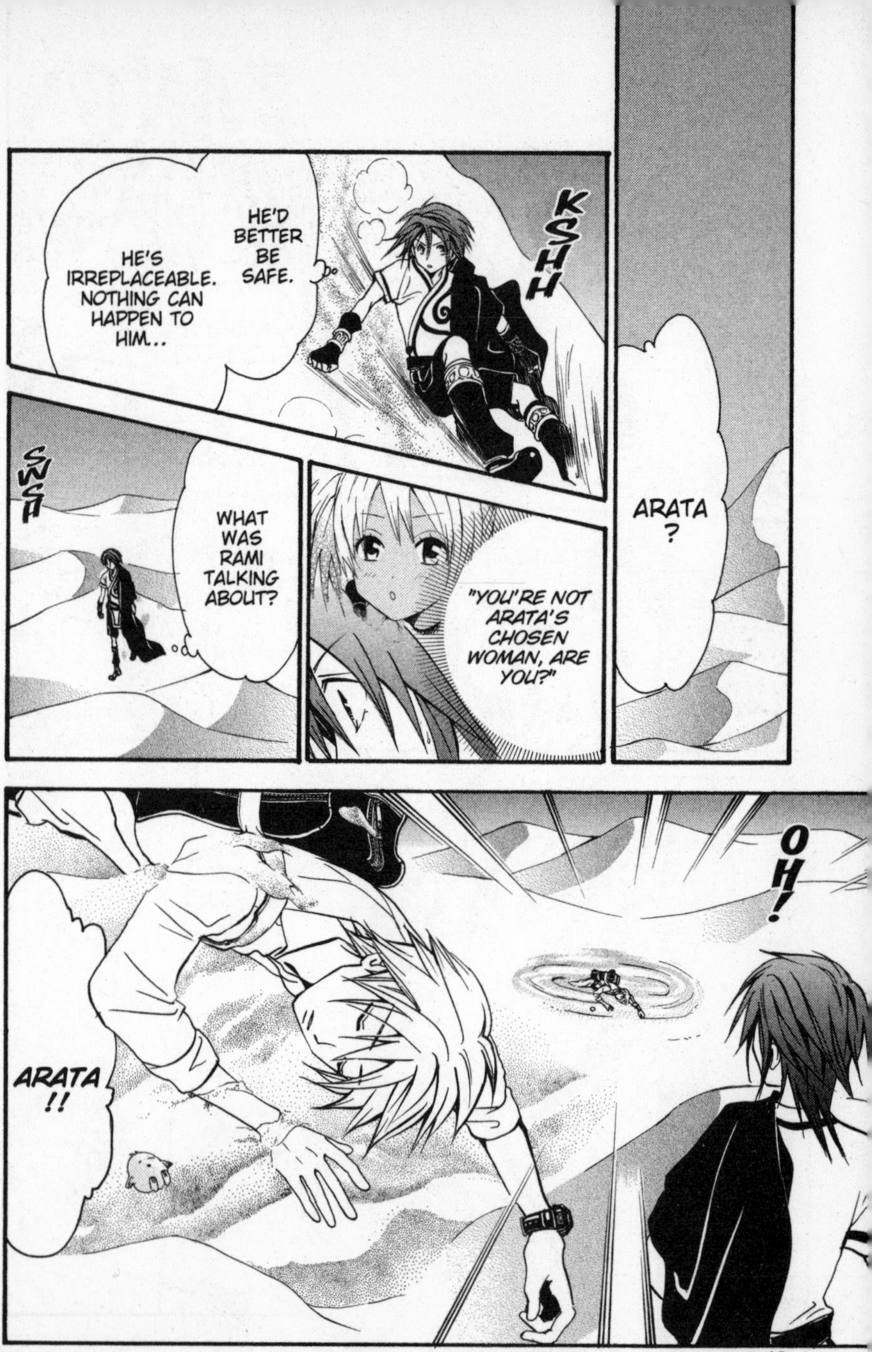
ARATA?
KSHH
HE'D BETTER BE SAFE.
HE'S IRREPLACEABLE. NOTHING CAN HAPPEN TO HIM...
"YOU'RE NOT ARATA'S CHOSEN WOMAN, ARE YOU?"
WHAT WAS RAMI TALKING ABOUT?
SWSH
OH!
ARATA!!

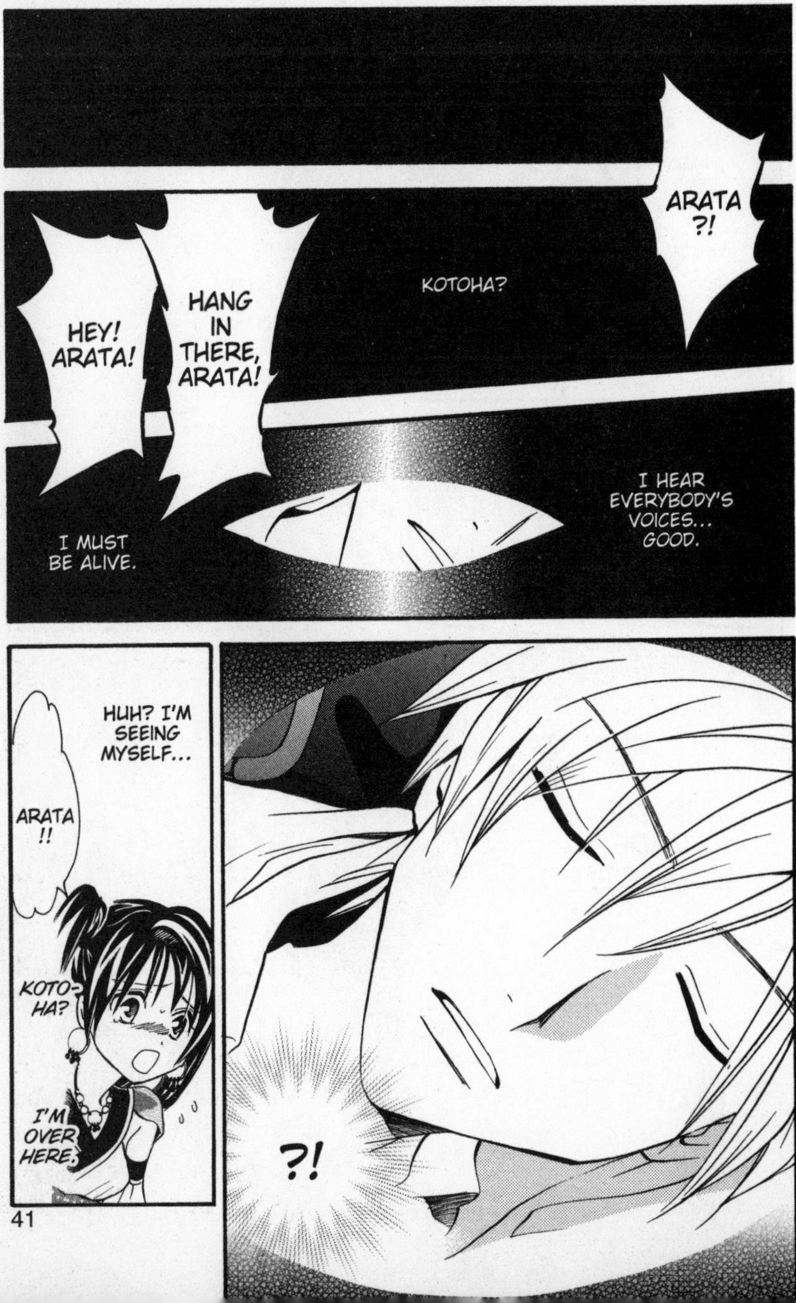
ARATA?!
KOTOHA?
HANG IN THERE, ARATA!
HEY! ARATA!
I HEAR EVERYBODY'S VOICES... GOOD.
I MUST BE ALIVE.
?!
HUH? I'M SEEING MYSELF...
ARATA!!
KOTOHA?
I'M OVER HERE.

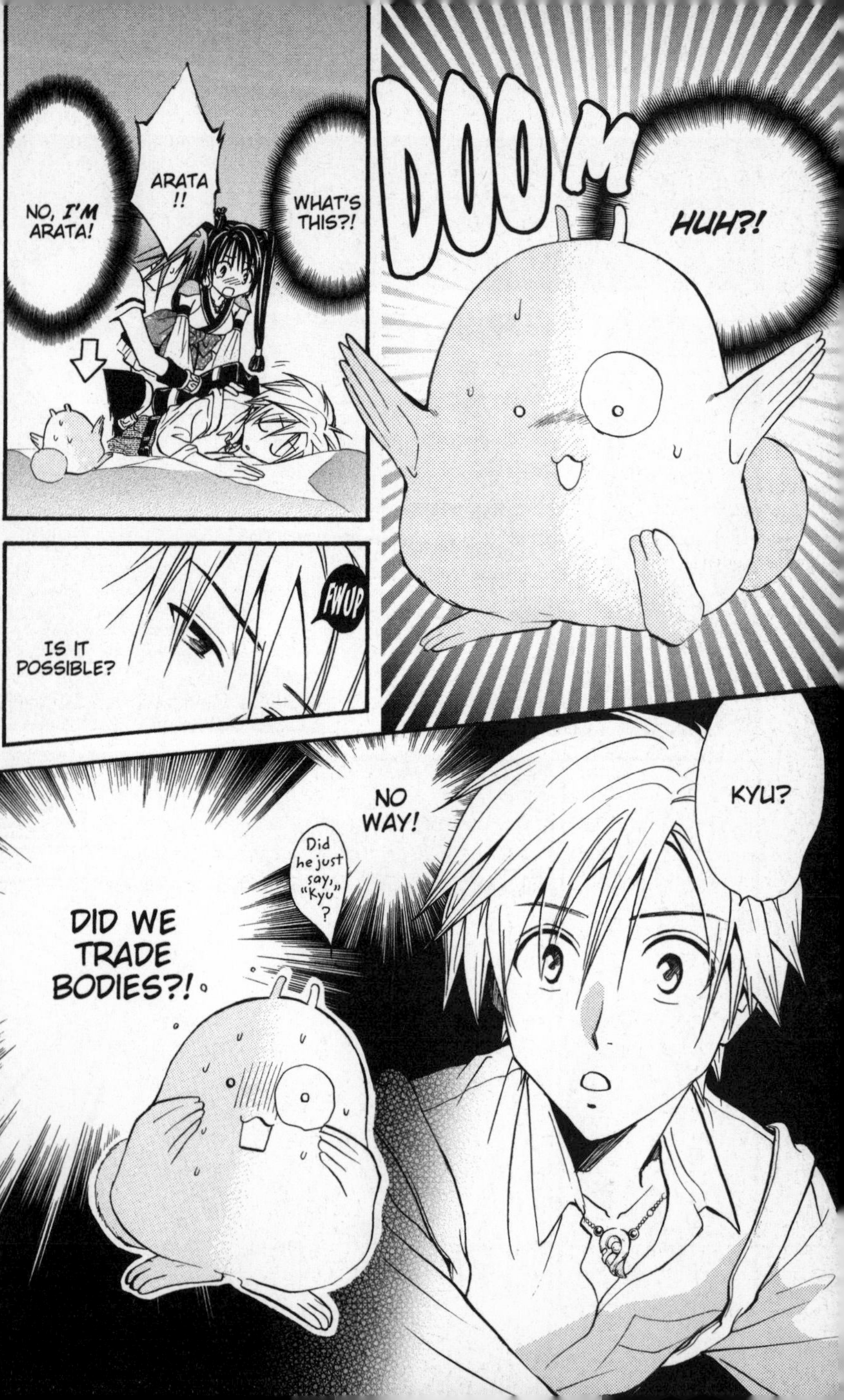
DOOOM
HUH?!
WHAT'S THIS?!
ARATA!!
NO, I'M ARATA!
FWUP
IS IT POSSIBLE?
KYU?
NO WAY!
Did he just say, "Kyu"?
DID WE TRADE BODIES?!

Arata
THE LEGEND

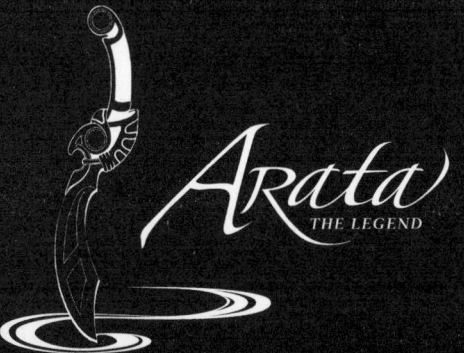

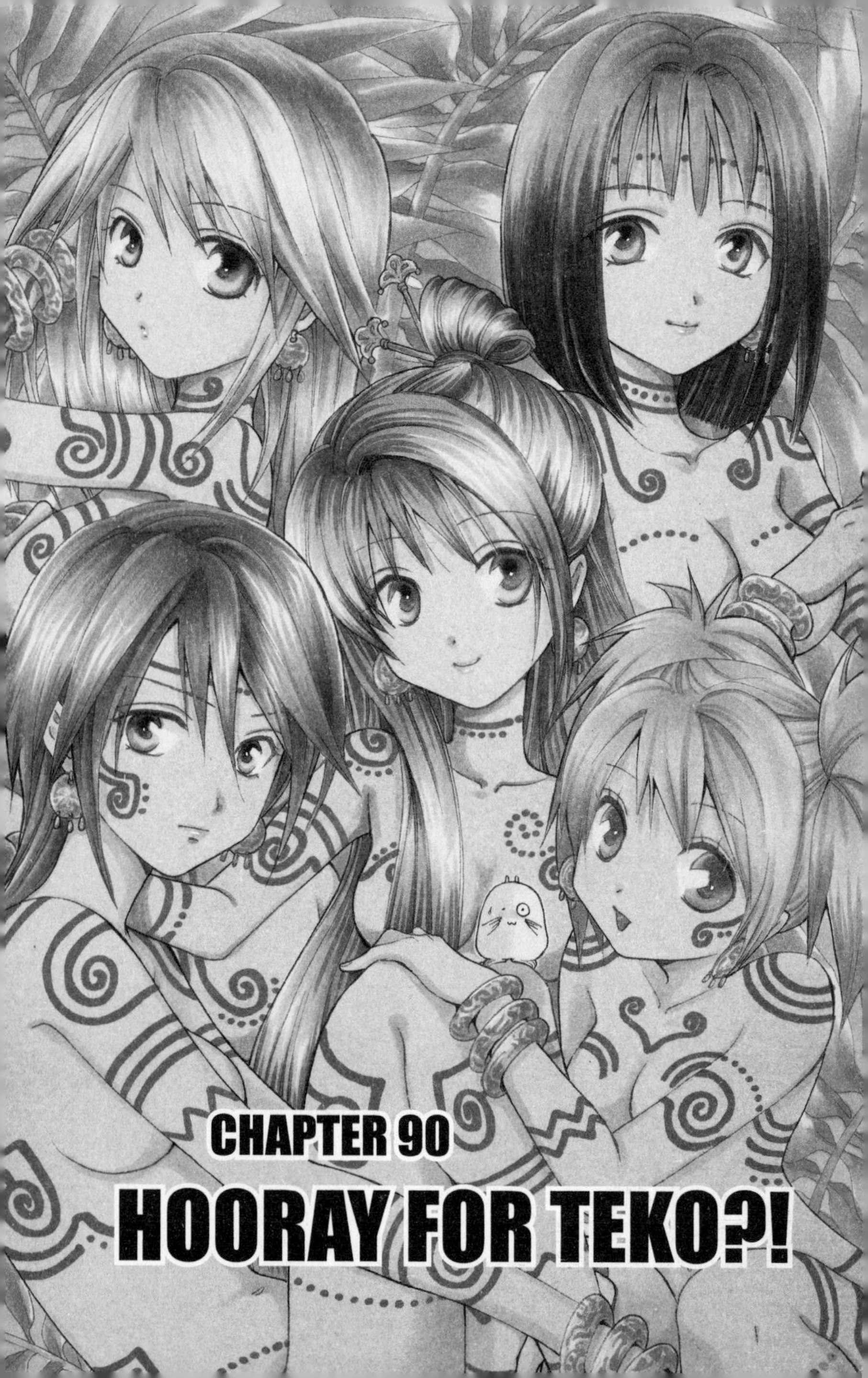
CHAPTER 90
HOORAY FOR TEKO?!

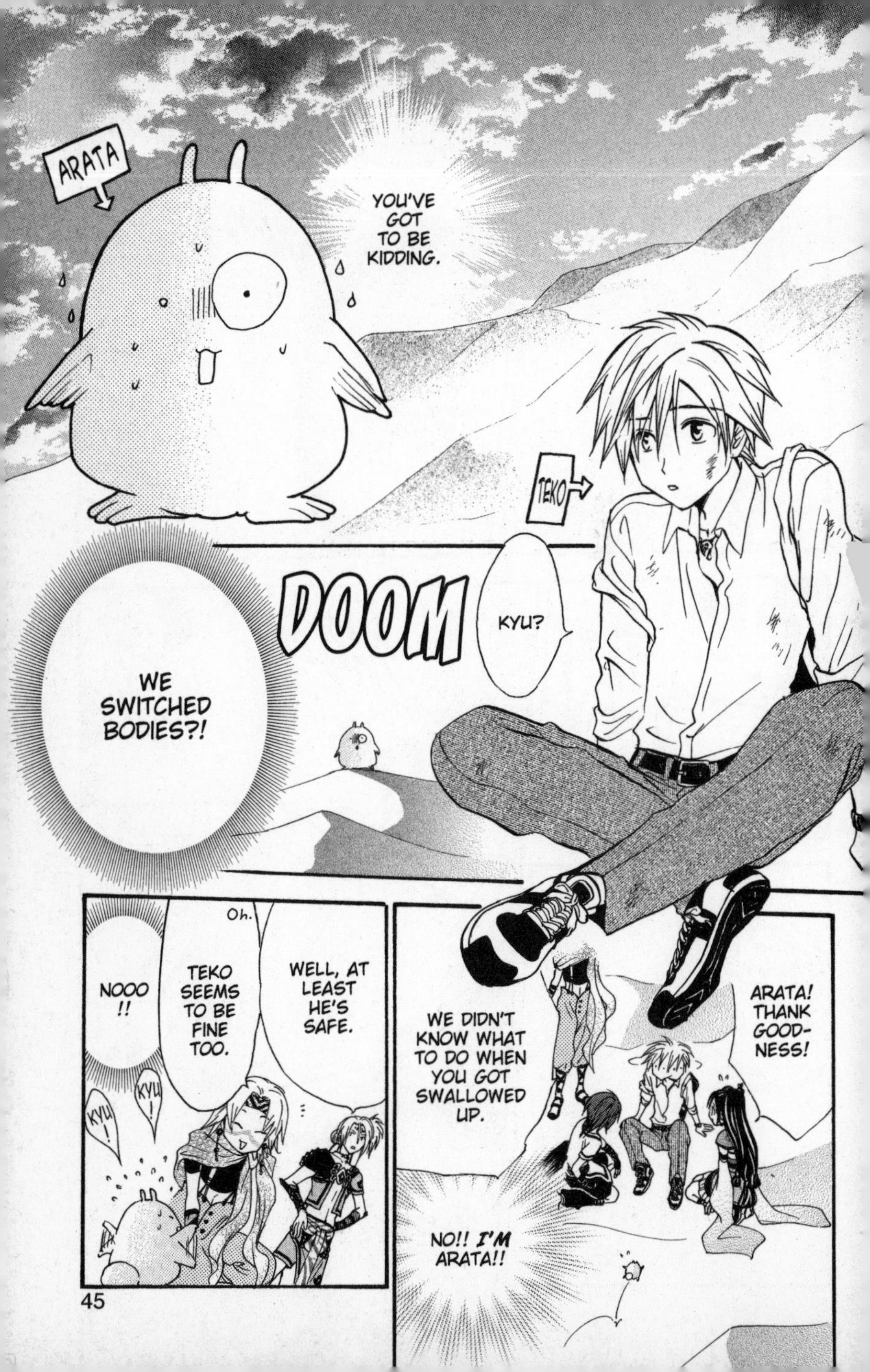

ARATA
YOU'VE GOT TO BE KIDDING.
TEKO
KYU?
DOOM
WE SWITCHED BODIES?!
ARATA! THANK GOOD-NESS!
WE DIDN'T KNOW WHAT TO DO WHEN YOU GOT SWALLOWED UP.
NO!! *I'M* ARATA!!
WELL, AT LEAST HE'S SAFE.
Oh.
TEKO SEEMS TO BE FINE TOO.
NOOO !!
KYU !
KYU !

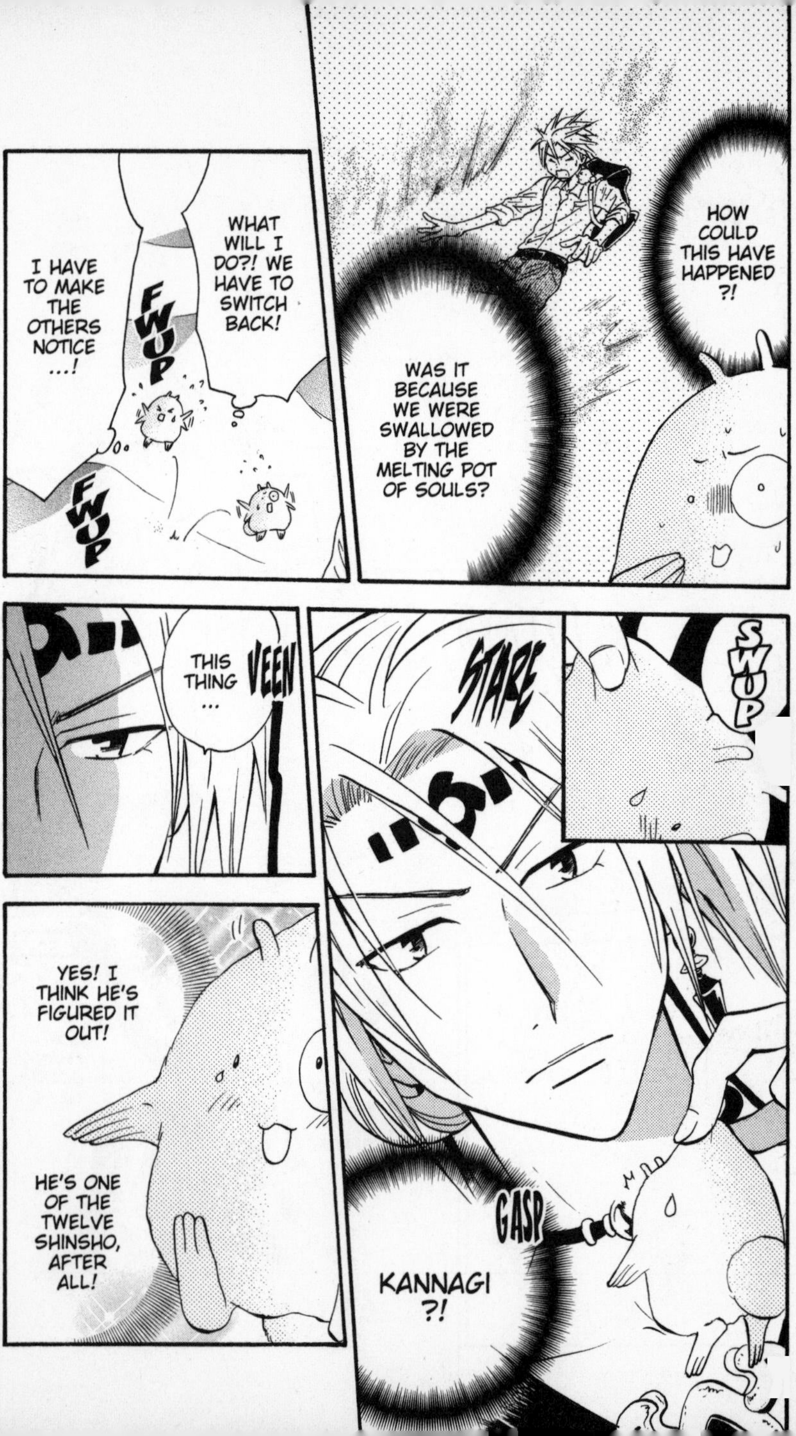
HOW COULD THIS HAVE HAPPENED?!
WAS IT BECAUSE WE WERE SWALLOWED BY THE MELTING POT OF SOULS?
WHAT WILL I DO?! WE HAVE TO SWITCH BACK!
I HAVE TO MAKE THE OTHERS NOTICE...!
FWUP
FWUP
SWUP
STARE
GASP
KANNAGI?!
THIS THING...
VEEN
YES! I THINK HE'S FIGURED IT OUT!
HE'S ONE OF THE TWELVE SHINSHO, AFTER ALL!

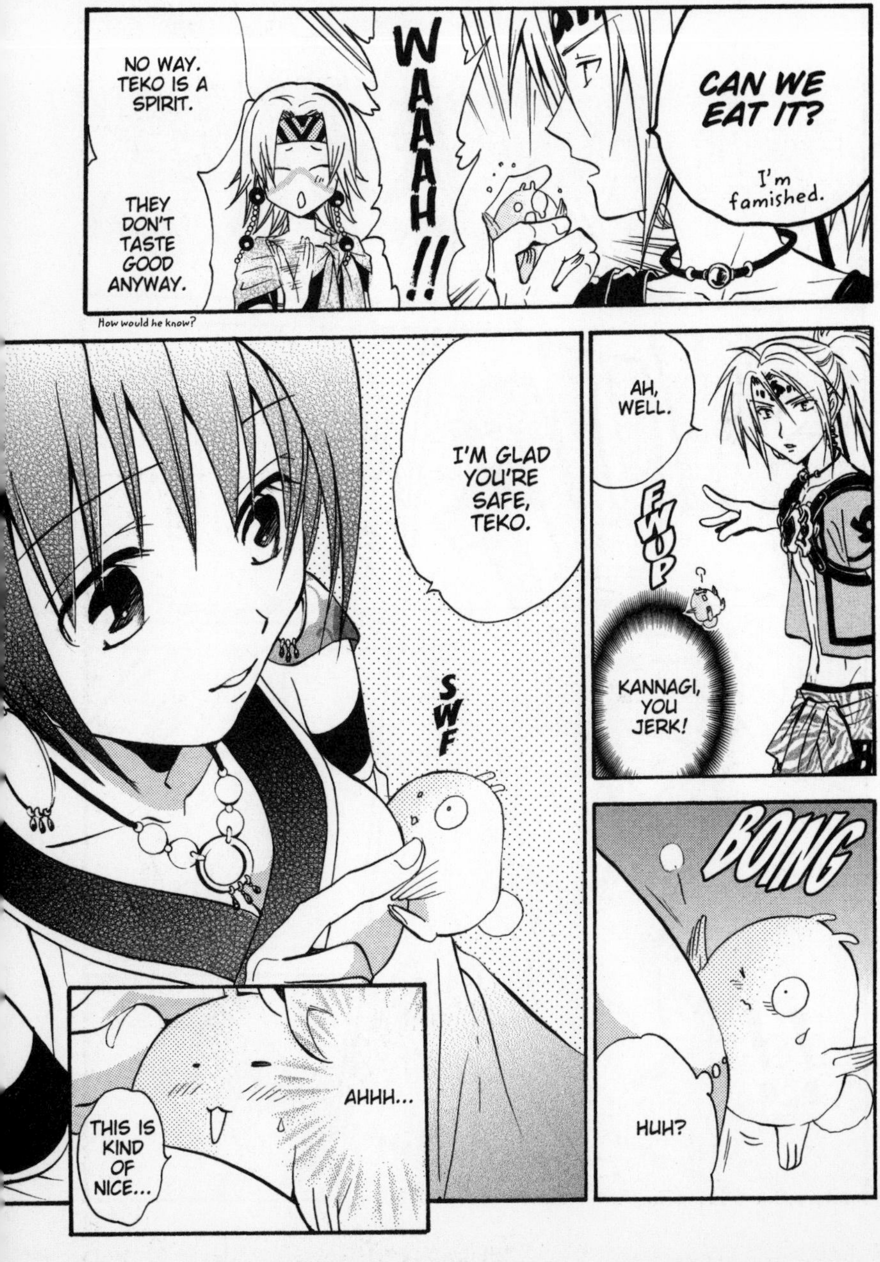
CAN WE EAT IT?
I'm famished.
WAAAH!!
NO WAY. TEKO IS A SPIRIT.
THEY DON'T TASTE GOOD ANYWAY.
How would he know?
AH, WELL.
FWUP
KANNAGI, YOU JERK!
BOING
HUH?
I'M GLAD YOU'RE SAFE, TEKO.
SWF
AHHH...
THIS IS KIND OF NICE...

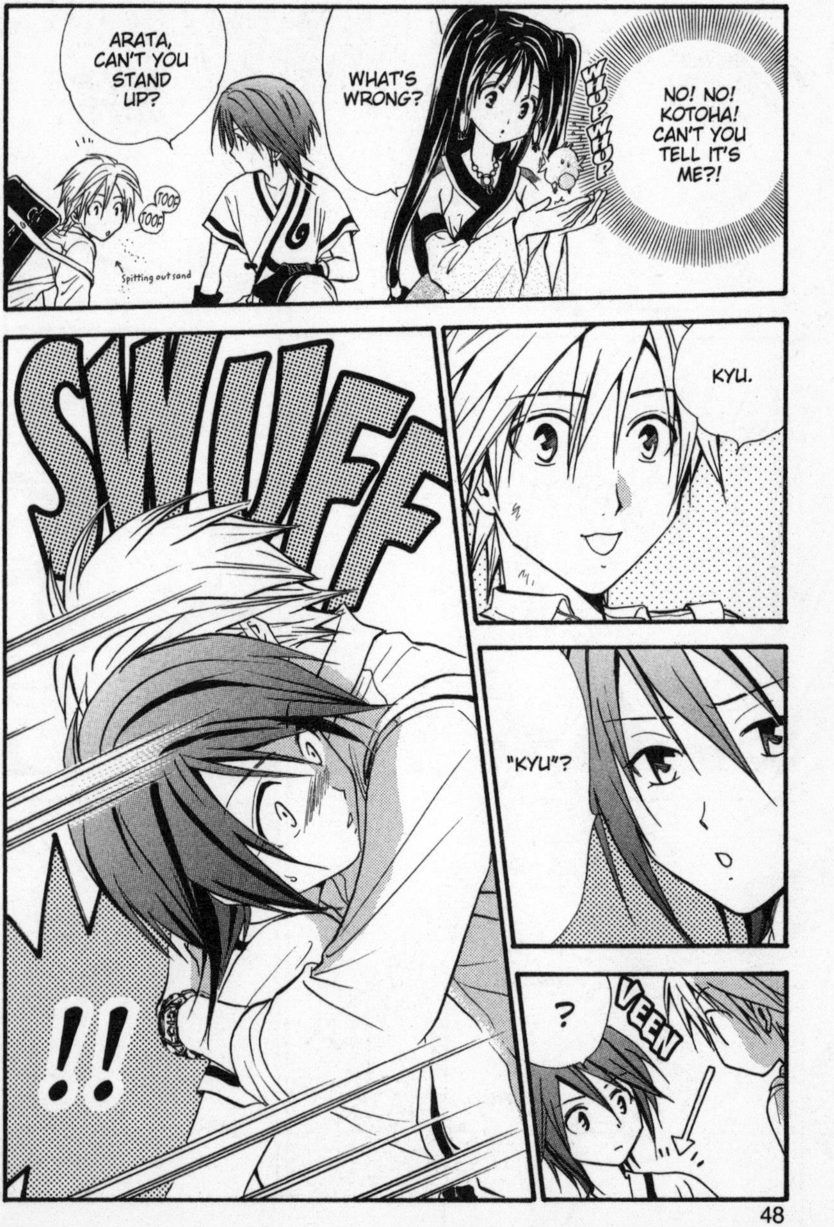
NO! NO! KOTOHA! CAN'T YOU TELL IT'S ME?!
WHUPWHUP
WHAT'S WRONG?
ARATA, CAN'T YOU STAND UP?
TOOF
TOOF
Spitting out sand
KYU.
"KYU"?
?
VEEN
SWUFF
!!

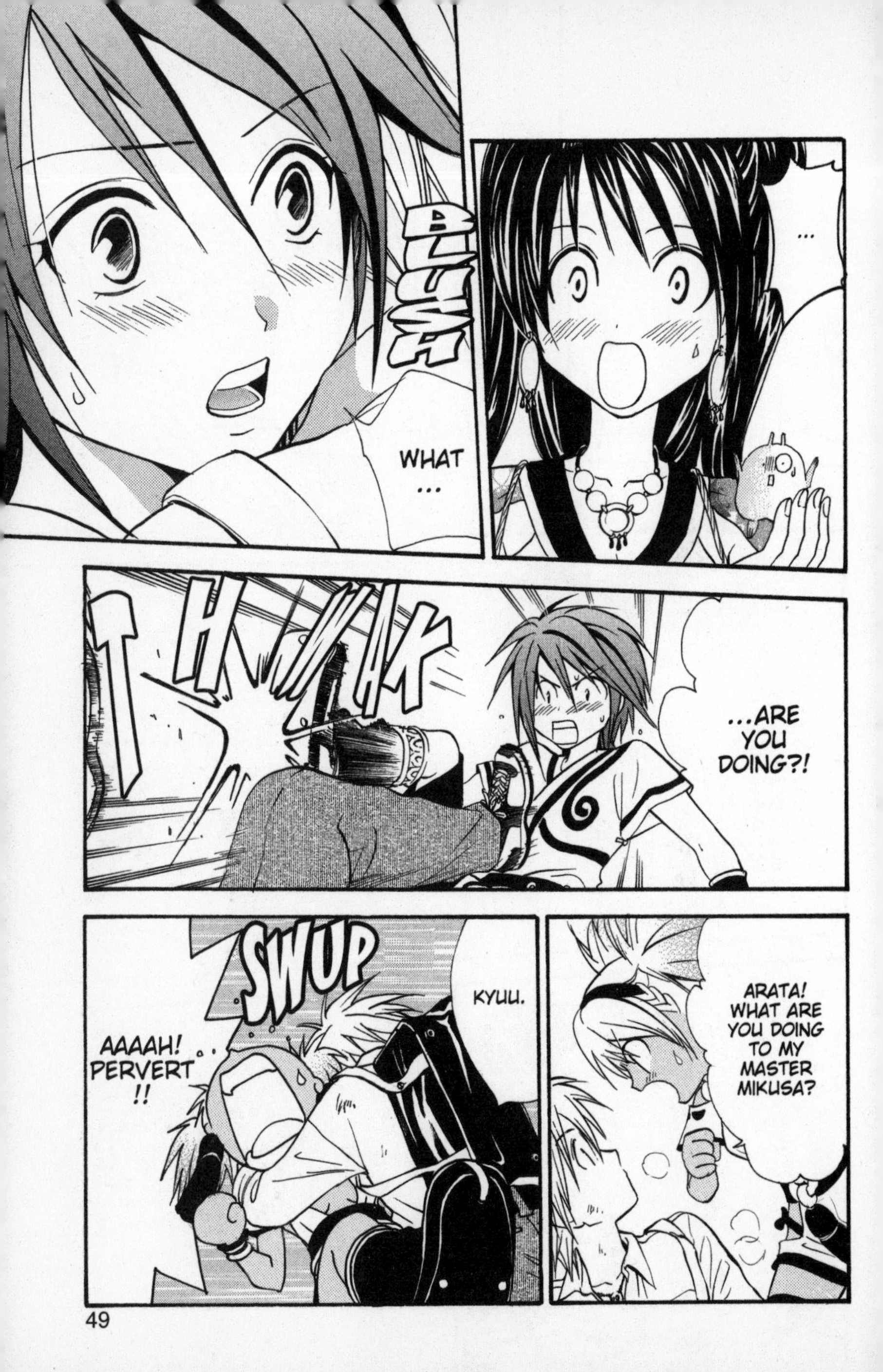
...
BLUSH
WHAT ...
THWAK
...ARE YOU DOING?!
ARATA! WHAT ARE YOU DOING TO MY MASTER MIKUSA?
SWUP
KYUU.
AAAAH! PERVERT!!

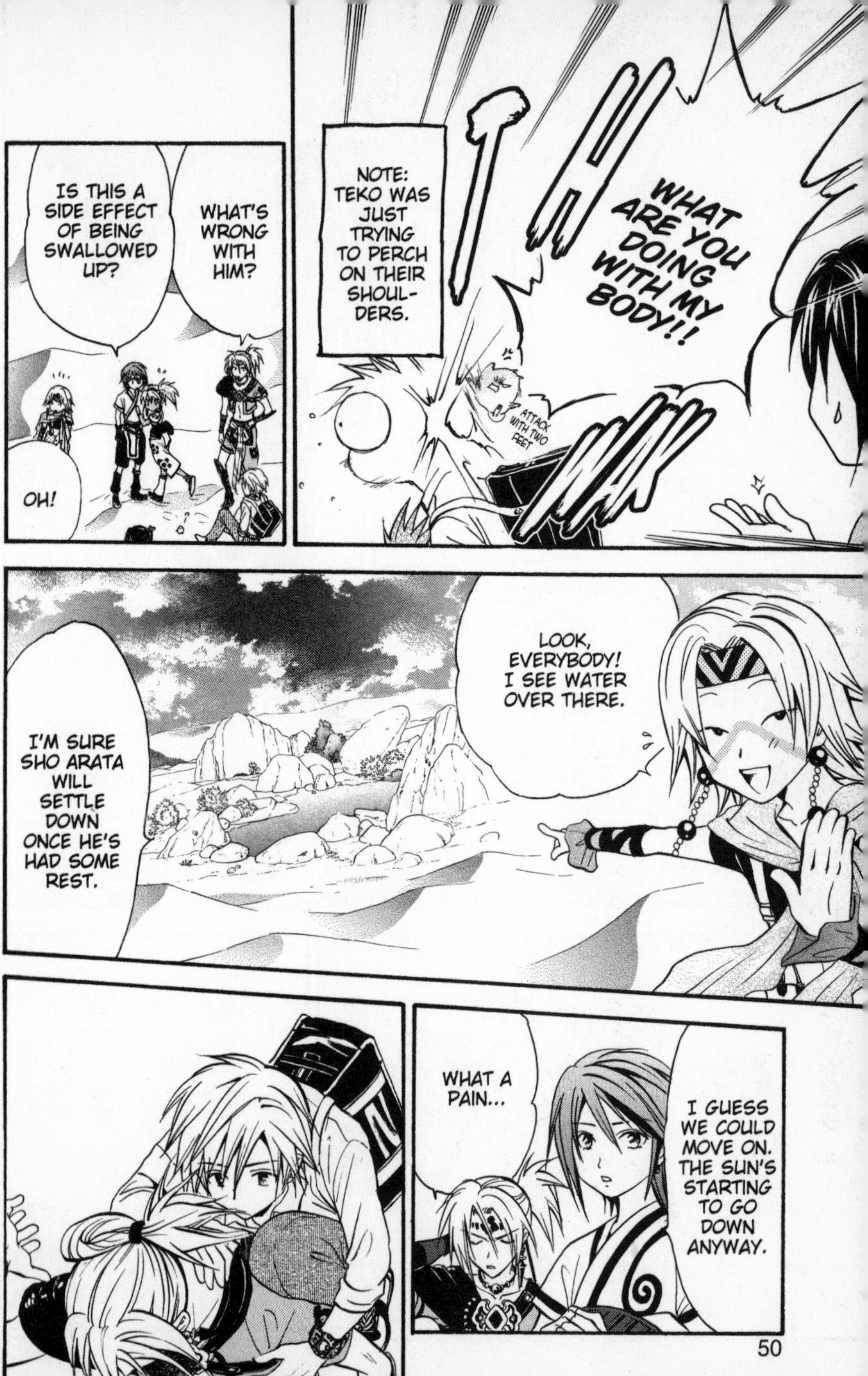
WHAT ARE YOU DOING WITH MY BODY!!
ATTACK WITH TWO FEET
NOTE: TEKO WAS JUST TRYING TO PERCH ON THEIR SHOULDERS.
WHAT'S WRONG WITH HIM?
IS THIS A SIDE EFFECT OF BEING SWALLOWED UP?
OH!
LOOK, EVERYBODY! I SEE WATER OVER THERE.
I'M SURE SHO ARATA WILL SETTLE DOWN ONCE HE'S HAD SOME REST.
I GUESS WE COULD MOVE ON. THE SUN'S STARTING TO GO DOWN ANYWAY.
WHAT A PAIN...

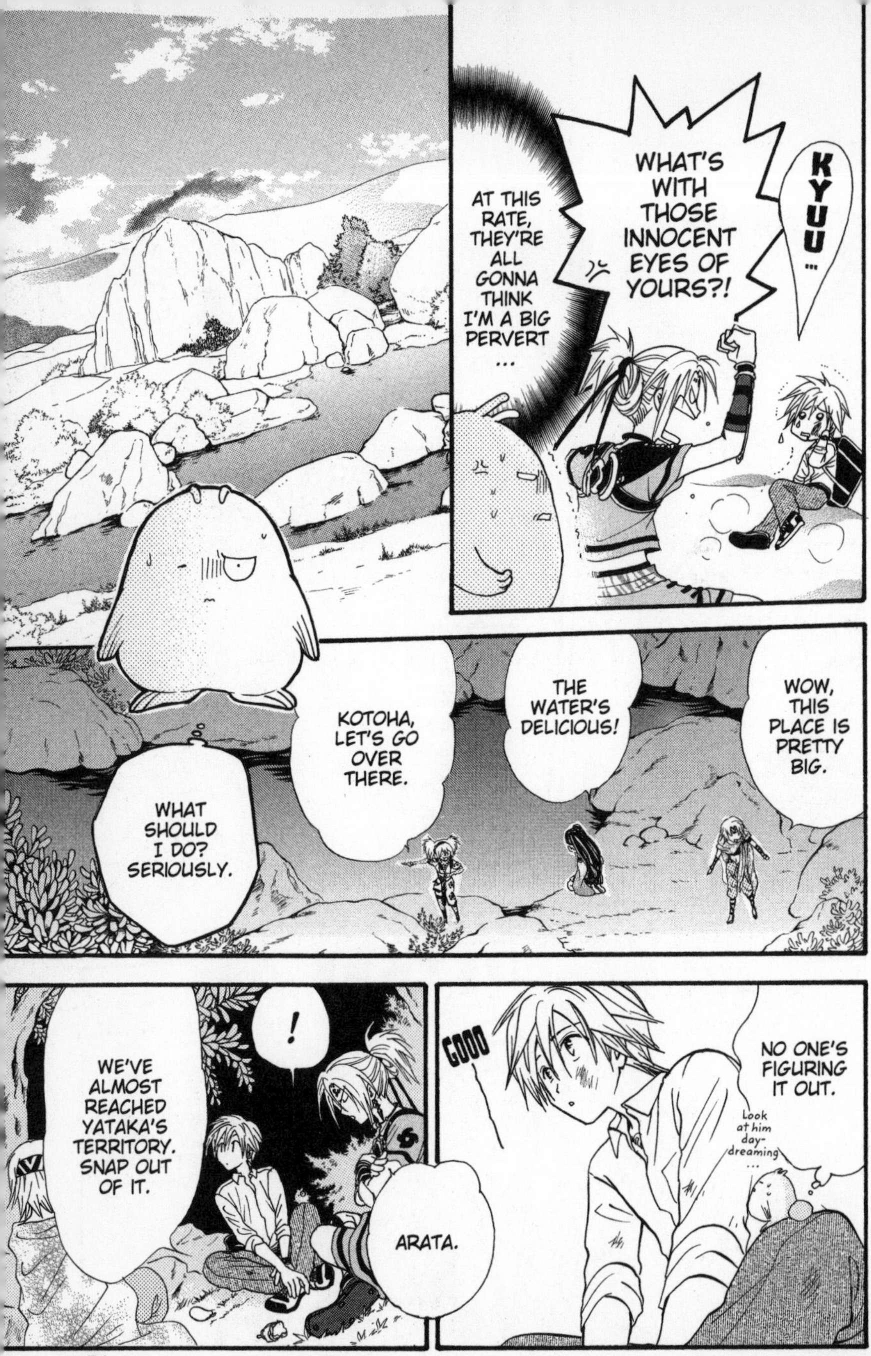
KYUU...
WHAT'S WITH THOSE INNOCENT EYES OF YOURS?!
AT THIS RATE, THEY'RE ALL GONNA THINK I'M A BIG PERVERT...
WOW, THIS PLACE IS PRETTY BIG.
THE WATER'S DELICIOUS!
KOTOHA, LET'S GO OVER THERE.
WHAT SHOULD I DO? SERIOUSLY.
NO ONE'S FIGURING IT OUT.
Look at him day-dreaming...
GOOO
!
ARATA.
WE'VE ALMOST REACHED YATAKA'S TERRITORY. SNAP OUT OF IT.

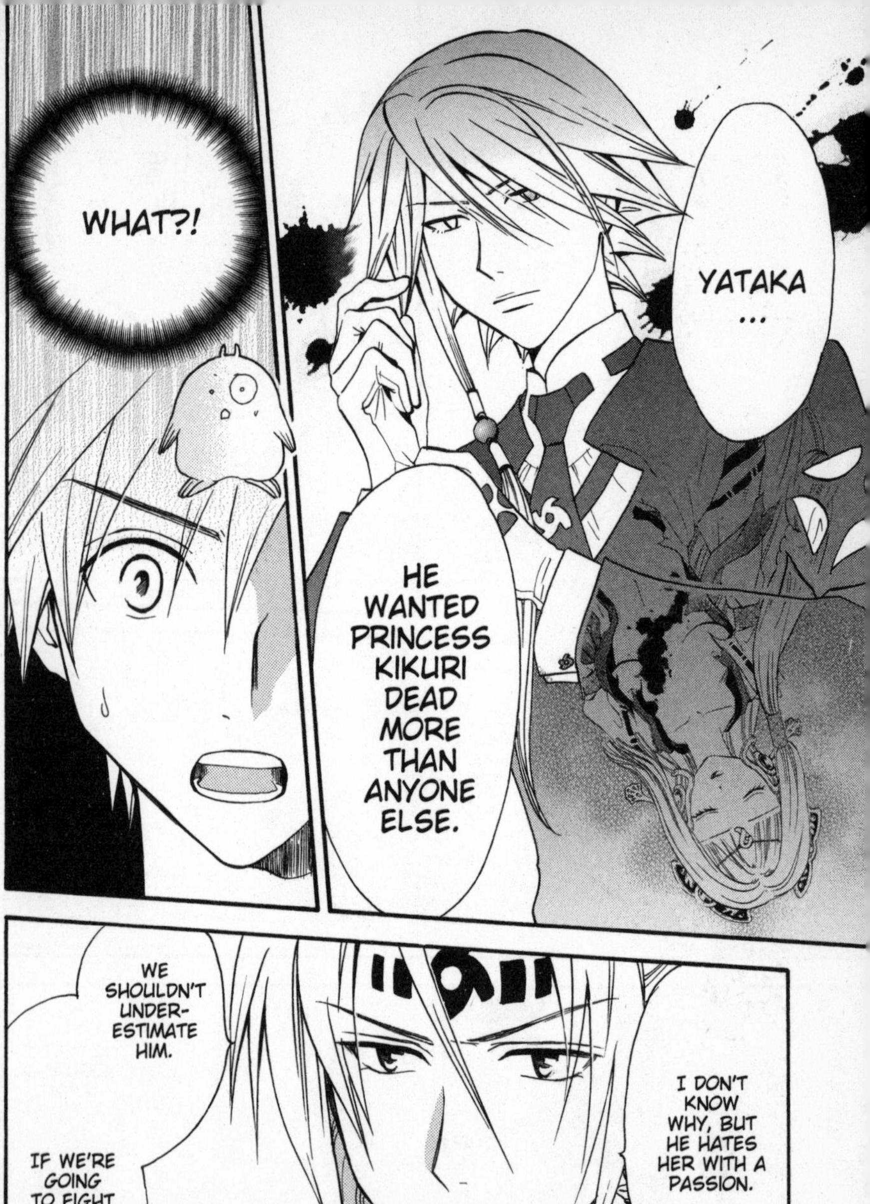
YATAKA ...
HE WANTED PRINCESS KIKURI DEAD MORE THAN ANYONE ELSE.
WHAT?!
I DON'T KNOW WHY, BUT HE HATES HER WITH A PASSION.
WE SHOULDN'T UNDER-ESTIMATE HIM.
IF WE'RE GOING TO FIGHT HIM, WE'D BETTER NOT...

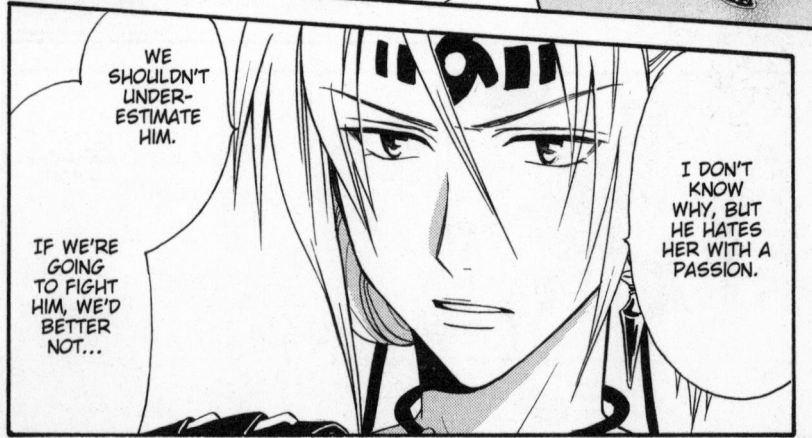

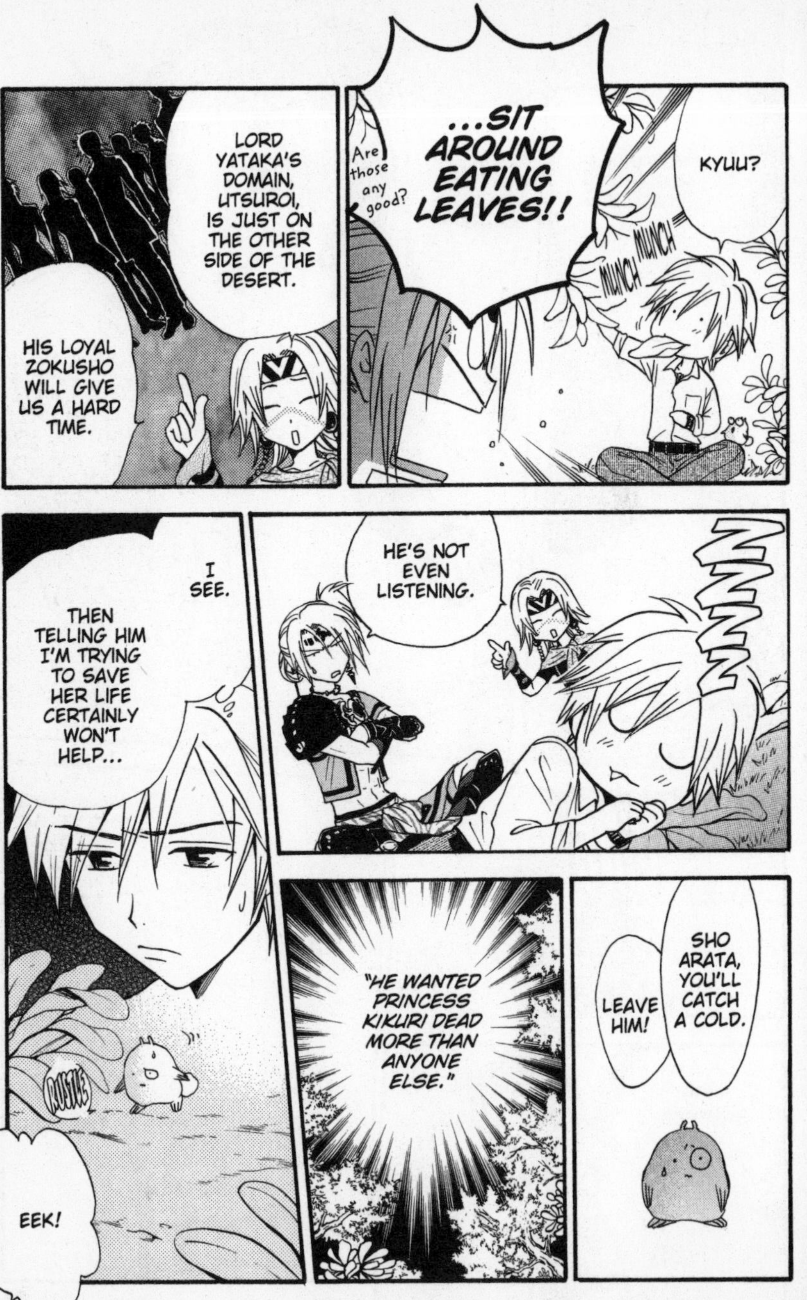
...SIT AROUND EATING LEAVES!!
Are those any good?
KYUU?
MUNCH MUNCH
LORD YATAKA'S DOMAIN, UTSUROI, IS JUST ON THE OTHER SIDE OF THE DESERT.
HIS LOYAL ZOKUSHO WILL GIVE US A HARD TIME.
ZZZZZ
HE'S NOT EVEN LISTENING.
SHO ARATA, YOU'LL CATCH A COLD.
LEAVE HIM!
"HE WANTED PRINCESS KIKURI DEAD MORE THAN ANYONE ELSE."
I SEE.
THEN TELLING HIM I'M TRYING TO SAVE HER LIFE CERTAINLY WON'T HELP...
RUSTLE
EEK!

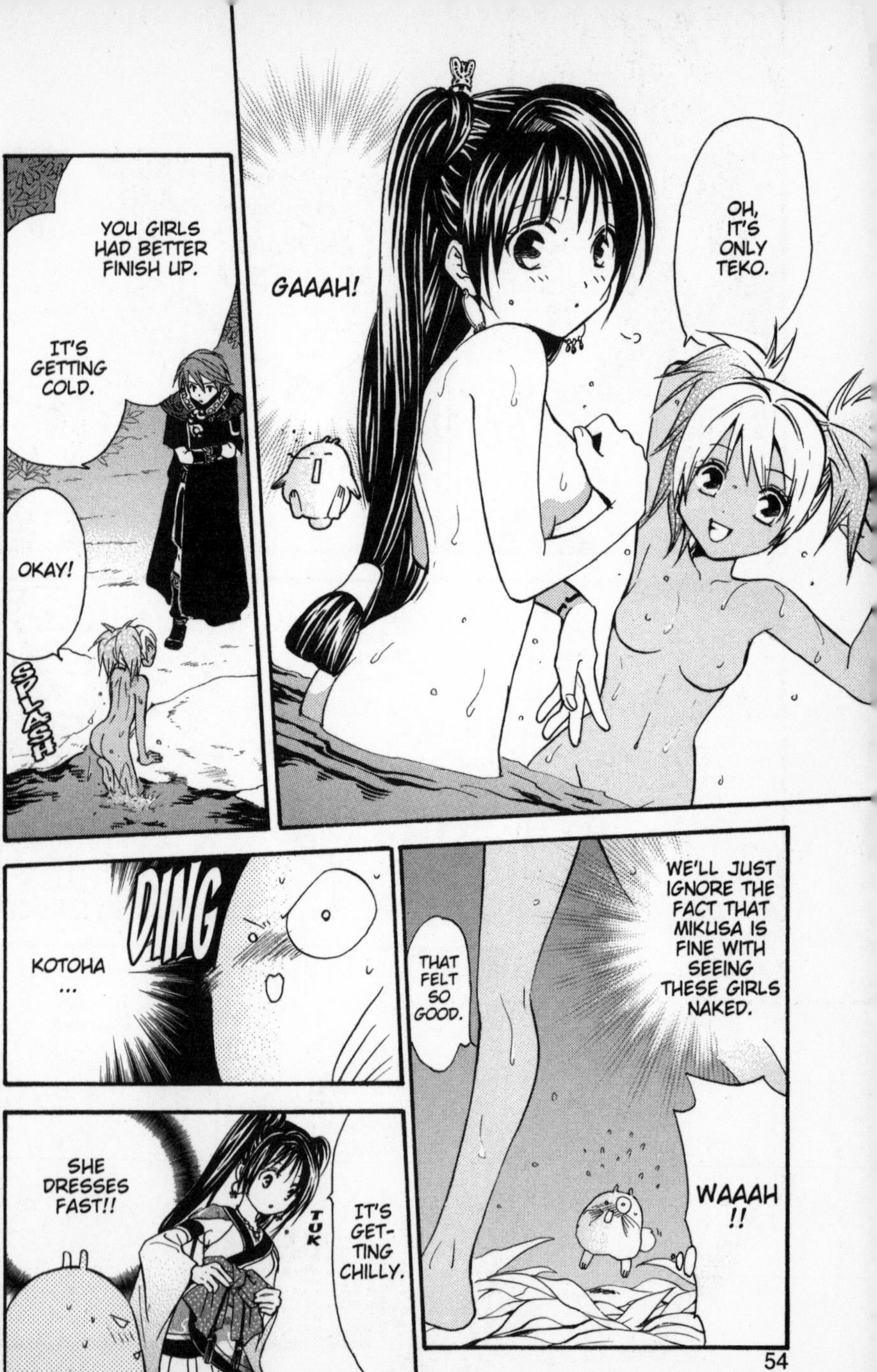
OH, IT'S ONLY TEKO.
GAAAH!
YOU GIRLS HAD BETTER FINISH UP.
IT'S GETTING COLD.
OKAY!
SPLASH
WE'LL JUST IGNORE THE FACT THAT MIKUSA IS FINE WITH SEEING THESE GIRLS NAKED.
THAT FELT SO GOOD.
WAAAH !!
DING
KOTOHA ...
IT'S GET-TING CHILLY.
TUK
SHE DRESSES FAST!!

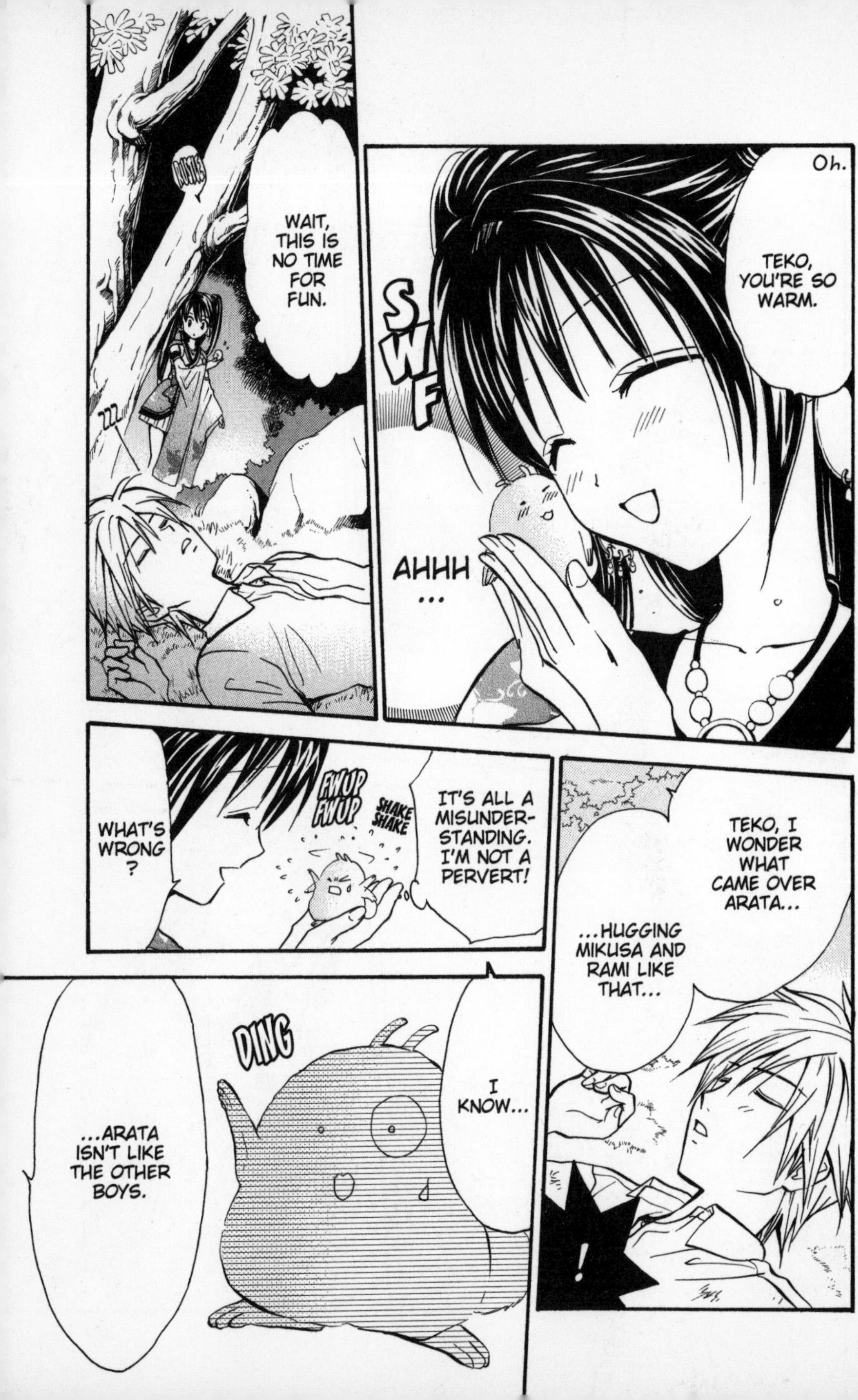
Oh.
TEKO, YOU'RE SO WARM.
SWF
AHHH ...
RUSTLE
WAIT, THIS IS NO TIME FOR FUN.
ZZZ
TEKO, I WONDER WHAT CAME OVER ARATA...
...HUGGING MIKUSA AND RAMI LIKE THAT...
!
IT'S ALL A MISUNDERSTANDING. I'M NOT A PERVERT!
SHAKE SHAKE
FWUP FWUP
WHAT'S WRONG?
I KNOW...
DING
...ARATA ISN'T LIKE THE OTHER BOYS.

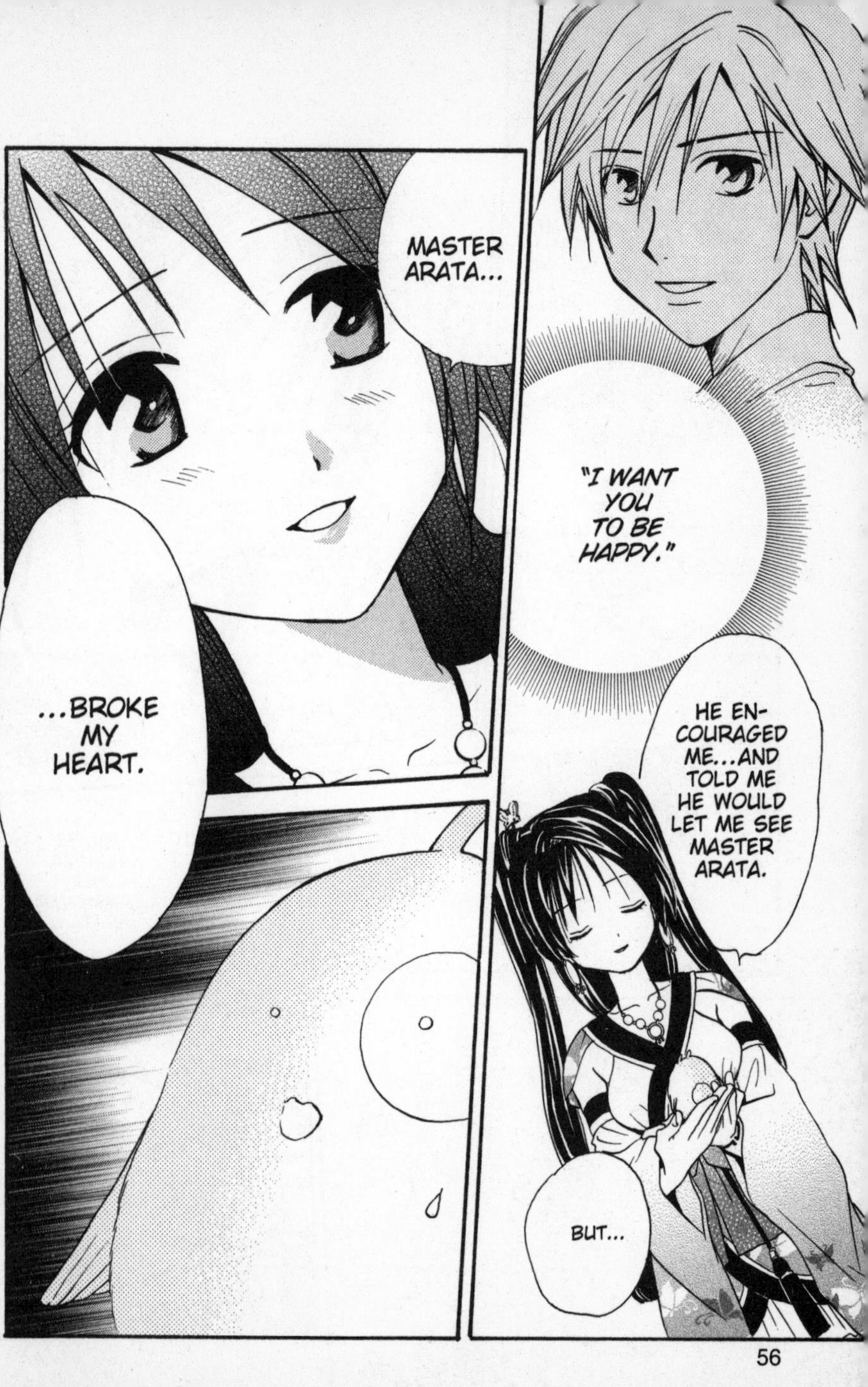
"I WANT YOU TO BE HAPPY."
HE EN-COURAGED ME...AND TOLD ME HE WOULD LET ME SEE MASTER ARATA.
BUT...
MASTER ARATA...
...BROKE MY HEART.

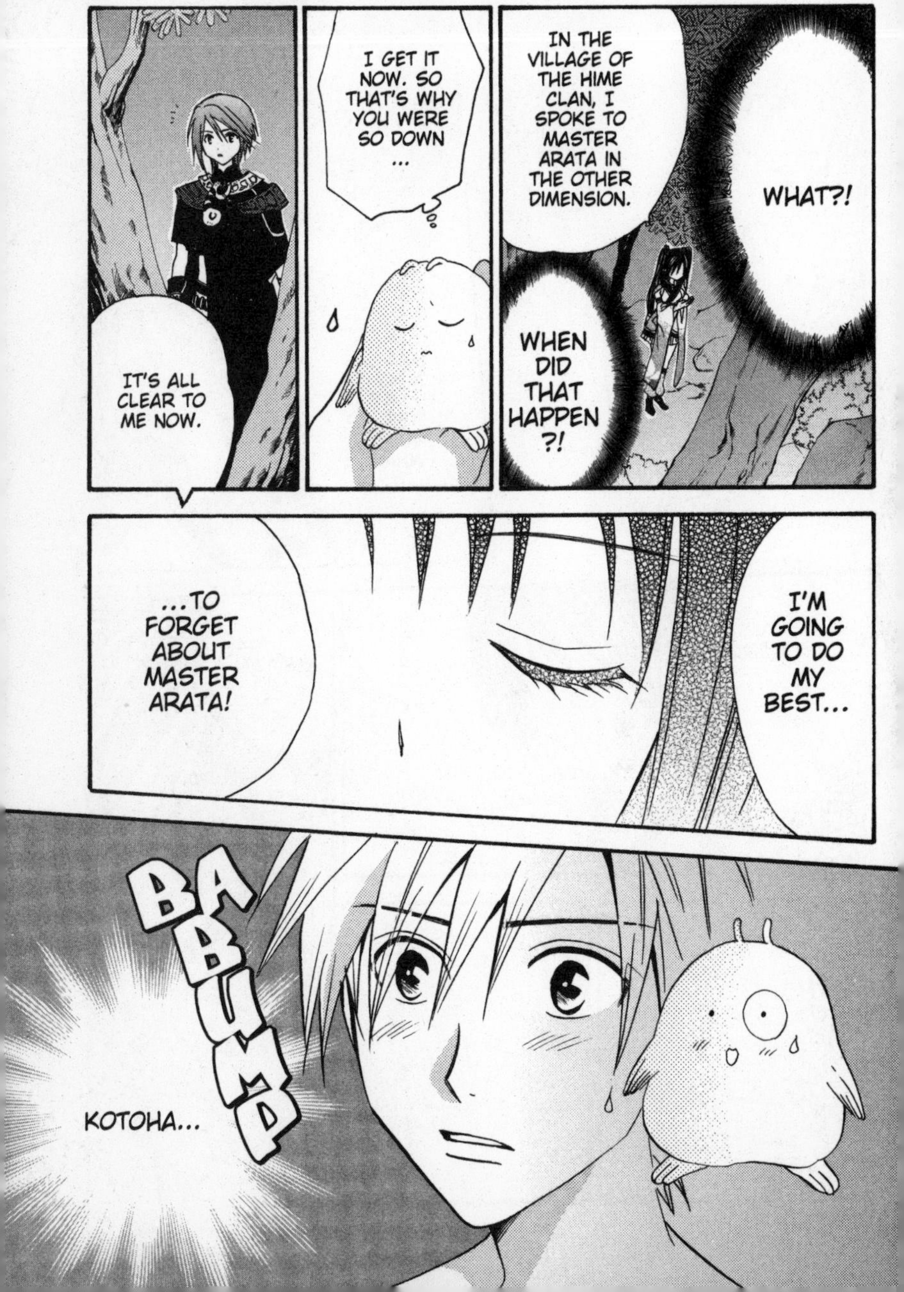
WHAT?!
IN THE VILLAGE OF THE HIME CLAN, I SPOKE TO MASTER ARATA IN THE OTHER DIMENSION.
WHEN DID THAT HAPPEN?!
I GET IT NOW. SO THAT'S WHY YOU WERE SO DOWN ...
IT'S ALL CLEAR TO ME NOW.
I'M GOING TO DO MY BEST...
...TO FORGET ABOUT MASTER ARATA!
BABUMP
KOTOHA...

KOTOHA...

MASTER ARATA WOULDN'T ABANDON ME.

HE SAID I'LL ALWAYS BE HIS LITTLE SISTER, NO MATTER WHAT.

THAT'S WEIRD!

?

WHY AM I TELLING YOU ALL THIS?

ANYWAY...

TUP

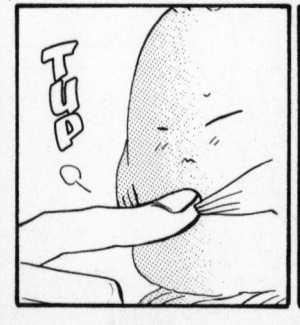

I GUESS...

...THERE'S NO ONE I CAN TALK TO ABOUT IT.

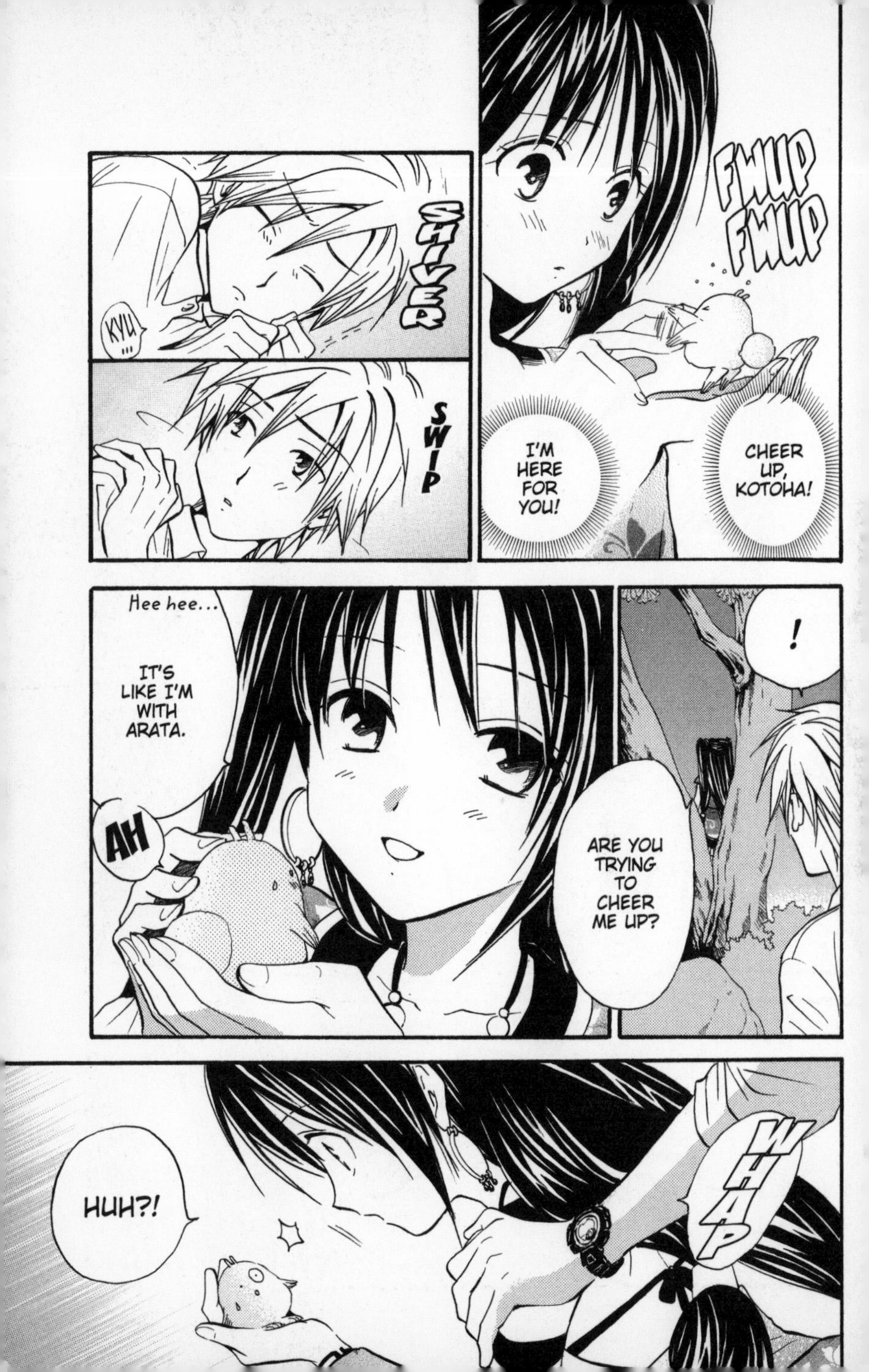
FWUP FWUP
CHEER UP, KOTOHA!
I'M HERE FOR YOU!
SHIVER
KYU...
SWIP
!
Hee hee...
ARE YOU TRYING TO CHEER ME UP?
IT'S LIKE I'M WITH ARATA.
AH
WHAP
HUH?!

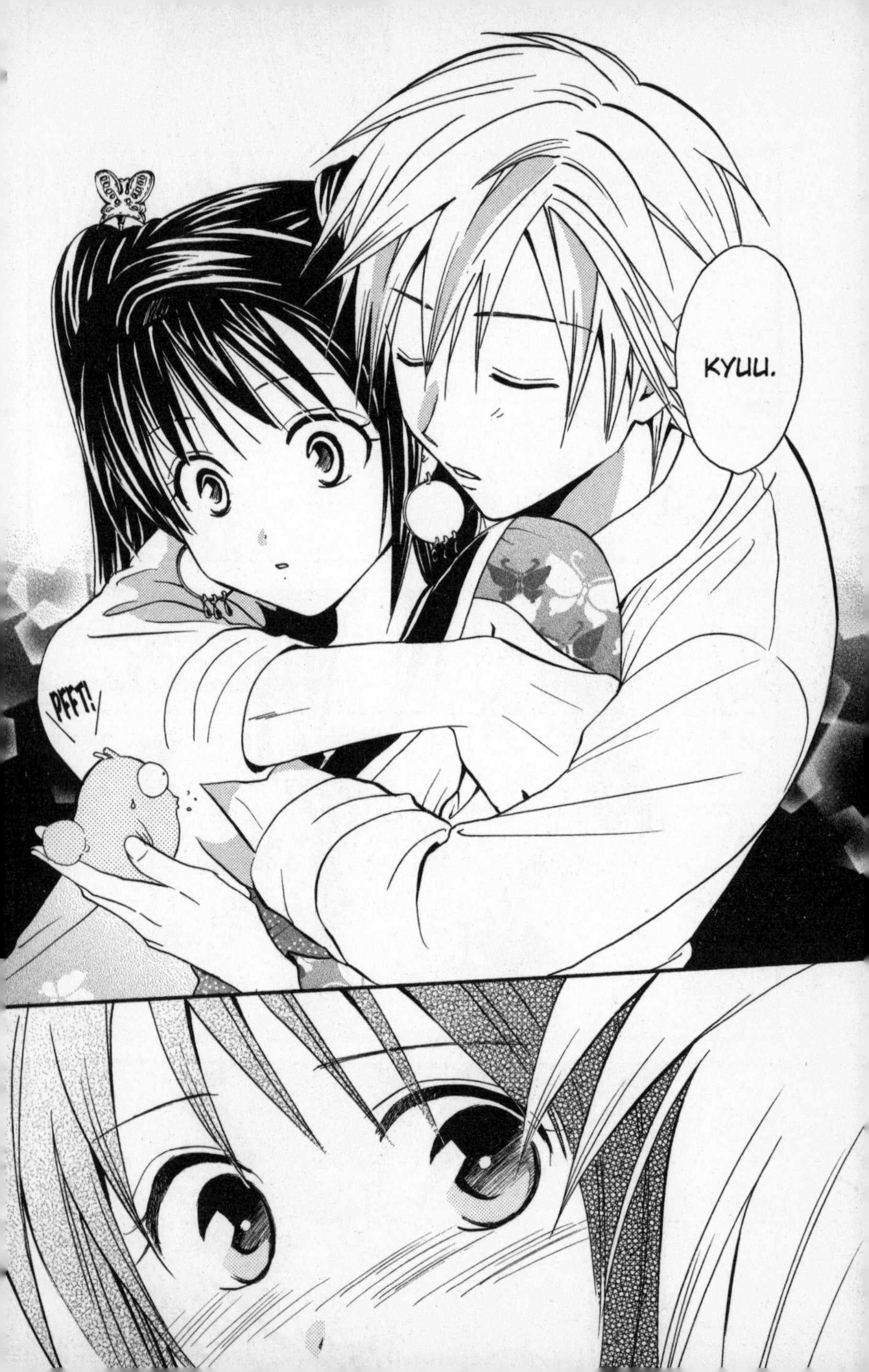
KYUU.
PFFT!

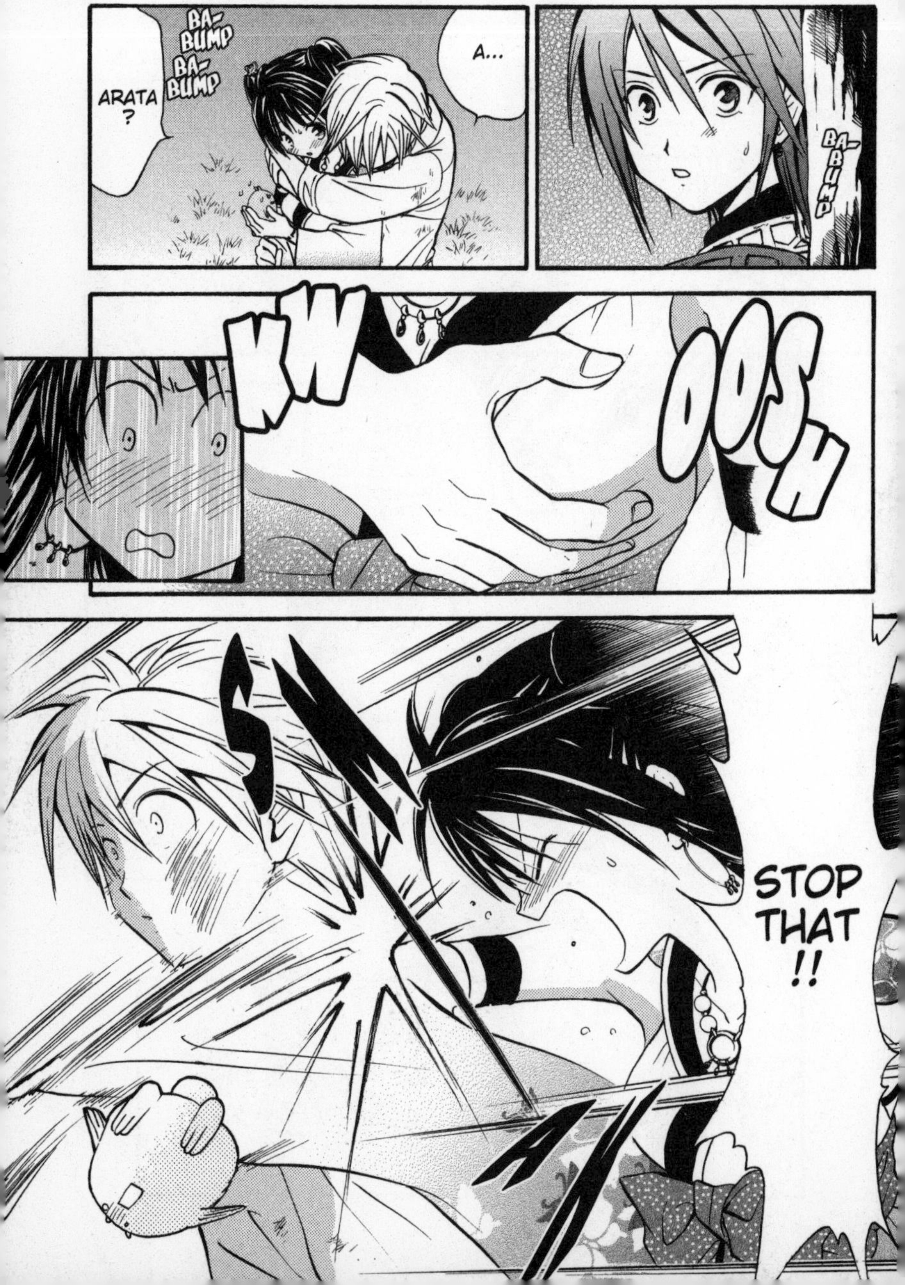
BA-BUMP
A...
BA-BUMP BA-BUMP
ARATA ?
WHOOSH
STOP THAT!!

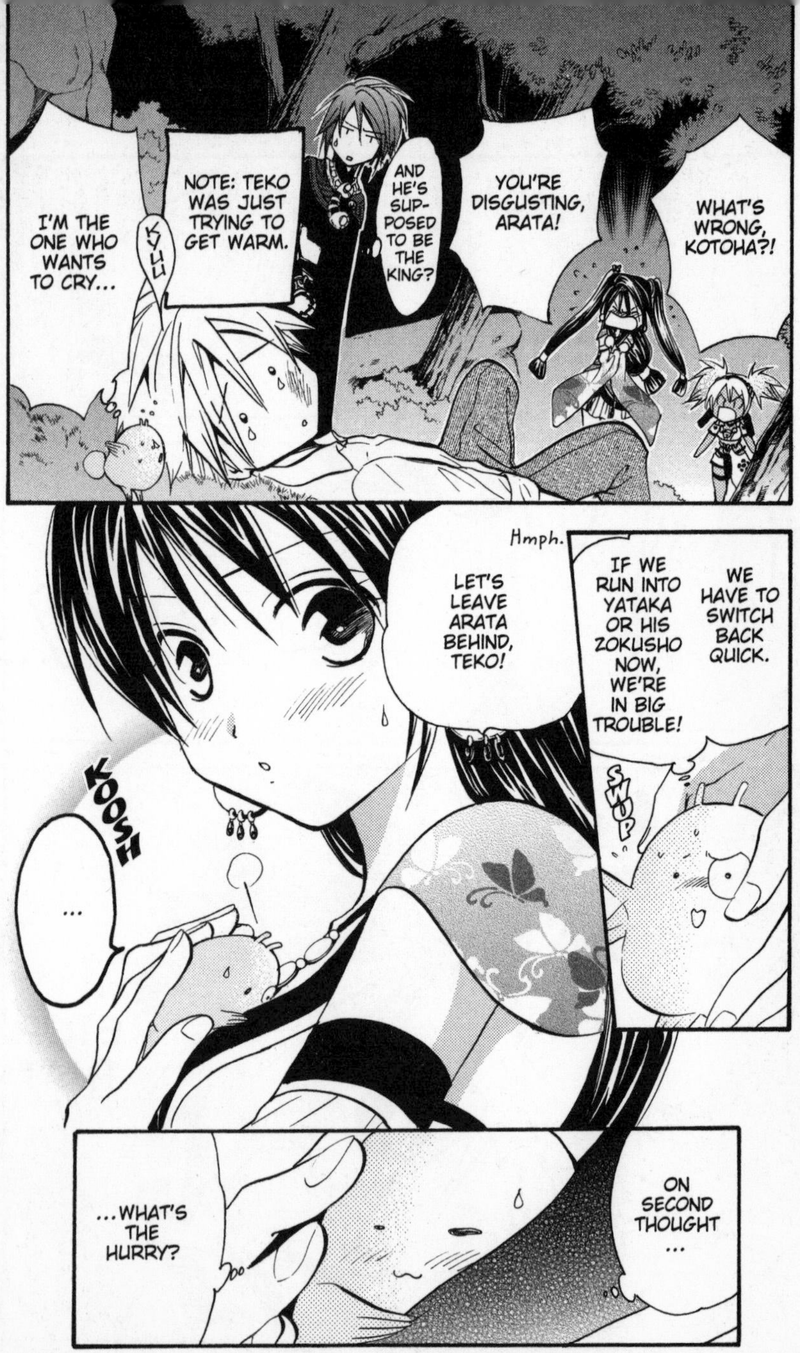
WHAT'S WRONG, KOTOHA?!
YOU'RE DISGUSTING, ARATA!
AND HE'S SUP-POSED TO BE THE KING?
NOTE: TEKO WAS JUST TRYING TO GET WARM.
KYUU
I'M THE ONE WHO WANTS TO CRY...
Hmph.
WE HAVE TO SWITCH BACK QUICK.
IF WE RUN INTO YATAKA OR HIS ZOKUSHO NOW, WE'RE IN BIG TROUBLE!
SWUP
LET'S LEAVE ARATA BEHIND, TEKO!
KOOSH
...
ON SECOND THOUGHT...
...WHAT'S THE HURRY?

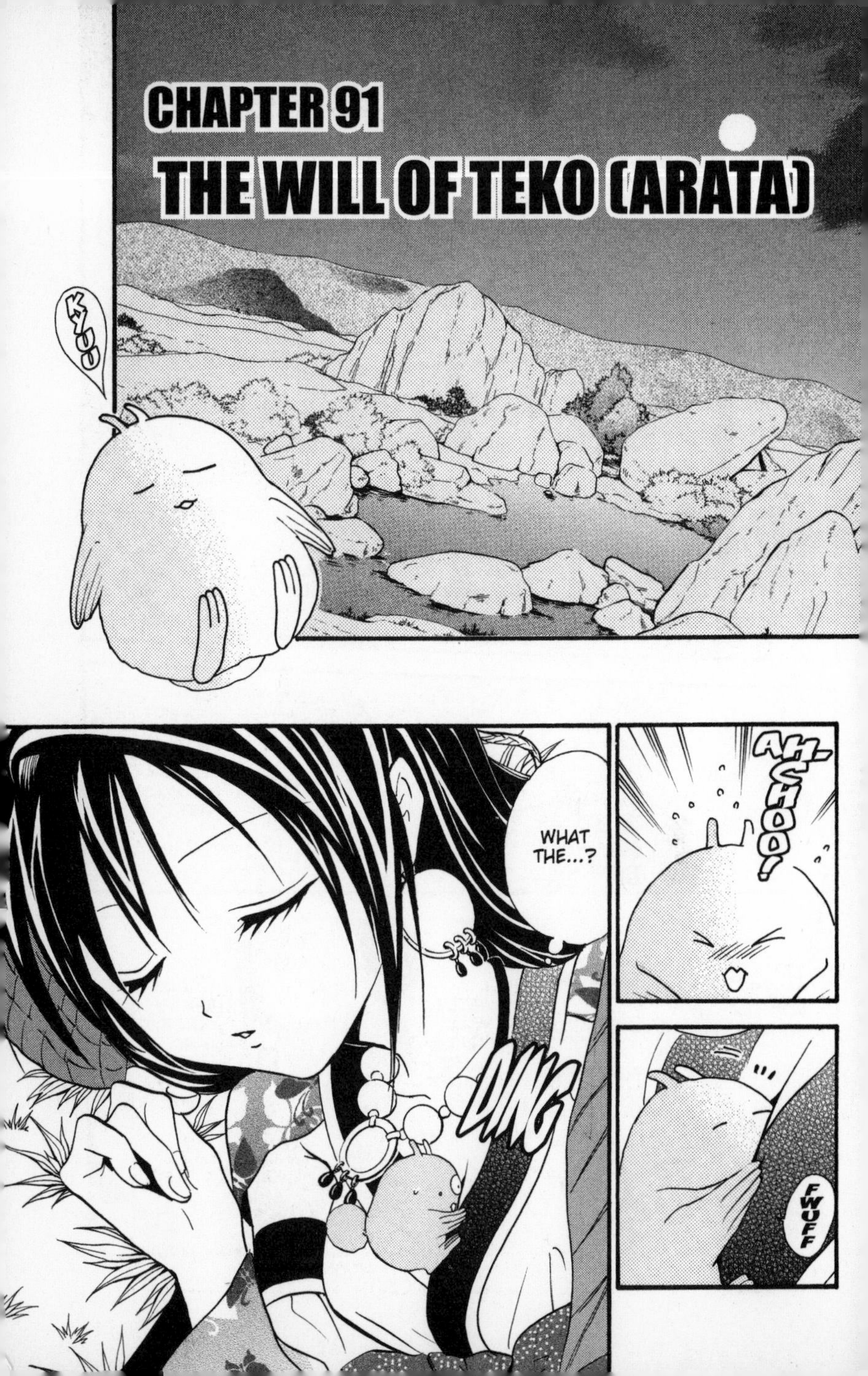
CHAPTER 91
THE WILL OF TEKO (ARATA)
KYUU
AH-CHOO!
...
FWUFF
WHAT THE...?
DING

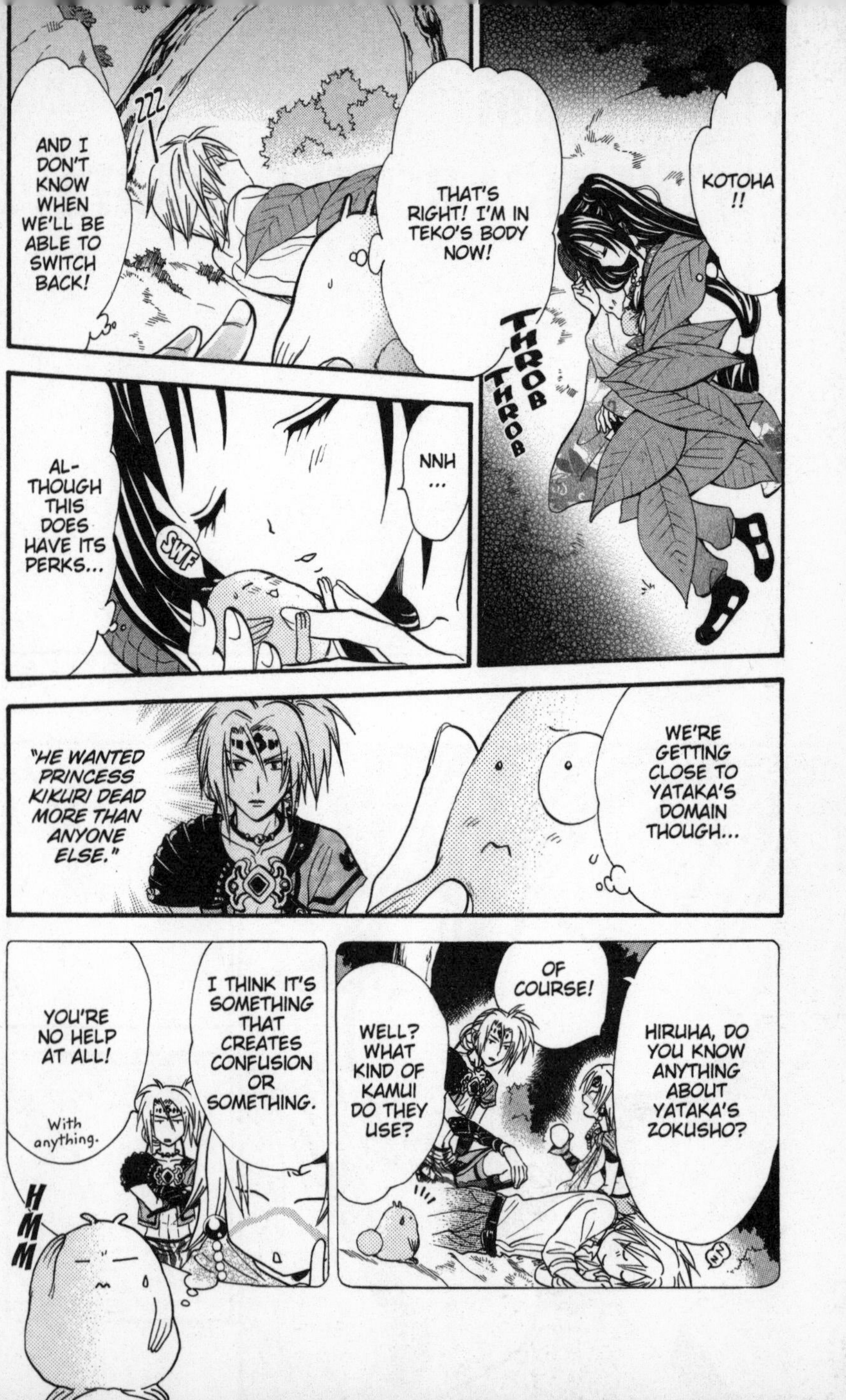
KOTOHA !!
THROB THROB
THAT'S RIGHT! I'M IN TEKO'S BODY NOW!
AND I DON'T KNOW WHEN WE'LL BE ABLE TO SWITCH BACK!
ZZZ
NNH ...
AL-THOUGH THIS DOES HAVE ITS PERKS...
SWF
WE'RE GETTING CLOSE TO YATAKA'S DOMAIN THOUGH...
"HE WANTED PRINCESS KIKURI DEAD MORE THAN ANYONE ELSE."
HIRUHA, DO YOU KNOW ANYTHING ABOUT YATAKA'S ZOKUSHO?
OF COURSE!
WELL? WHAT KIND OF KAMUI DO THEY USE?
NN
I THINK IT'S SOMETHING THAT CREATES CONFUSION OR SOMETHING.
YOU'RE NO HELP AT ALL!
With anything.
HMM

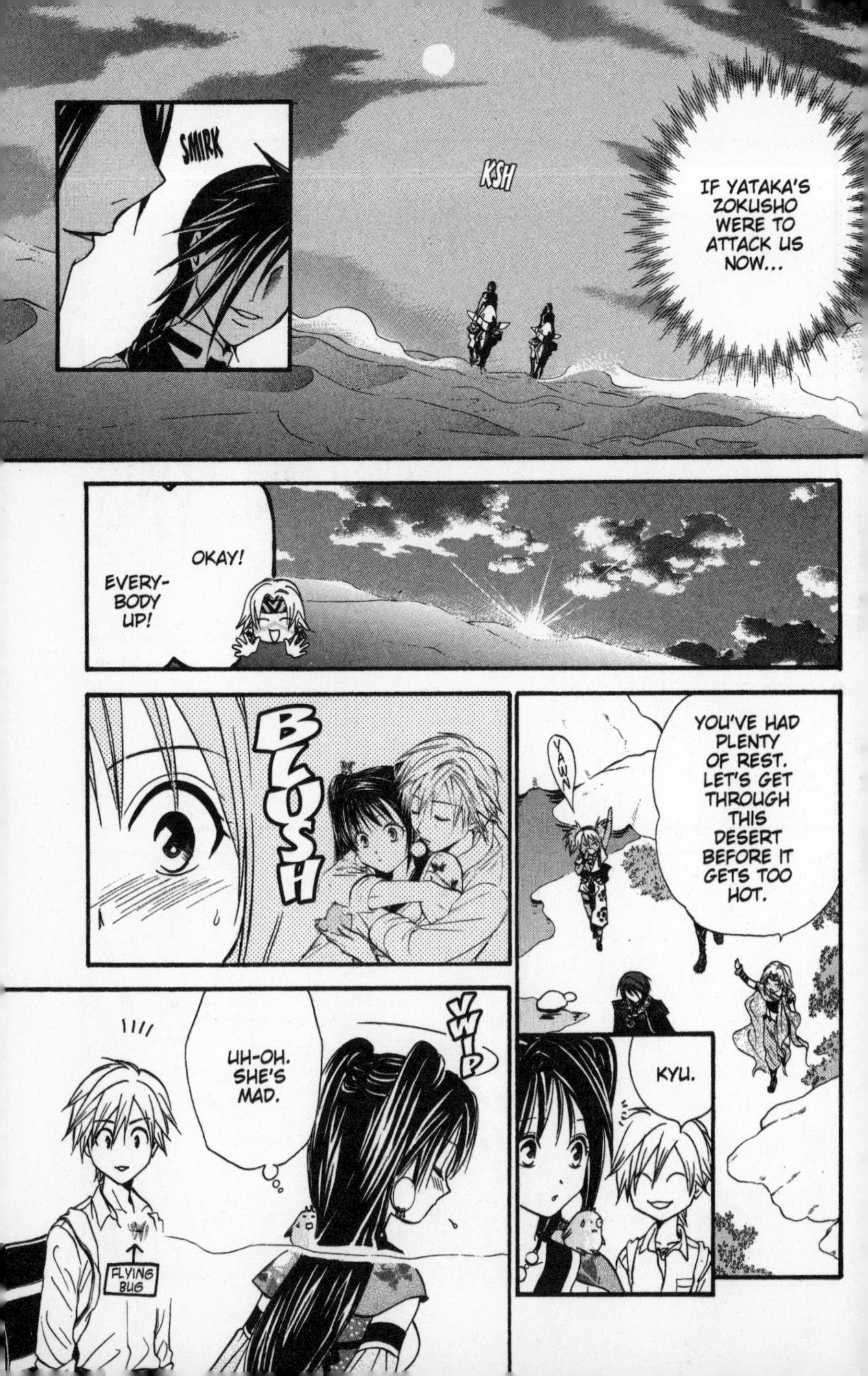
IF YATAKA'S ZOKUSHO WERE TO ATTACK US NOW...
KSH
SMIRK
OKAY!
EVERY-BODY UP!
YAWN
YOU'VE HAD PLENTY OF REST. LET'S GET THROUGH THIS DESERT BEFORE IT GETS TOO HOT.
BLUSH
KYU.
VWIP
UH-OH. SHE'S MAD.
FLYING BUG

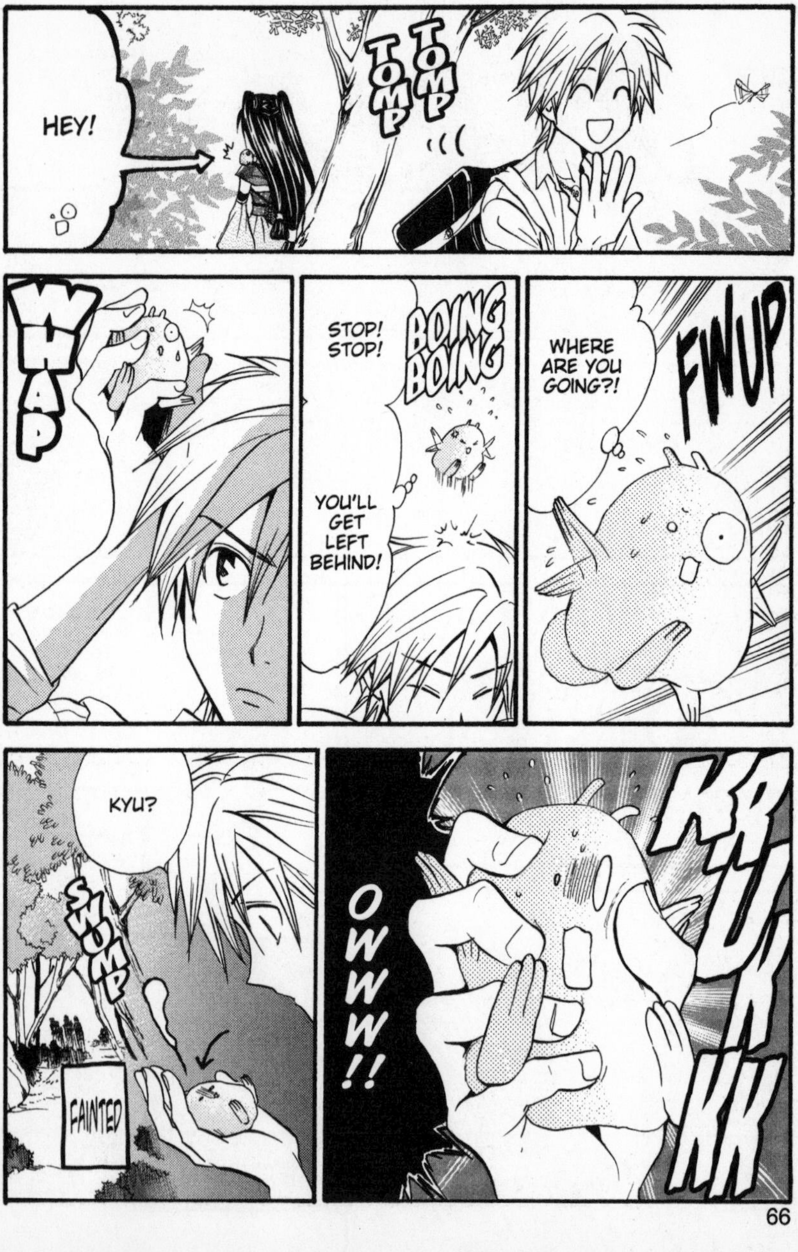
HEY!
TOMP TOMP
FWUP
WHERE ARE YOU GOING?!
STOP! STOP!
BOING BOING
YOU'LL GET LEFT BEHIND!
WHAP
KRUNKK
OWWW!!
KYU?
SWUMP
FAINTED

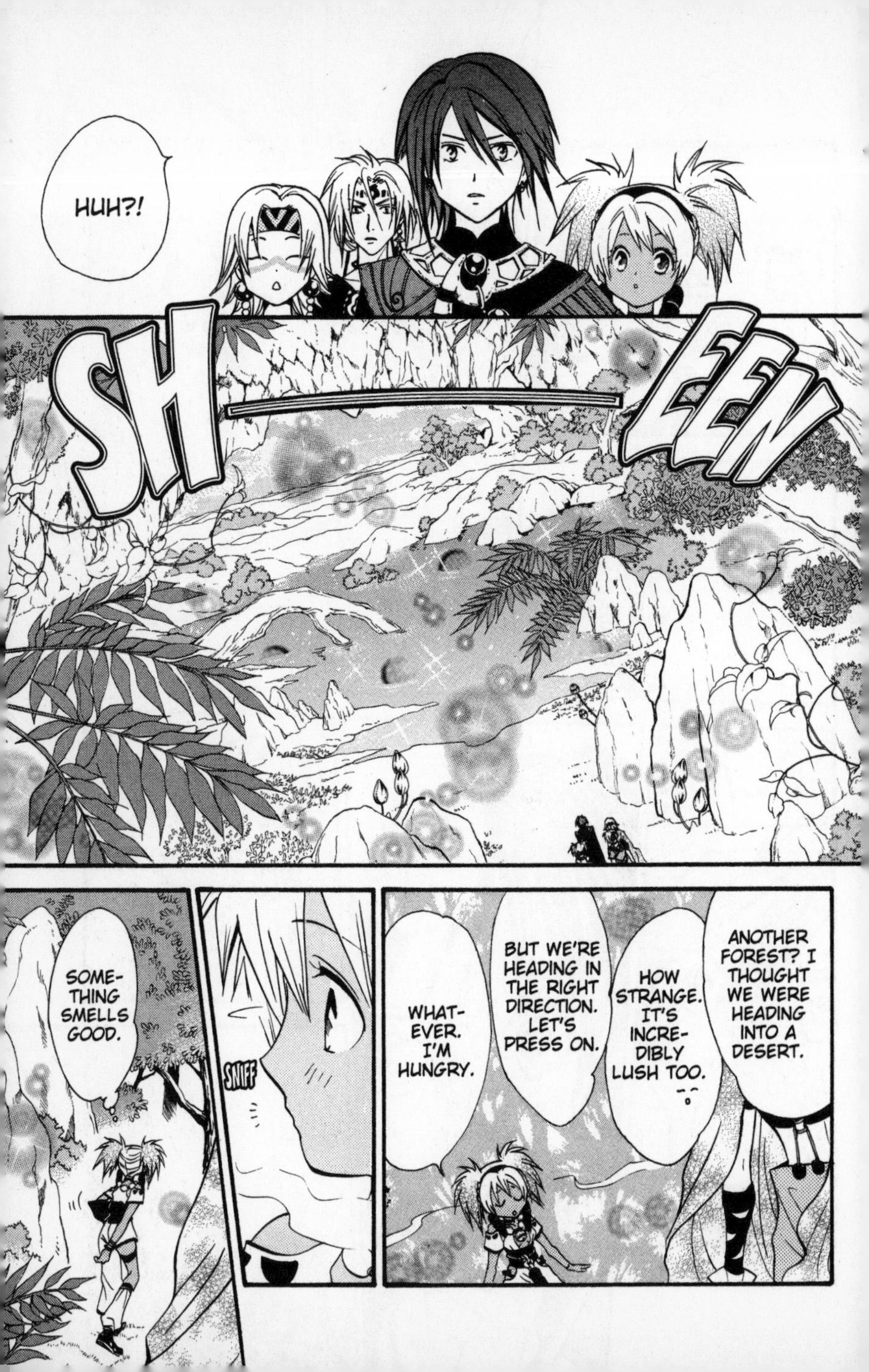
HUH?!
SH—EEN
ANOTHER FOREST? I THOUGHT WE WERE HEADING INTO A DESERT.
HOW STRANGE. IT'S INCREDIBLY LUSH TOO.
BUT WE'RE HEADING IN THE RIGHT DIRECTION. LET'S PRESS ON.
WHATEVER. I'M HUNGRY.
SNIFF
SOMETHING SMELLS GOOD.

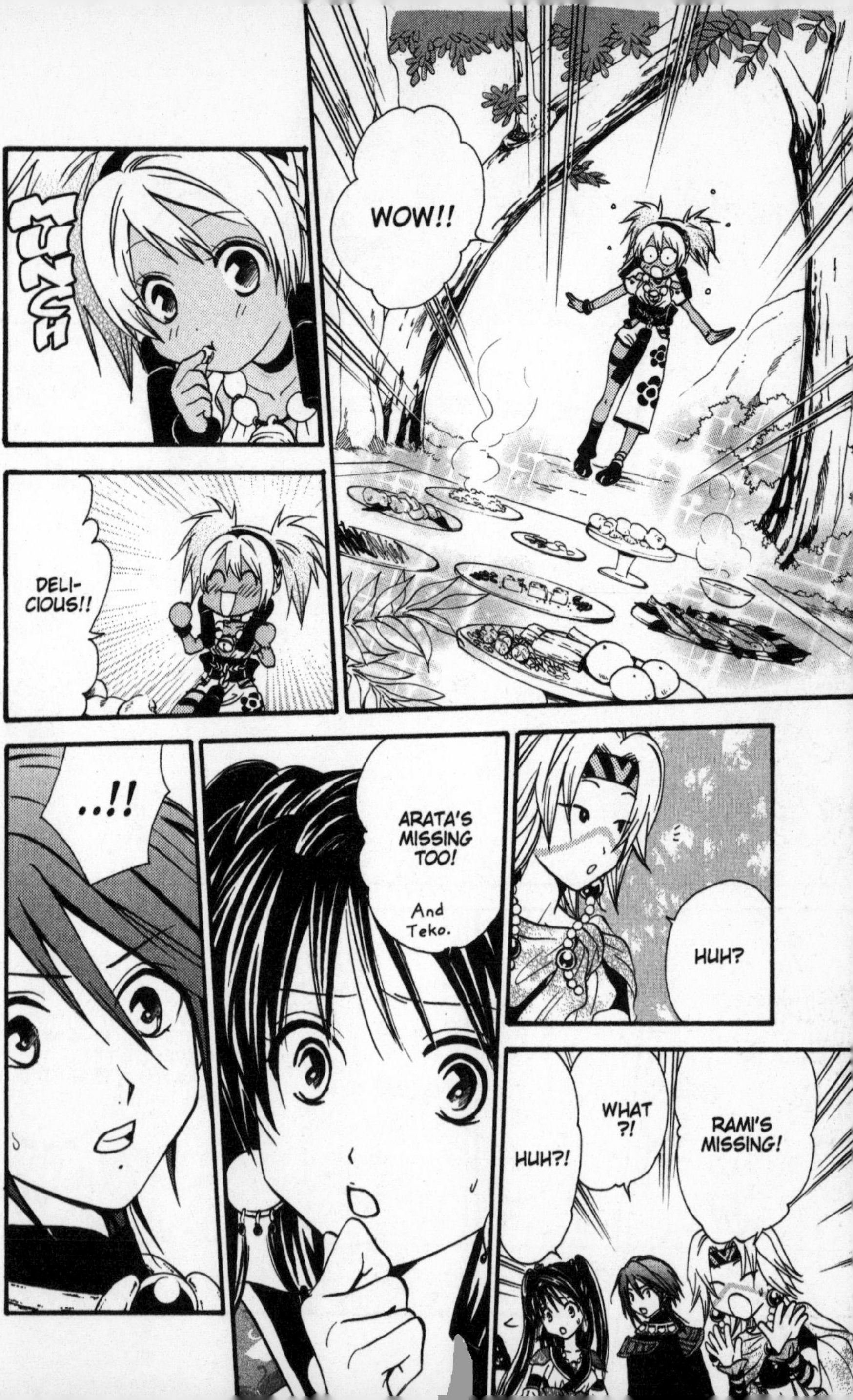
WOW!!
MUNCH
DELI-CIOUS!!
HUH?
RAMI'S MISSING!
WHAT ?!
HUH?!
ARATA'S MISSING TOO!
And Teko.
..!!

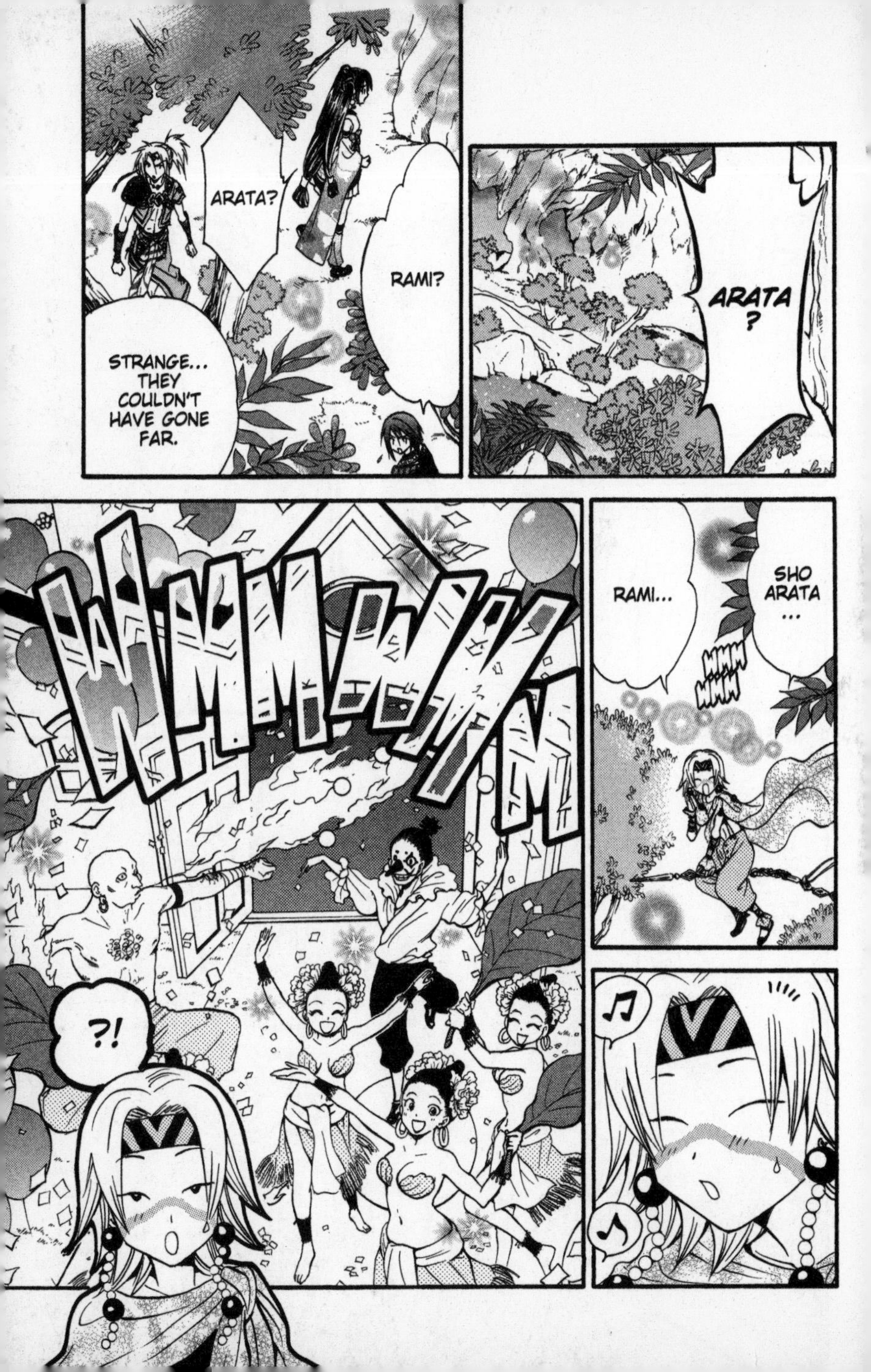
ARATA ?
RAMI?
ARATA?
STRANGE... THEY COULDN'T HAVE GONE FAR.
SHO ARATA ...
RAMI...
WMM WMM
?!

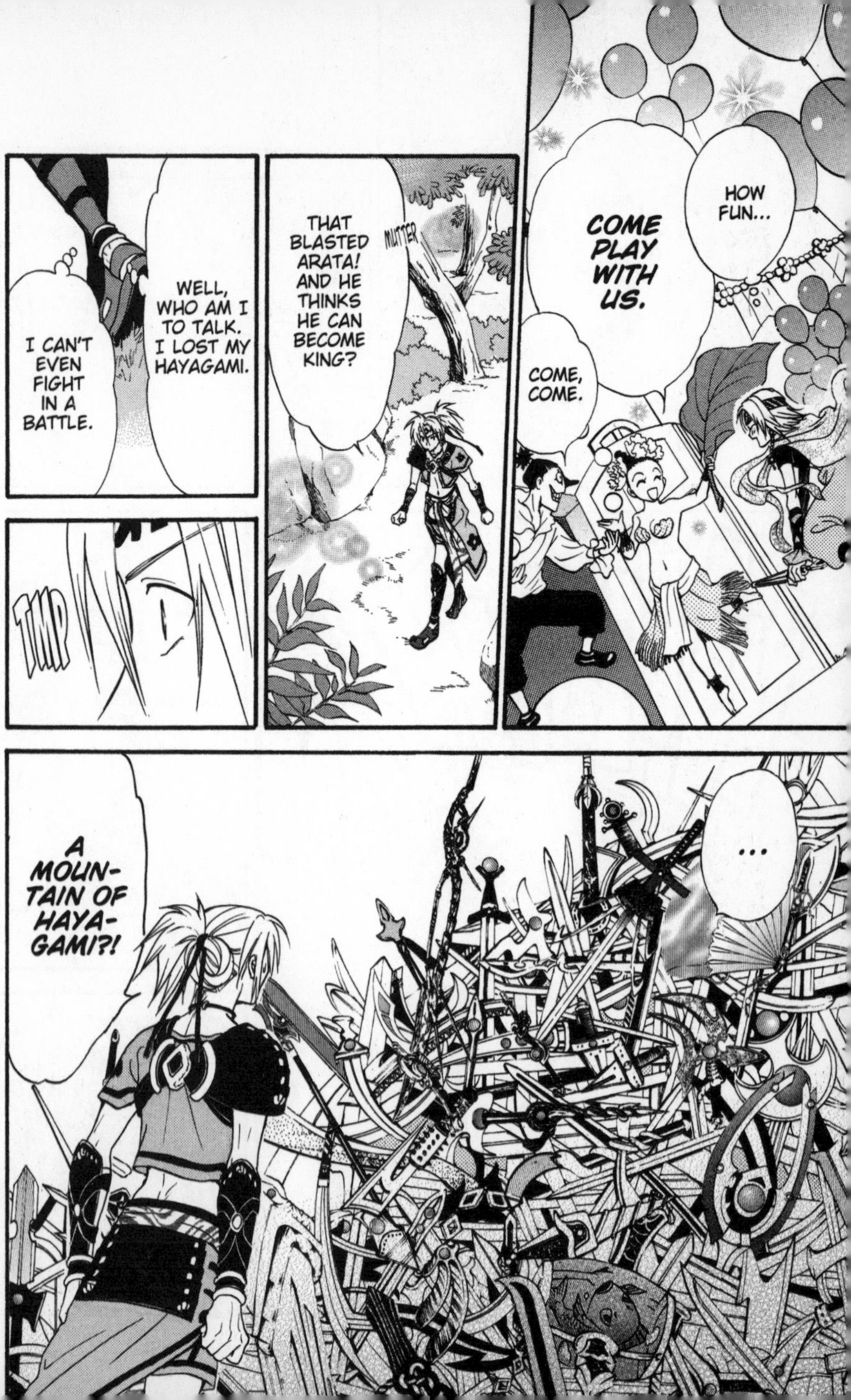
HOW FUN...
COME PLAY WITH US.
COME, COME.
MUTTER
THAT BLASTED ARATA! AND HE THINKS HE CAN BECOME KING?
WELL, WHO AM I TO TALK. I LOST MY HAYAGAMI.
I CAN'T EVEN FIGHT IN A BATTLE.
TMP
...
A MOUN-TAIN OF HAYA-GAMI?!

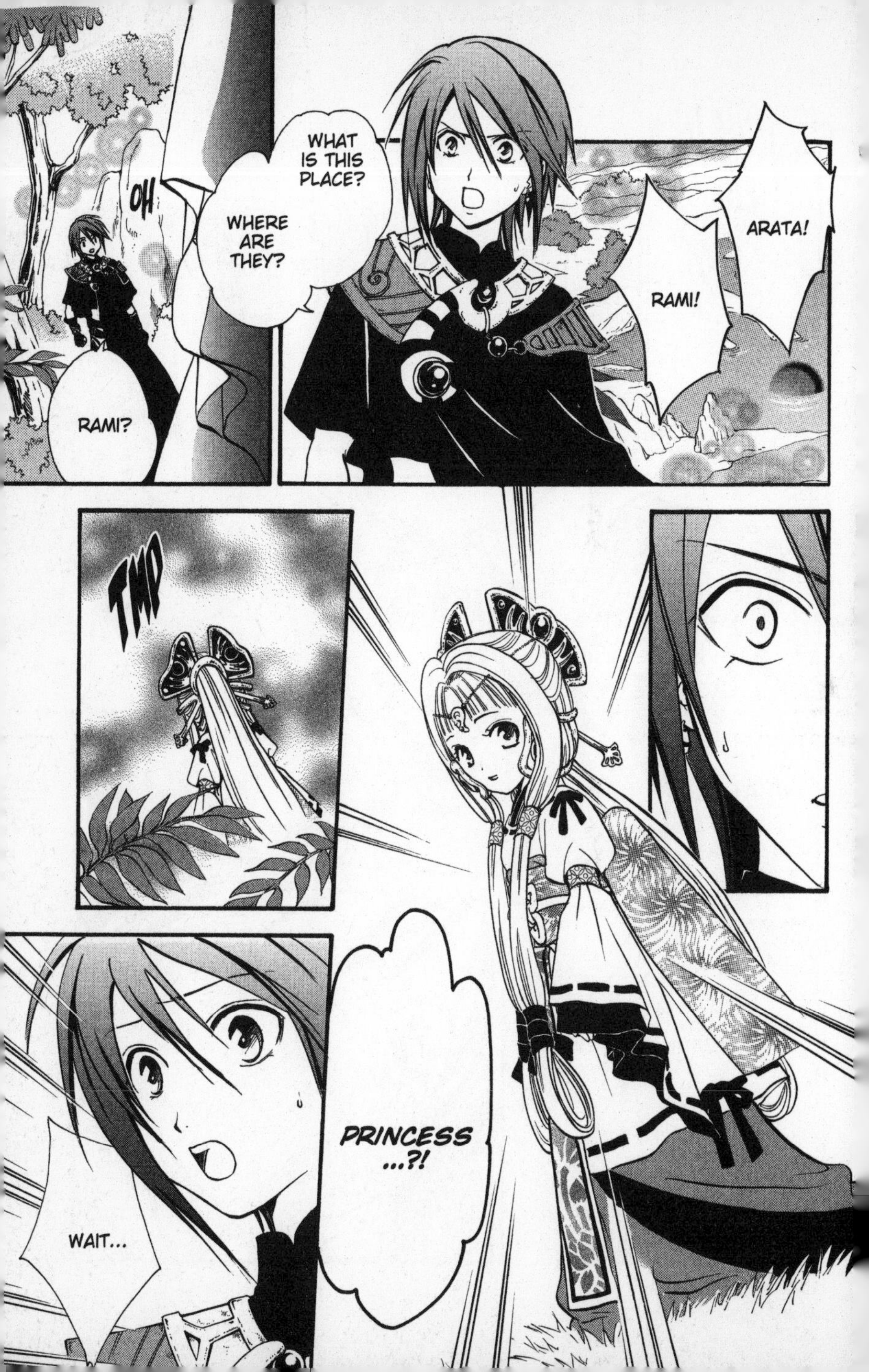
ARATA!
RAMI!
WHAT IS THIS PLACE?
WHERE ARE THEY?
OH
RAMI?
TMP
PRINCESS ...?!
WAIT...

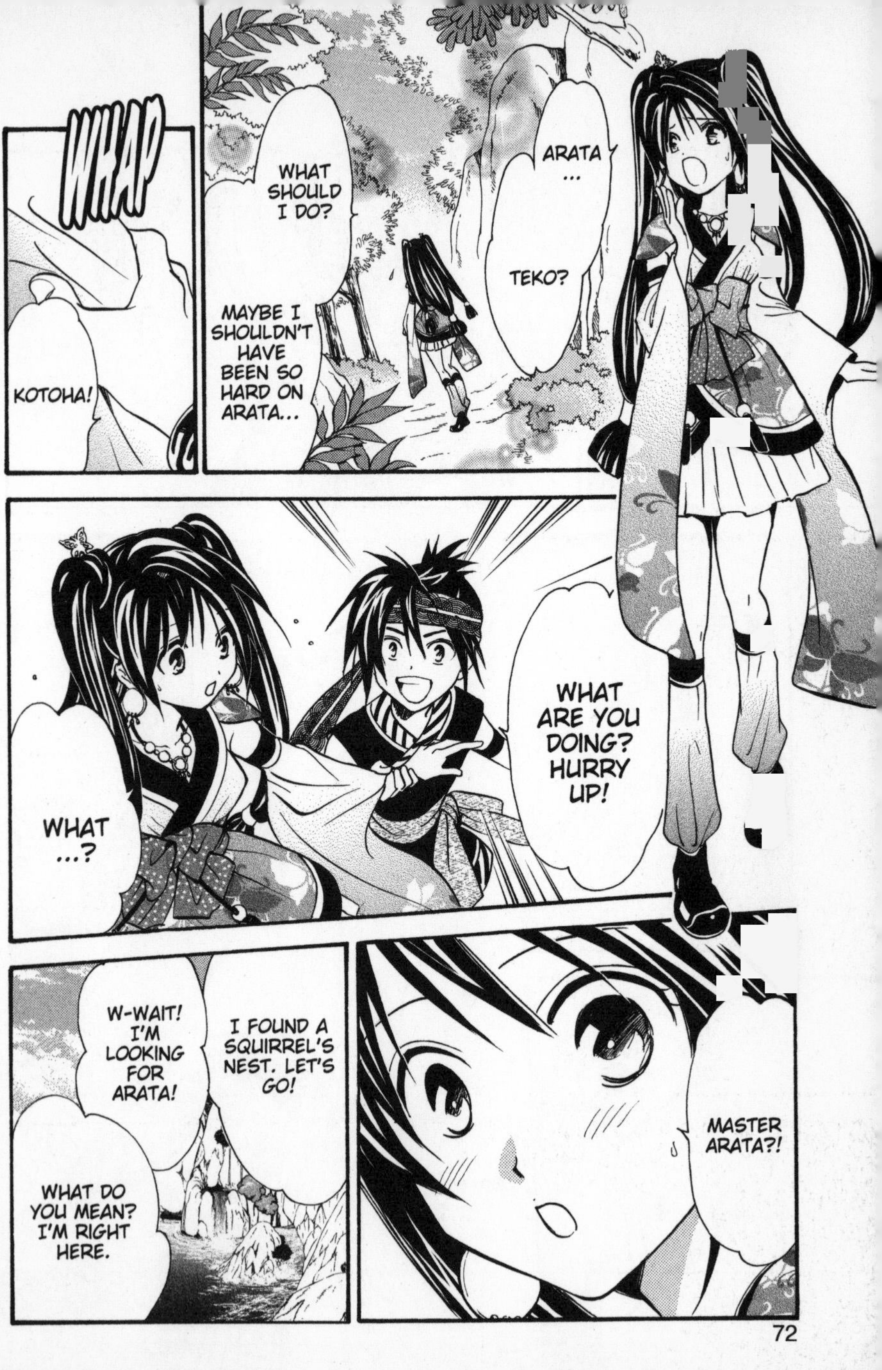
ARATA ...
TEKO?
WHAT SHOULD I DO?
MAYBE I SHOULDN'T HAVE BEEN SO HARD ON ARATA...
WHAP
KOTOHA!
WHAT ARE YOU DOING? HURRY UP!
WHAT ...?
MASTER ARATA?!
I FOUND A SQUIRREL'S NEST. LET'S GO!
W-WAIT! I'M LOOKING FOR ARATA!
WHAT DO YOU MEAN? I'M RIGHT HERE.

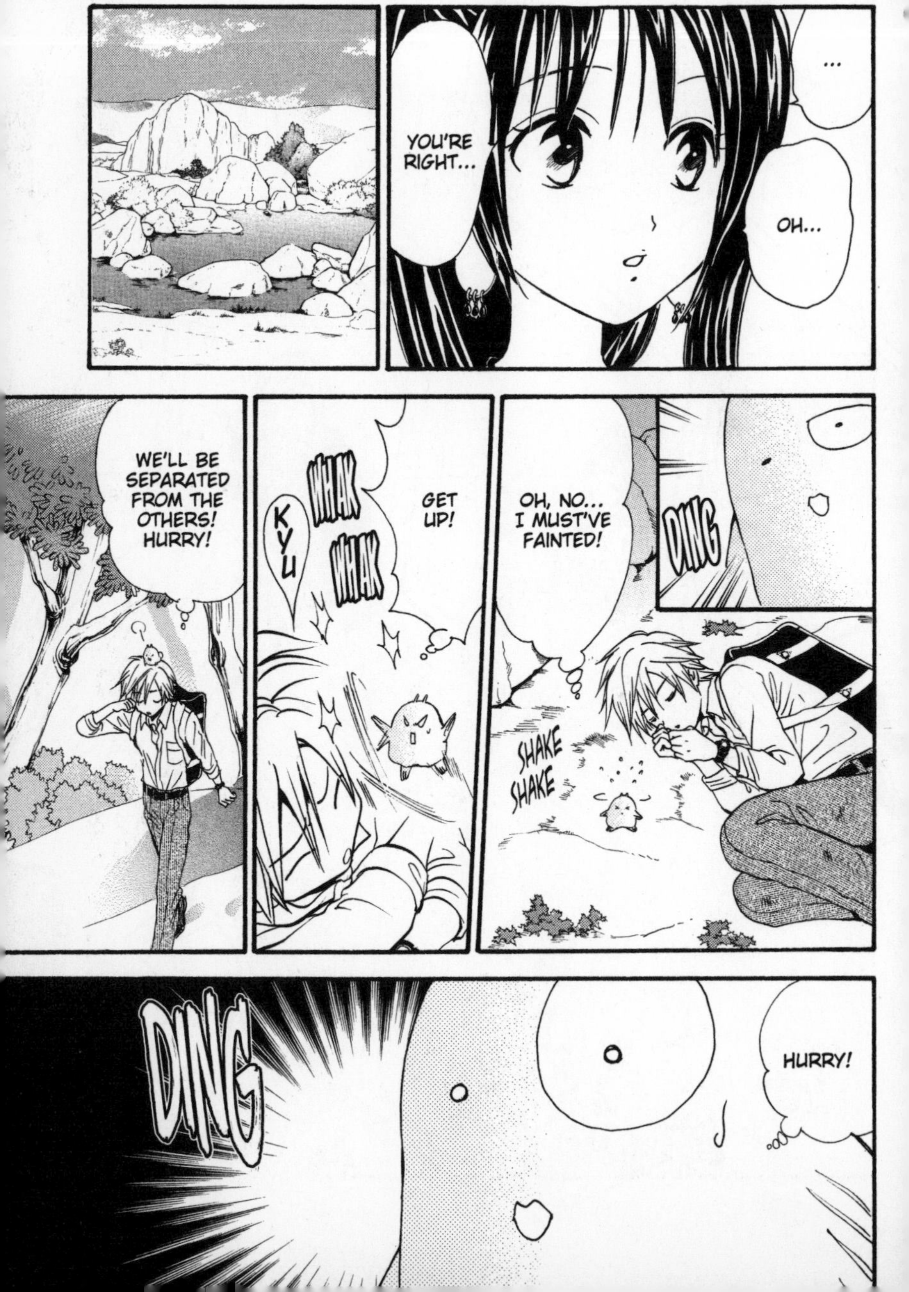
...
OH...
YOU'RE RIGHT...
DING
OH, NO... I MUST'VE FAINTED!
SHAKE SHAKE
GET UP!
WHAK WHAK
KYU
WE'LL BE SEPARATED FROM THE OTHERS! HURRY!
HURRY!
DING

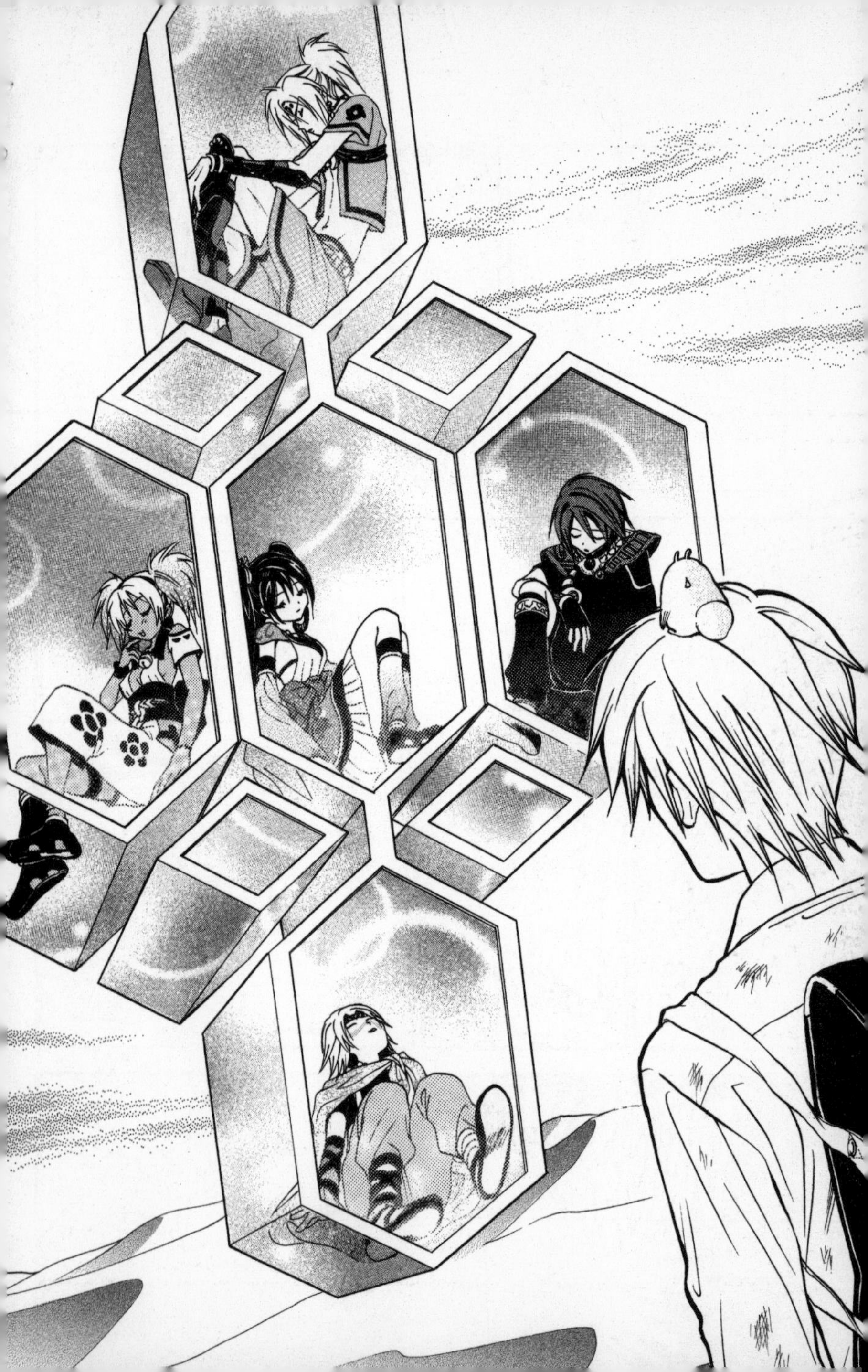

WHAT'S GOING ON?!

EVERY-ONE'S...

APPEAR...

...SOKARA!!

KYU!

WHA

DOOM

WHAT THE...?

SWUSH

SO THERE YOU ARE.

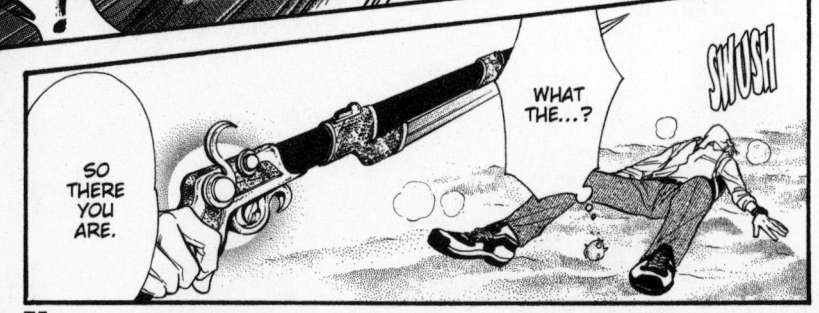

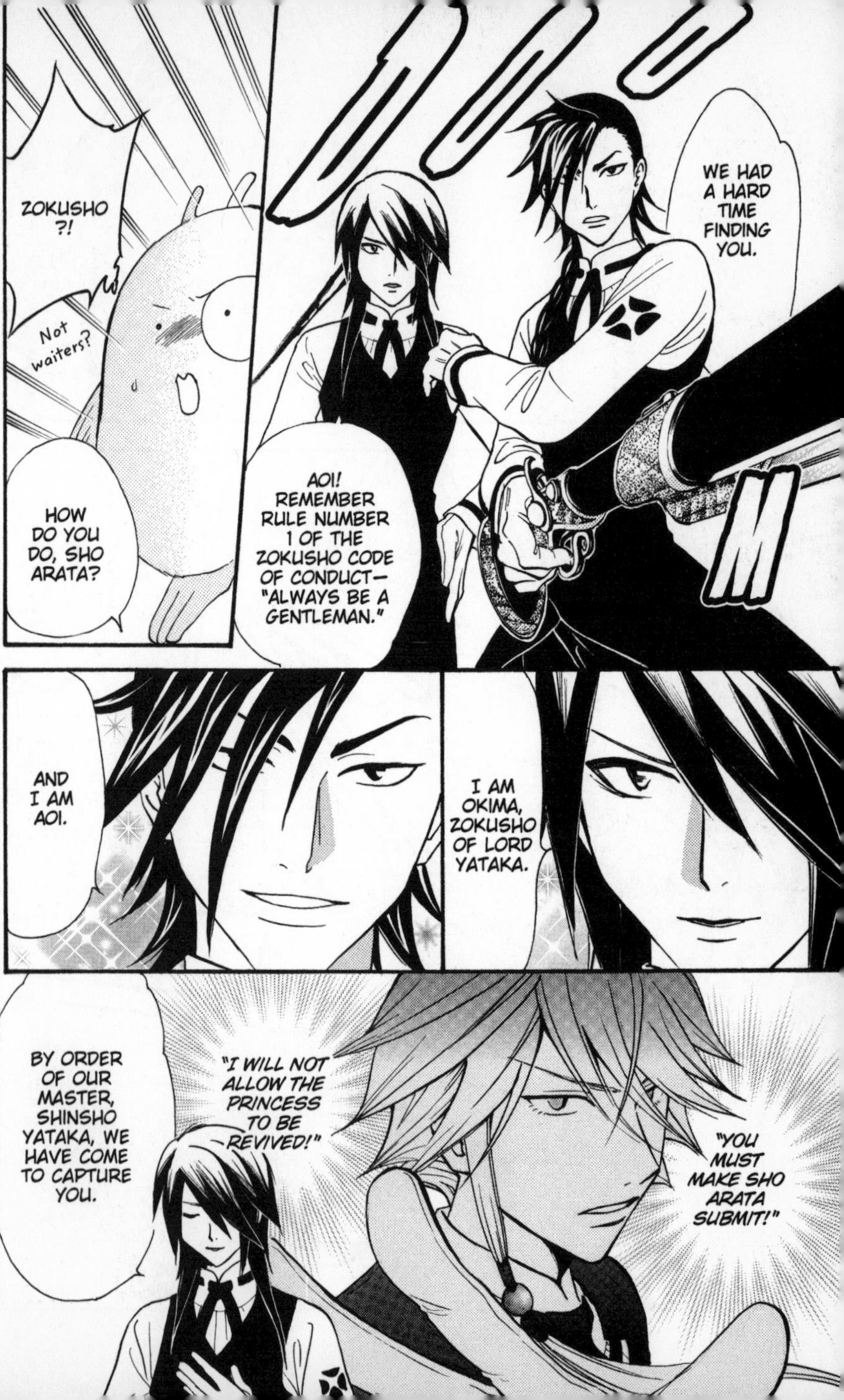

WE HAD A HARD TIME FINDING YOU.
AOI! REMEMBER RULE NUMBER 1 OF THE ZOKUSHO CODE OF CONDUCT—"ALWAYS BE A GENTLEMAN."
ZOKUSHO ?!
Not waiters?
HOW DO YOU DO, SHO ARATA?
I AM OKIMA, ZOKUSHO OF LORD YATAKA.
AND I AM AOI.
BY ORDER OF OUR MASTER, SHINSHO YATAKA, WE HAVE COME TO CAPTURE YOU.
"I WILL NOT ALLOW THE PRINCESS TO BE REVIVED!"
"YOU MUST MAKE SHO ARATA SUBMIT!"

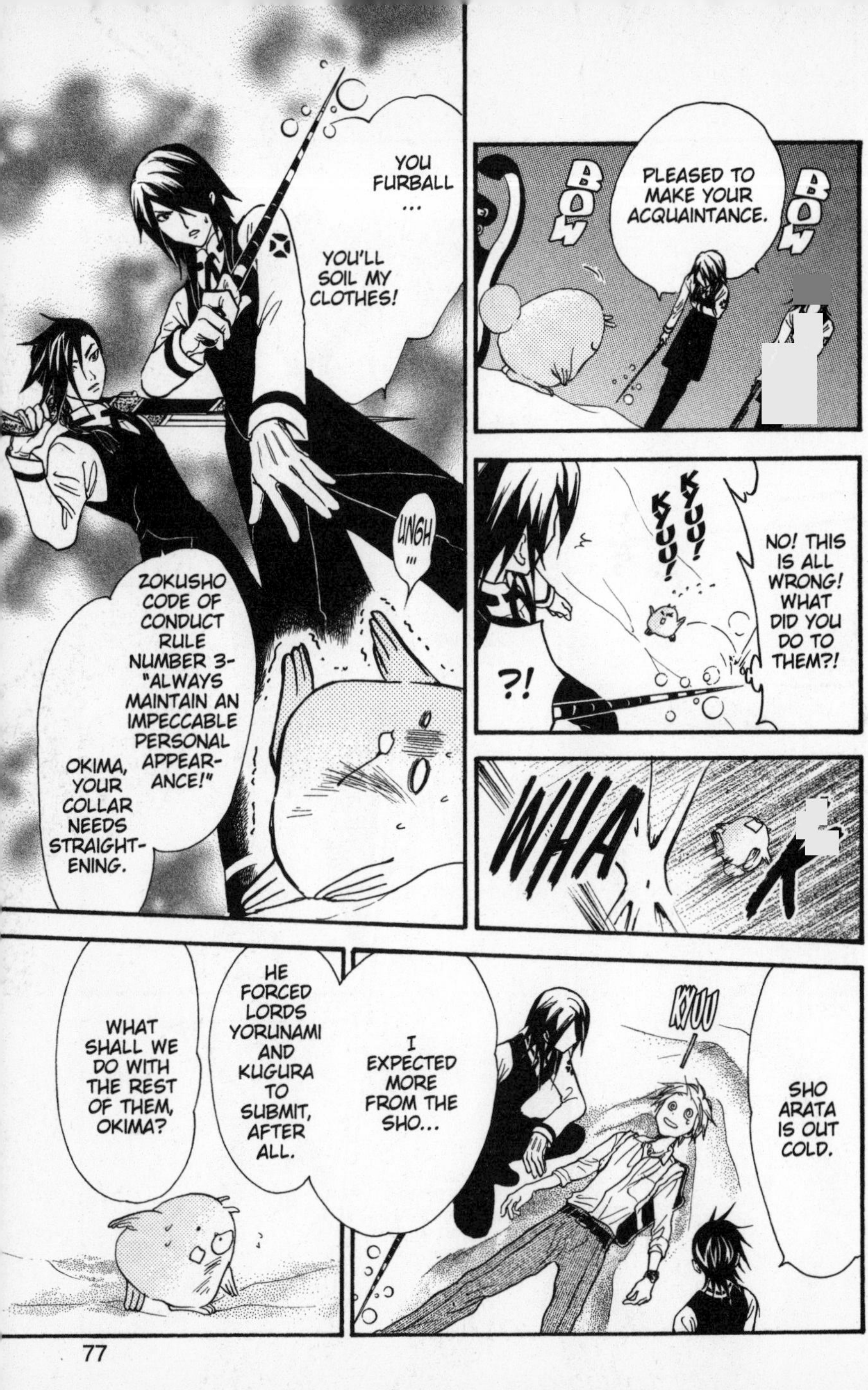
BOW
PLEASED TO MAKE YOUR ACQUAINTANCE.
BOW
NO! THIS IS ALL WRONG! WHAT DID YOU DO TO THEM?!
KYUU! KYUU!
?!
WHA
YOU FURBALL...
YOU'LL SOIL MY CLOTHES!
UNGH!!
ZOKUSHO CODE OF CONDUCT RULE NUMBER 3- "ALWAYS MAINTAIN AN IMPECCABLE PERSONAL APPEAR-ANCE!"
OKIMA, YOUR COLLAR NEEDS STRAIGHT-ENING.
SHO ARATA IS OUT COLD.
KYUU
I EXPECTED MORE FROM THE SHO...
HE FORCED LORDS YORUNAMI AND KUGURA TO SUBMIT, AFTER ALL.
WHAT SHALL WE DO WITH THE REST OF THEM, OKIMA?

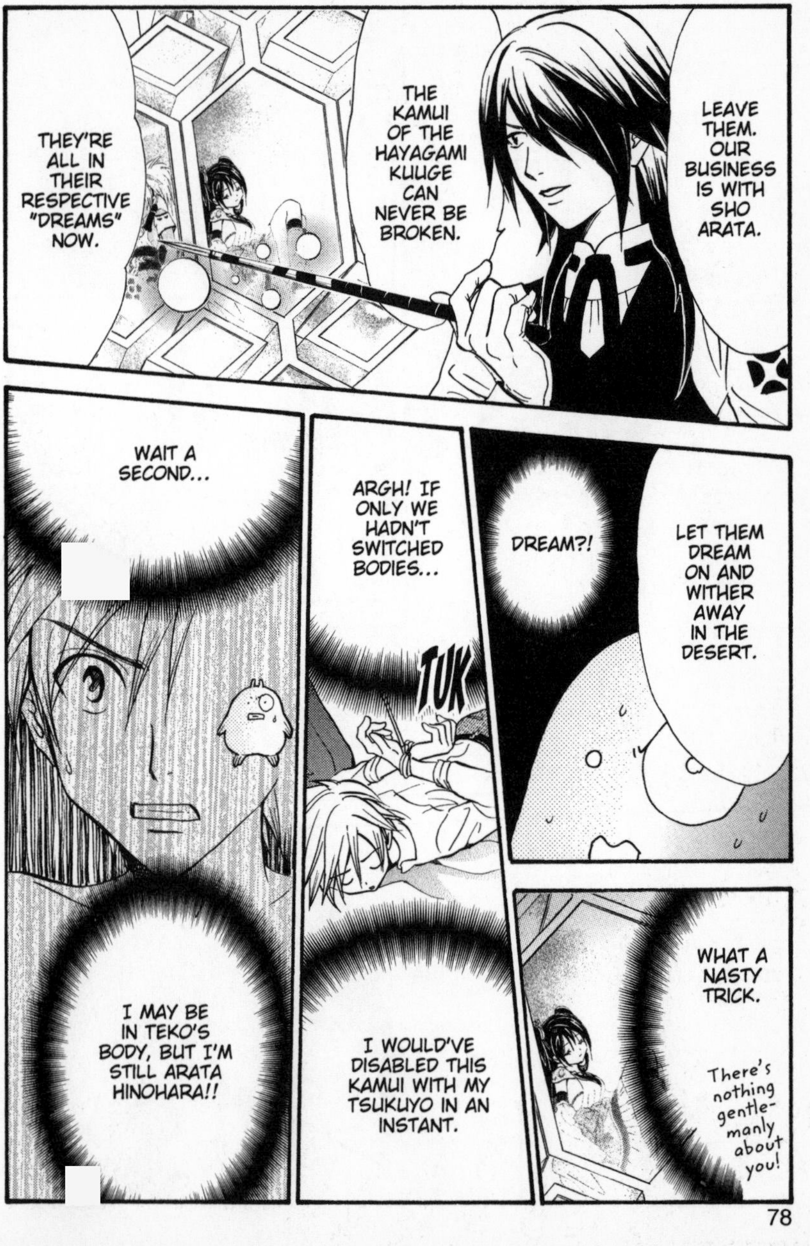
LEAVE THEM. OUR BUSINESS IS WITH SHO ARATA.
THE KAMUI OF THE HAYAGAMI KUUGE CAN NEVER BE BROKEN.
THEY'RE ALL IN THEIR RESPECTIVE "DREAMS" NOW.
LET THEM DREAM ON AND WITHER AWAY IN THE DESERT.
DREAM?!
WHAT A NASTY TRICK.
There's nothing gentle-manly about you!
ARGH! IF ONLY WE HADN'T SWITCHED BODIES...
TUK
I WOULD'VE DISABLED THIS KAMUI WITH MY TSUKUYO IN AN INSTANT.
WAIT A SECOND...
I MAY BE IN TEKO'S BODY, BUT I'M STILL ARATA HINOHARA!!

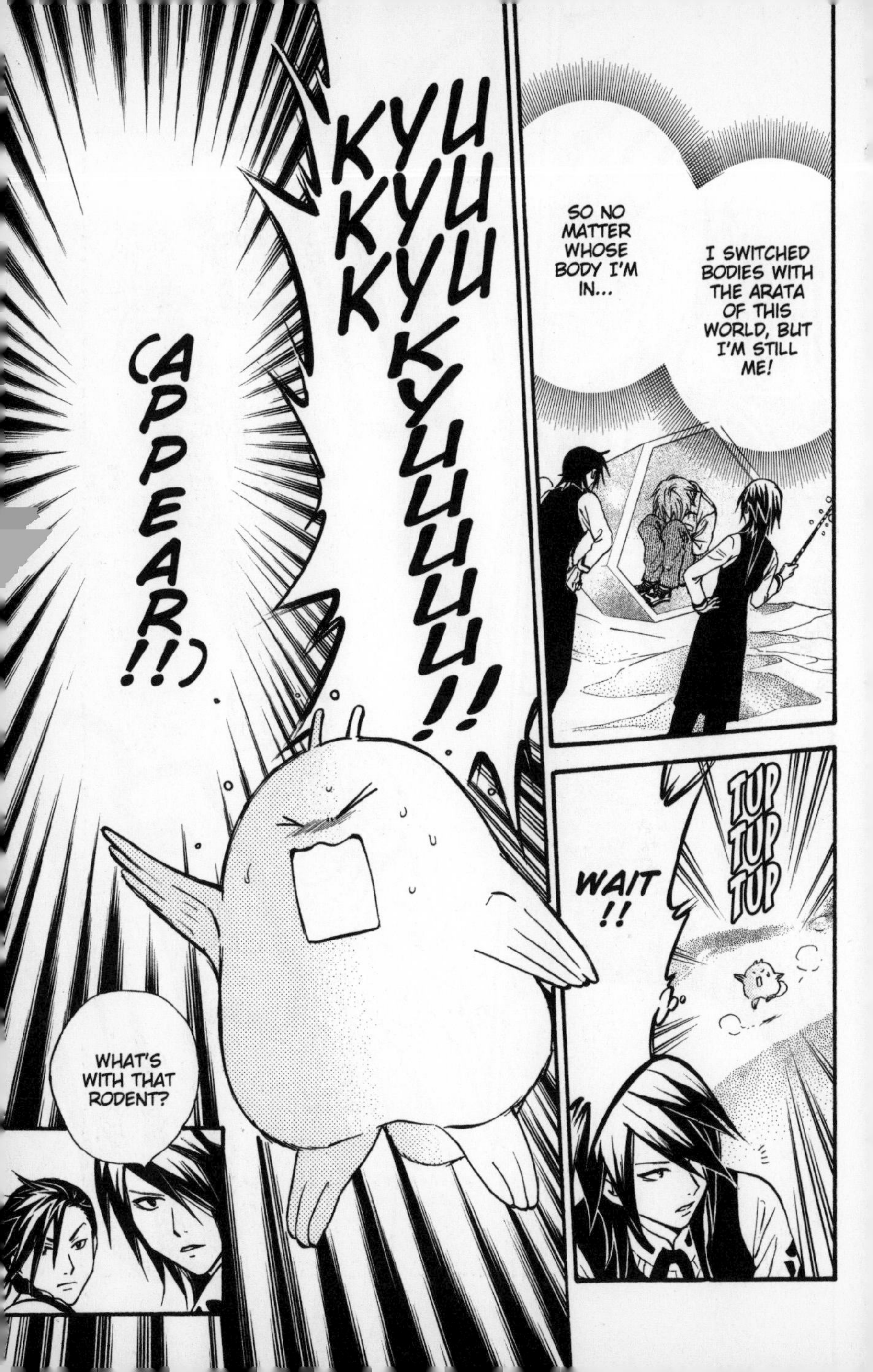
I SWITCHED BODIES WITH THE ARATA OF THIS WORLD, BUT I'M STILL ME!
SO NO MATTER WHOSE BODY I'M IN...
TUP TUP TUP
WAIT !!
KYU KYU KYU KYUUUUUU!!
(APPEAR!!)
WHAT'S WITH THAT RODENT?

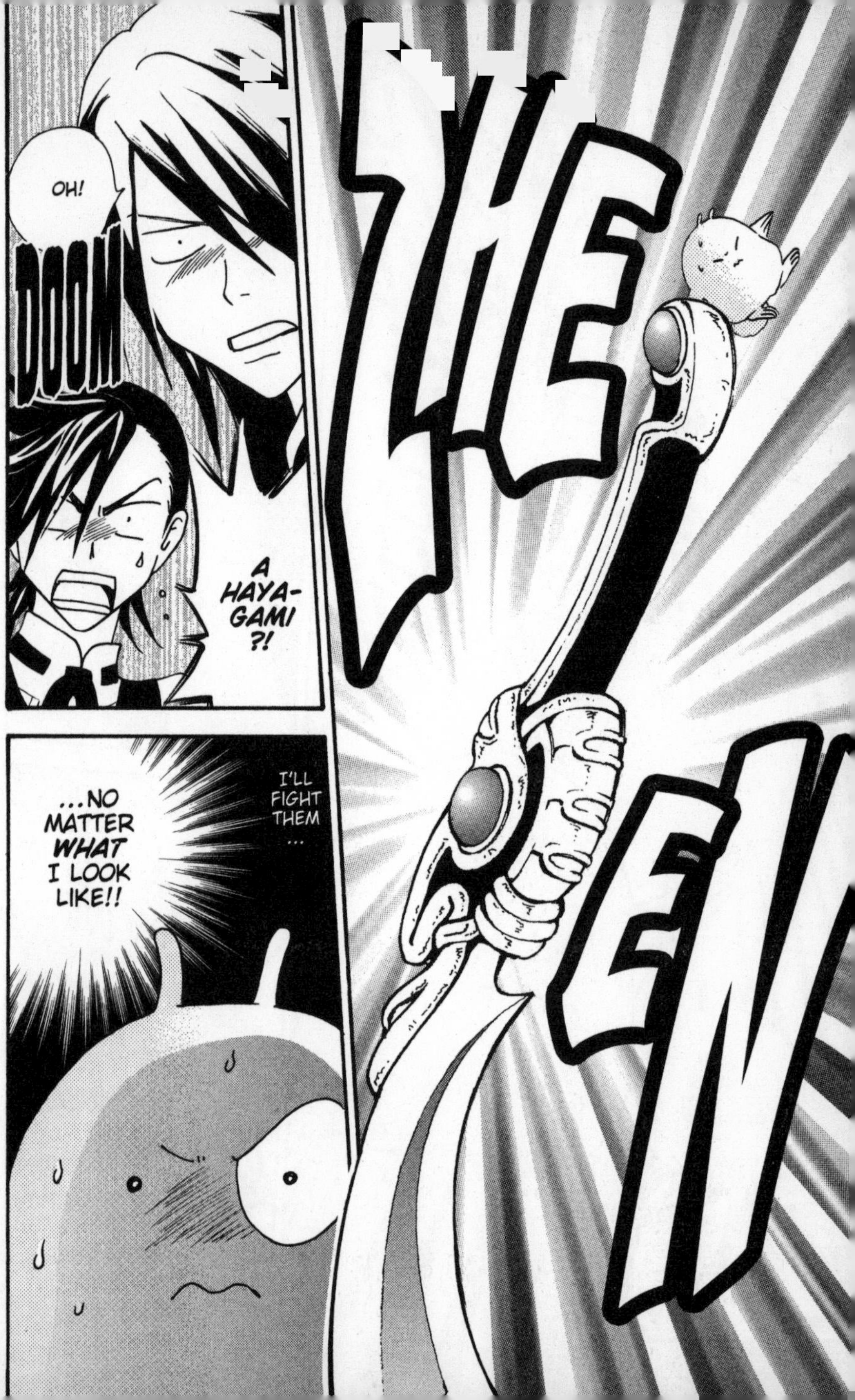
OH!
DOOM
A HAYA-GAMI?!
I'LL FIGHT THEM...
...NO MATTER WHAT I LOOK LIKE!!

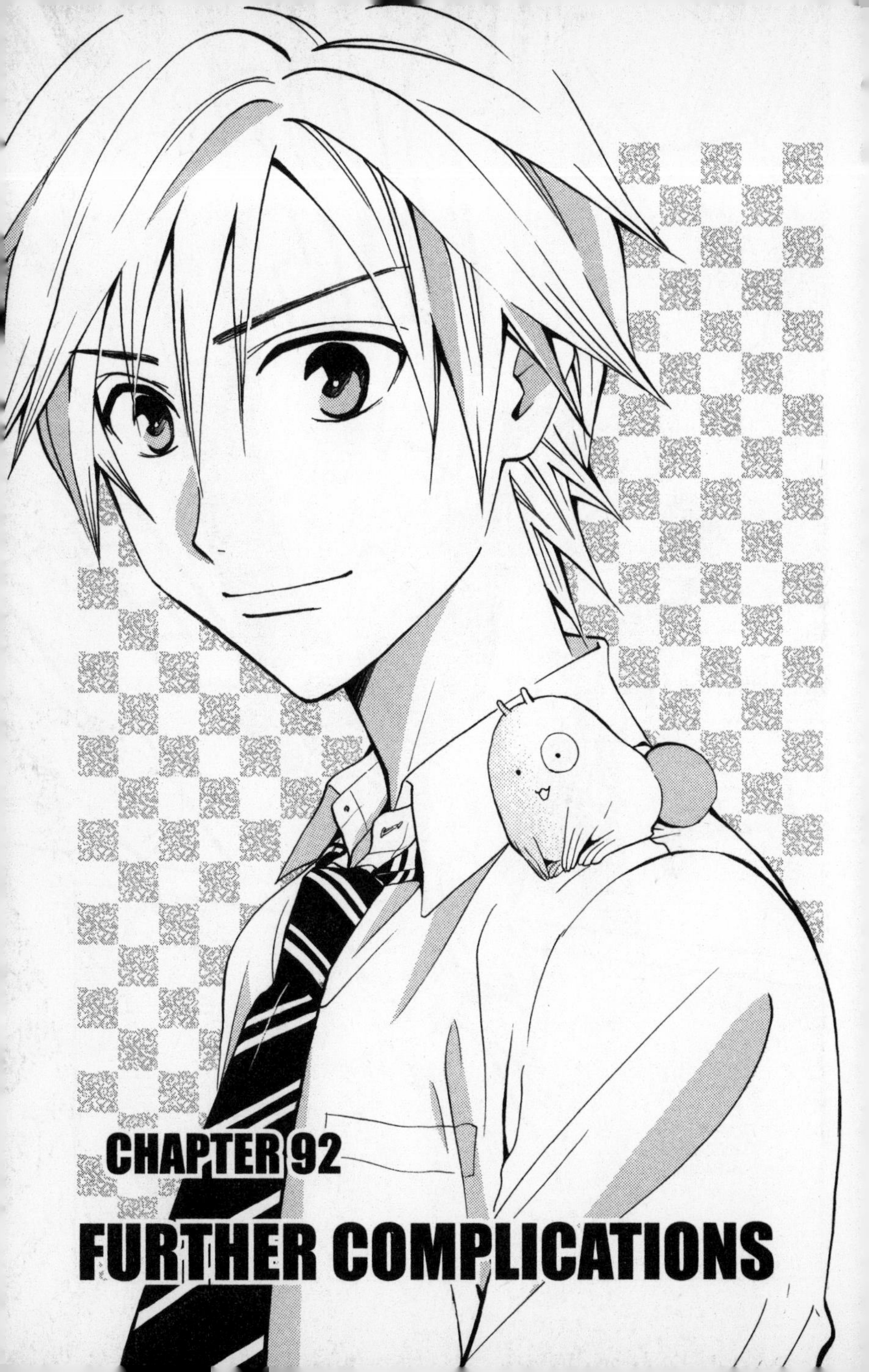
CHAPTER 92
FURTHER COMPLICATIONS

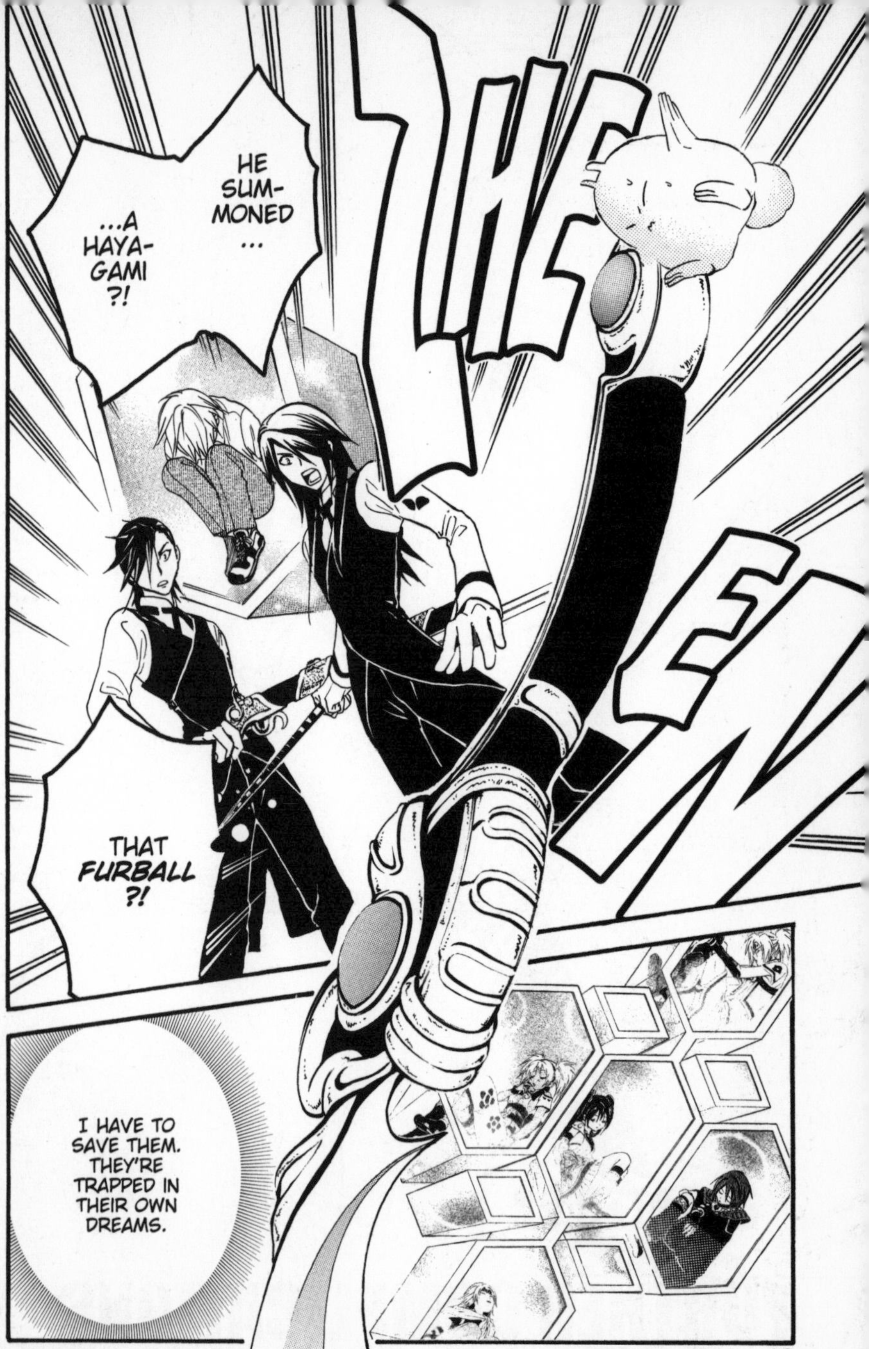
HE SUM- MONED ...
...A HAYA- GAMI ?!
THAT FURBALL ?!
I HAVE TO SAVE THEM. THEY'RE TRAPPED IN THEIR OWN DREAMS.

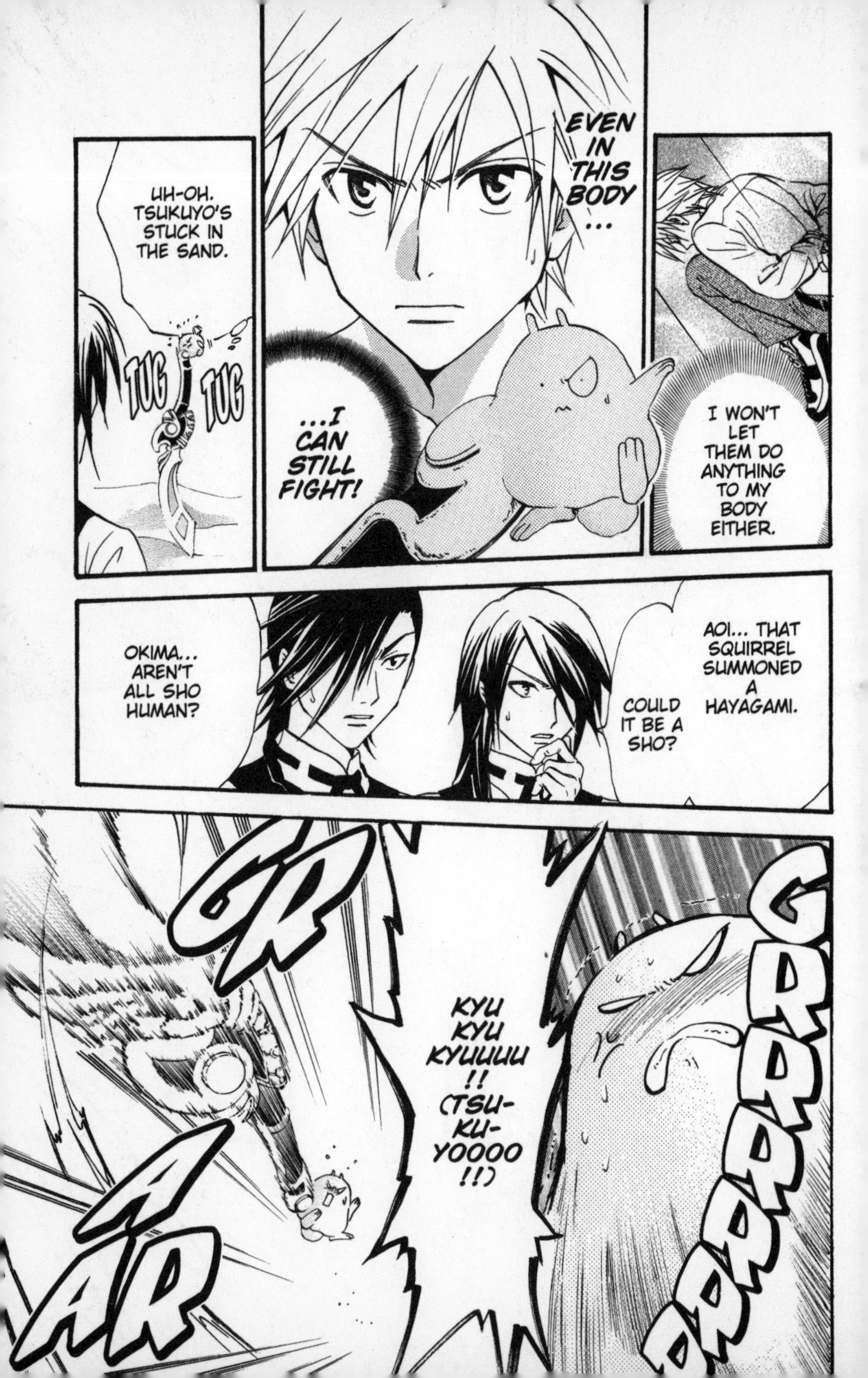
I WON'T LET THEM DO ANYTHING TO MY BODY EITHER.
EVEN IN THIS BODY...
...I CAN STILL FIGHT!
UH-OH. TSUKUYO'S STUCK IN THE SAND.
TUG TUG
AOI... THAT SQUIRREL SUMMONED A HAYAGAMI.
COULD IT BE A SHO?
OKIMA... AREN'T ALL SHO HUMAN?
GRRRRRR
KYU KYU KYUUUU!! (TSU-KU-YOOOO!!)
GRAR

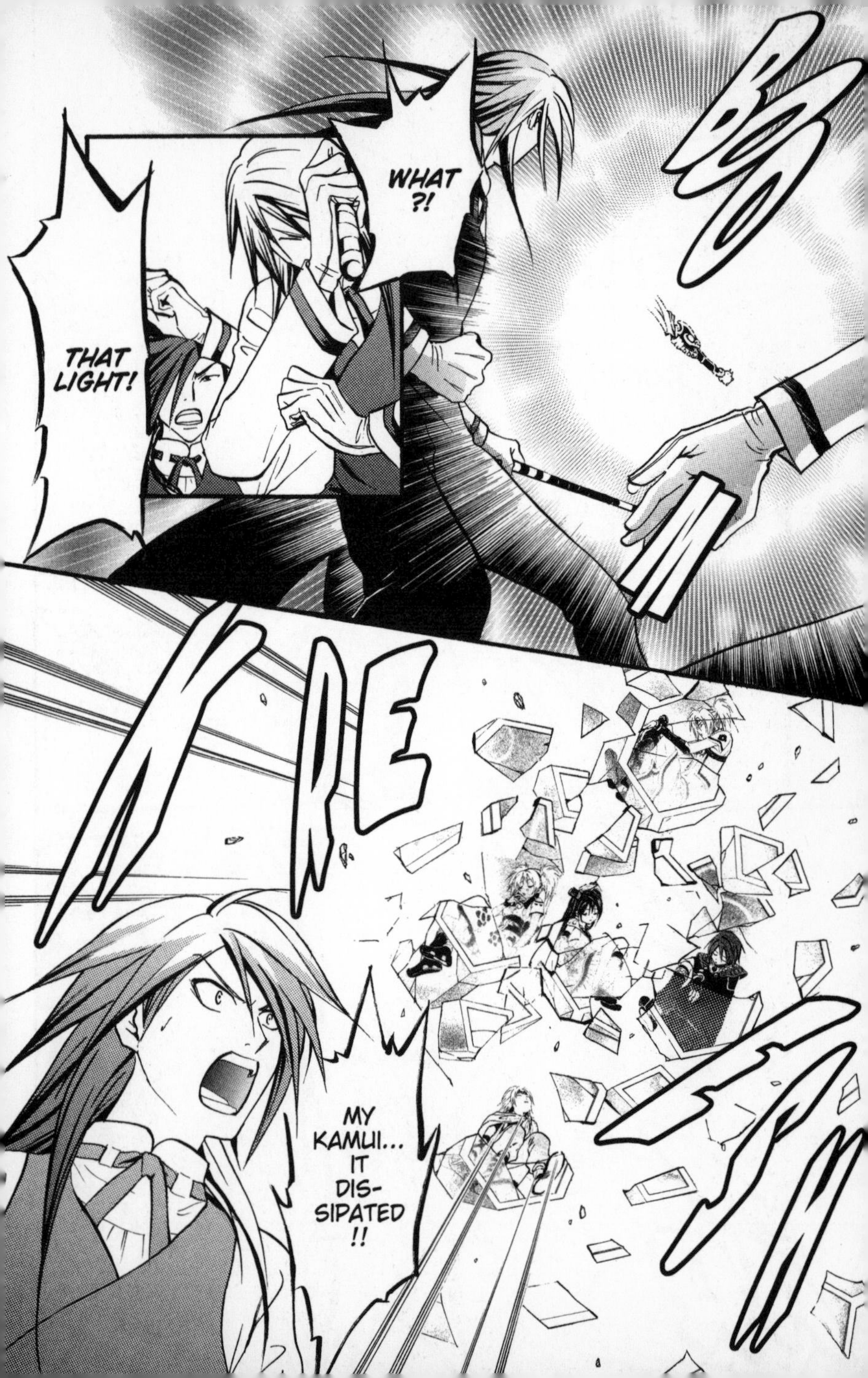
WHAT ?!
THAT LIGHT!
MY KAMUI... IT DIS- SIPATED !!

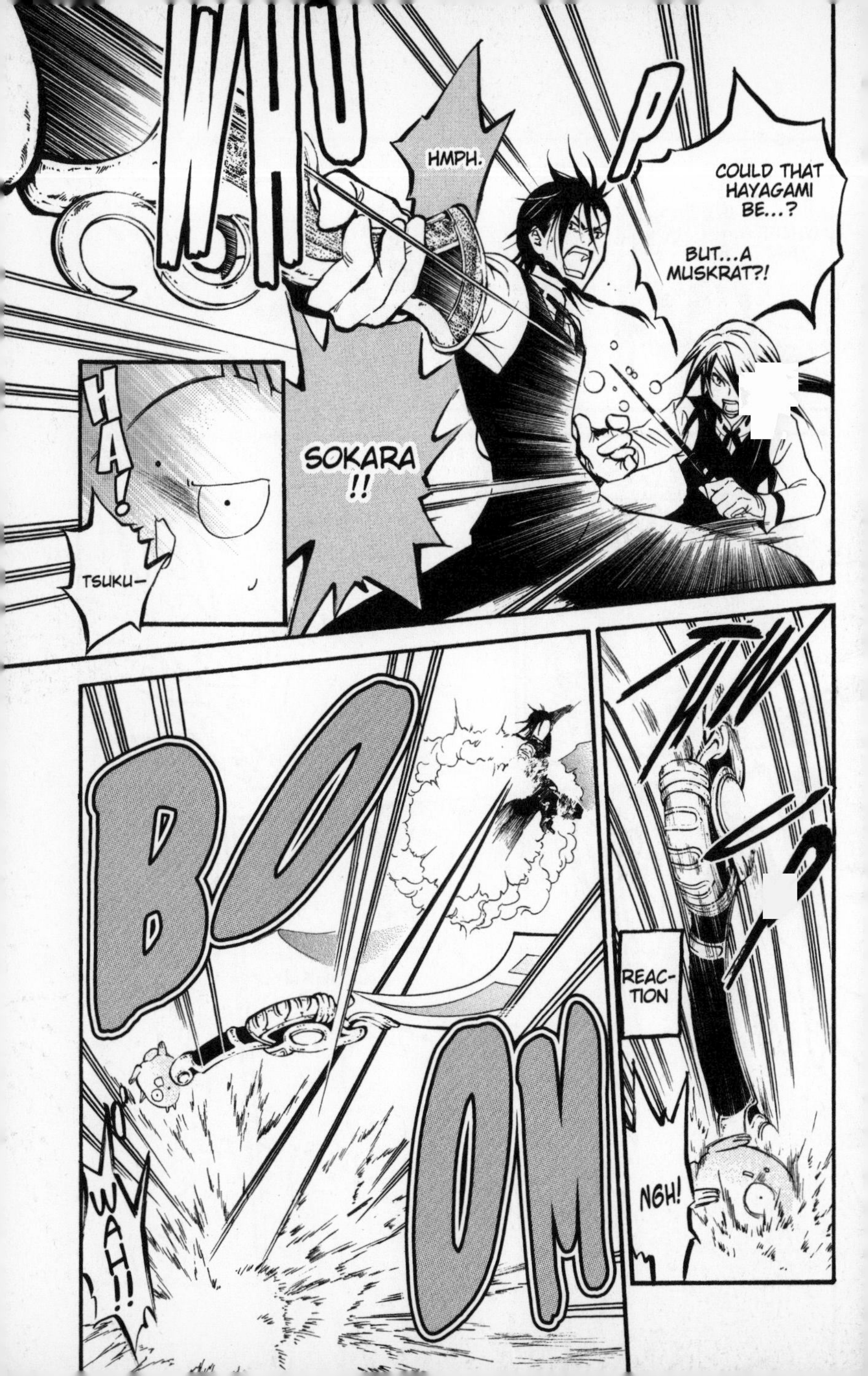
COULD THAT HAYAGAMI BE...?
BUT...A MUSKRAT?!
HMPH.
SOKARA !!
HA!
TSUKU-
REAC-TION
NGH!
BOOM
WAH!!

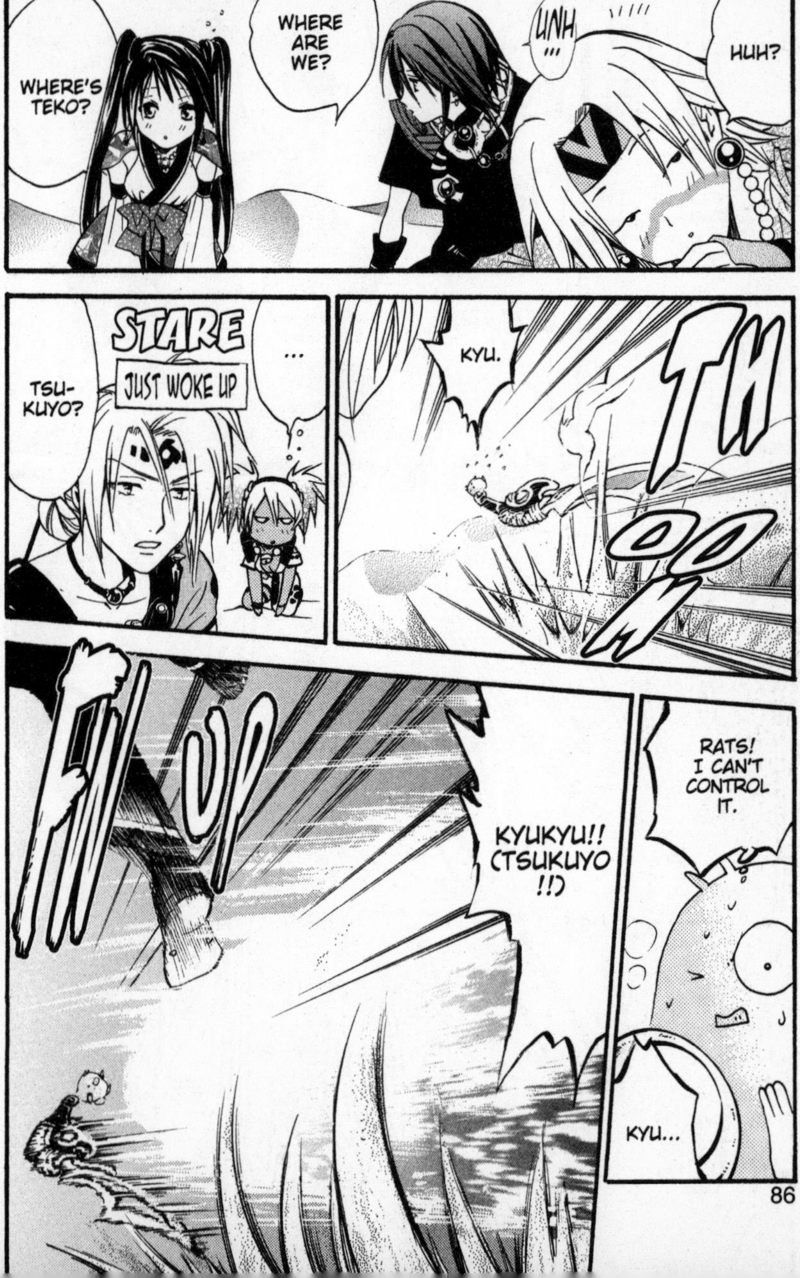
HUH?
UNH...
WHERE ARE WE?
WHERE'S TEKO?
KYU.
THOOM
...
STARE
JUST WOKE UP
TSU-KUYO?
RATS! I CAN'T CONTROL IT.
KYU...
KYUKYU!! (TSUKUYO!!)
WHUP

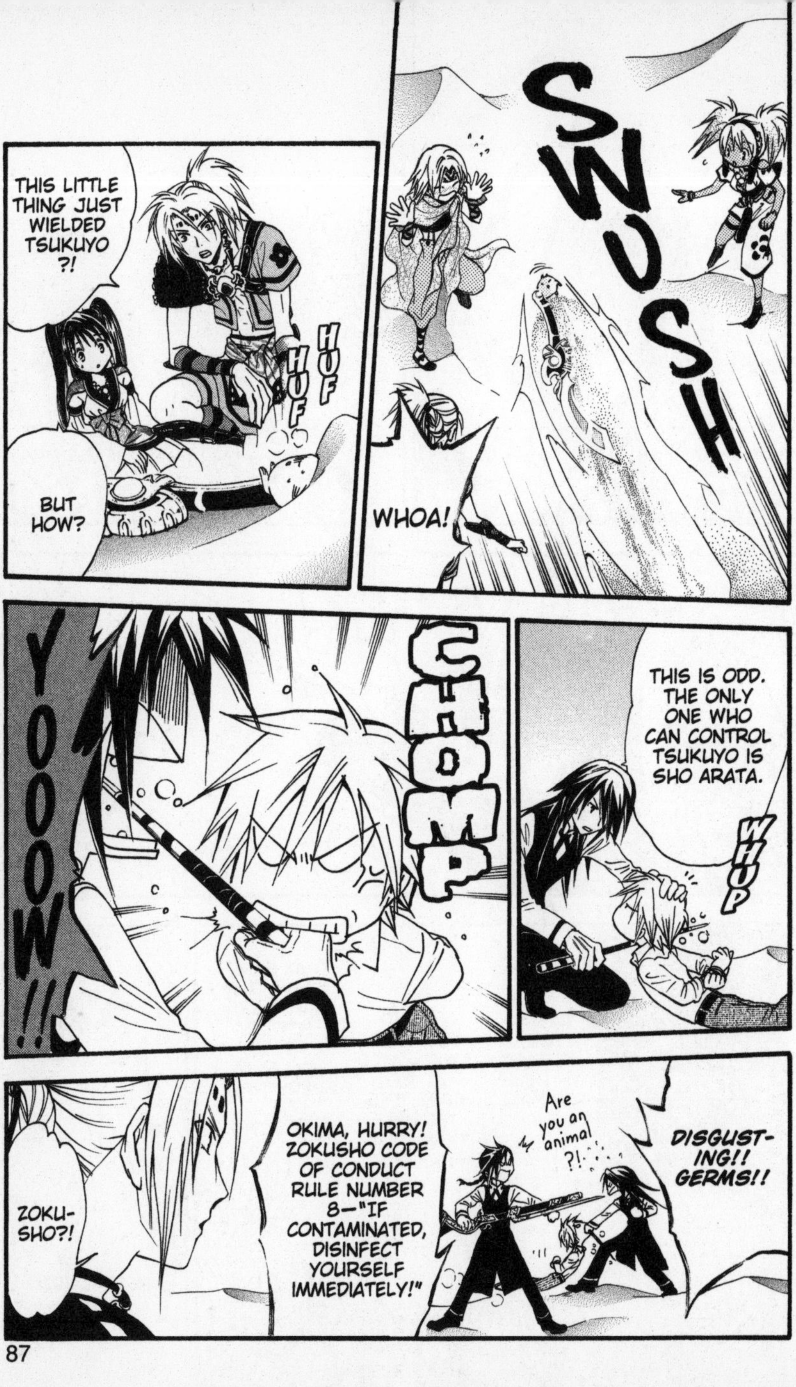
SWUSH
WHOA!
THIS LITTLE THING JUST WIELDED TSUKUYO ?!
HUF HUF
BUT HOW?
THIS IS ODD. THE ONLY ONE WHO CAN CONTROL TSUKUYO IS SHO ARATA.
WHUP
CHOMP
YOOOOW!!
DISGUST-ING!! GERMS!!
Are you an animal ?!
OKIMA, HURRY! ZOKUSHO CODE OF CONDUCT RULE NUMBER 8—"IF CONTAMINATED, DISINFECT YOURSELF IMMEDIATELY!"
ZOKU-SHO?!

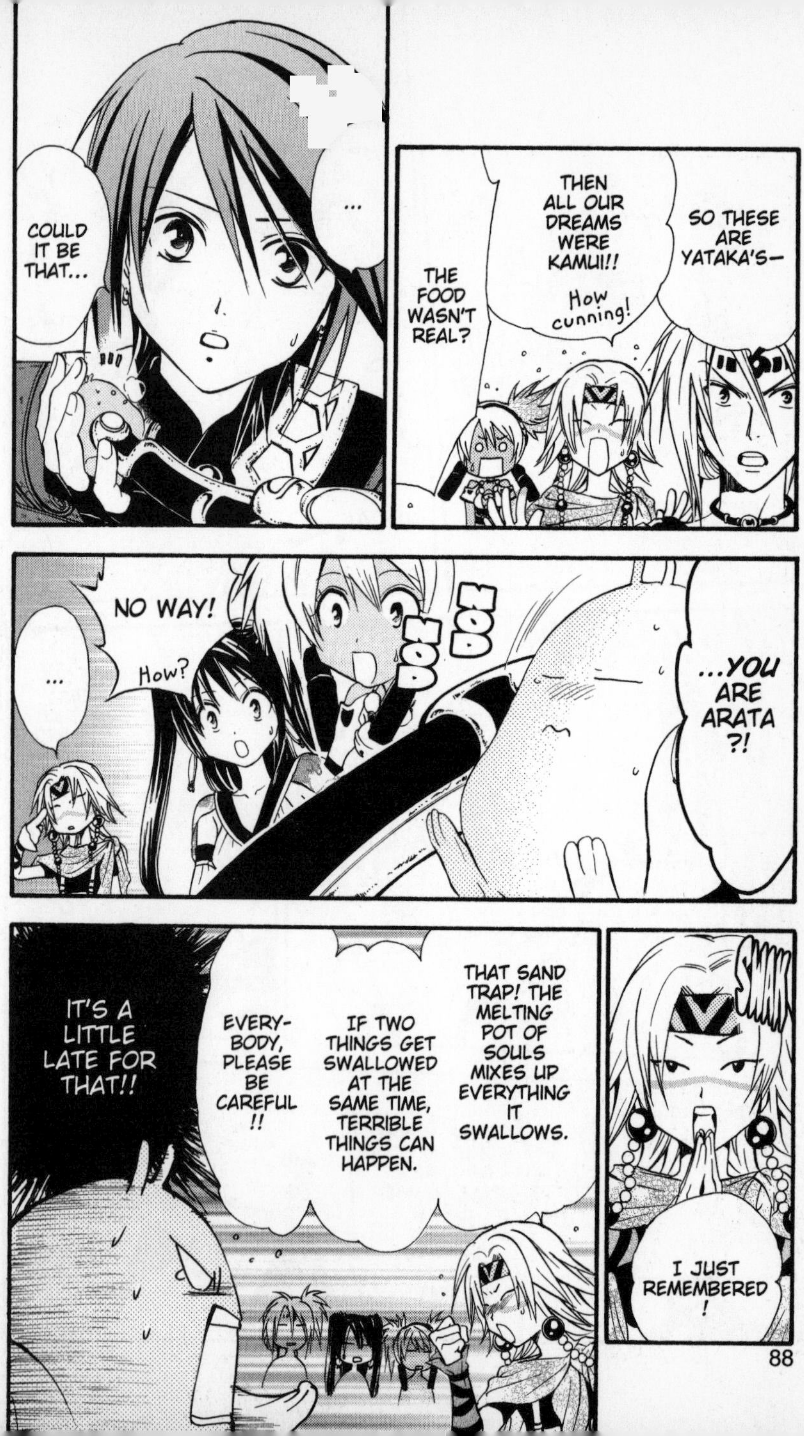
SO THESE ARE YATAKA'S—
THEN ALL OUR DREAMS WERE KAMUI!!
How cunning!
THE FOOD WASN'T REAL?
...
COULD IT BE THAT...
...YOU ARE ARATA?!
NOD NOD
NO WAY!
How?
...
I JUST REMEMBERED!
THAT SAND TRAP! THE MELTING POT OF SOULS MIXES UP EVERYTHING IT SWALLOWS.
IF TWO THINGS GET SWALLOWED AT THE SAME TIME, TERRIBLE THINGS CAN HAPPEN.
EVERY-BODY, PLEASE BE CAREFUL!!
IT'S A LITTLE LATE FOR THAT!!

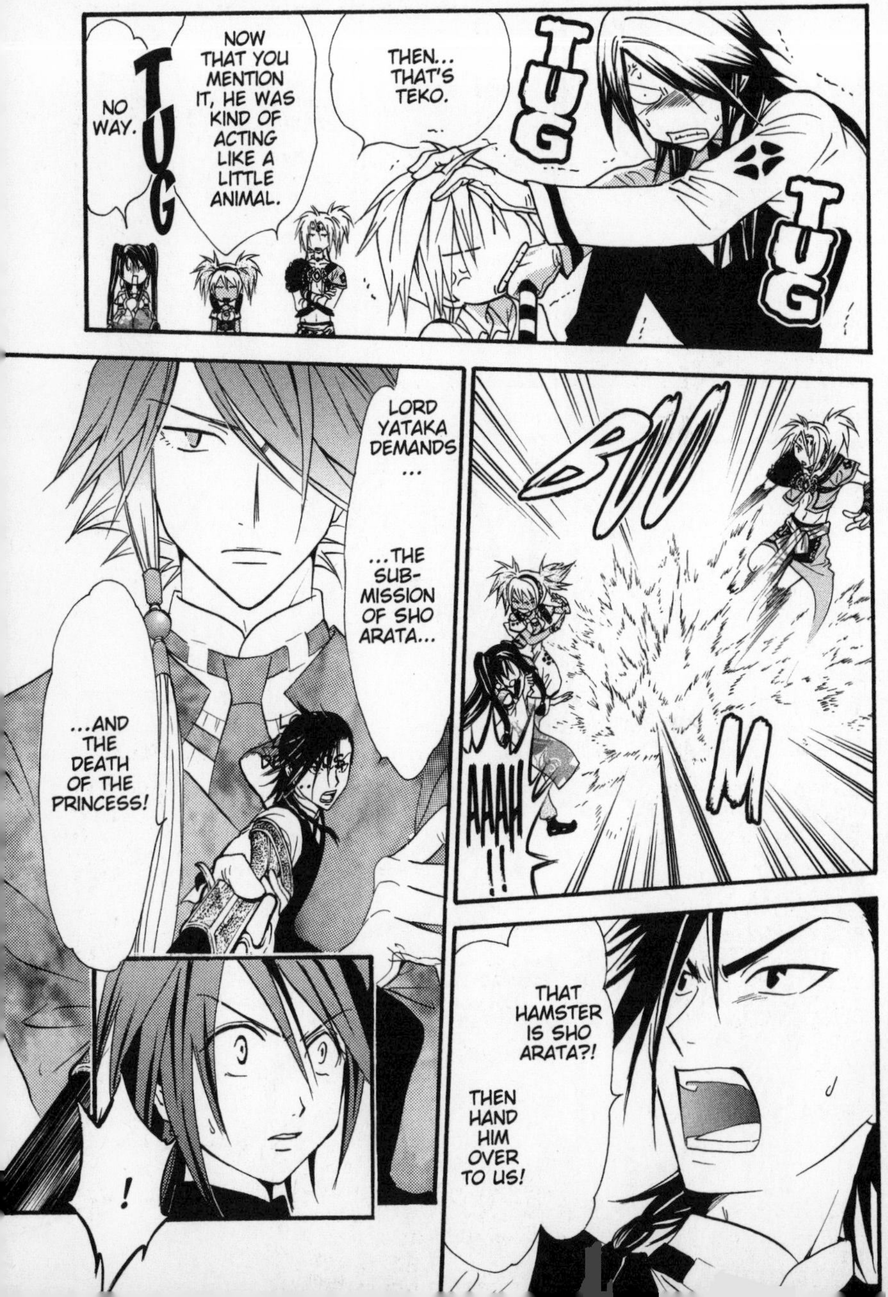
TUG TUG
TUG TUG
THEN... THAT'S TEKO.
NOW THAT YOU MENTION IT, HE WAS KIND OF ACTING LIKE A LITTLE ANIMAL.
TUG
NO WAY.
BOOM
AAAH!!
THAT HAMSTER IS SHO ARATA?!
THEN HAND HIM OVER TO US!
LORD YATAKA DEMANDS...
...THE SUBMISSION OF SHO ARATA...
...AND THE DEATH OF THE PRINCESS!
!

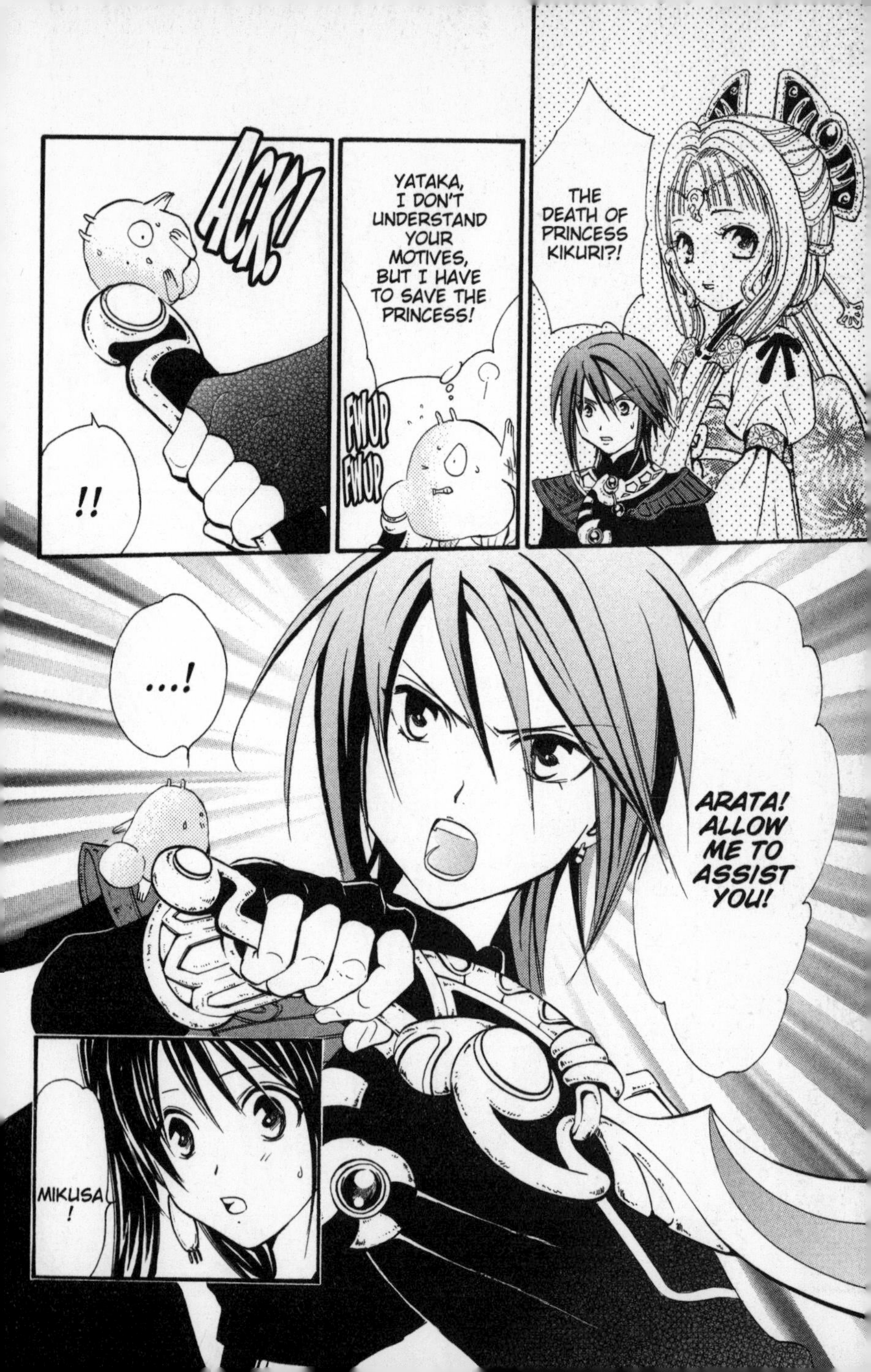
THE DEATH OF PRINCESS KIKURI?!
YATAKA, I DON'T UNDERSTAND YOUR MOTIVES, BUT I HAVE TO SAVE THE PRINCESS!
FWUP FWUP
ACK!
!!
ARATA! ALLOW ME TO ASSIST YOU!
...!
MIKUSA!

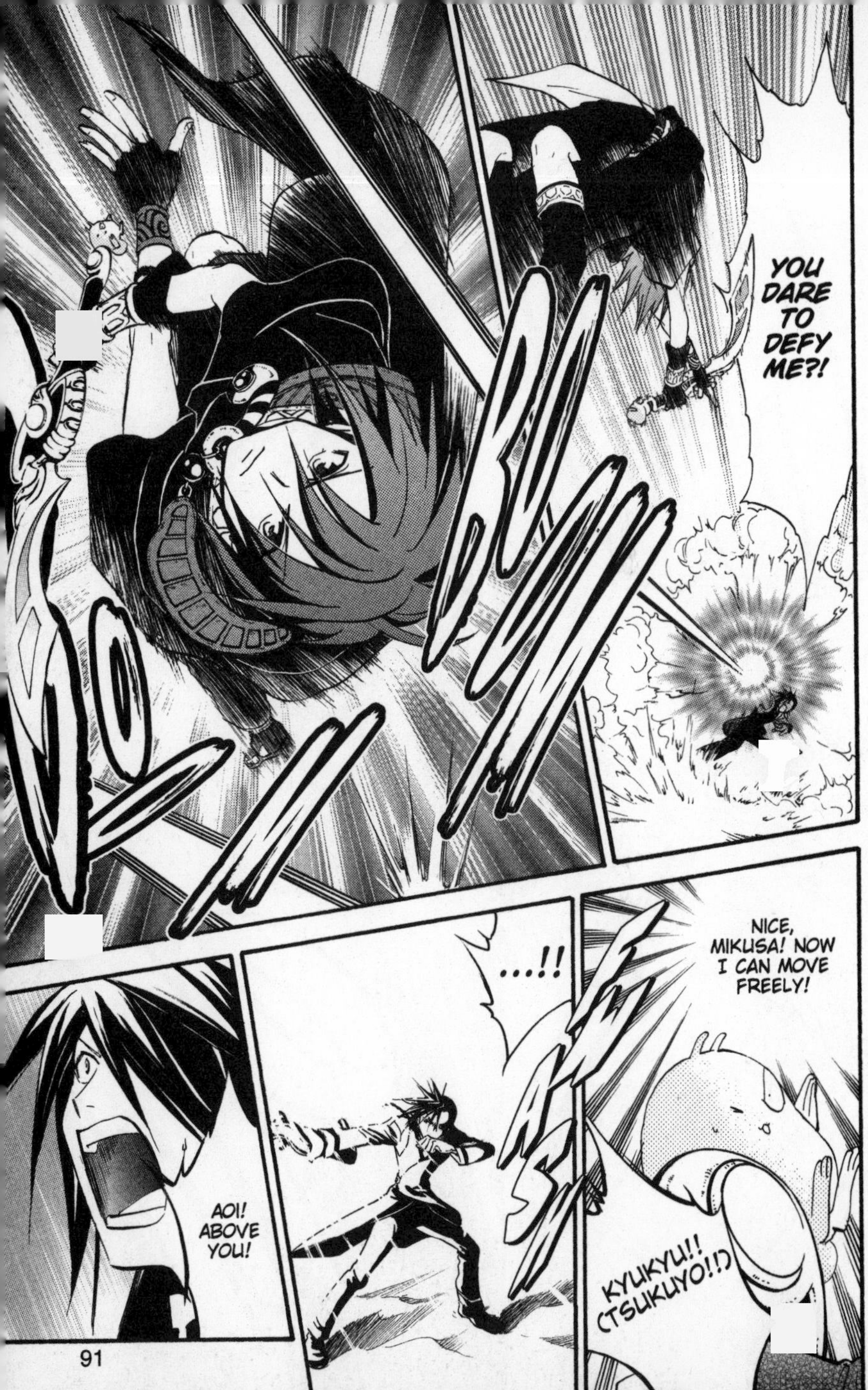
YOU DARE TO DEFY ME?!
NICE, MIKUSA! NOW I CAN MOVE FREELY!
KYUKYU!! (TSUKUYO!!)
...!!
AOI! ABOVE YOU!

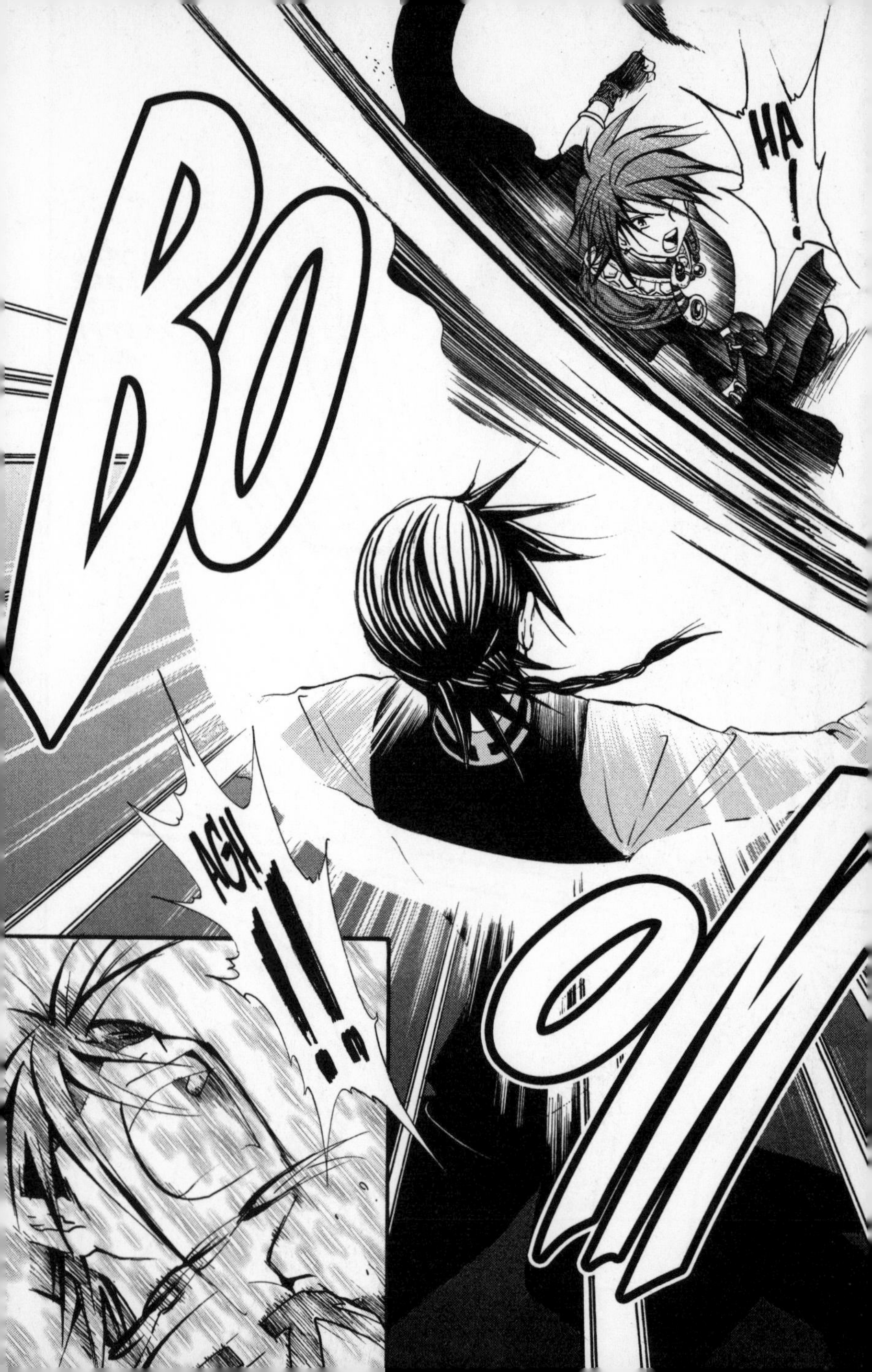
HA!
BO
AGH!!

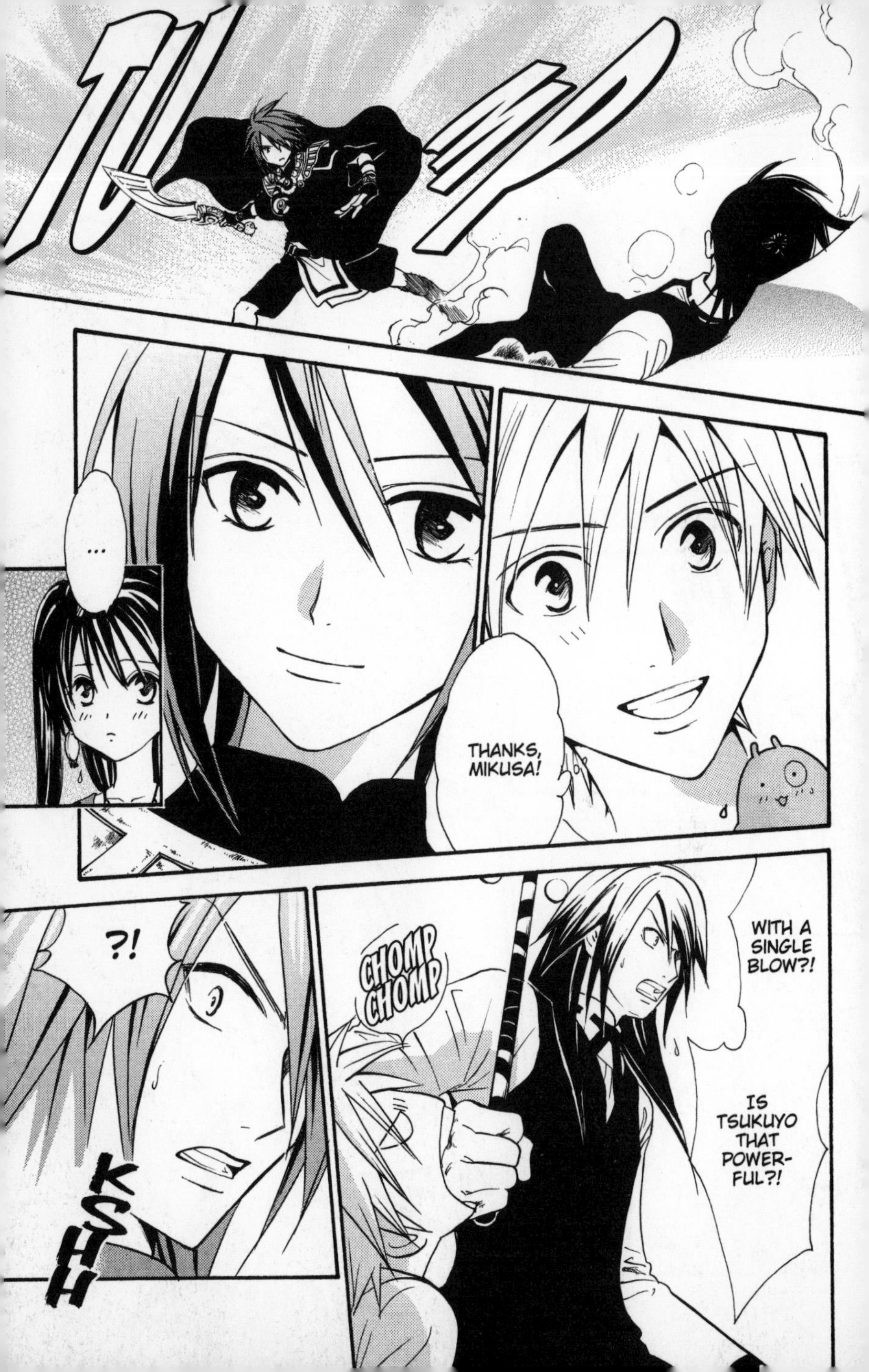
THANKS, MIKUSA!
...
WITH A SINGLE BLOW?!
IS TSUKUYO THAT POWERFUL?!
CHOMP CHOMP
?!
KSHH

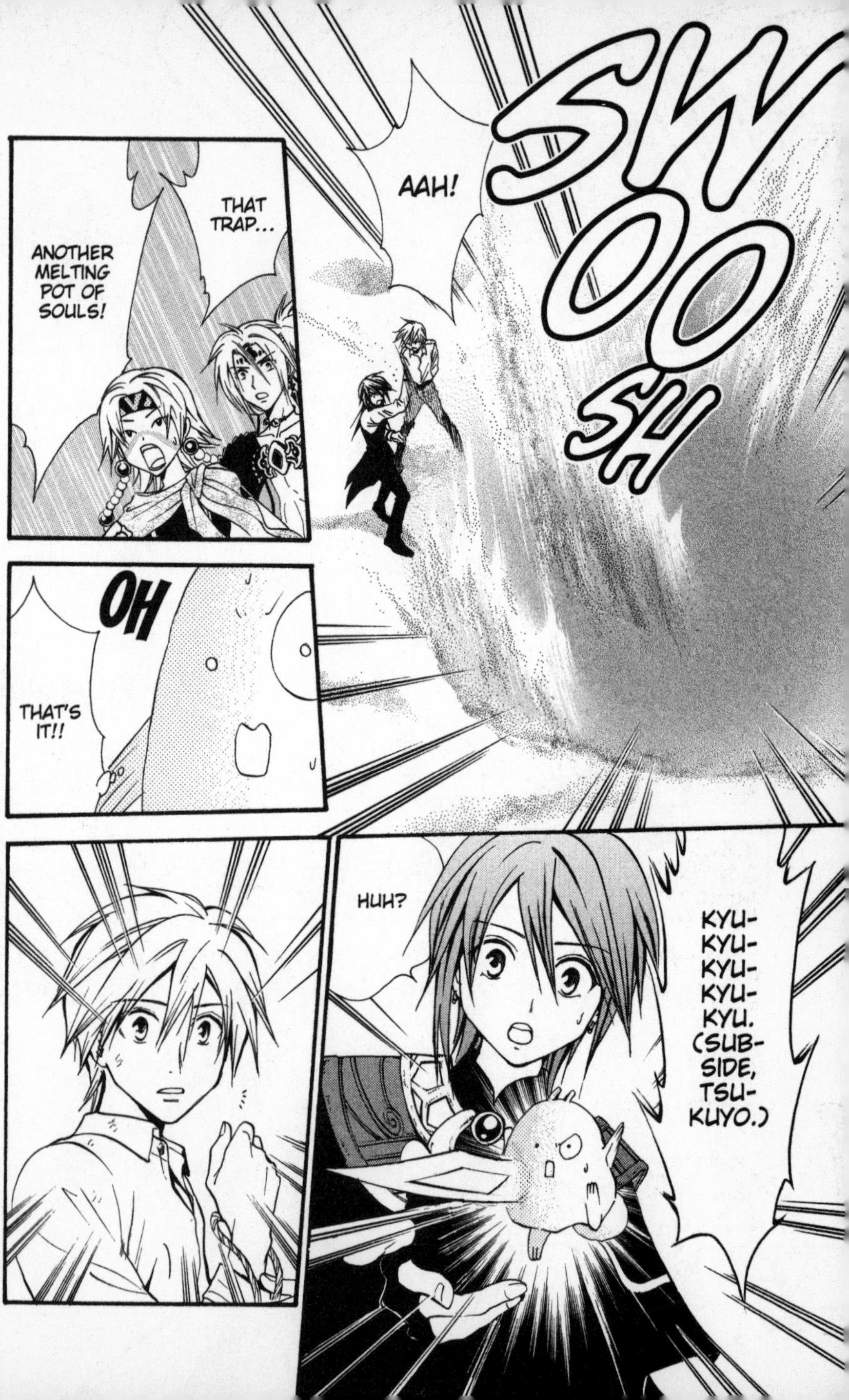

SWOOSH
AAH!
THAT TRAP...
ANOTHER MELTING POT OF SOULS!
OH
THAT'S IT!!
KYU-KYU-KYU-KYU-KYU. (SUB-SIDE, TSU-KUYO.)
HUH?

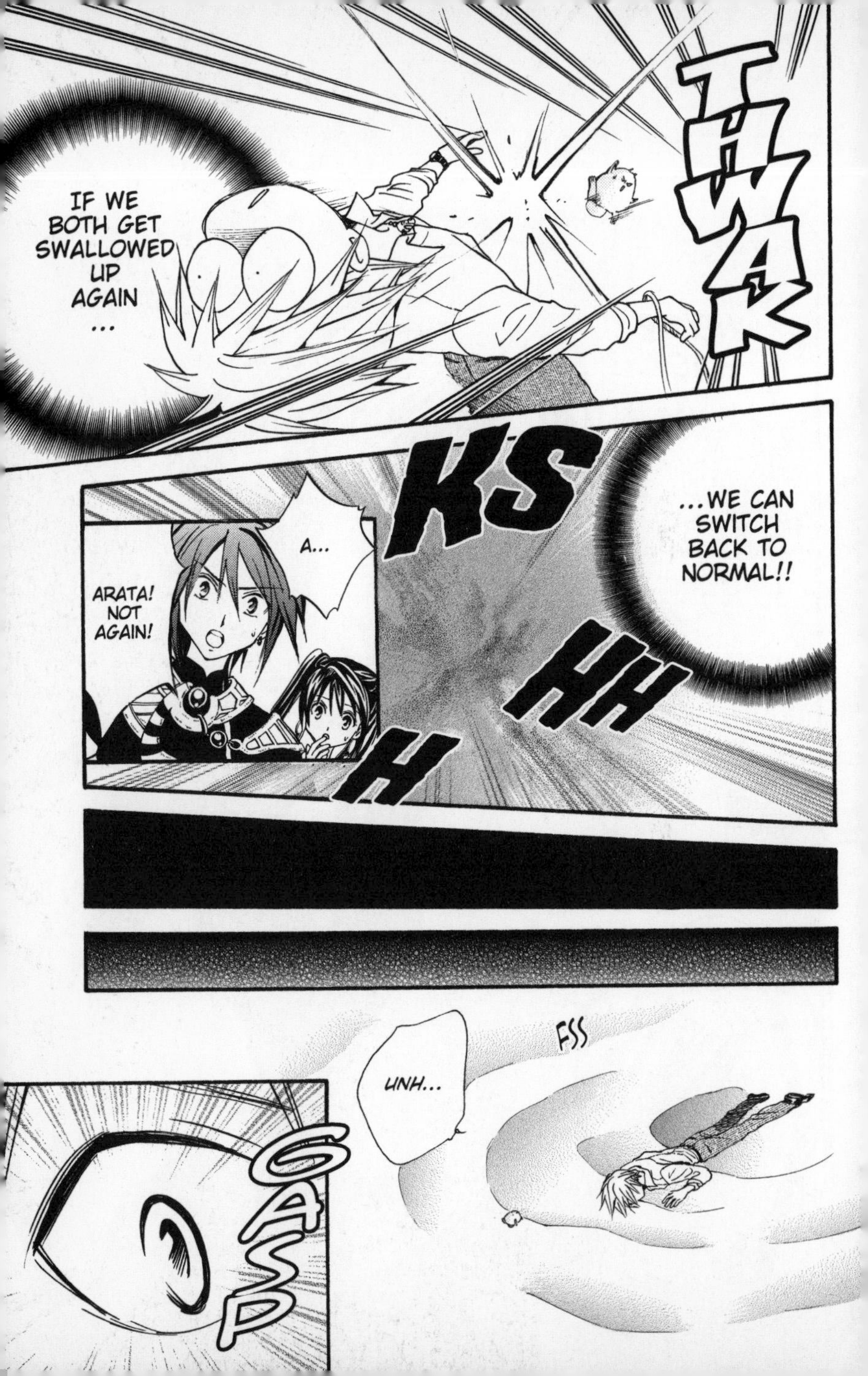
THWAK
IF WE BOTH GET SWALLOWED UP AGAIN ...
...WE CAN SWITCH BACK TO NORMAL!!
KSHHH
A...
ARATA! NOT AGAIN!
FSS
UNH...
GASP

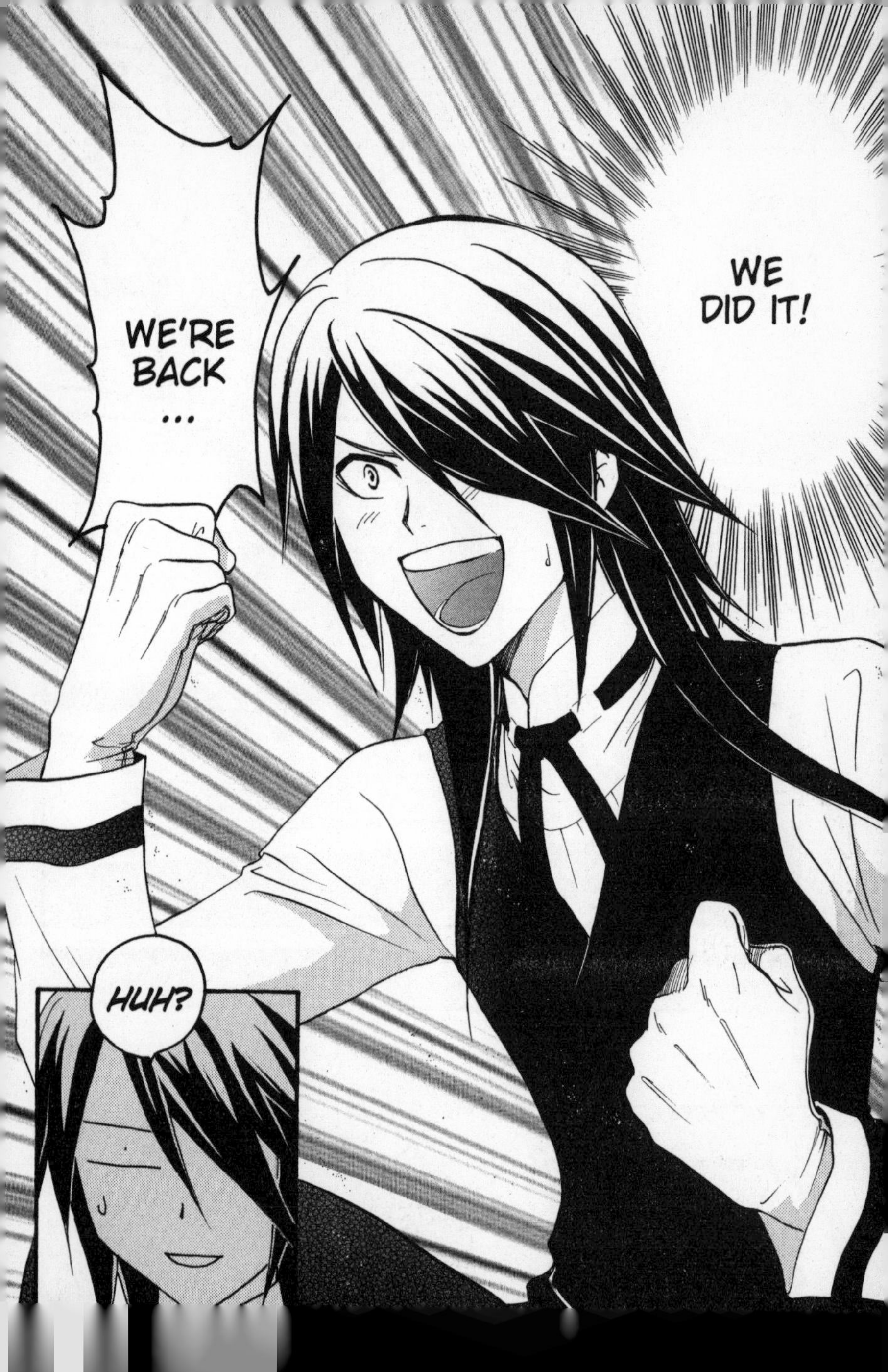
WE DID IT!
WE'RE BACK ...
HUH?

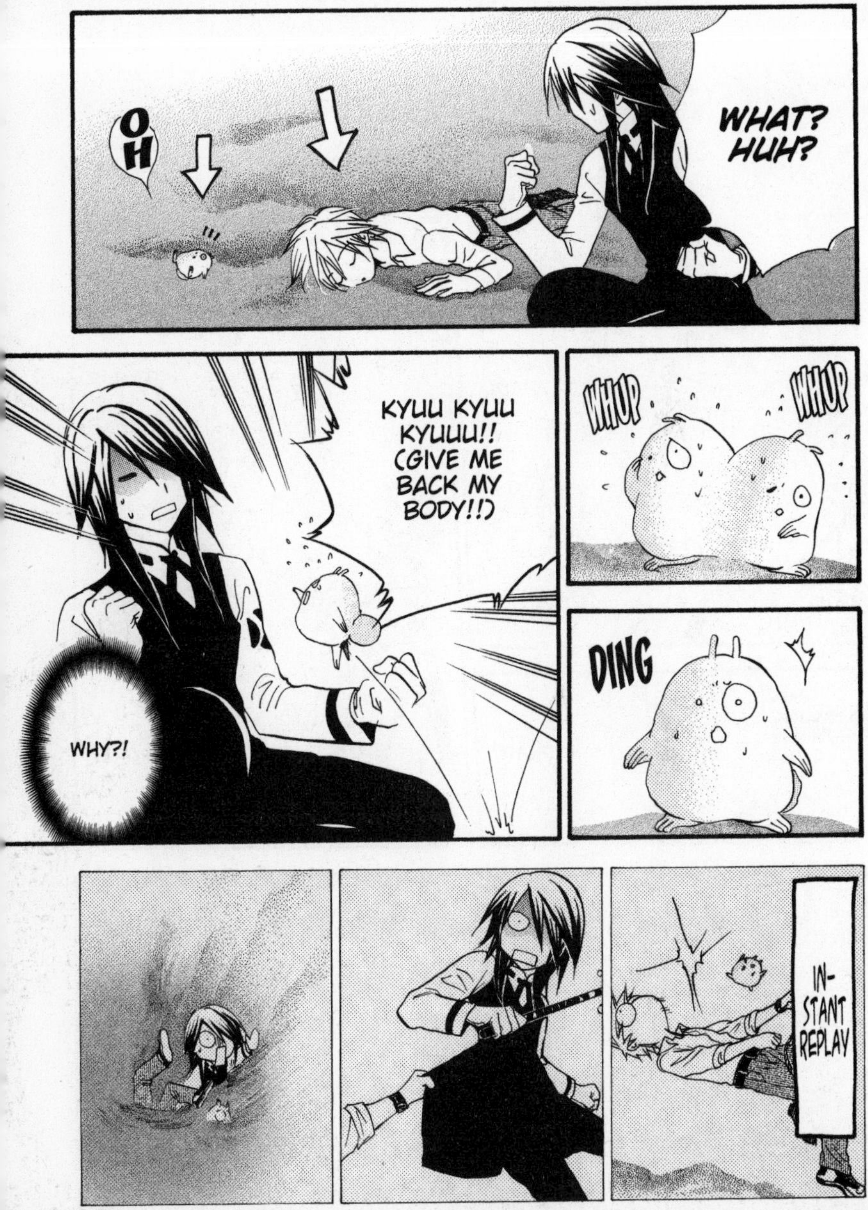
WHAT? HUH?
OH
WHUP
WHUP
DING
KYUU KYUU KYUUU!! (GIVE ME BACK MY BODY!!)
WHY?!
IN-STANT REPLAY

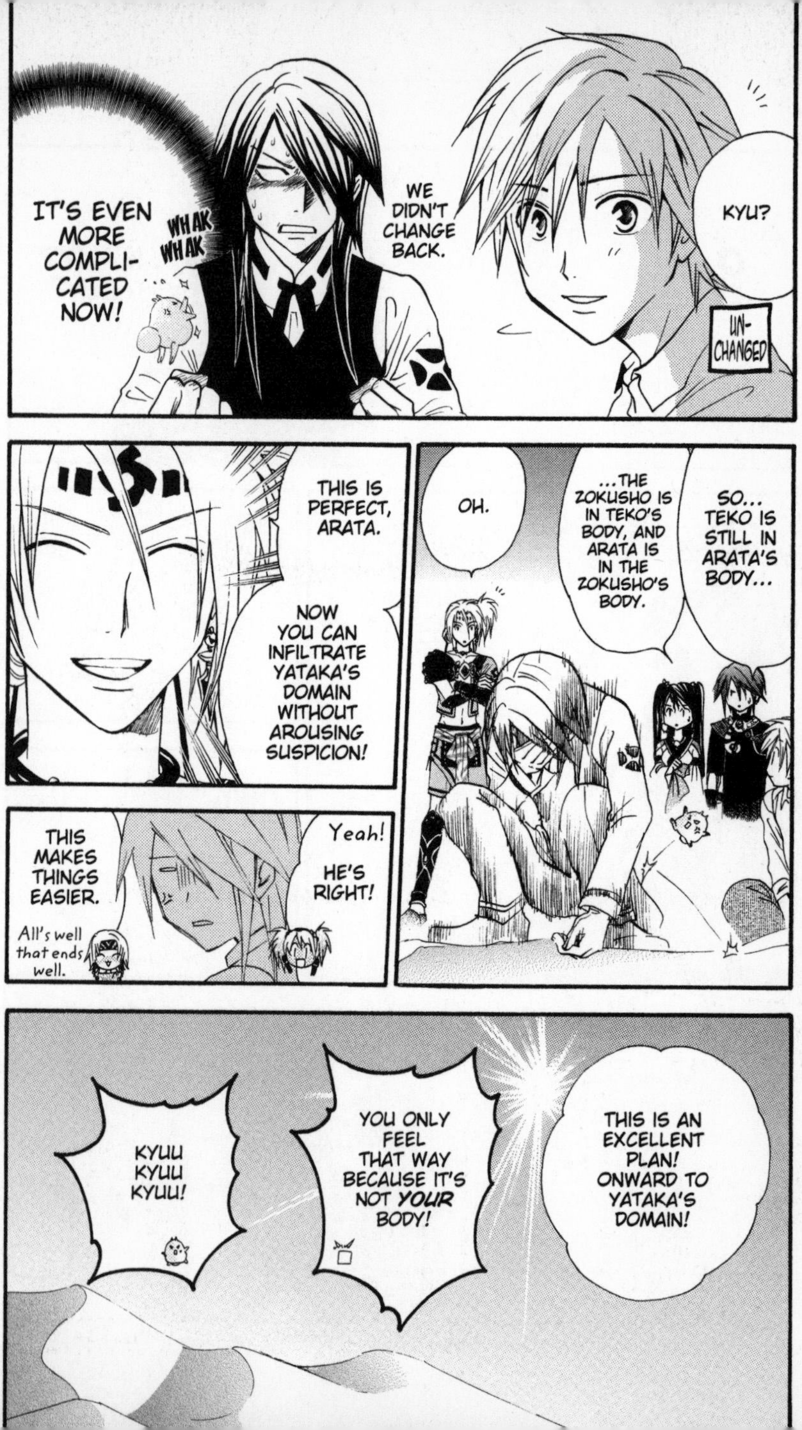
KYU?
UN-CHANGED
WE DIDN'T CHANGE BACK.
WHAK WHAK
IT'S EVEN MORE COMPLI-CATED NOW!
SO... TEKO IS STILL IN ARATA'S BODY...
...THE ZOKUSHO IS IN TEKO'S BODY, AND ARATA IS IN THE ZOKUSHO'S BODY.
OH.
THIS IS PERFECT, ARATA.
NOW YOU CAN INFILTRATE YATAKA'S DOMAIN WITHOUT AROUSING SUSPICION!
Yeah!
HE'S RIGHT!
THIS MAKES THINGS EASIER.
All's well that ends well.
THIS IS AN EXCELLENT PLAN! ONWARD TO YATAKA'S DOMAIN!
YOU ONLY FEEL THAT WAY BECAUSE IT'S NOT *YOUR* BODY!
KYUU KYUU KYUU!

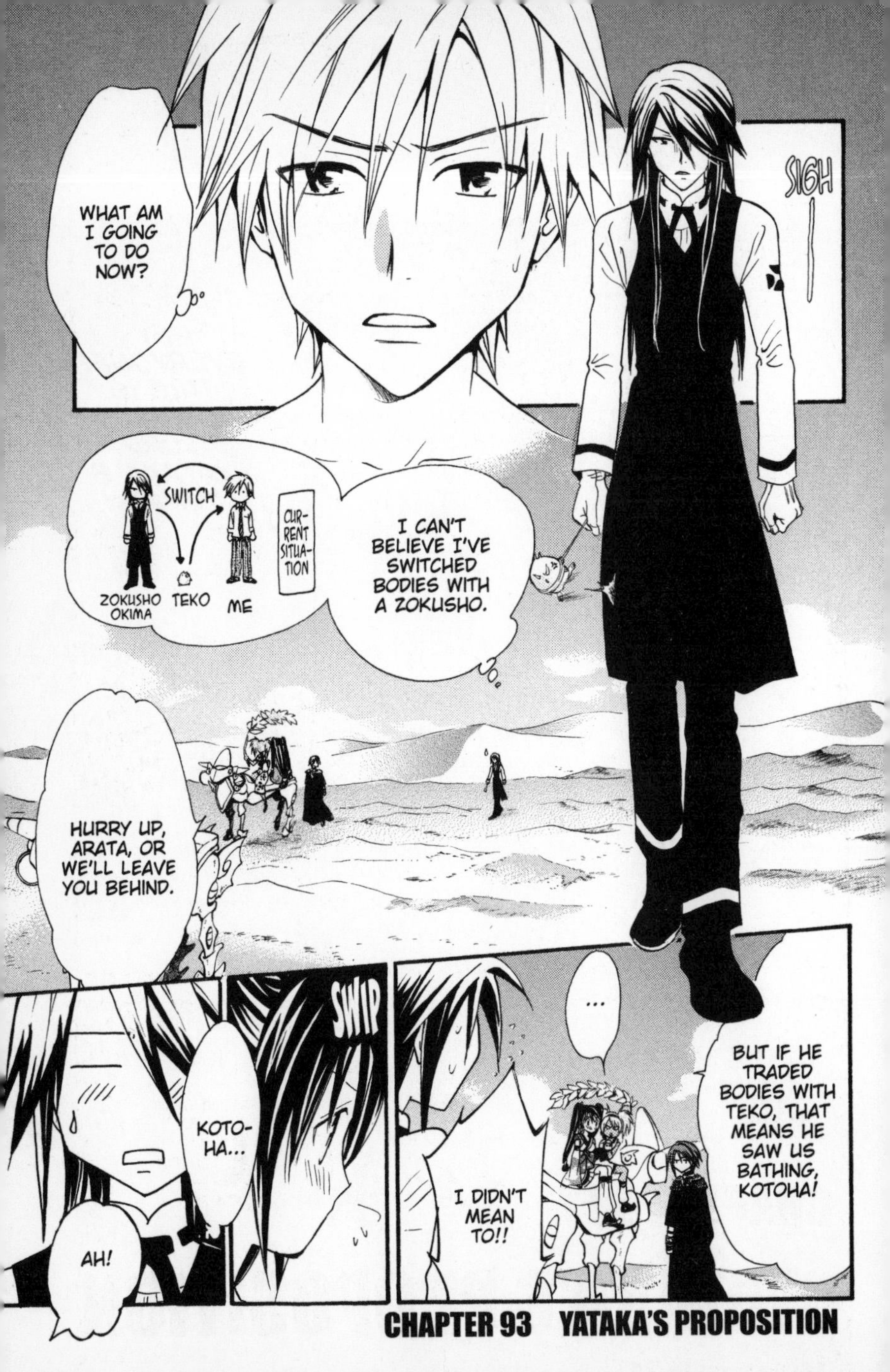
SIGH
WHAT AM I GOING TO DO NOW?
I CAN'T BELIEVE I'VE SWITCHED BODIES WITH A ZOKUSHO.
CURRENT SITUATION
SWITCH
ME
TEKO
ZOKUSHO OKIMA
HURRY UP, ARATA, OR WE'LL LEAVE YOU BEHIND.
BUT IF HE TRADED BODIES WITH TEKO, THAT MEANS HE SAW US BATHING, KOTOHA!
...
I DIDN'T MEAN TO!!
SWIP
KOTO-HA...
AH!

CHAPTER 93 YATAKA'S PROPOSITION

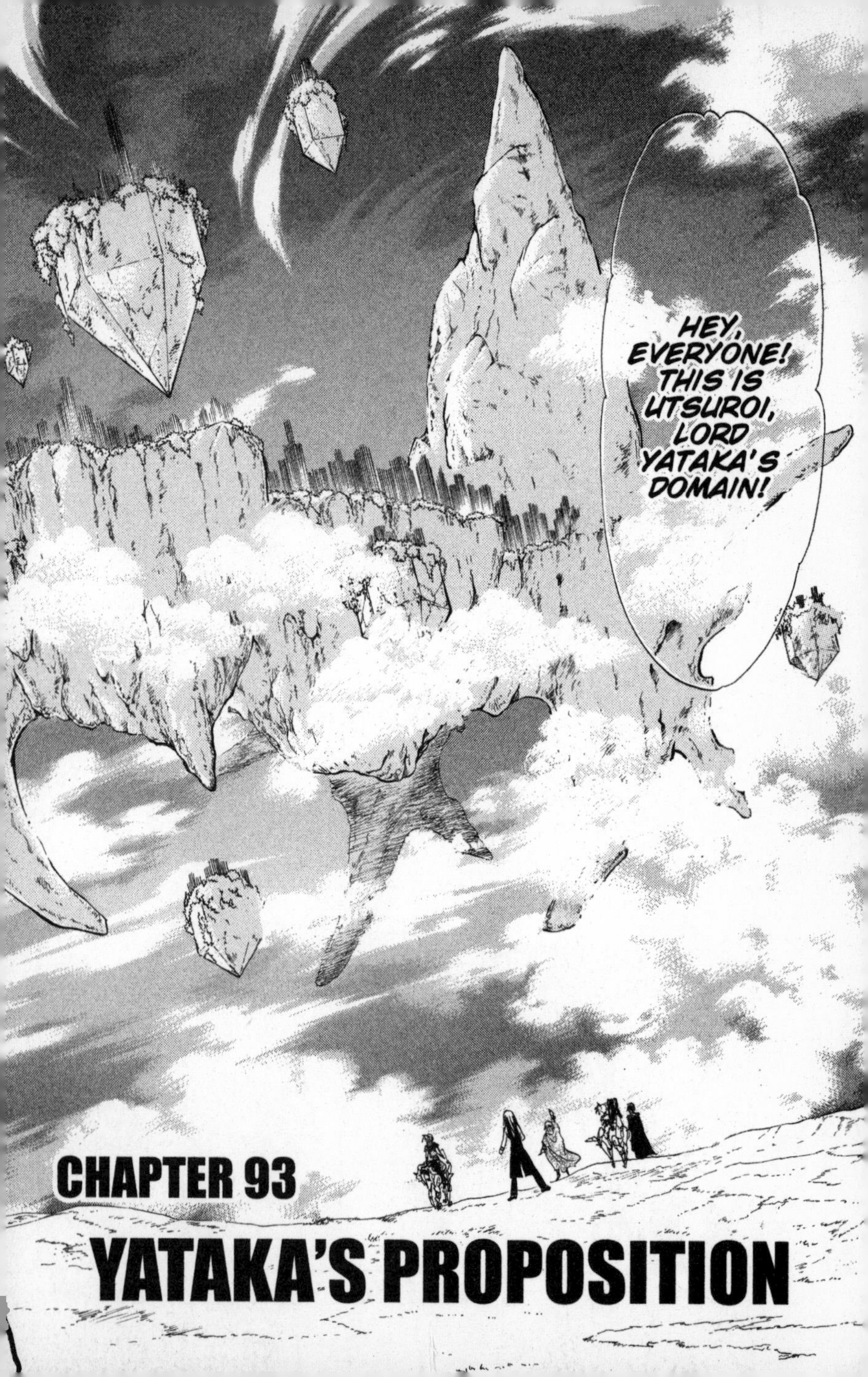
HEY, EVERYONE! THIS IS UTSUROI, LORD YATAKA'S DOMAIN!
CHAPTER 93
YATAKA'S PROPOSITION

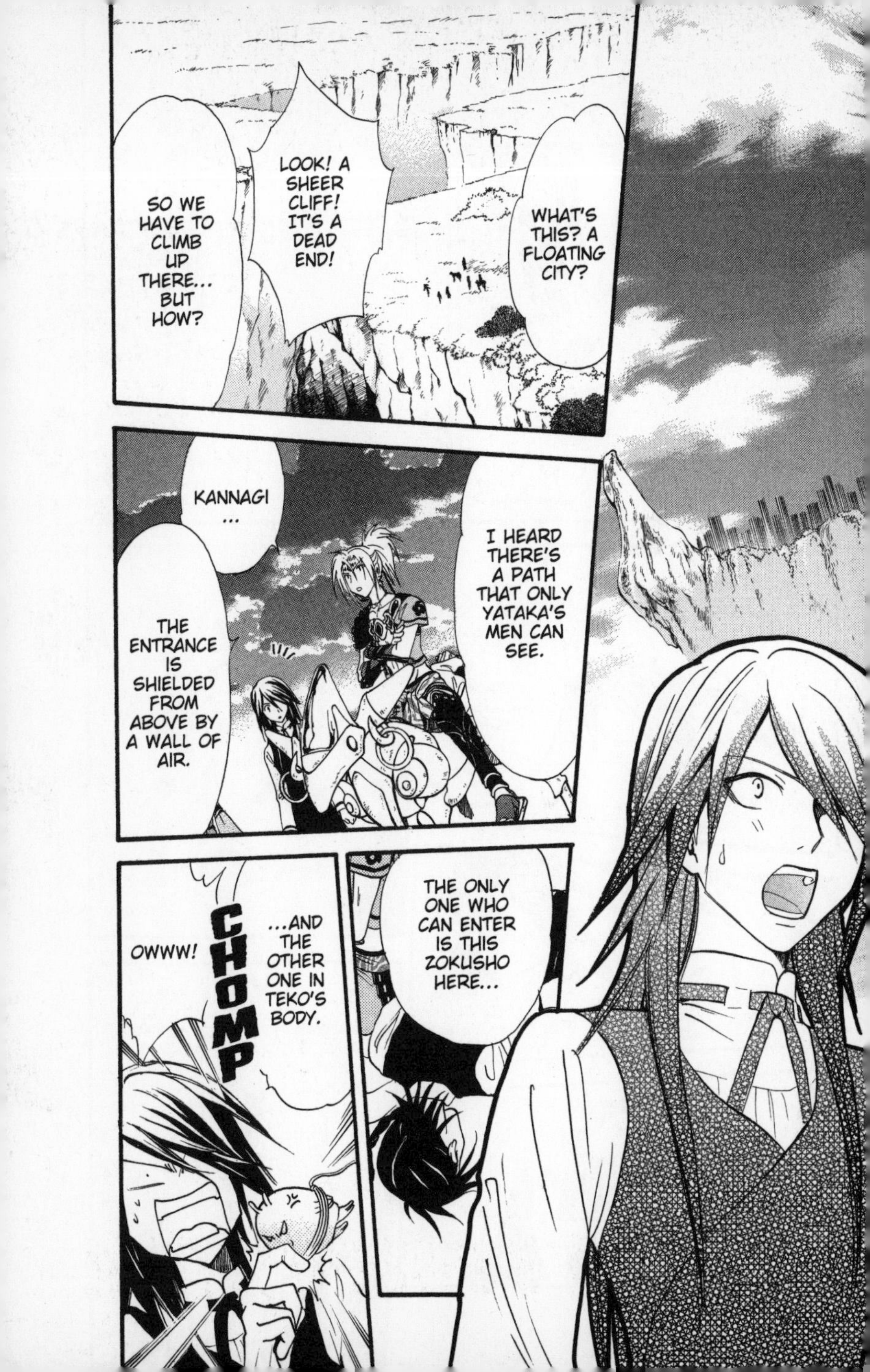
WHAT'S THIS? A FLOATING CITY?
LOOK! A SHEER CLIFF! IT'S A DEAD END!
SO WE HAVE TO CLIMB UP THERE... BUT HOW?
I HEARD THERE'S A PATH THAT ONLY YATAKA'S MEN CAN SEE.
KANNAGI ...
THE ENTRANCE IS SHIELDED FROM ABOVE BY A WALL OF AIR.
THE ONLY ONE WHO CAN ENTER IS THIS ZOKUSHO HERE...
...AND THE OTHER ONE IN TEKO'S BODY.
CHOMP
OWWW!

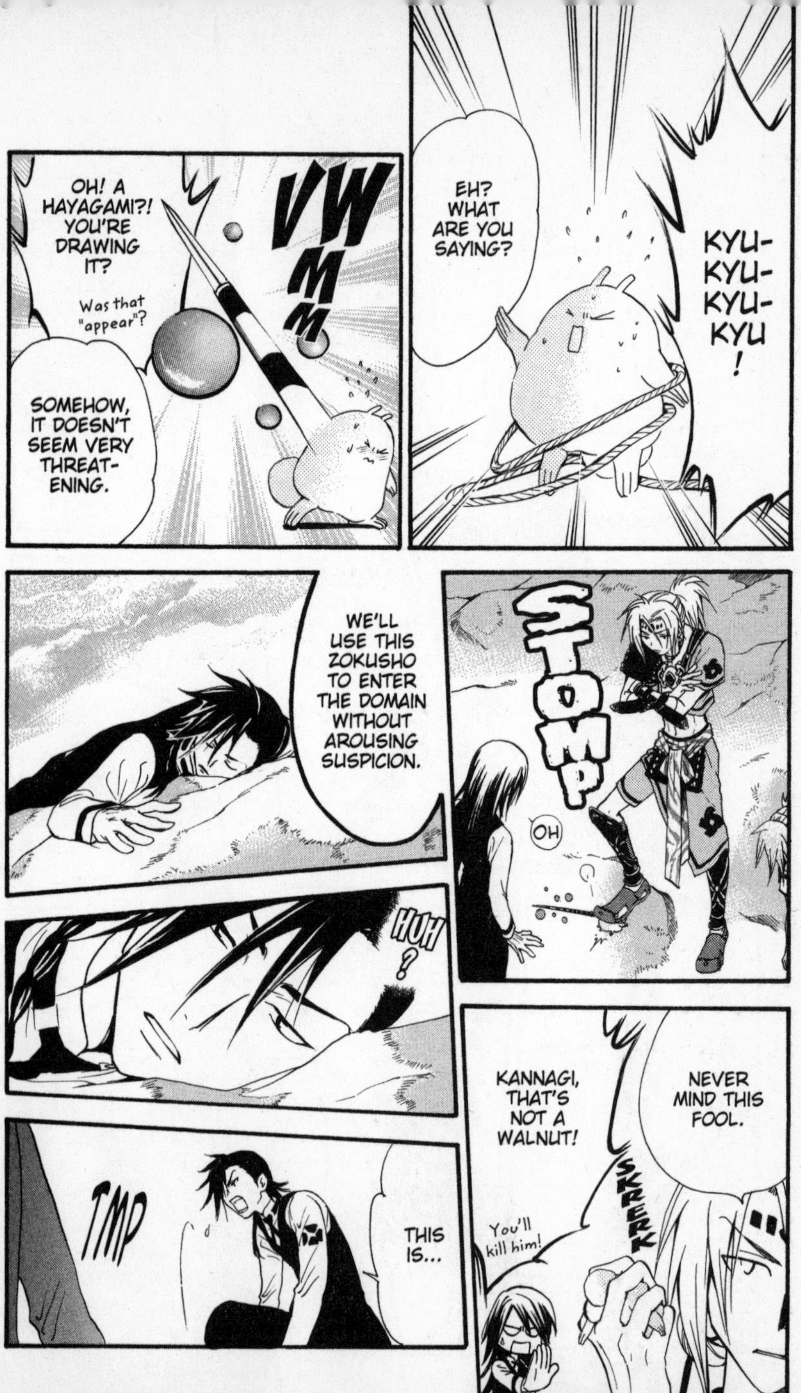
KYU-KYU-KYU-KYU!
EH? WHAT ARE YOU SAYING?
VWMM
OH! A HAYAGAMI?! YOU'RE DRAWING IT?
Was that "appear"?
SOMEHOW, IT DOESN'T SEEM VERY THREAT-ENING.
STOMP
OH
WE'LL USE THIS ZOKUSHO TO ENTER THE DOMAIN WITHOUT AROUSING SUSPICION.
NEVER MIND THIS FOOL.
KANNAGI, THAT'S NOT A WALNUT!
SKRERK
You'll kill him!
HUH?
THIS IS...
TMP

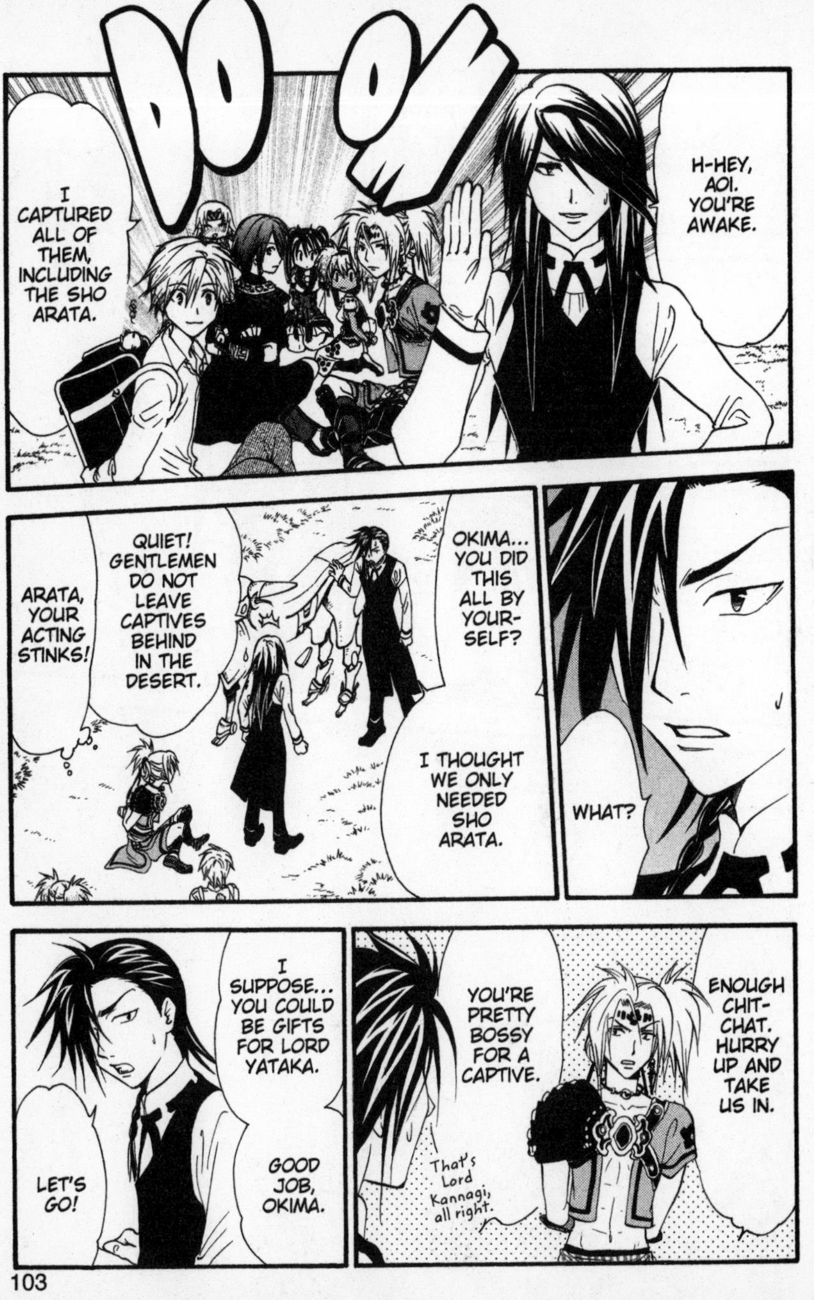
DO-ON
H-HEY, AOI. YOU'RE AWAKE.
I CAPTURED ALL OF THEM, INCLUDING THE SHO ARATA.
WHAT?
OKIMA... YOU DID THIS ALL BY YOURSELF?
I THOUGHT WE ONLY NEEDED SHO ARATA.
QUIET! GENTLEMEN DO NOT LEAVE CAPTIVES BEHIND IN THE DESERT.
ARATA, YOUR ACTING STINKS!
ENOUGH CHIT-CHAT. HURRY UP AND TAKE US IN.
YOU'RE PRETTY BOSSY FOR A CAPTIVE.
That's Lord Kannagi, all right.
I SUPPOSE... YOU COULD BE GIFTS FOR LORD YATAKA.
GOOD JOB, OKIMA.
LET'S GO!

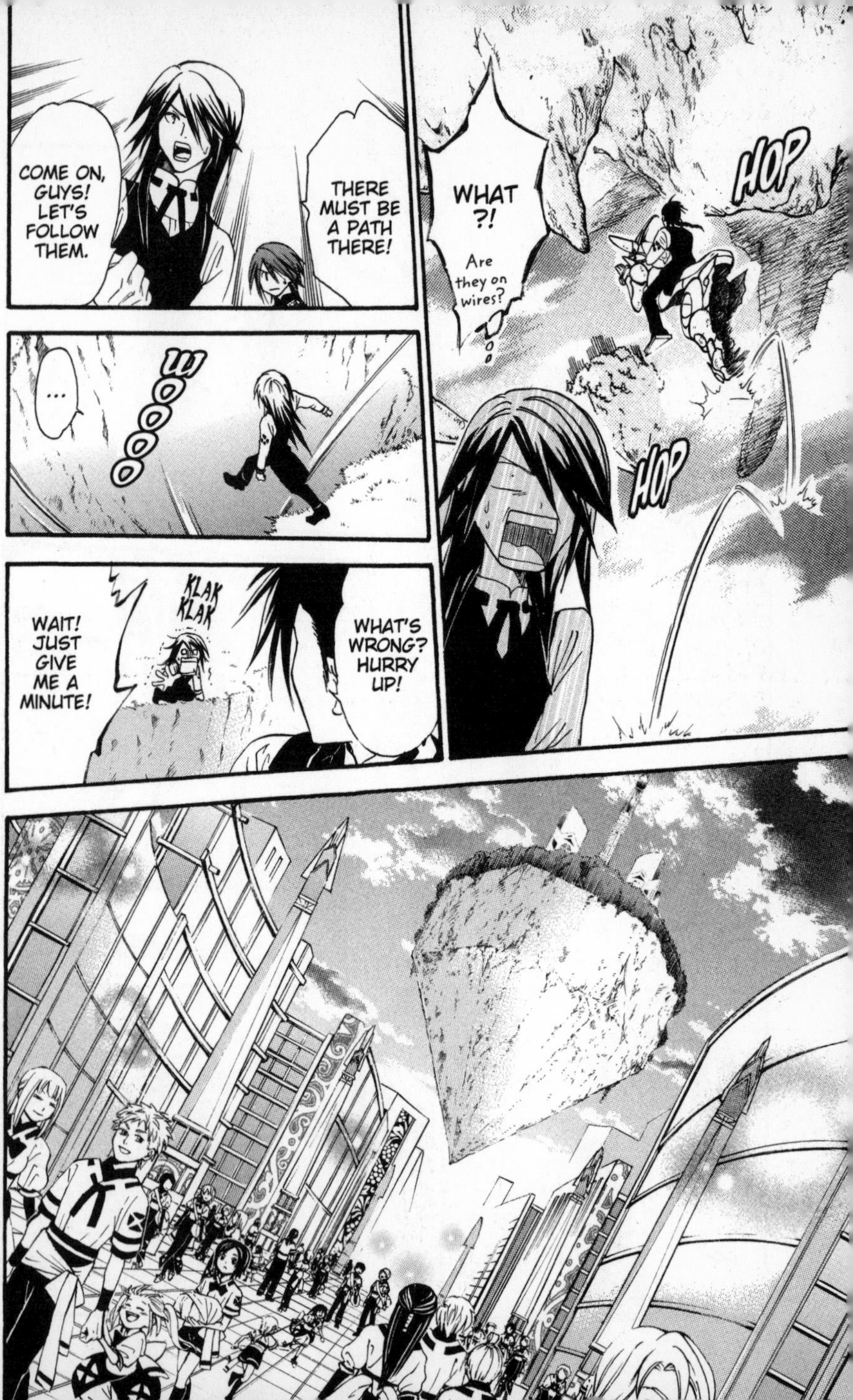
WHAT ?!
Are they on wires?
HOP
HOP
THERE MUST BE A PATH THERE!
COME ON, GUYS! LET'S FOLLOW THEM.
WOOOOOO
...
WHAT'S WRONG? HURRY UP!
KLAK KLAK
WAIT! JUST GIVE ME A MINUTE!

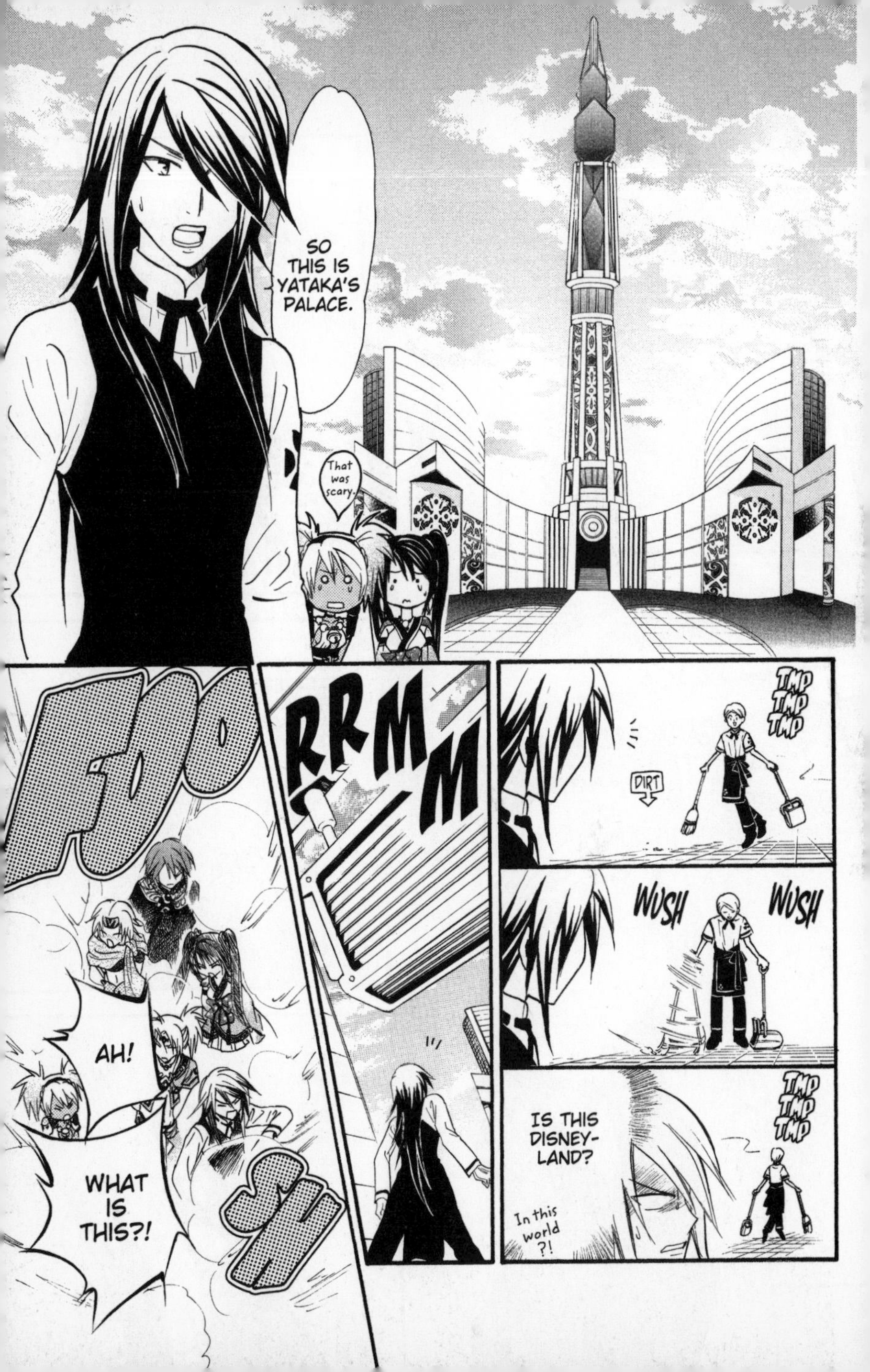
SO THIS IS YATAKA'S PALACE.
That was scary.
TMP TMP TMP
DIRT
WUSH WUSH
IS THIS DISNEY-LAND?
In this world ?!
TMP TMP TMP
RRMM
FOO
AH!
WHAT IS THIS?!
SH

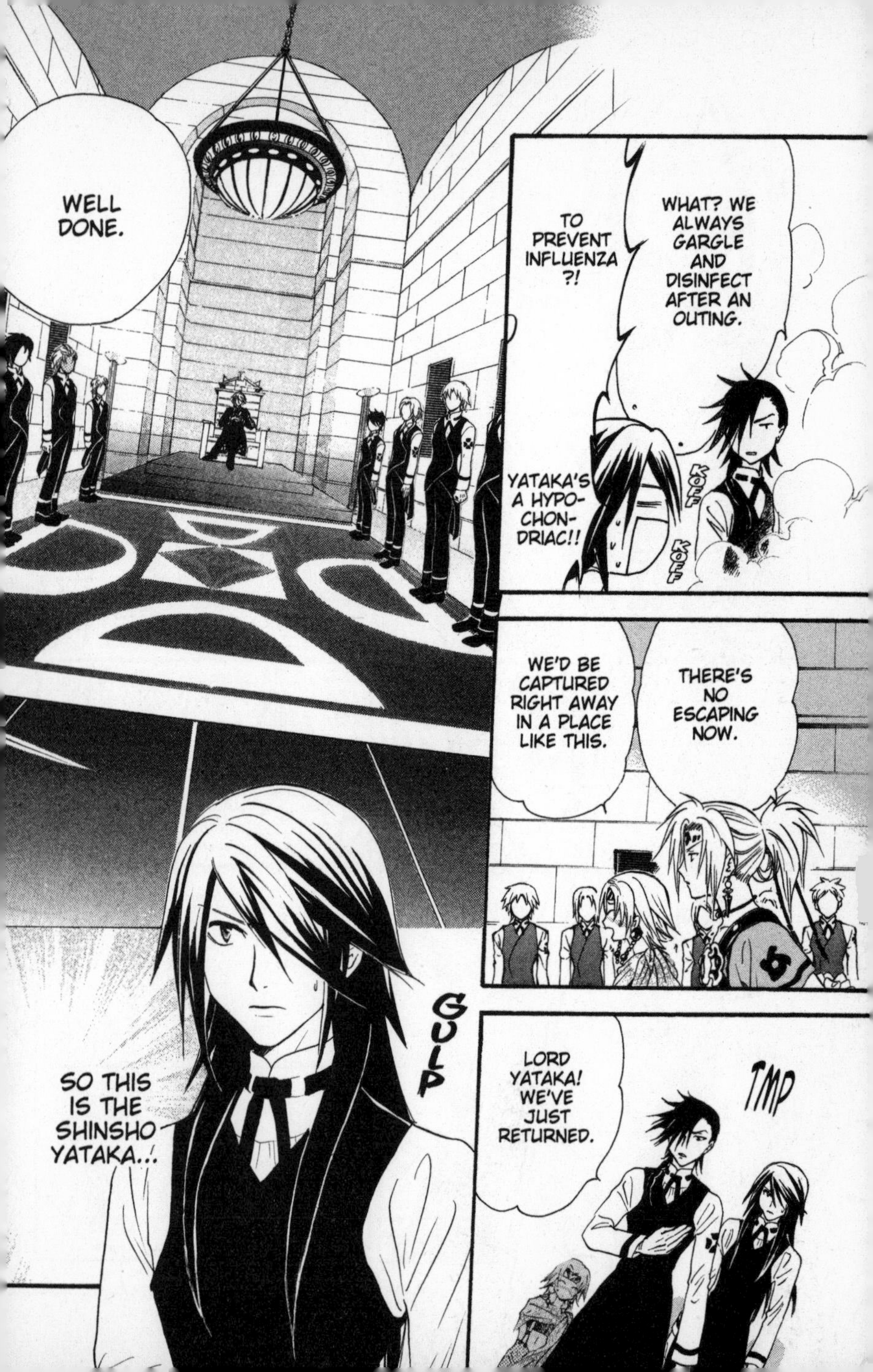
WHAT? WE ALWAYS GARGLE AND DISINFECT AFTER AN OUTING.
TO PREVENT INFLUENZA ?!
KOFF
KOFF
YATAKA'S A HYPOCHONDRIAC!!
THERE'S NO ESCAPING NOW.
WE'D BE CAPTURED RIGHT AWAY IN A PLACE LIKE THIS.
TMP
LORD YATAKA! WE'VE JUST RETURNED.
WELL DONE.
GULP
SO THIS IS THE SHINSHO YATAKA..!

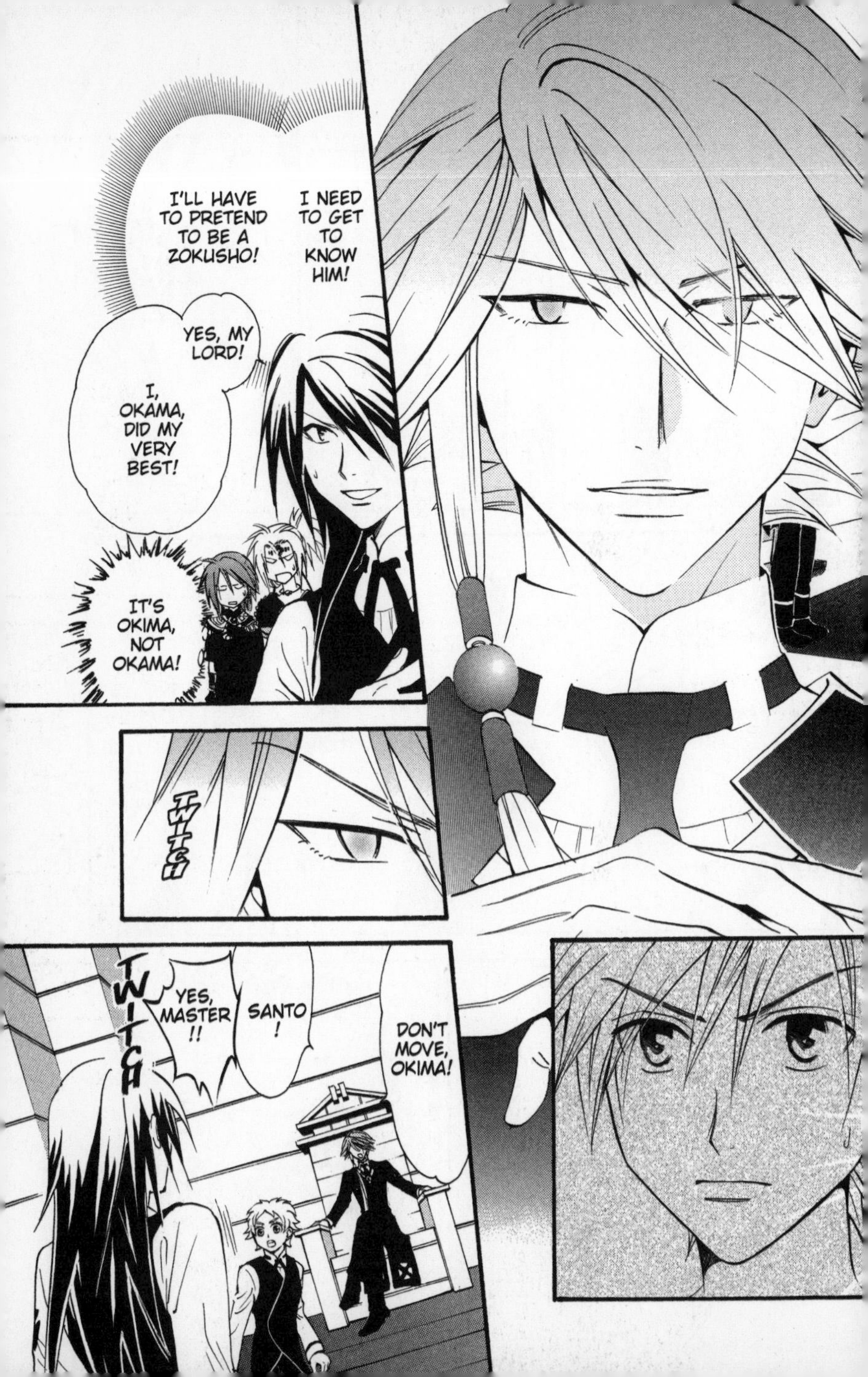
I NEED TO GET TO KNOW HIM!
I'LL HAVE TO PRETEND TO BE A ZOKUSHO!
YES, MY LORD!
I, OKAMA, DID MY VERY BEST!
IT'S OKIMA, NOT OKAMA!
TWITCH
DON'T MOVE, OKIMA!
SANTO!
YES, MASTER!!
TWITCH

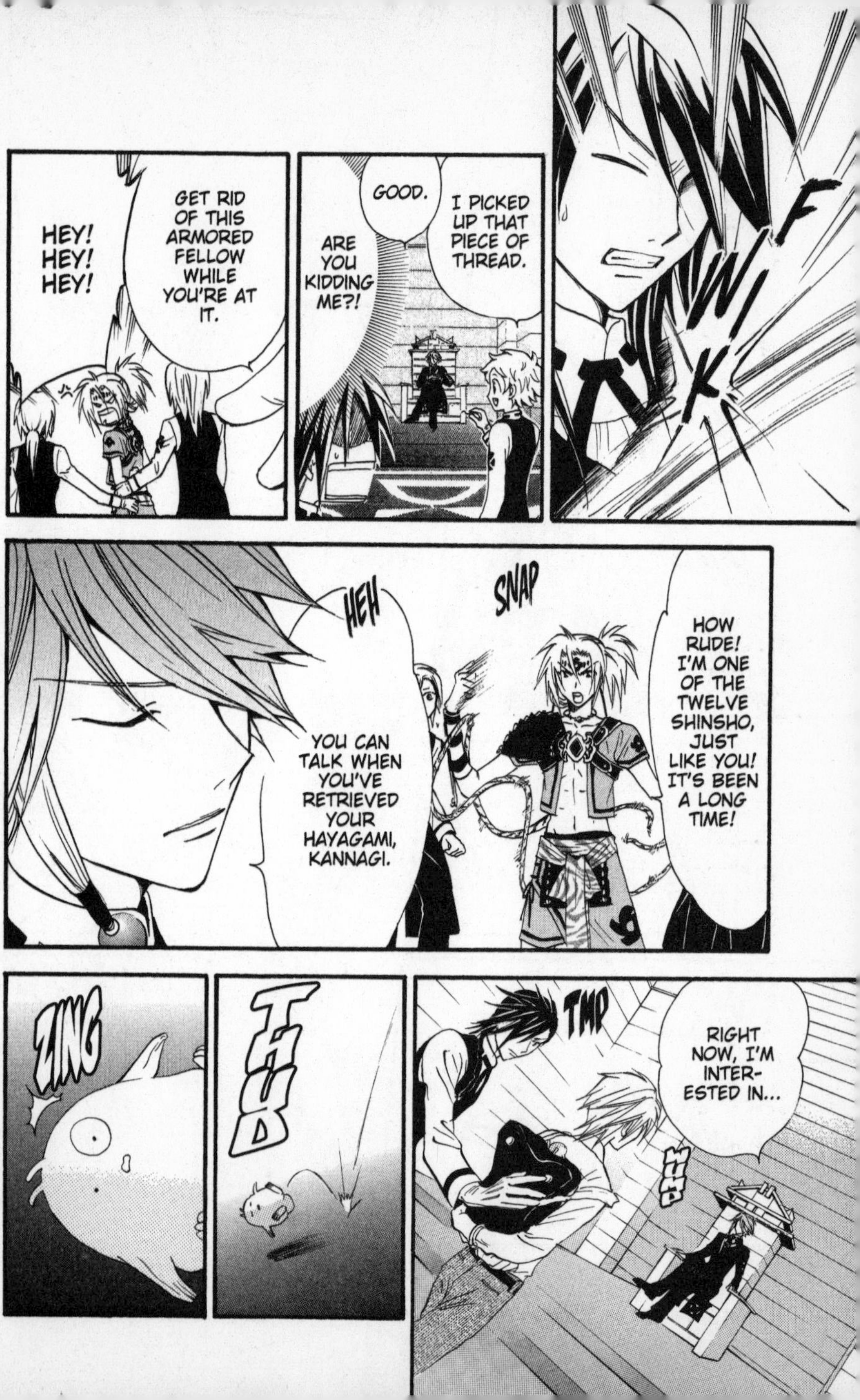
FWIK
I PICKED UP THAT PIECE OF THREAD.
GOOD.
ARE YOU KIDDING ME?!
GET RID OF THIS ARMORED FELLOW WHILE YOU'RE AT IT.
HEY! HEY! HEY!
HOW RUDE! I'M ONE OF THE TWELVE SHINSHO, JUST LIKE YOU! IT'S BEEN A LONG TIME!
SNAP
HEH
YOU CAN TALK WHEN YOU'VE RETRIEVED YOUR HAYAGAMI, KANNAGI.
RIGHT NOW, I'M INTERESTED IN...
TMP
WUMP
THUD
ZING

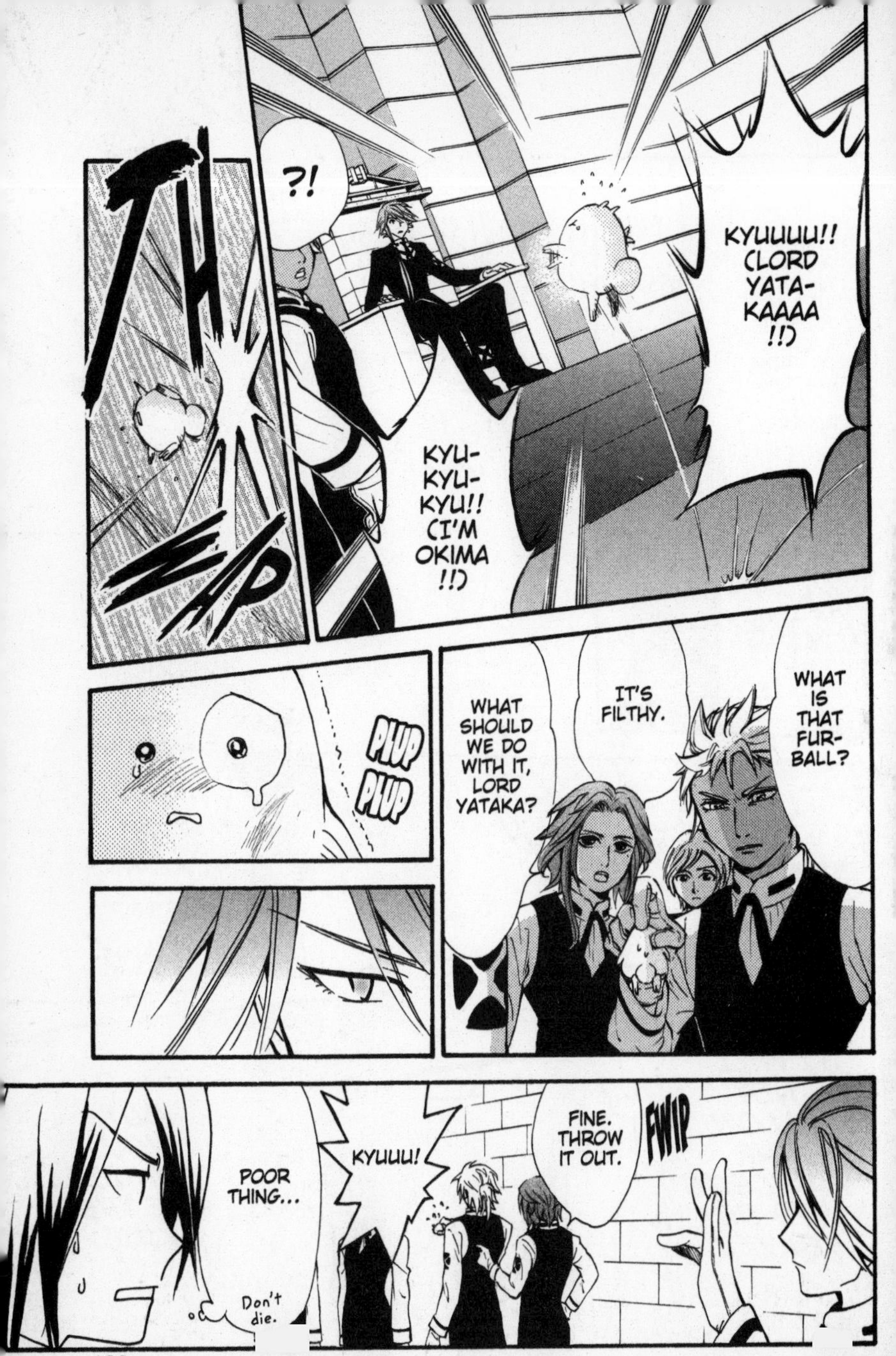

KYUUUU!! (LORD YATA-KAAAA!!)
?!
KYU-KYU-KYU!! (I'M OKIMA!!)
THWAP
WHAT IS THAT FUR-BALL?
IT'S FILTHY.
WHAT SHOULD WE DO WITH IT, LORD YATAKA?
PLUP PLUP
FWIP
FINE. THROW IT OUT.
KYUUU!
POOR THING...
Don't die.

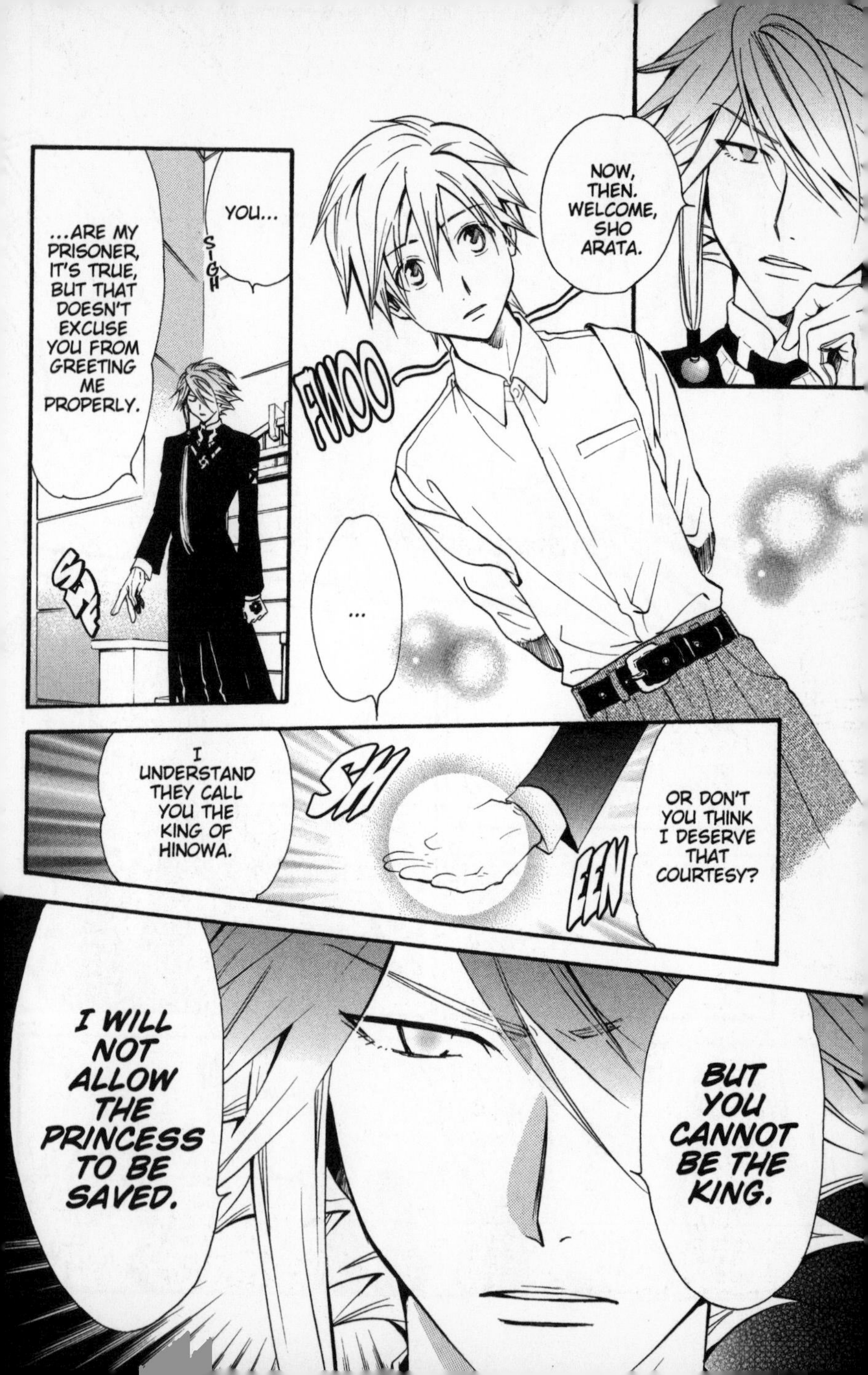
NOW, THEN. WELCOME, SHO ARATA.
FWOO
...
YOU...
SIGH
...ARE MY PRISONER, IT'S TRUE, BUT THAT DOESN'T EXCUSE YOU FROM GREETING ME PROPERLY.
OR DON'T YOU THINK I DESERVE THAT COURTESY?
SH
EEN
I UNDERSTAND THEY CALL YOU THE KING OF HINOWA.
BUT YOU CANNOT BE THE KING.
I WILL NOT ALLOW THE PRINCESS TO BE SAVED.

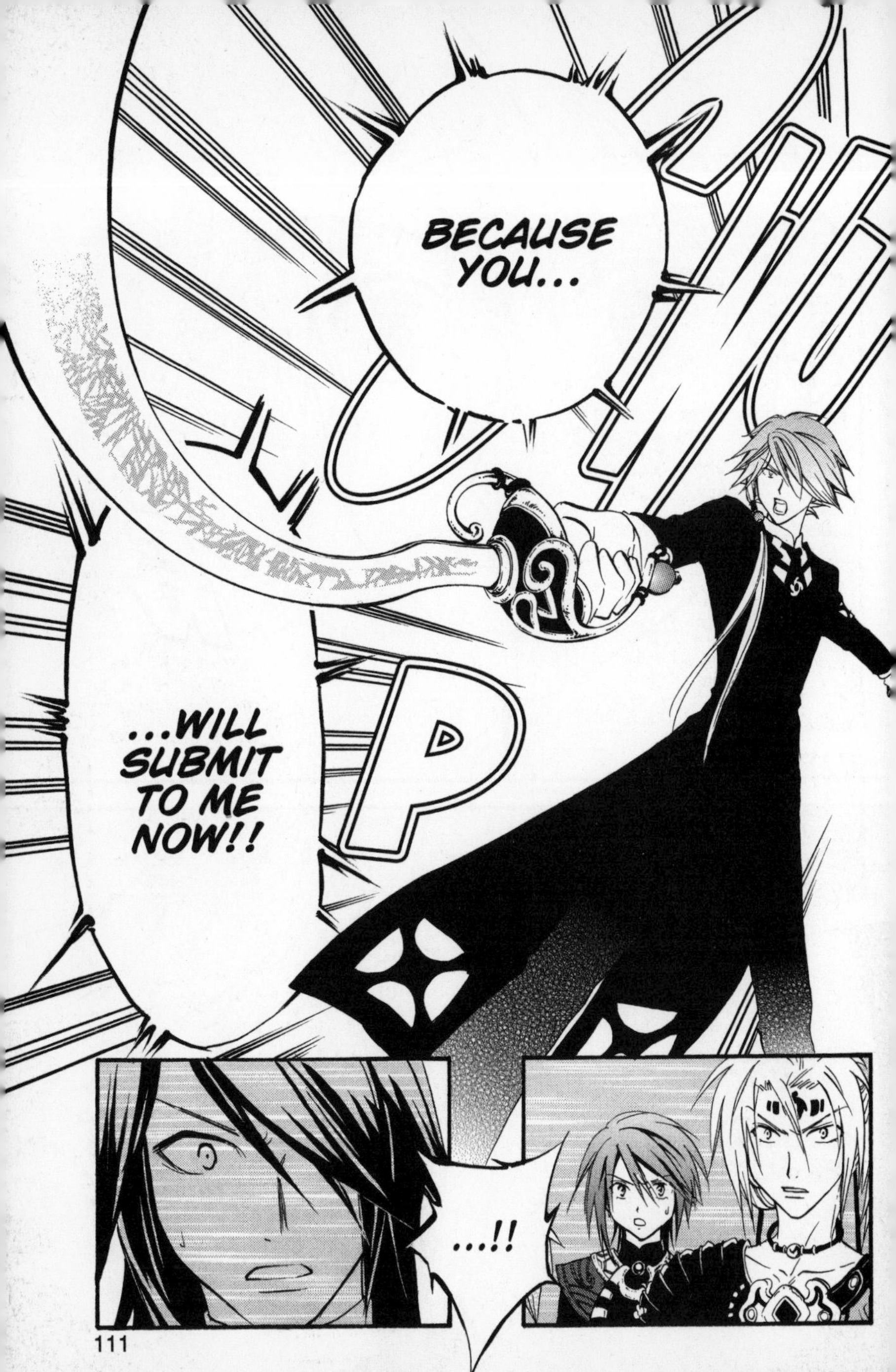
BECAUSE YOU...
...WILL SUBMIT TO ME NOW!!
...!!

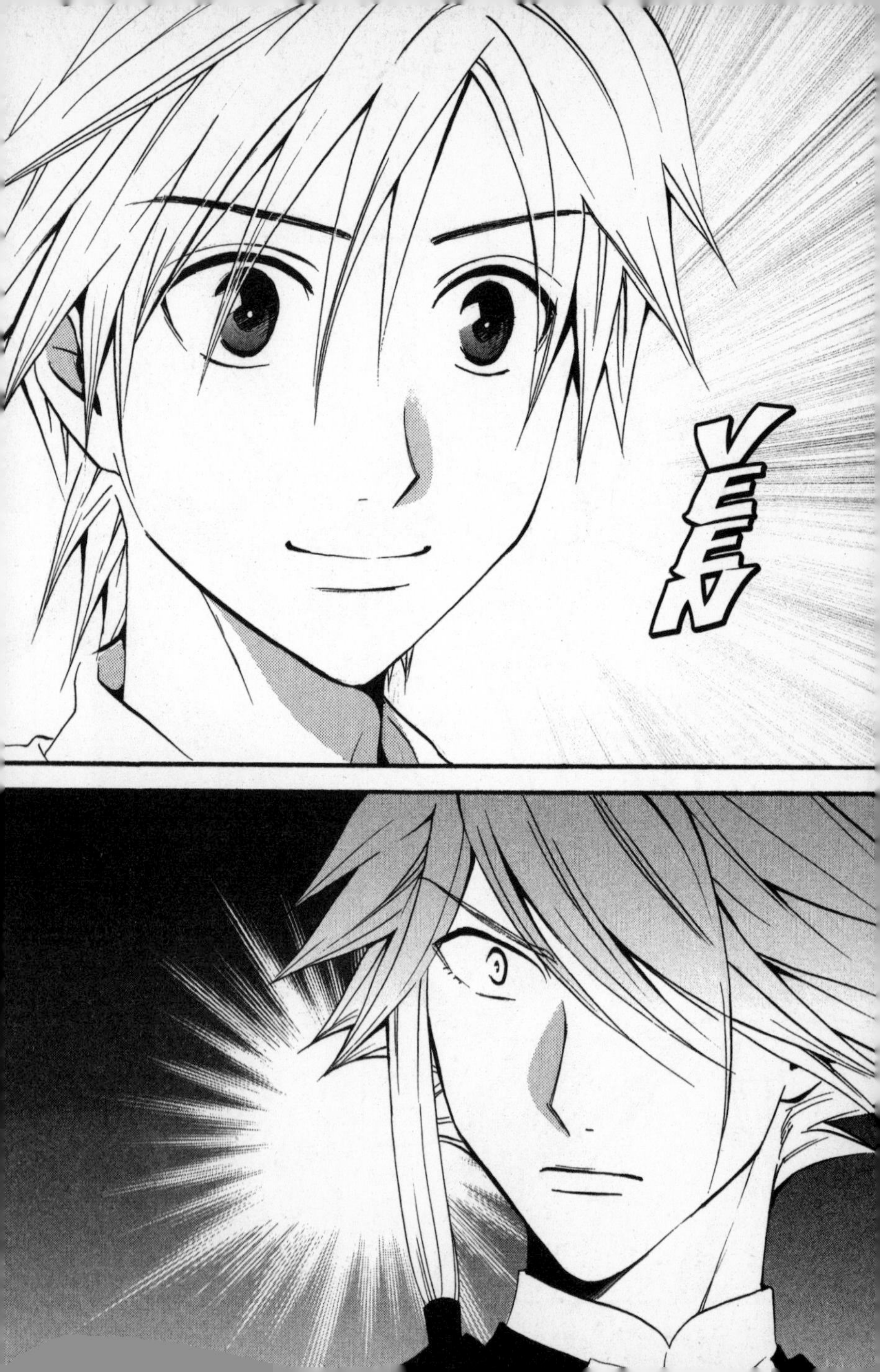
VEEN

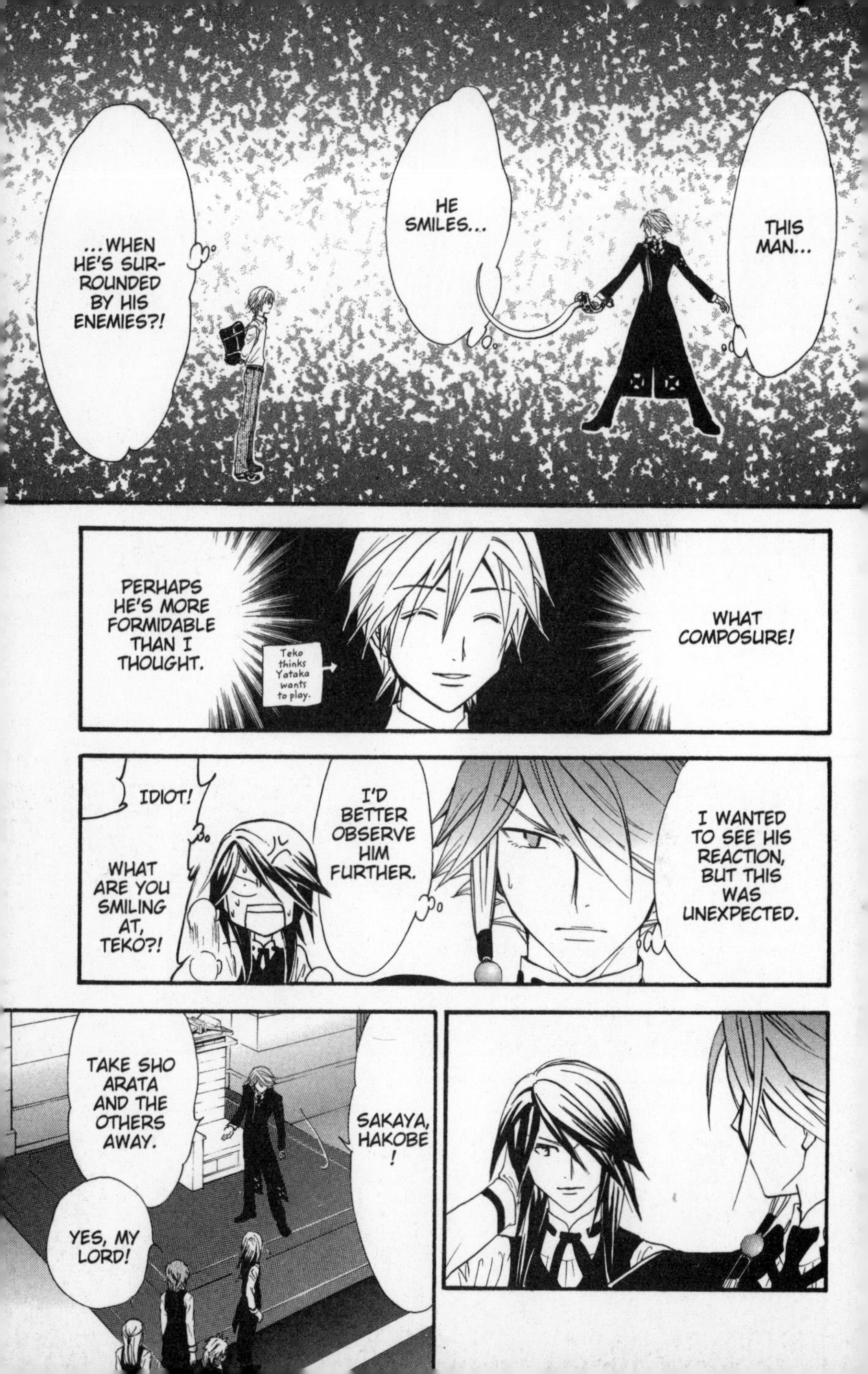
THIS MAN...
HE SMILES...
...WHEN HE'S SURROUNDED BY HIS ENEMIES?!
WHAT COMPOSURE!
PERHAPS HE'S MORE FORMIDABLE THAN I THOUGHT.
Teko thinks Yataka wants to play.
I WANTED TO SEE HIS REACTION, BUT THIS WAS UNEXPECTED.
I'D BETTER OBSERVE HIM FURTHER.
IDIOT!
WHAT ARE YOU SMILING AT, TEKO?!
SAKAYA, HAKOBE!
TAKE SHO ARATA AND THE OTHERS AWAY.
YES, MY LORD!

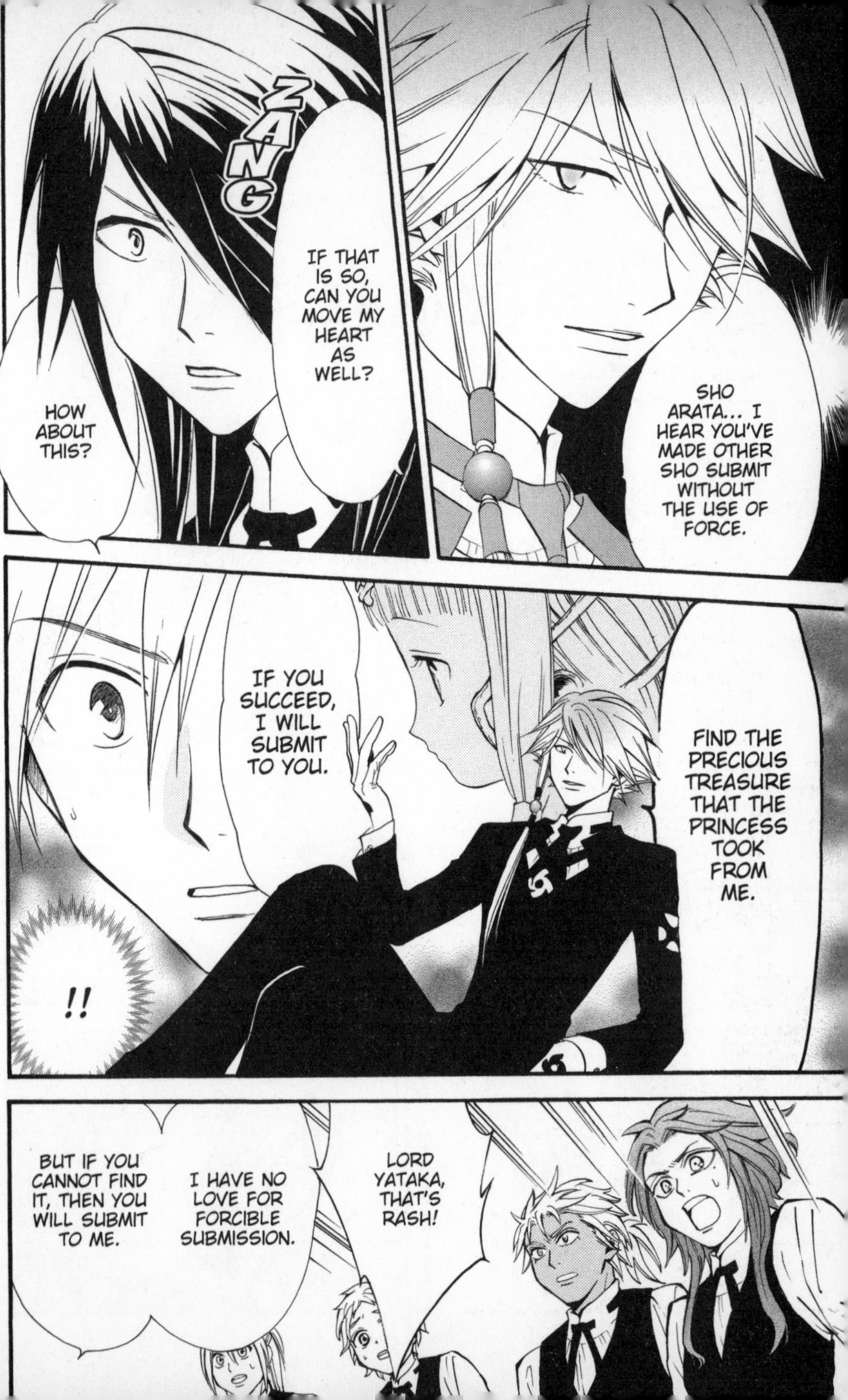
SHO ARATA... I HEAR YOU'VE MADE OTHER SHO SUBMIT WITHOUT THE USE OF FORCE.
IF THAT IS SO, CAN YOU MOVE MY HEART AS WELL?
ZANG
HOW ABOUT THIS?
FIND THE PRECIOUS TREASURE THAT THE PRINCESS TOOK FROM ME.
IF YOU SUCCEED, I WILL SUBMIT TO YOU.
!!
LORD YATAKA, THAT'S RASH!
I HAVE NO LOVE FOR FORCIBLE SUBMISSION.
BUT IF YOU CANNOT FIND IT, THEN YOU WILL SUBMIT TO ME.

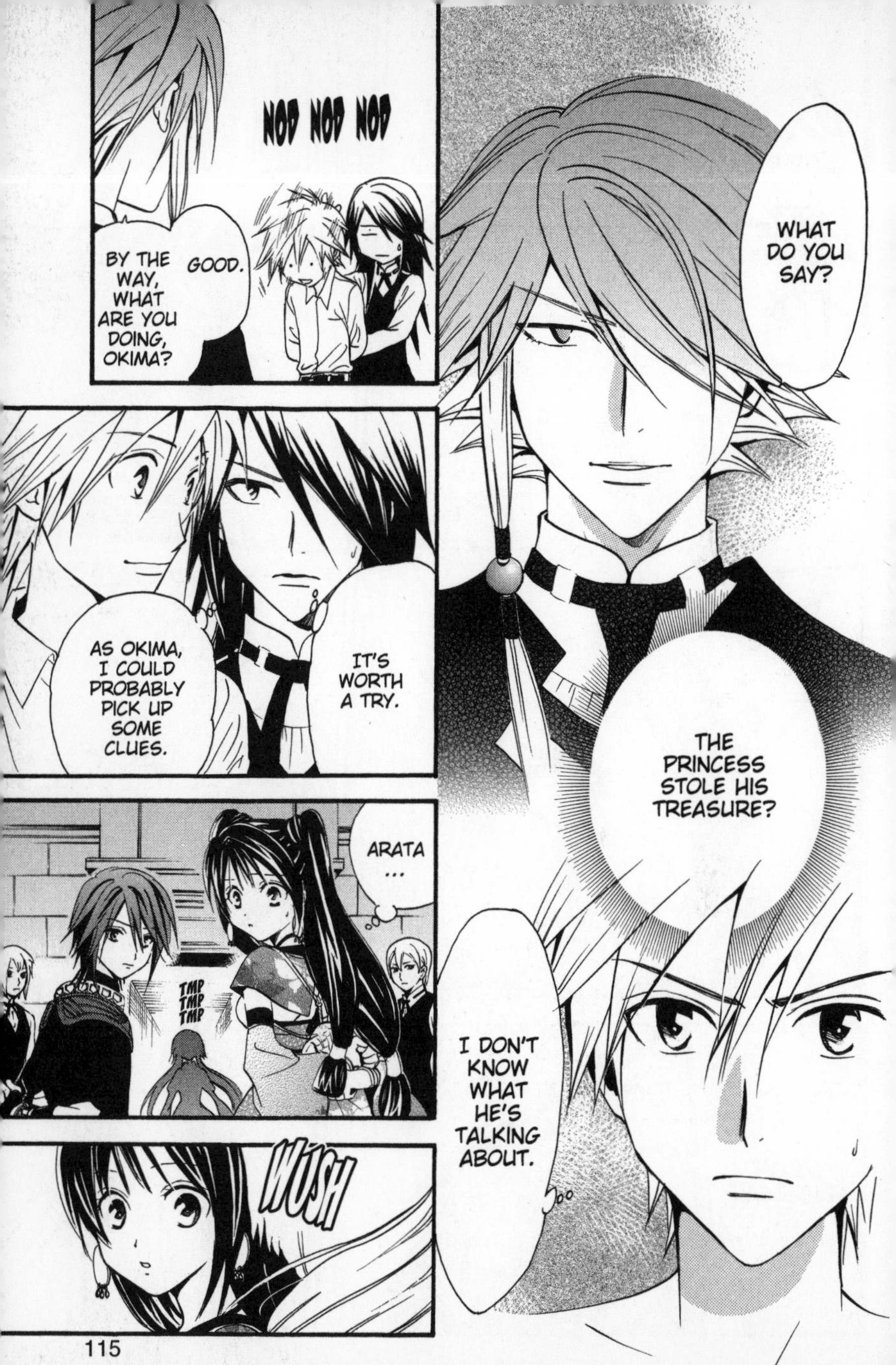
WHAT DO YOU SAY?
THE PRINCESS STOLE HIS TREASURE?
I DON'T KNOW WHAT HE'S TALKING ABOUT.
NOD NOD NOD
GOOD.
BY THE WAY, WHAT ARE YOU DOING, OKIMA?
IT'S WORTH A TRY.
AS OKIMA, I COULD PROBABLY PICK UP SOME CLUES.
ARATA ...
TMP TMP TMP
WUSH

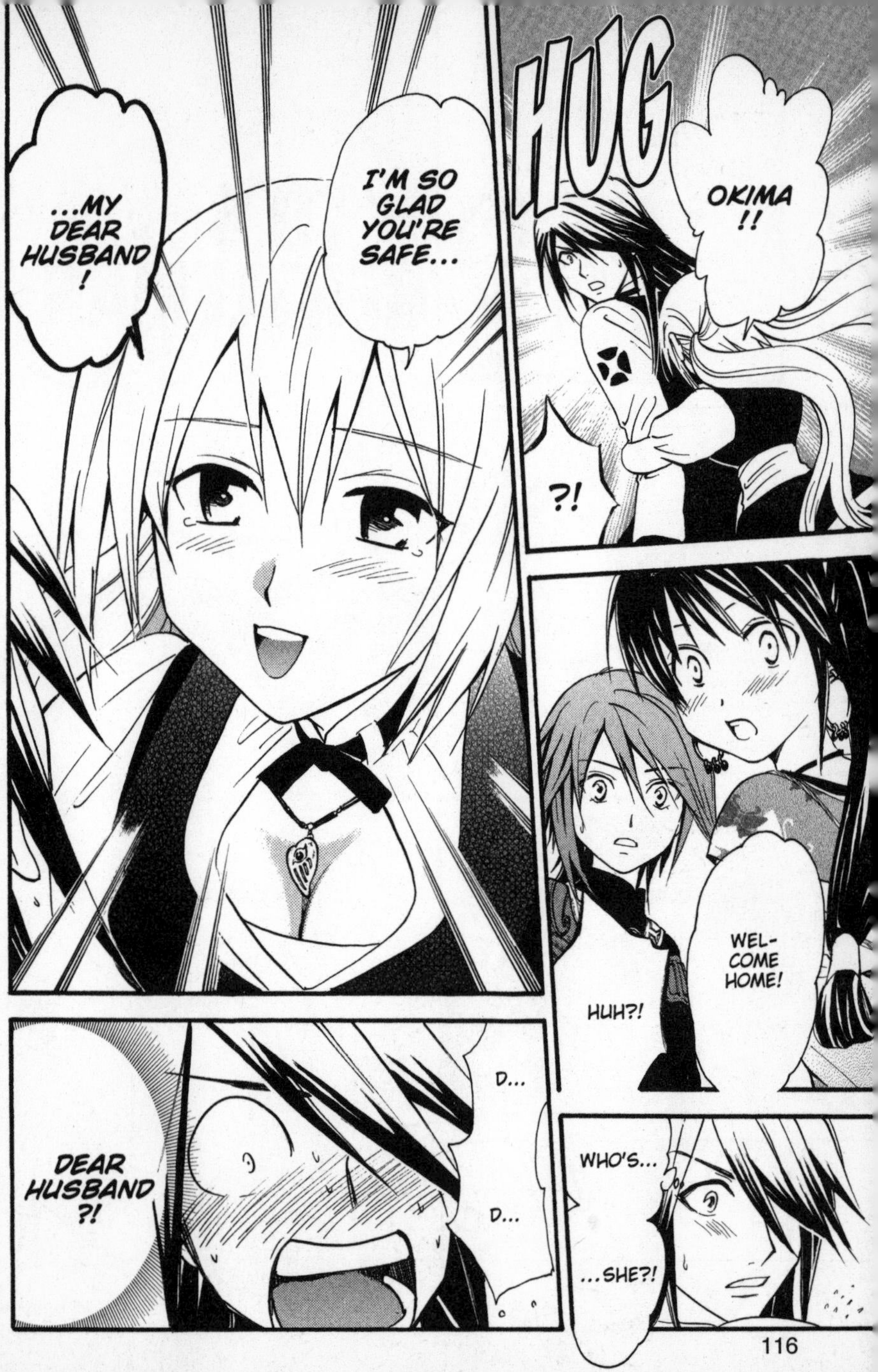
HUG
OKIMA!!
?!
WEL-COME HOME!
HUH?!
I'M SO GLAD YOU'RE SAFE...
...MY DEAR HUSBAND!
WHO'S...
...SHE?!
D...
D...
DEAR HUSBAND?!

CHAPTER 94
TO BE A GENTLEMAN

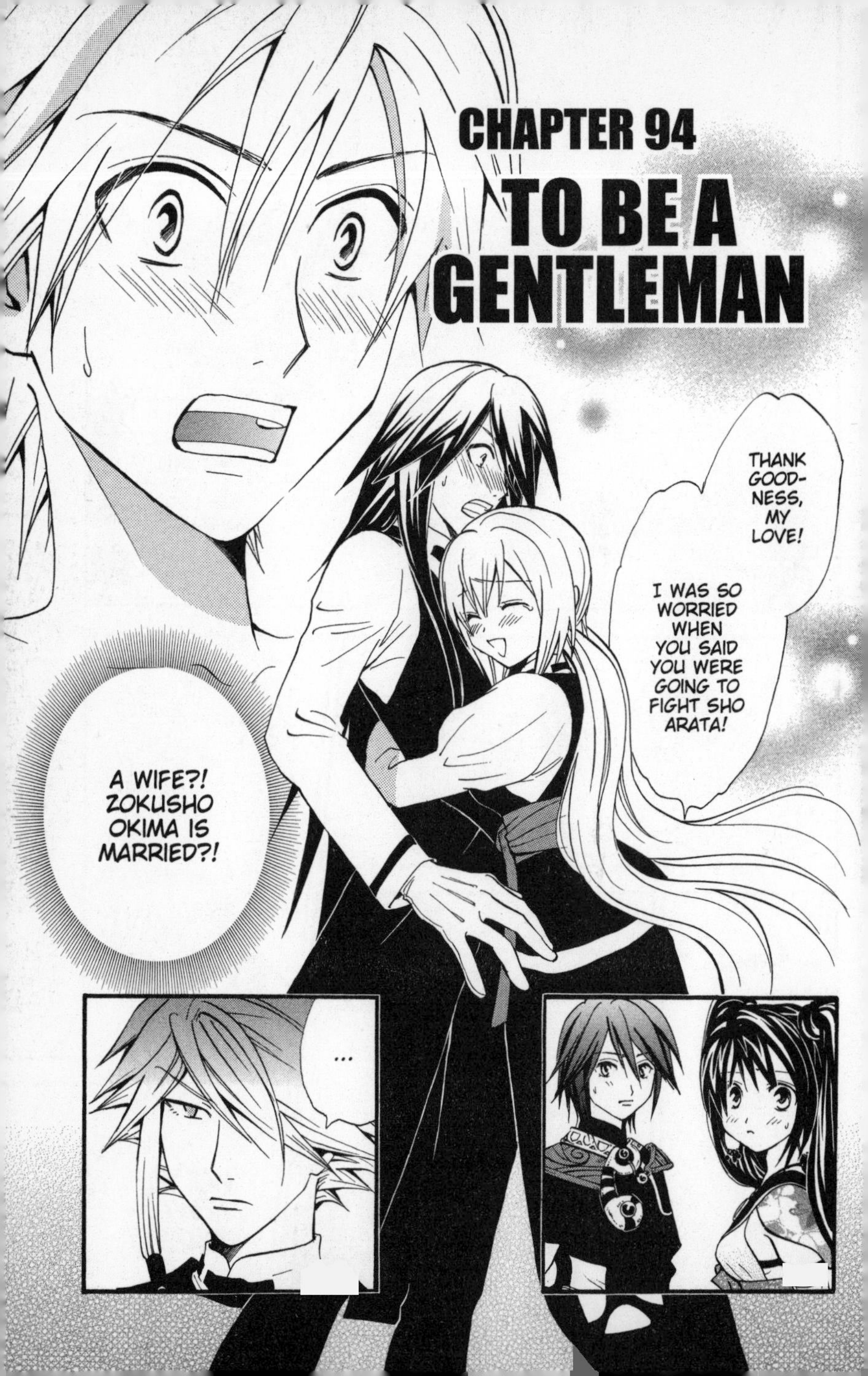
THANK GOODNESS, MY LOVE!
I WAS SO WORRIED WHEN YOU SAID YOU WERE GOING TO FIGHT SHO ARATA!
A WIFE?! ZOKUSHO OKIMA IS MARRIED?!
...

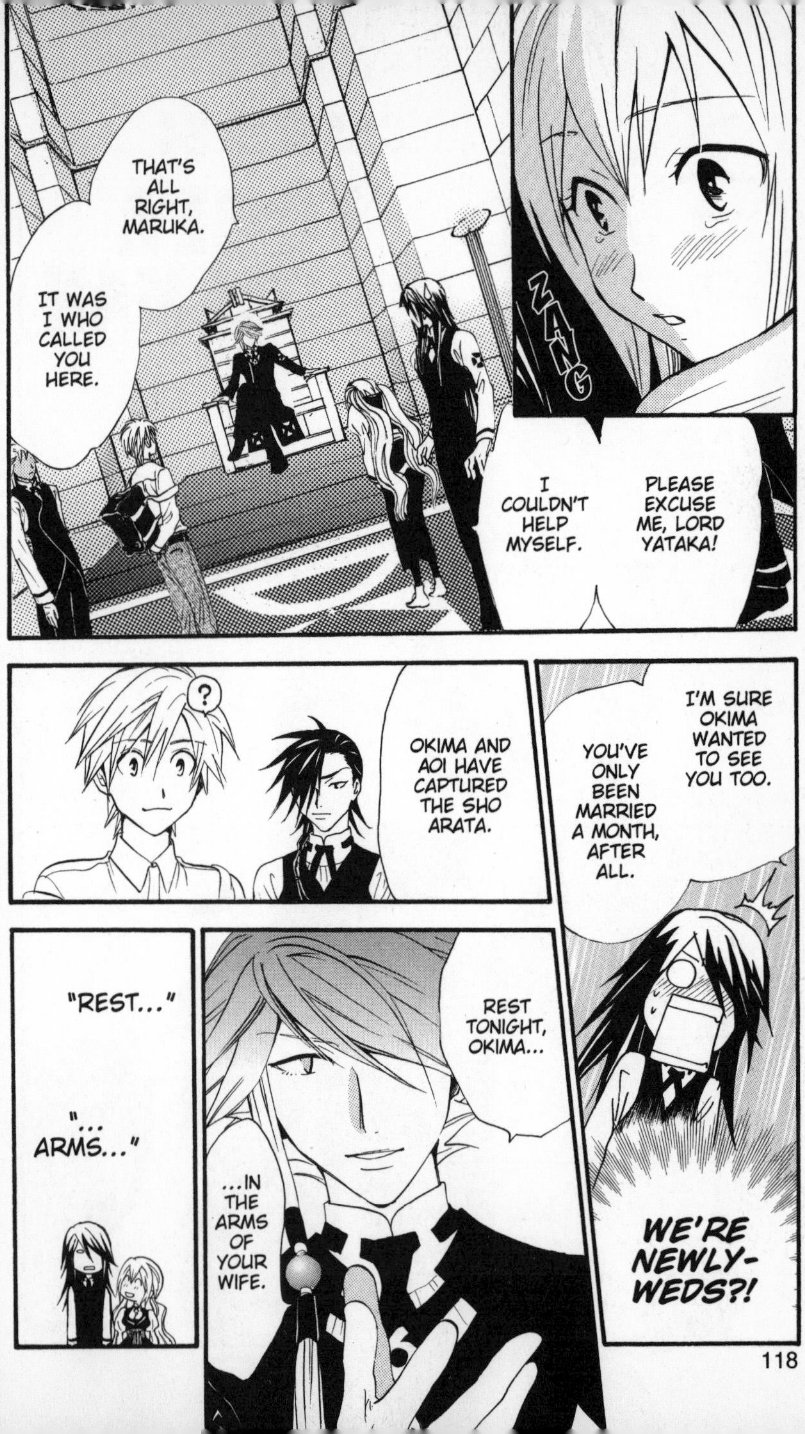
ZANG
PLEASE EXCUSE ME, LORD YATAKA!
I COULDN'T HELP MYSELF.
THAT'S ALL RIGHT, MARUKA.
IT WAS I WHO CALLED YOU HERE.
I'M SURE OKIMA WANTED TO SEE YOU TOO.
YOU'VE ONLY BEEN MARRIED A MONTH, AFTER ALL.
?
OKIMA AND AOI HAVE CAPTURED THE SHO ARATA.
WE'RE NEWLY-WEDS?!
REST TONIGHT, OKIMA...
...IN THE ARMS OF YOUR WIFE.
"REST..."
"...ARMS..."

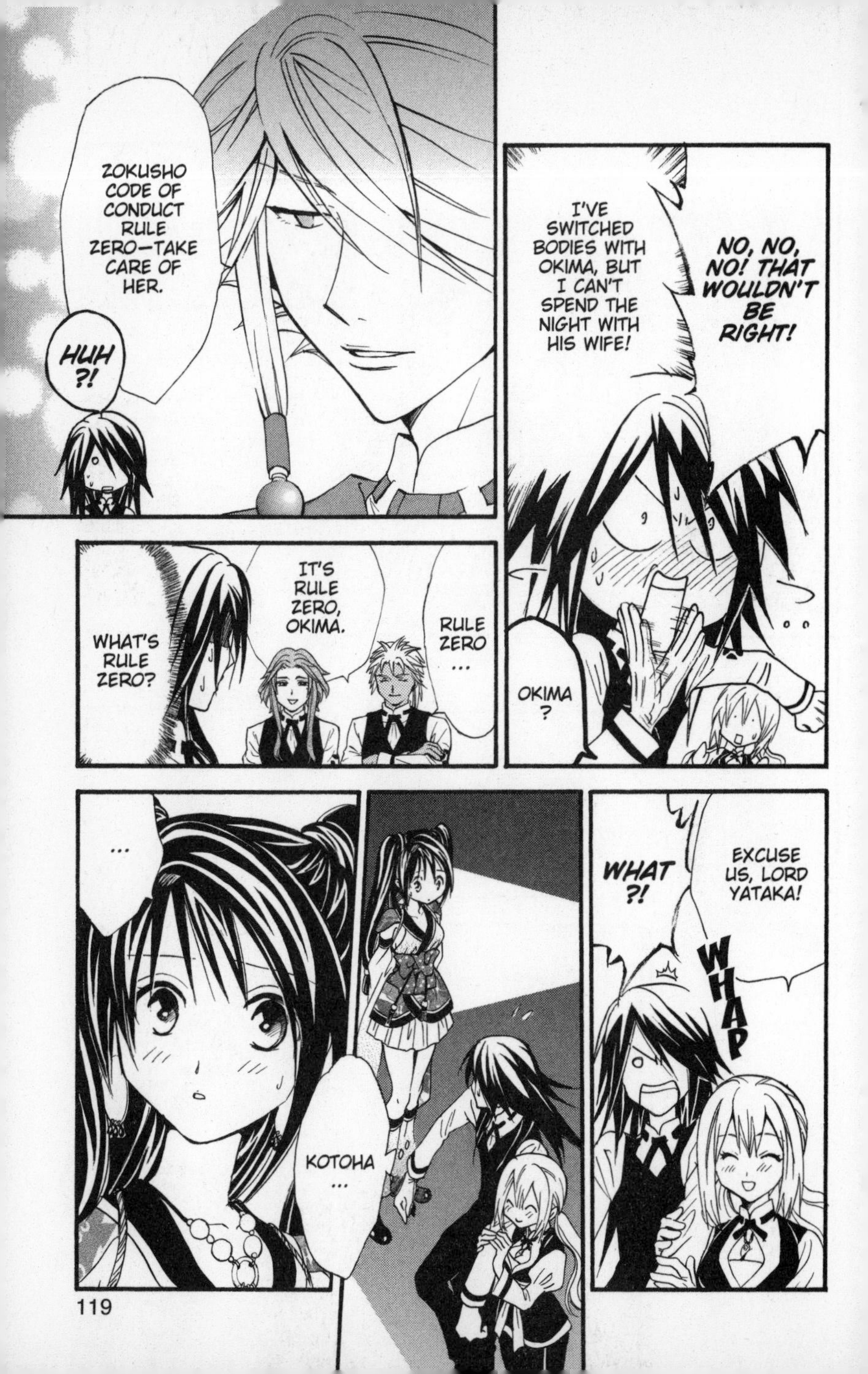

I'VE SWITCHED BODIES WITH OKIMA, BUT I CAN'T SPEND THE NIGHT WITH HIS WIFE!
NO, NO, NO! THAT WOULDN'T BE RIGHT!
OKIMA?
ZOKUSHO CODE OF CONDUCT RULE ZERO—TAKE CARE OF HER.
HUH?!
RULE ZERO...
IT'S RULE ZERO, OKIMA.
WHAT'S RULE ZERO?
EXCUSE US, LORD YATAKA!
WHAT?!
WHAP
...
KOTOHA...

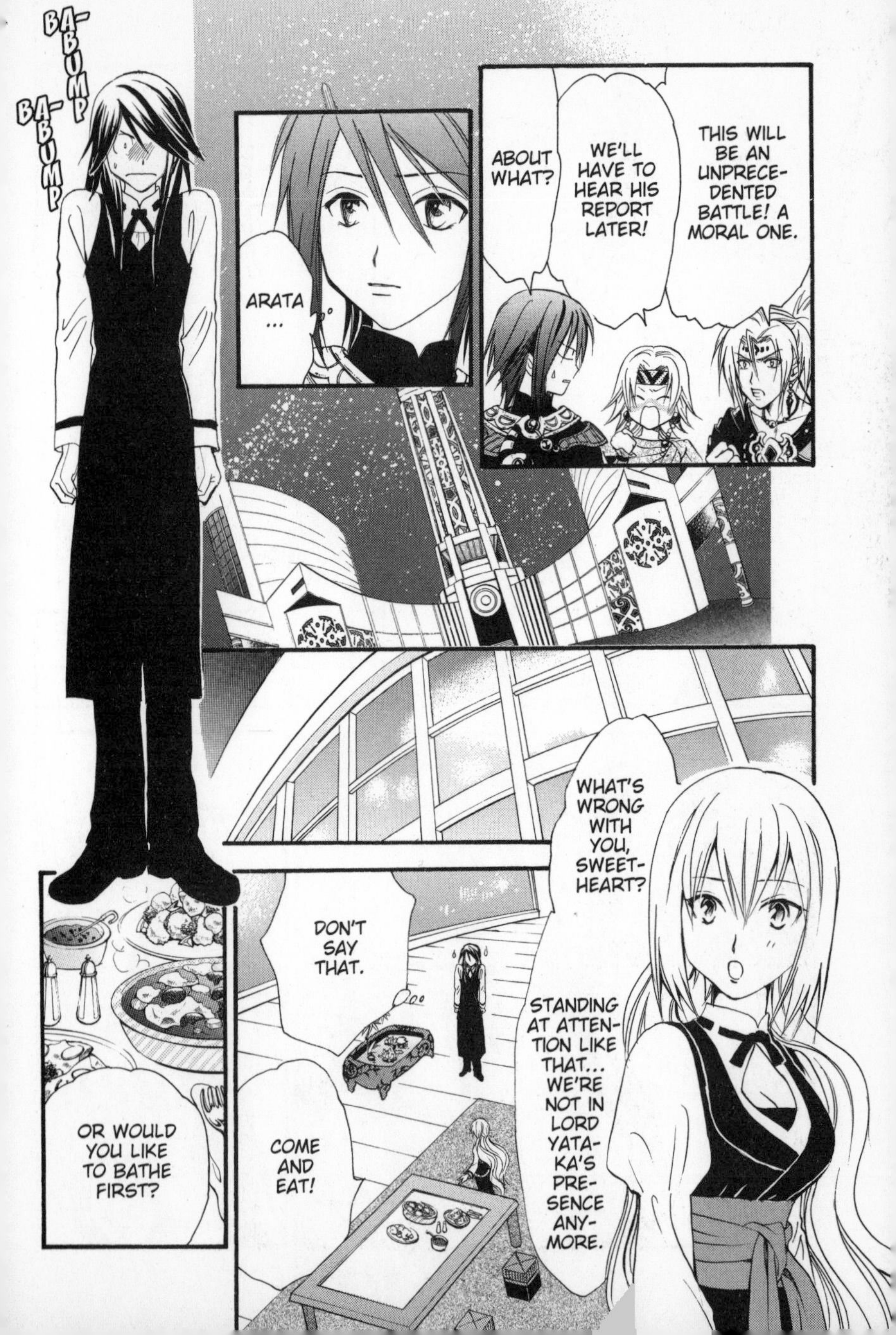
THIS WILL BE AN UNPRECEDENTED BATTLE! A MORAL ONE.
WE'LL HAVE TO HEAR HIS REPORT LATER!
ABOUT WHAT?
ARATA ...
WHAT'S WRONG WITH YOU, SWEETHEART?
STANDING AT ATTENTION LIKE THAT... WE'RE NOT IN LORD YATAKA'S PRESENCE ANYMORE.
DON'T SAY THAT.
COME AND EAT!
OR WOULD YOU LIKE TO BATHE FIRST?
BA-BUMP BA-BUMP

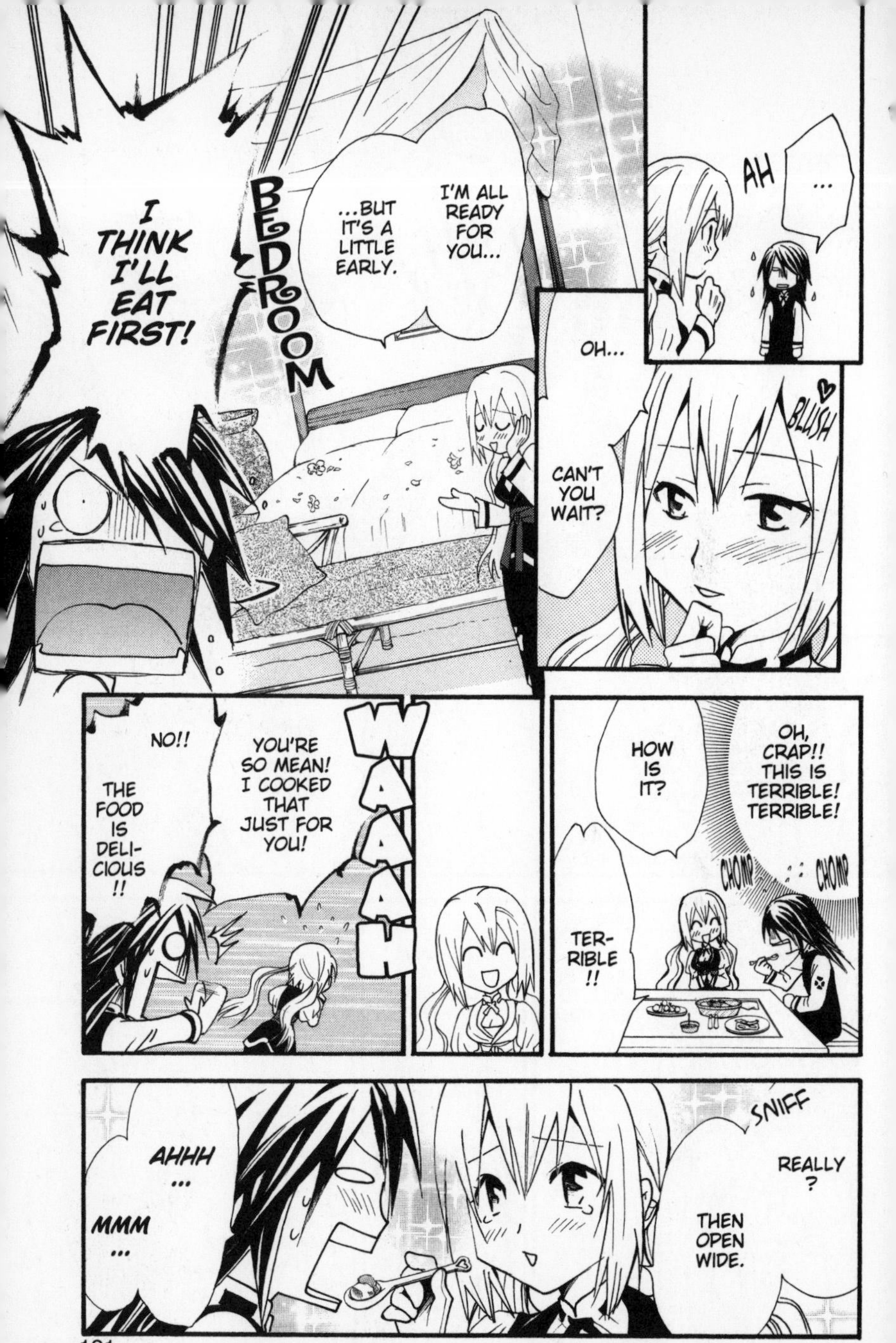
AH
...
OH...
CAN'T YOU WAIT?
BLUSH
I'M ALL READY FOR YOU...
...BUT IT'S A LITTLE EARLY.
BEDROOM
I THINK I'LL EAT FIRST!
OH, CRAP!! THIS IS TERRIBLE! TERRIBLE!
HOW IS IT?
CHOMP
CHOMP
TERRIBLE!!
WAAAAH
YOU'RE SO MEAN! I COOKED THAT JUST FOR YOU!
NO!!
THE FOOD IS DELICIOUS!!
SNIFF
REALLY?
THEN OPEN WIDE.
AHHH...
MMM...

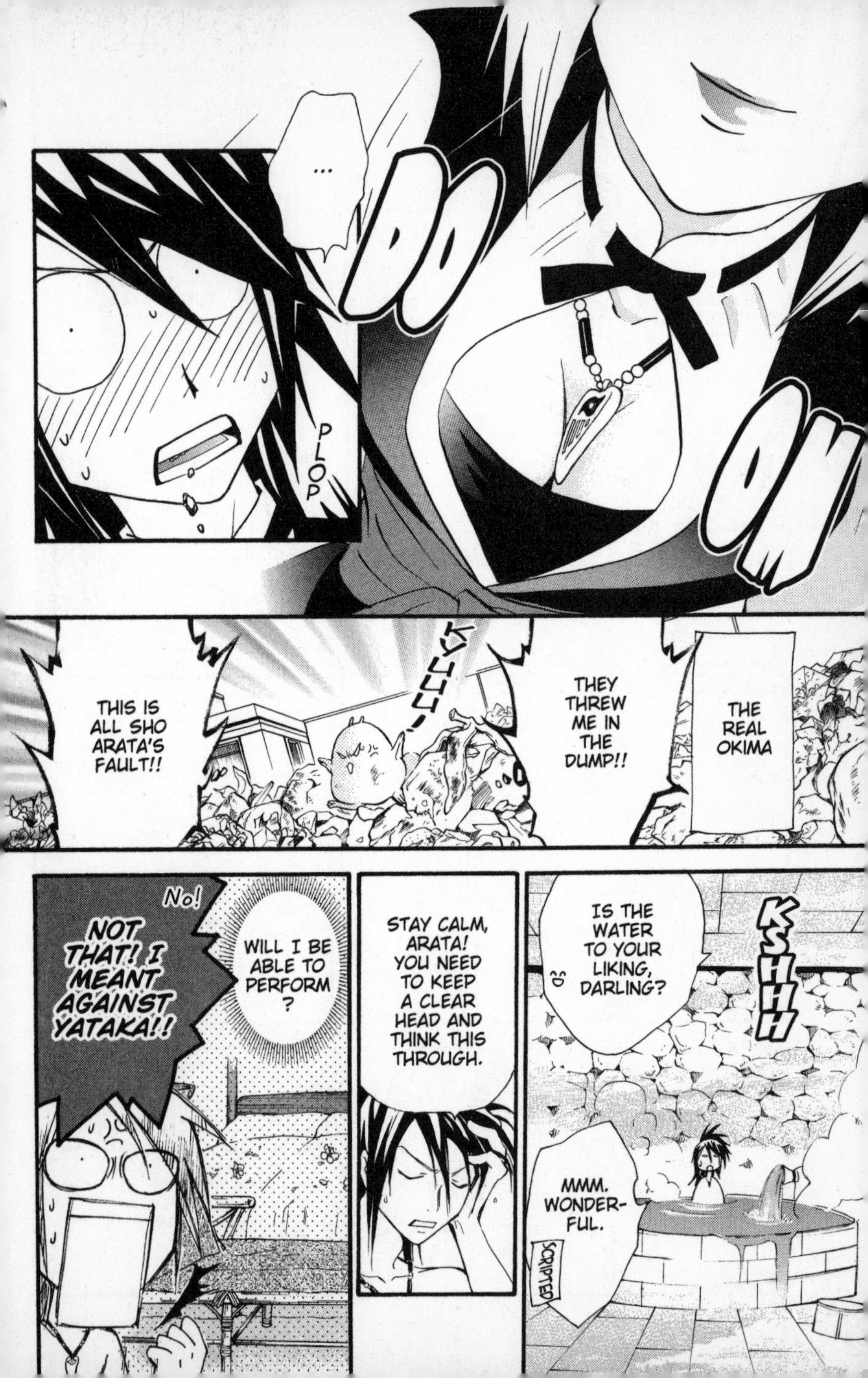
DOOM
...
PLOP
THE REAL OKIMA
THEY THREW ME IN THE DUMP!!
KYUUU!
THIS IS ALL SHO ARATA'S FAULT!!
KSHHH
IS THE WATER TO YOUR LIKING, DARLING?
MMM. WONDERFUL.
SCRIPTED
STAY CALM, ARATA! YOU NEED TO KEEP A CLEAR HEAD AND THINK THIS THROUGH.
WILL I BE ABLE TO PERFORM?
No!
NOT THAT! I MEANT AGAINST YATAKA!!

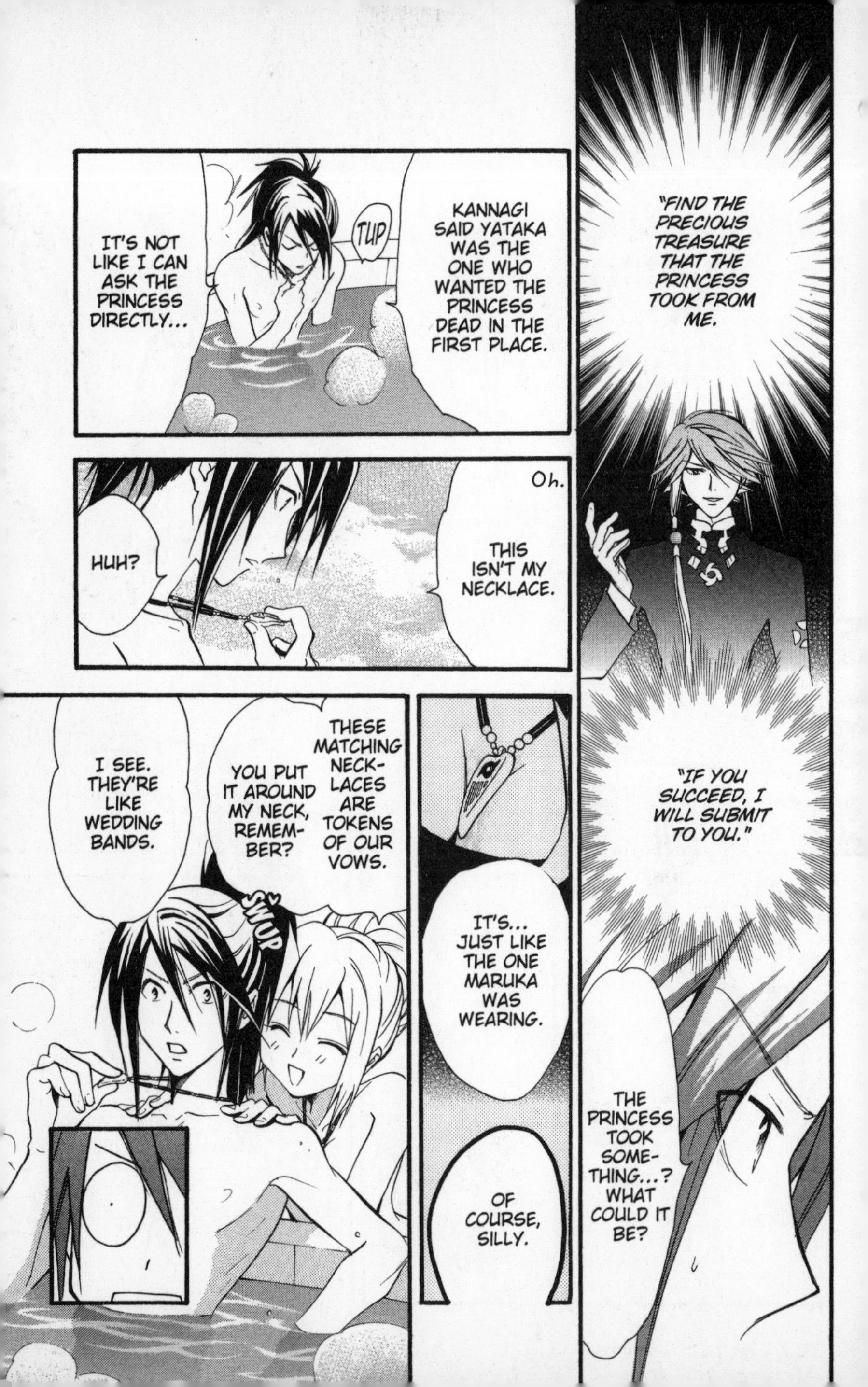
"FIND THE PRECIOUS TREASURE THAT THE PRINCESS TOOK FROM ME.
"IF YOU SUCCEED, I WILL SUBMIT TO YOU."
THE PRINCESS TOOK SOMETHING...? WHAT COULD IT BE?
KANNAGI SAID YATAKA WAS THE ONE WHO WANTED THE PRINCESS DEAD IN THE FIRST PLACE.
TUP
IT'S NOT LIKE I CAN ASK THE PRINCESS DIRECTLY...
Oh.
THIS ISN'T MY NECKLACE.
HUH?
IT'S... JUST LIKE THE ONE MARUKA WAS WEARING.
OF COURSE, SILLY.
THESE MATCHING NECK-LACES ARE TOKENS OF OUR VOWS.
YOU PUT IT AROUND MY NECK, REMEM-BER?
SWUP
I SEE. THEY'RE LIKE WEDDING BANDS.

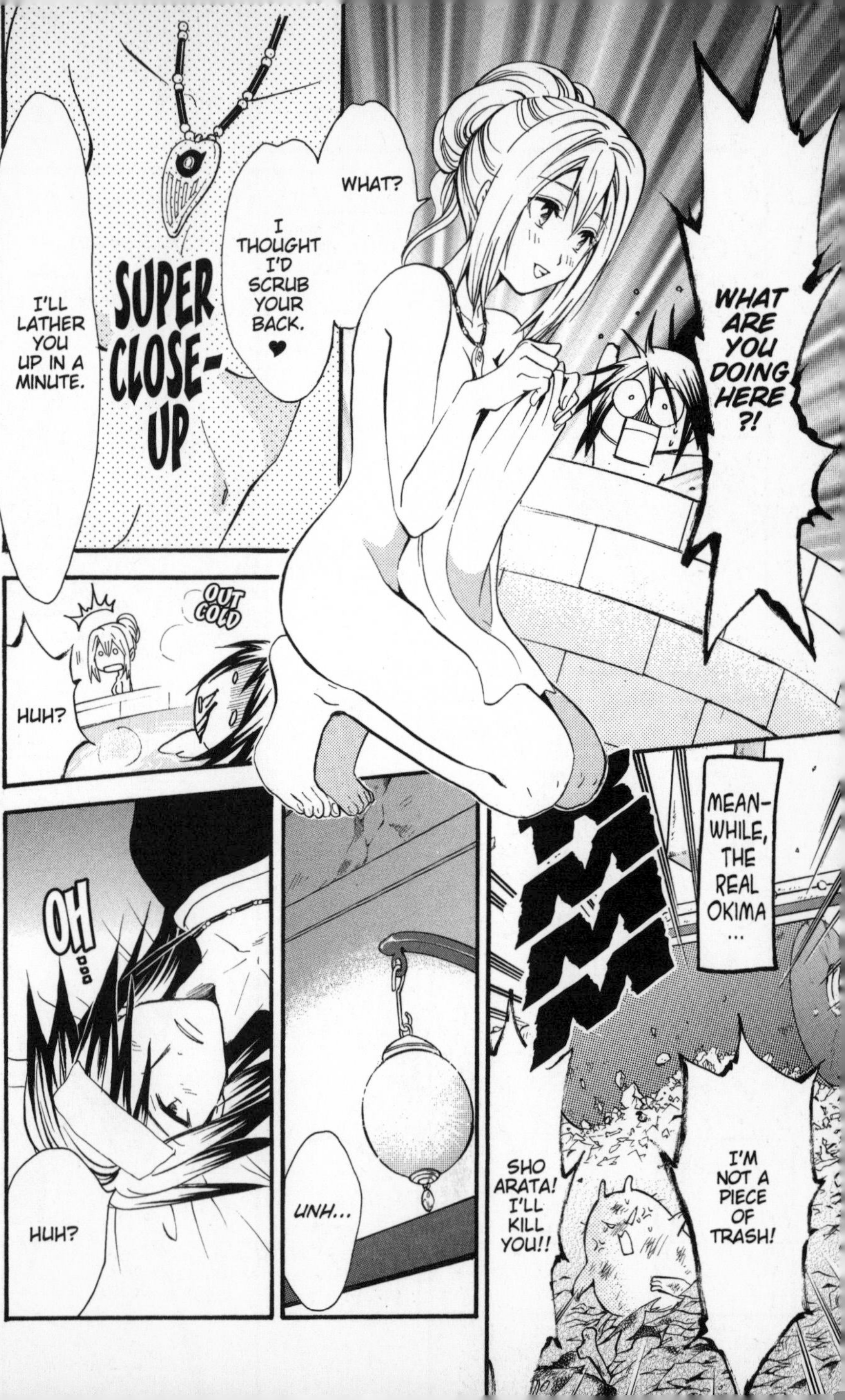
WHAT ARE YOU DOING HERE?!
WHAT?
I THOUGHT I'D SCRUB YOUR BACK. ♥
SUPER CLOSE-UP
I'LL LATHER YOU UP IN A MINUTE.
OUT COLD
HUH?
MEAN-WHILE, THE REAL OKIMA...
I'M NOT A PIECE OF TRASH!
SHO ARATA! I'LL KILL YOU!!
UNH...
OH...
HUH?

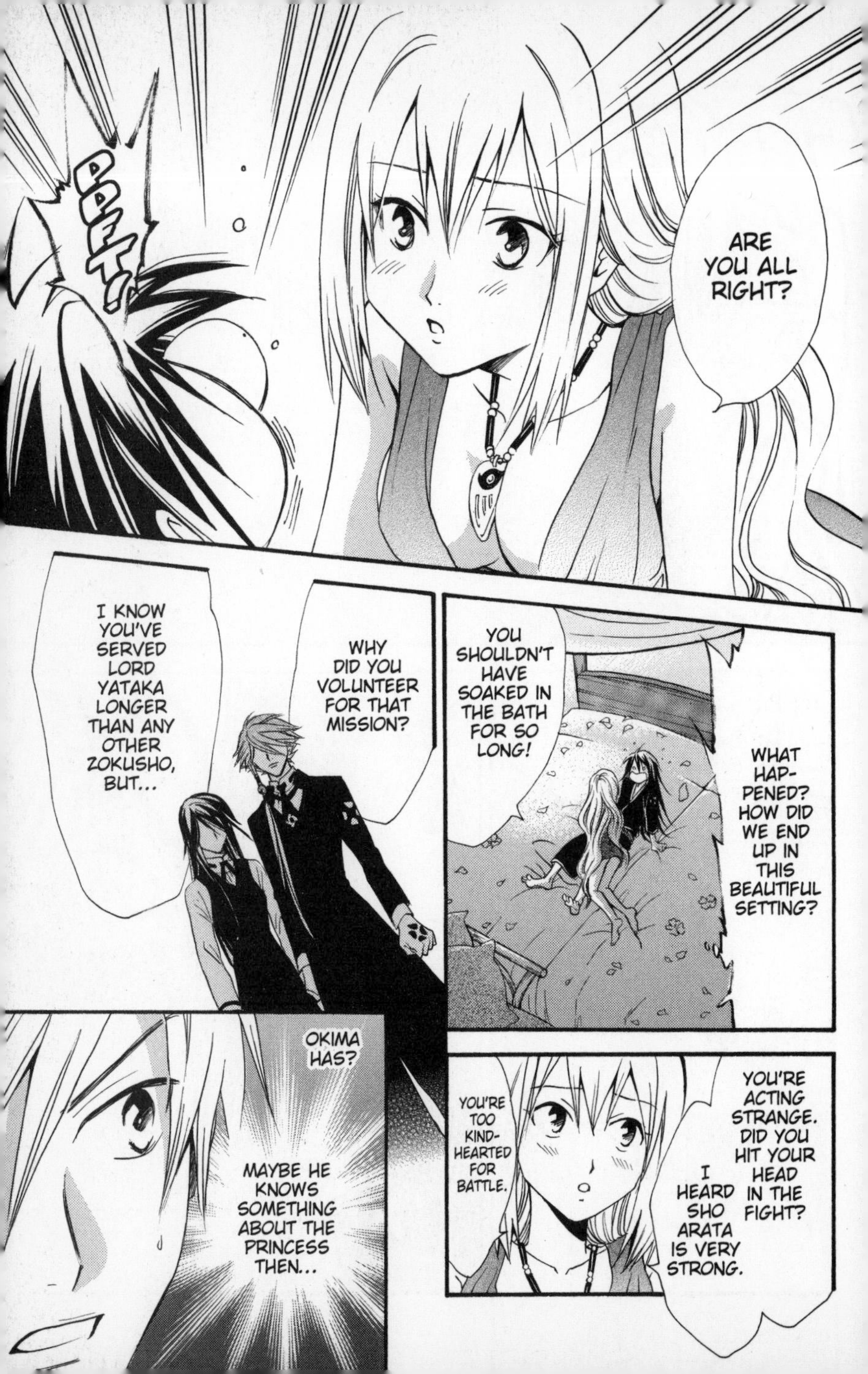
ARE YOU ALL RIGHT?
PAFT!
WHAT HAPPENED? HOW DID WE END UP IN THIS BEAUTIFUL SETTING?
YOU SHOULDN'T HAVE SOAKED IN THE BATH FOR SO LONG!
WHY DID YOU VOLUNTEER FOR THAT MISSION?
I KNOW YOU'VE SERVED LORD YATAKA LONGER THAN ANY OTHER ZOKUSHO, BUT...
YOU'RE ACTING STRANGE. DID YOU HIT YOUR HEAD IN THE FIGHT?
I HEARD SHO ARATA IS VERY STRONG.
YOU'RE TOO KIND-HEARTED FOR BATTLE.
OKIMA HAS?
MAYBE HE KNOWS SOMETHING ABOUT THE PRINCESS THEN...

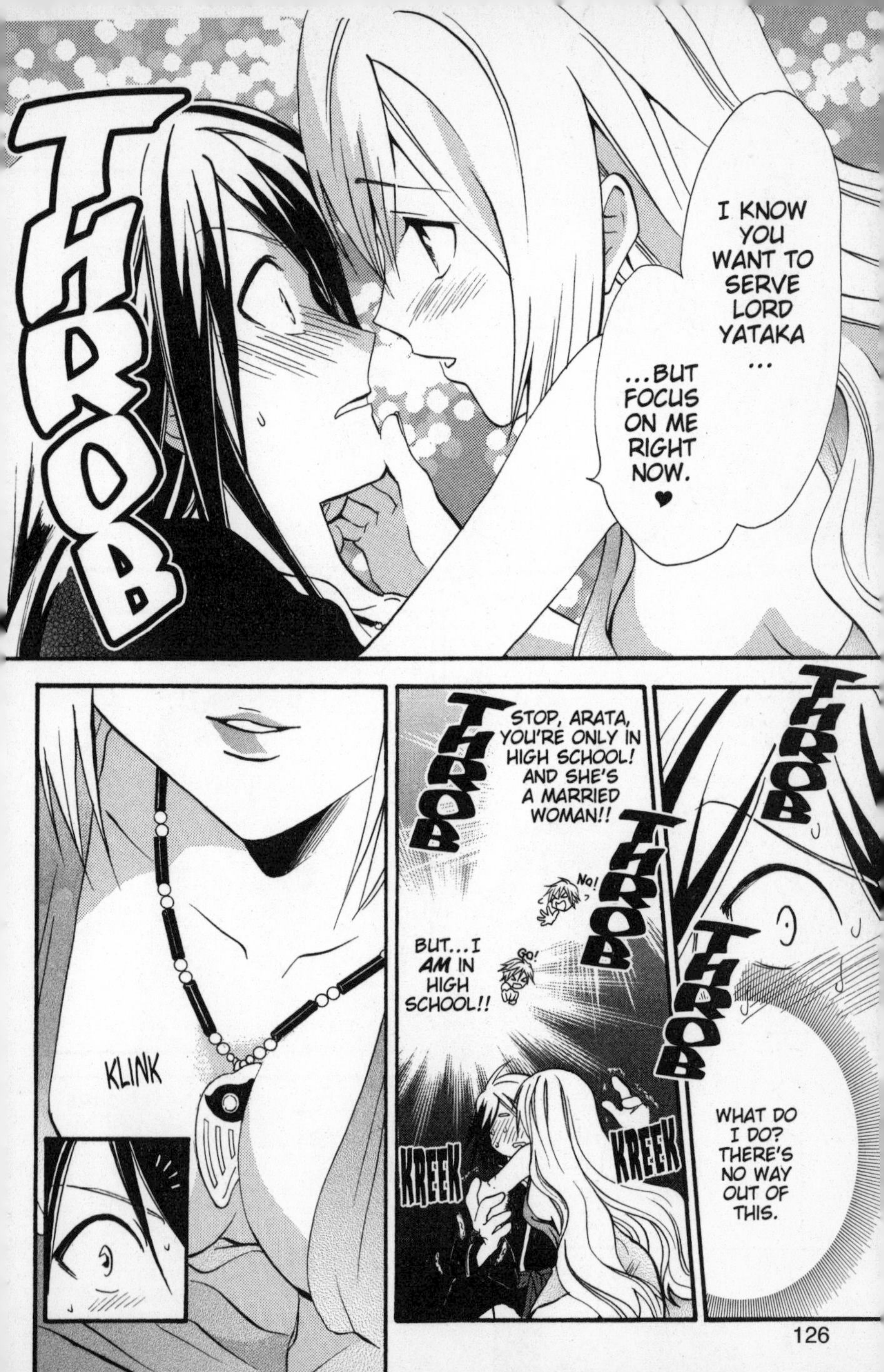
I KNOW YOU WANT TO SERVE LORD YATAKA ...
...BUT FOCUS ON ME RIGHT NOW. ♥
THROB
THROB
THROB
WHAT DO I DO? THERE'S NO WAY OUT OF THIS.
STOP, ARATA, YOU'RE ONLY IN HIGH SCHOOL! AND SHE'S A MARRIED WOMAN!!
THROB
THROB
No!
Go!
BUT...I *AM* IN HIGH SCHOOL!!
KREEK
KREEK
KLINK

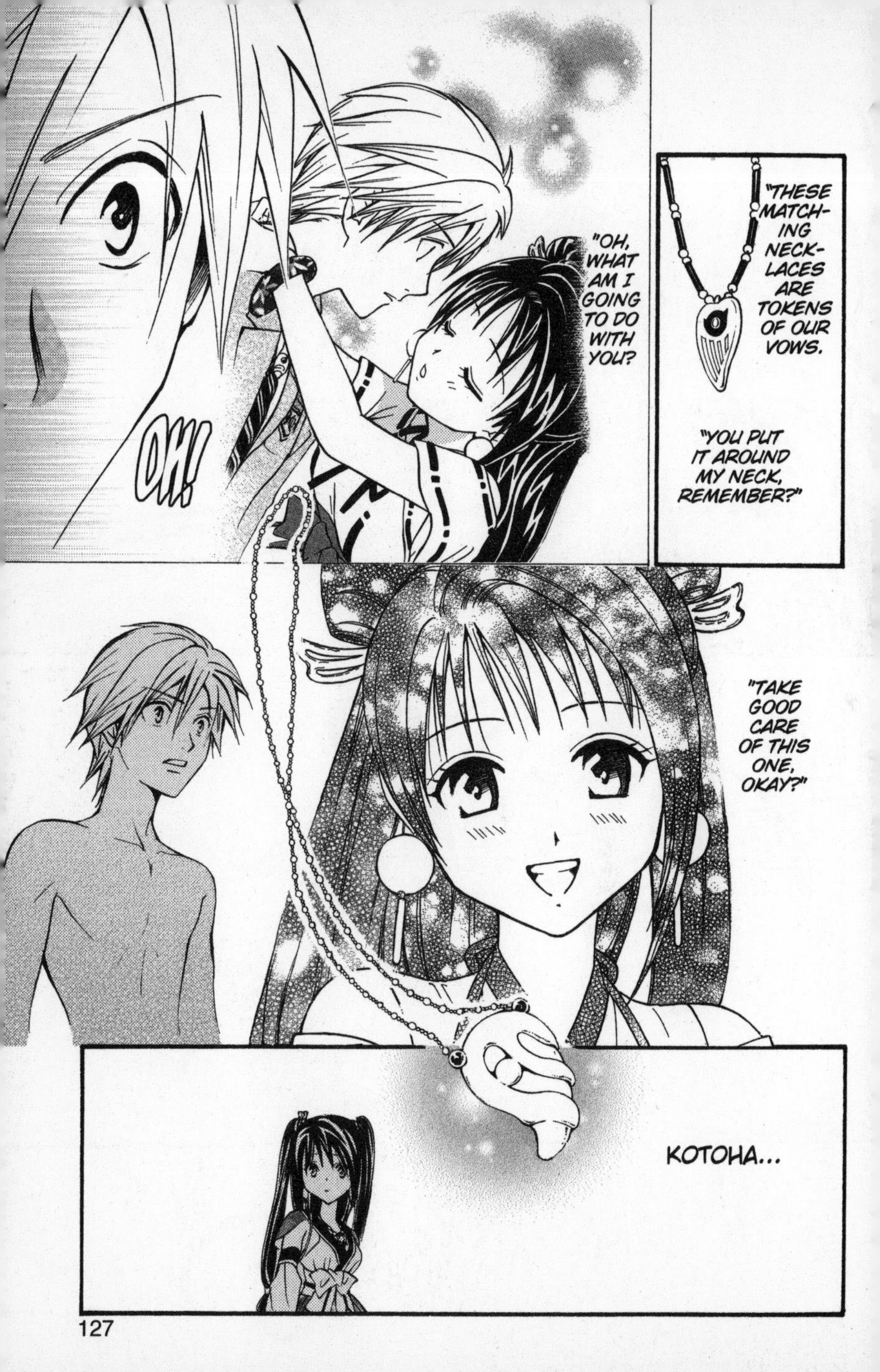
"THESE MATCHING-NECKLACES ARE TOKENS OF OUR VOWS.
"YOU PUT IT AROUND MY NECK, REMEMBER?"
"OH, WHAT AM I GOING TO DO WITH YOU?
OH!
"TAKE GOOD CARE OF THIS ONE, OKAY?"
KOTOHA...

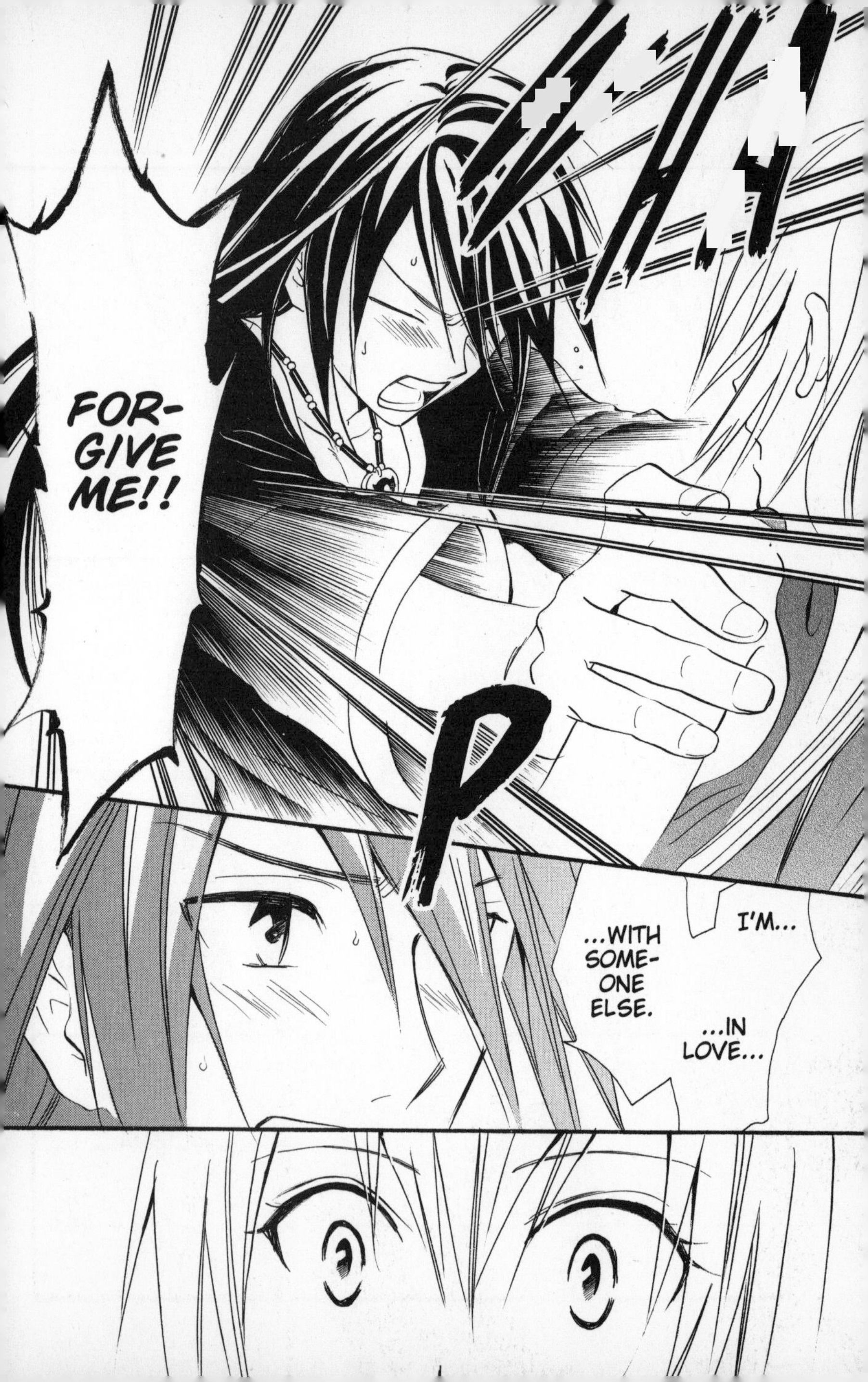
FOR-
GIVE
ME!!
P
I'M...
...IN
LOVE...
...WITH
SOME-
ONE
ELSE.

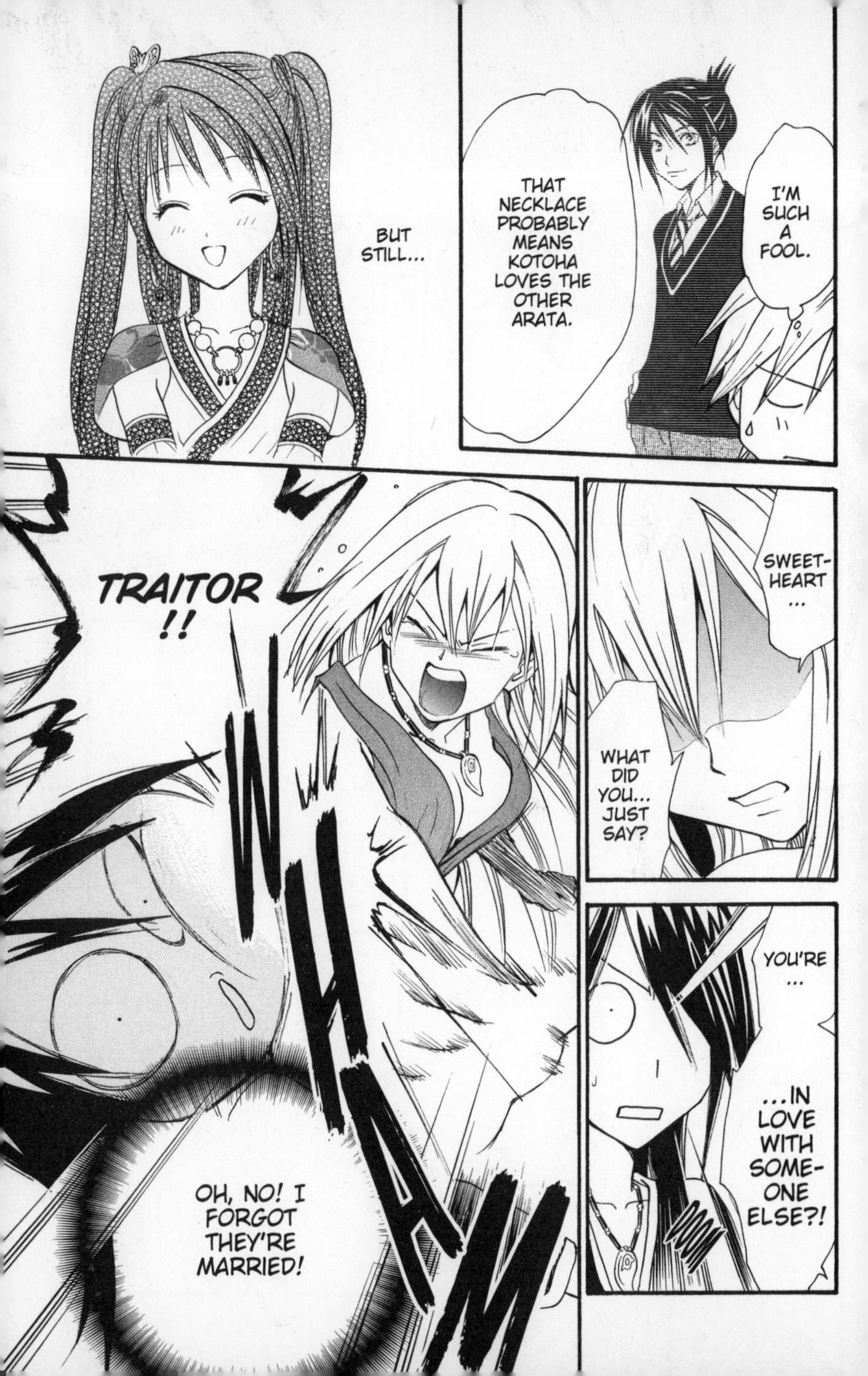
I'M SUCH A FOOL.
THAT NECKLACE PROBABLY MEANS KOTOHA LOVES THE OTHER ARATA.
BUT STILL...
SWEET-HEART ...
WHAT DID YOU... JUST SAY?
YOU'RE ...
...IN LOVE WITH SOME-ONE ELSE?!
TRAITOR !!
WHAM
OH, NO! I FORGOT THEY'RE MARRIED!

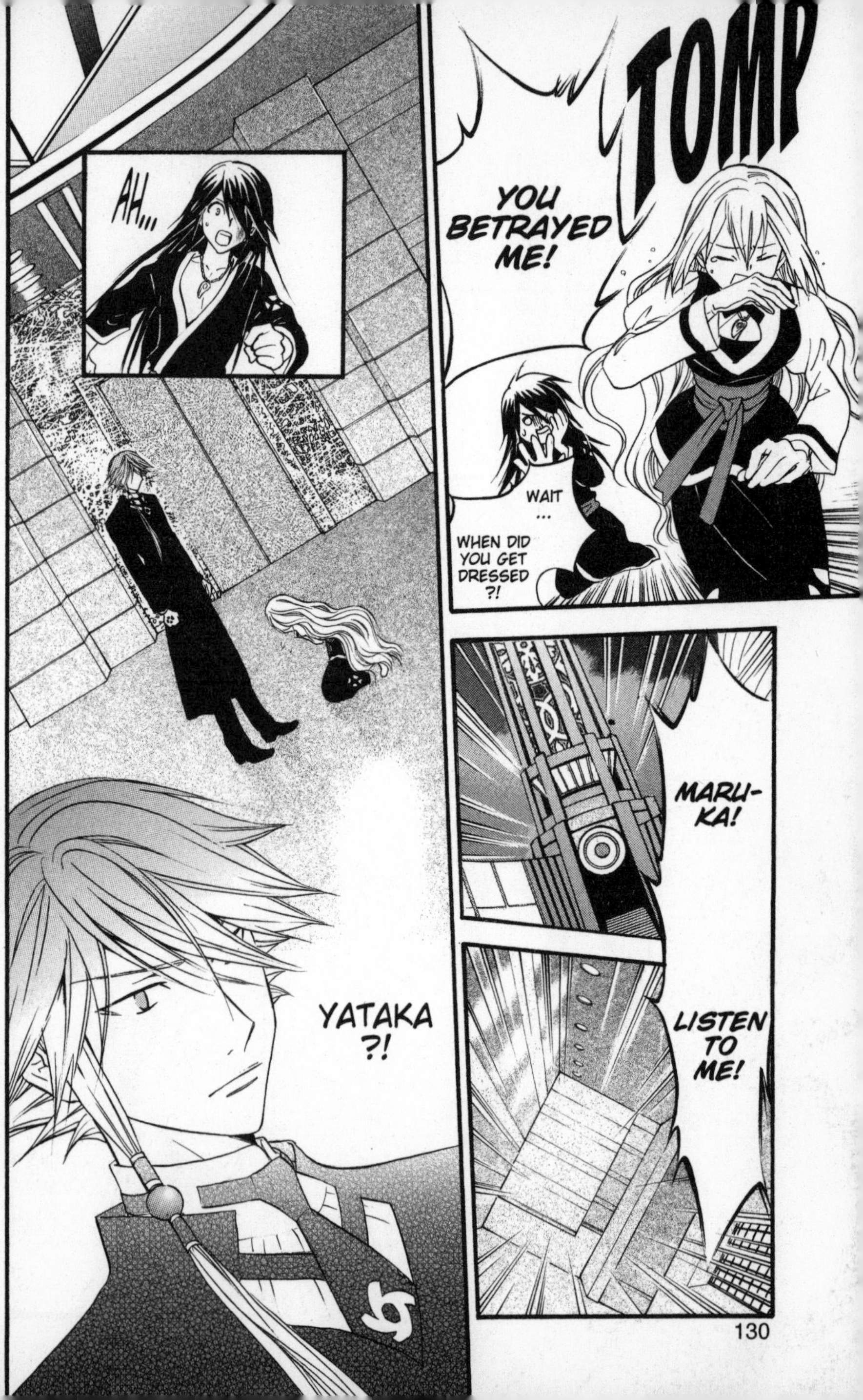
TOMP
YOU BETRAYED ME!
WAIT ...
WHEN DID YOU GET DRESSED ?!
MARU-KA!
LISTEN TO ME!
AH...
YATAKA ?!

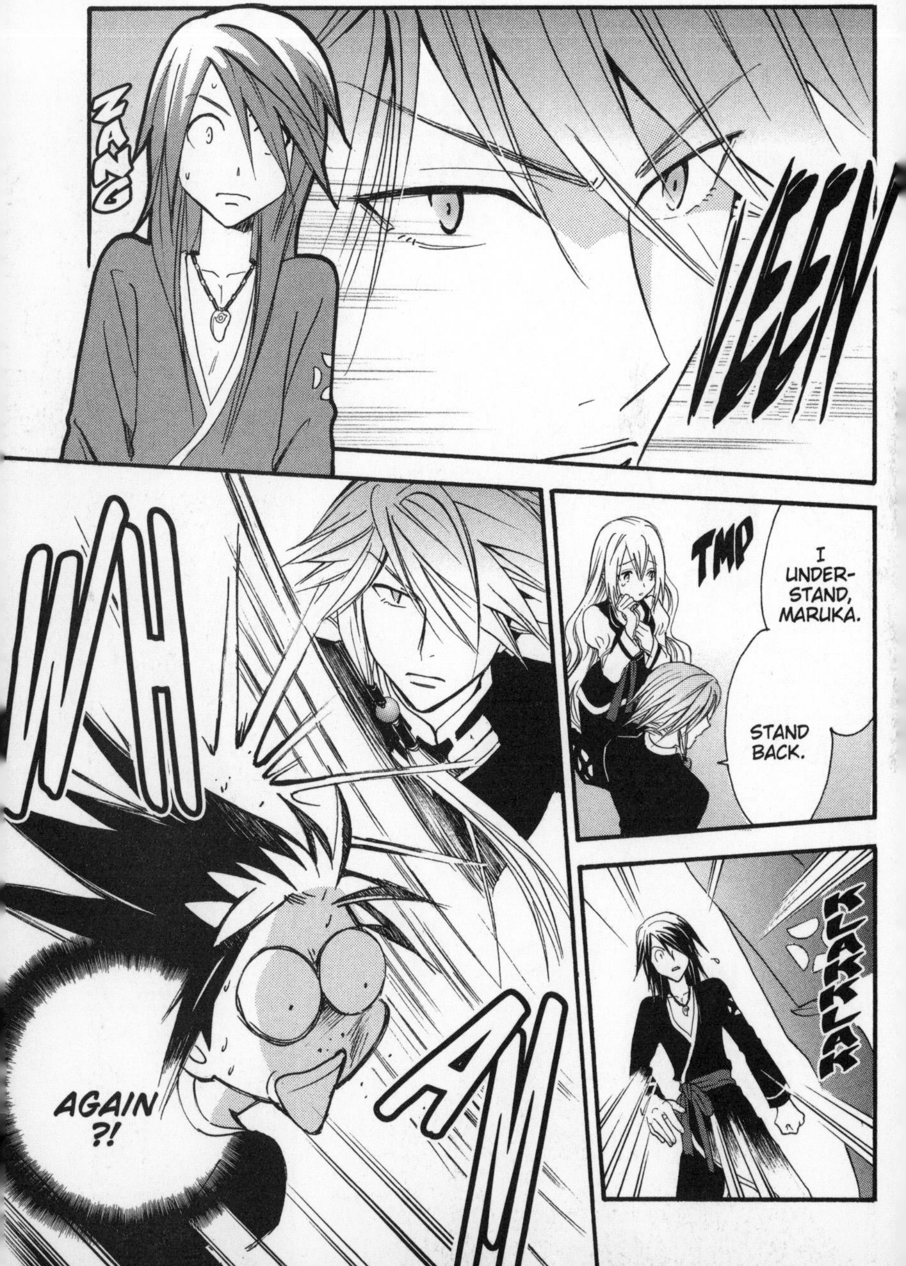
VEEN
ZANG
TMP
I UNDER-STAND, MARUKA.
STAND BACK.
KLAKKLAK
WH
AM
AGAIN ?!

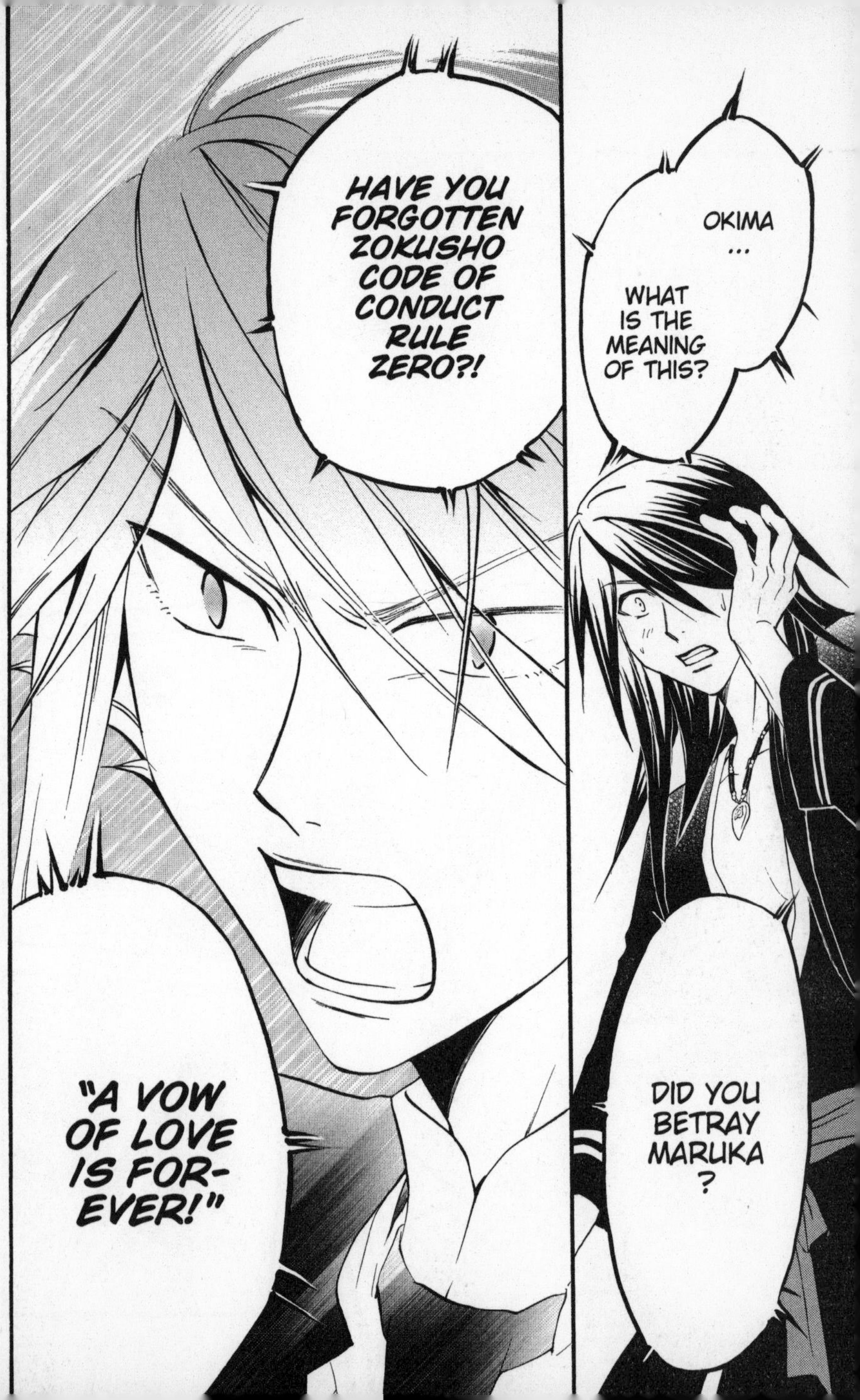
OKIMA ...
WHAT IS THE MEANING OF THIS?
DID YOU BETRAY MARUKA?
HAVE YOU FORGOTTEN ZOKUSHO CODE OF CONDUCT RULE ZERO?!
"A VOW OF LOVE IS FOR-EVER!"

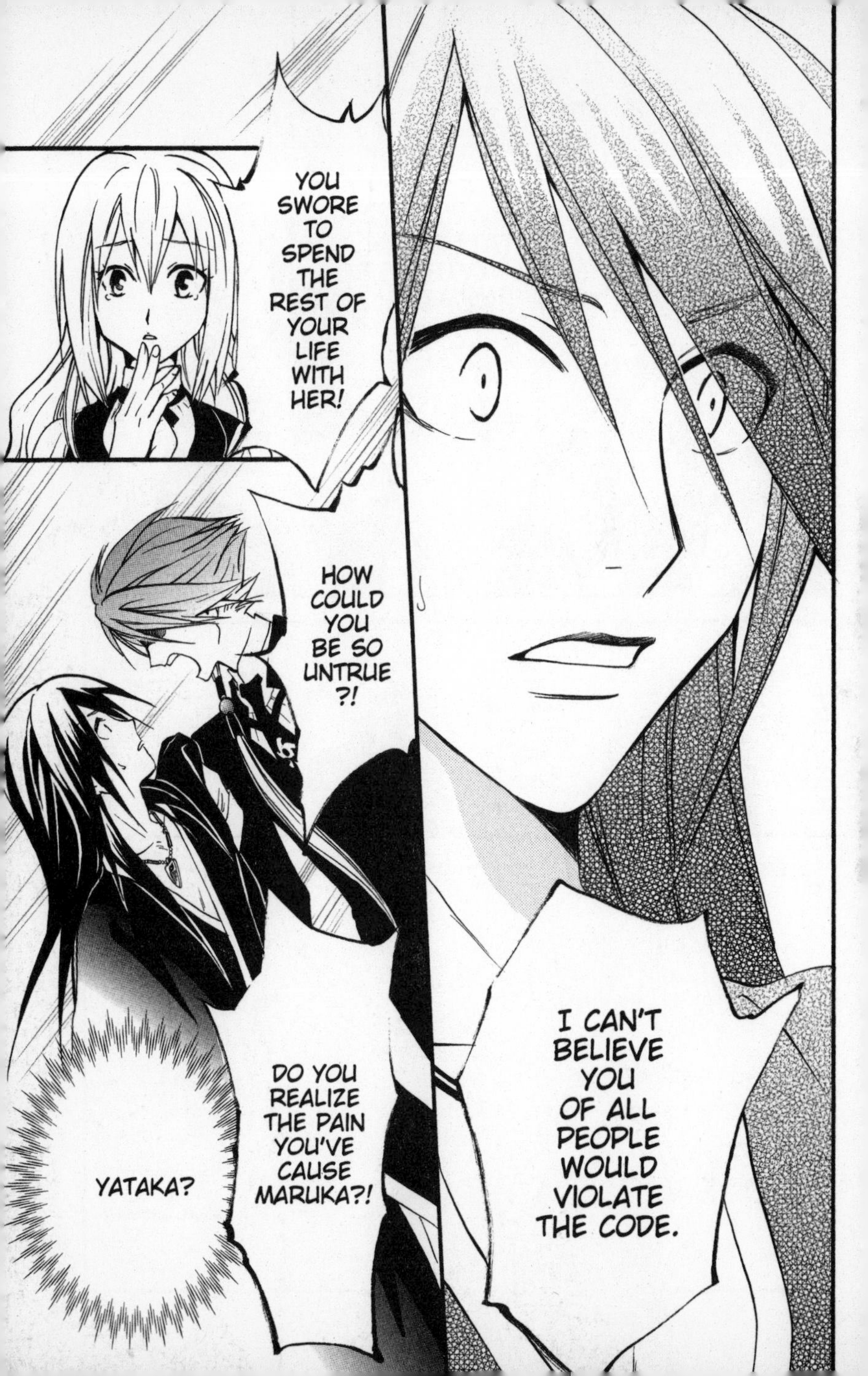
I CAN'T BELIEVE YOU OF ALL PEOPLE WOULD VIOLATE THE CODE.
YOU SWORE TO SPEND THE REST OF YOUR LIFE WITH HER!
HOW COULD YOU BE SO UNTRUE?!
DO YOU REALIZE THE PAIN YOU'VE CAUSE MARUKA?!
YATAKA?

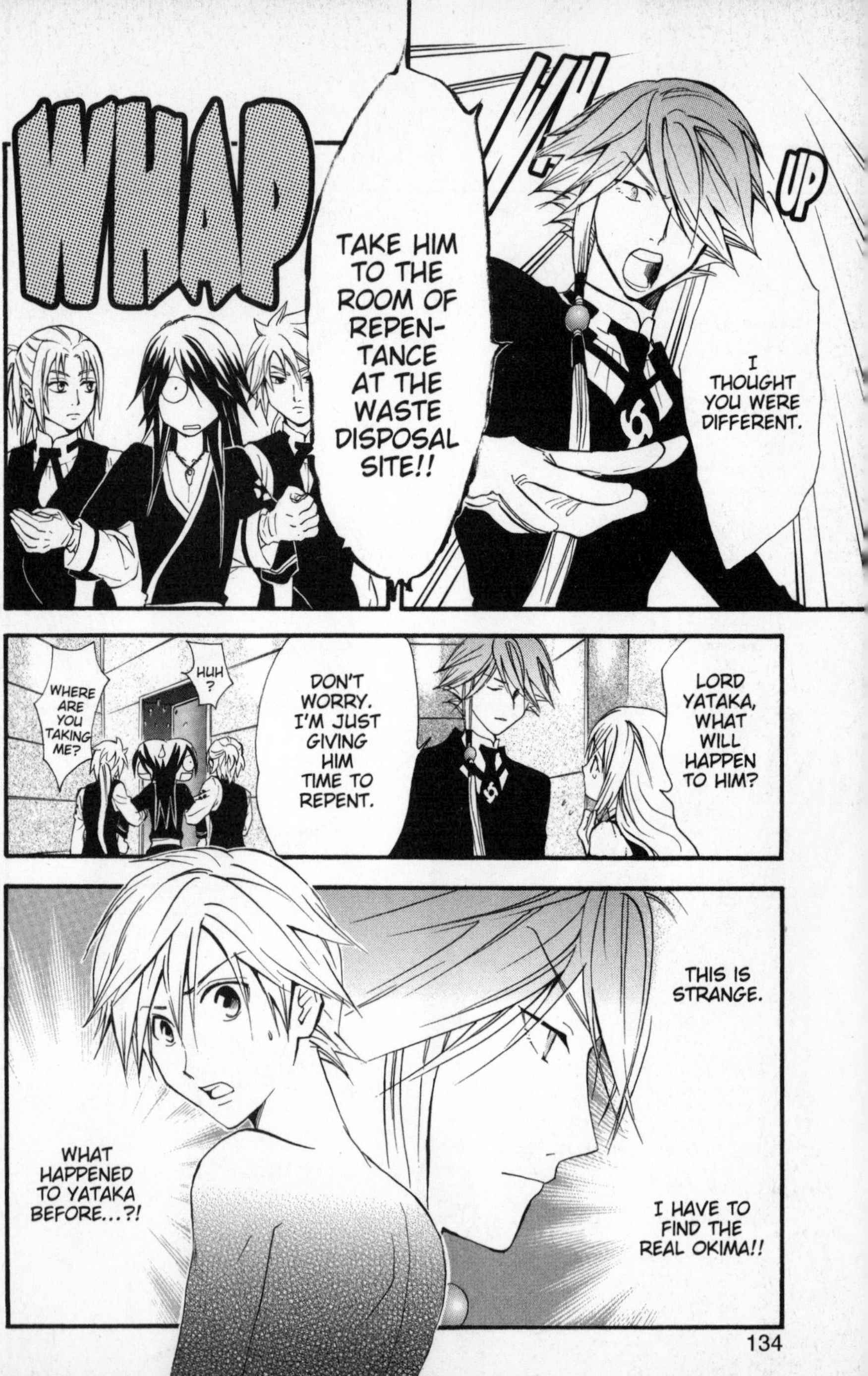
UP
I THOUGHT YOU WERE DIFFERENT.
TAKE HIM TO THE ROOM OF REPEN-TANCE AT THE WASTE DISPOSAL SITE!!
WHAP
LORD YATAKA, WHAT WILL HAPPEN TO HIM?
DON'T WORRY. I'M JUST GIVING HIM TIME TO REPENT.
HUH?
WHERE ARE YOU TAKING ME?
THIS IS STRANGE.
I HAVE TO FIND THE REAL OKIMA!!
WHAT HAPPENED TO YATAKA BEFORE...?!

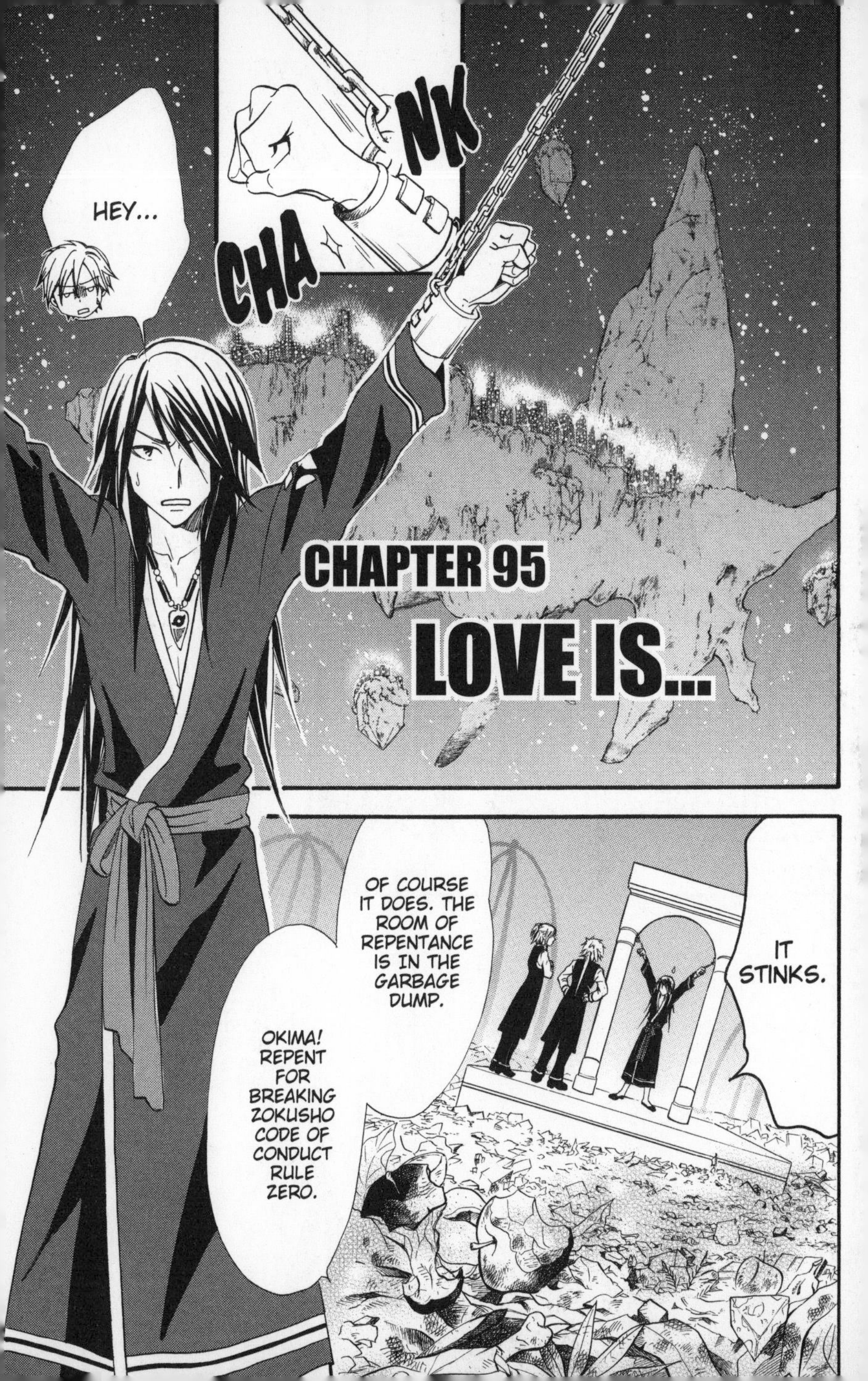
CHANK
CHAPTER 95
LOVE IS...
HEY...
IT STINKS.
OF COURSE IT DOES. THE ROOM OF REPENTANCE IS IN THE GARBAGE DUMP.
OKIMA! REPENT FOR BREAKING ZOKUSHO CODE OF CONDUCT RULE ZERO.

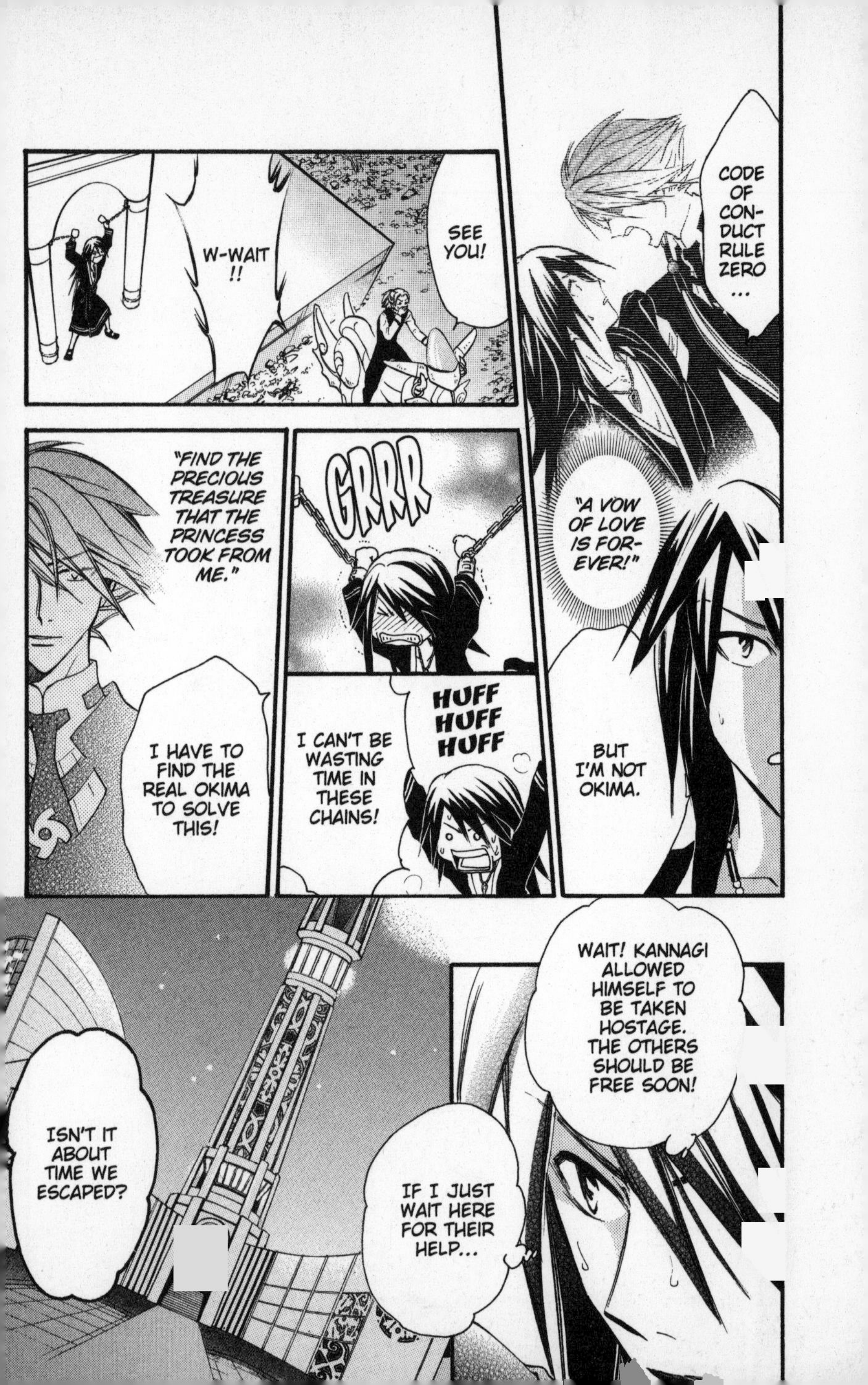
CODE OF CON-DUCT RULE ZERO...
"A VOW OF LOVE IS FOR-EVER!"
BUT I'M NOT OKIMA.
SEE YOU!
W-WAIT!!
GRRR
HUFF HUFF HUFF
I CAN'T BE WASTING TIME IN THESE CHAINS!
"FIND THE PRECIOUS TREASURE THAT THE PRINCESS TOOK FROM ME."
I HAVE TO FIND THE REAL OKIMA TO SOLVE THIS!
WAIT! KANNAGI ALLOWED HIMSELF TO BE TAKEN HOSTAGE. THE OTHERS SHOULD BE FREE SOON!
IF I JUST WAIT HERE FOR THEIR HELP...
ISN'T IT ABOUT TIME WE ESCAPED?

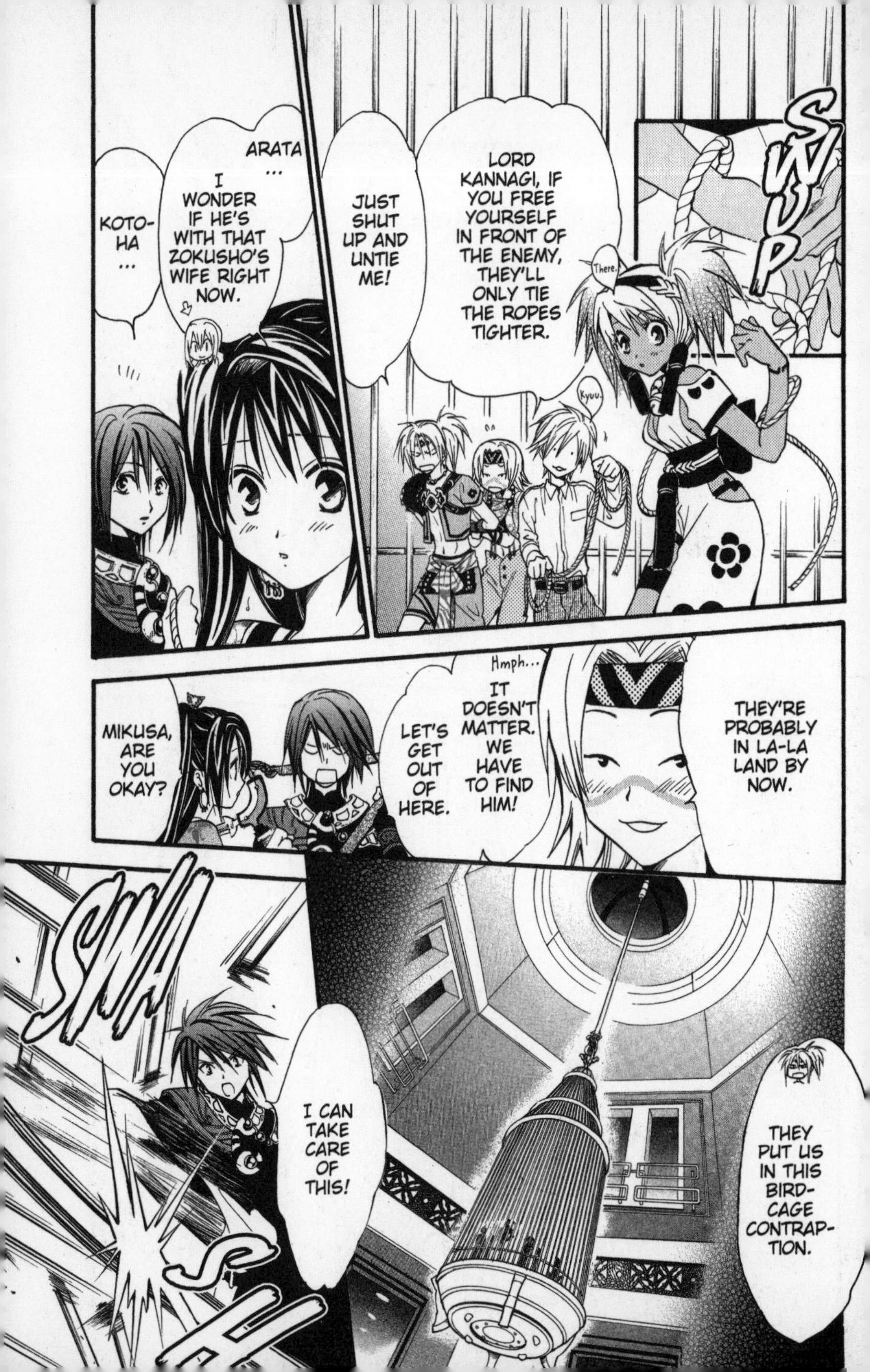
SWUP
There.
LORD KANNAGI, IF YOU FREE YOURSELF IN FRONT OF THE ENEMY, THEY'LL ONLY TIE THE ROPES TIGHTER.
Kyuu.
JUST SHUT UP AND UNTIE ME!
ARATA ...
I WONDER IF HE'S WITH THAT ZOKUSHO'S WIFE RIGHT NOW.
KOTO-HA ...
THEY'RE PROBABLY IN LA-LA LAND BY NOW.
Hmph...
IT DOESN'T MATTER. WE HAVE TO FIND HIM!
LET'S GET OUT OF HERE.
MIKUSA, ARE YOU OKAY?
THEY PUT US IN THIS BIRD-CAGE CONTRAPTION.
SHH
I CAN TAKE CARE OF THIS!

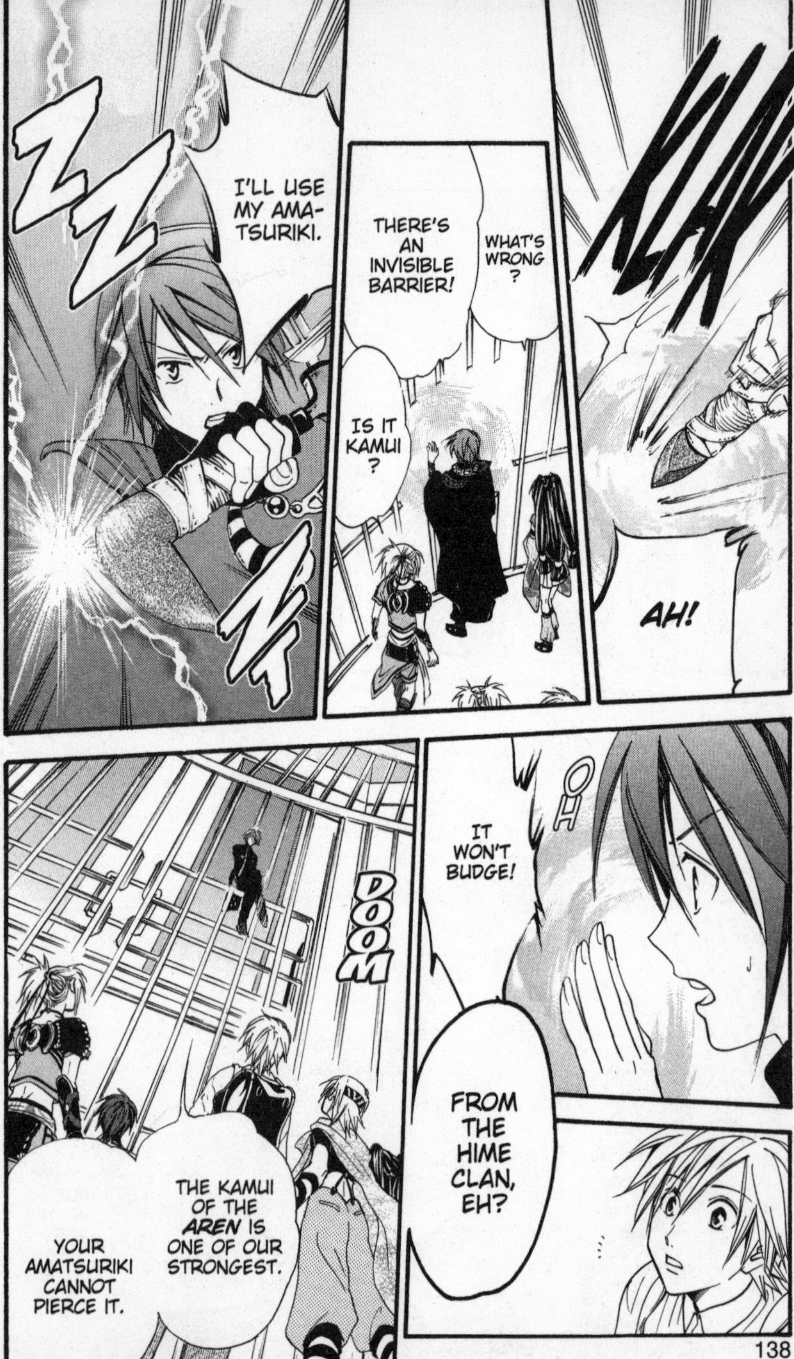
KLAK
AH!
WHAT'S WRONG?
THERE'S AN INVISIBLE BARRIER!
IS IT KAMUI?
ZZZ
I'LL USE MY AMA-TSURIKI.
ZZNT
OH
IT WON'T BUDGE!
FROM THE HIME CLAN, EH?
...
DOOM
THE KAMUI OF THE *AREN* IS ONE OF OUR STRONGEST.
YOUR AMATSURIKI CANNOT PIERCE IT.

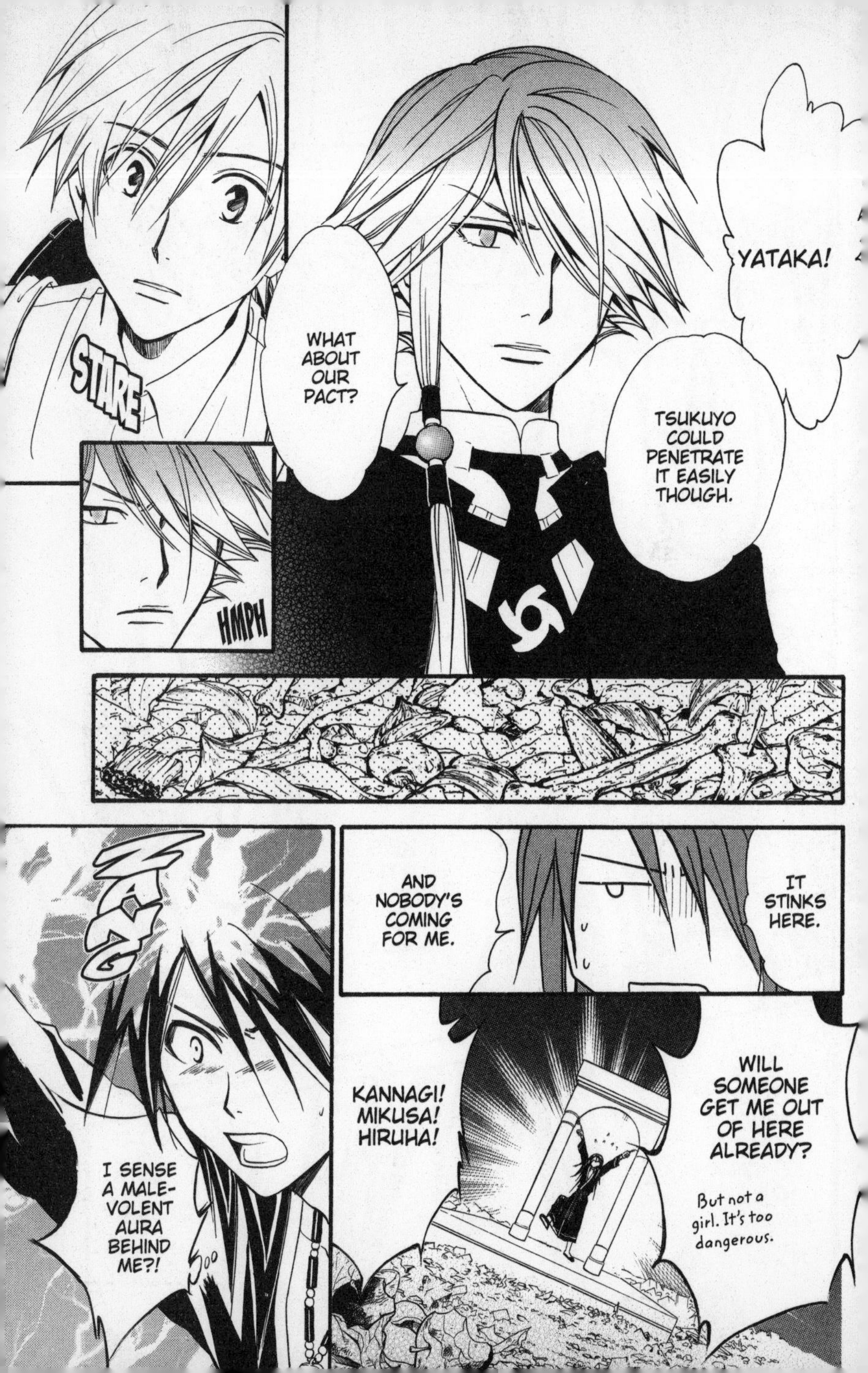

YATAKA!
TSUKUYO COULD PENETRATE IT EASILY THOUGH.
WHAT ABOUT OUR PACT?
STARE
HMPH
IT STINKS HERE.
AND NOBODY'S COMING FOR ME.
WILL SOMEONE GET ME OUT OF HERE ALREADY?
KANNAGI! MIKUSA! HIRUHA!
But not a girl. It's too dangerous.
I SENSE A MALE-VOLENT AURA BEHIND ME?!

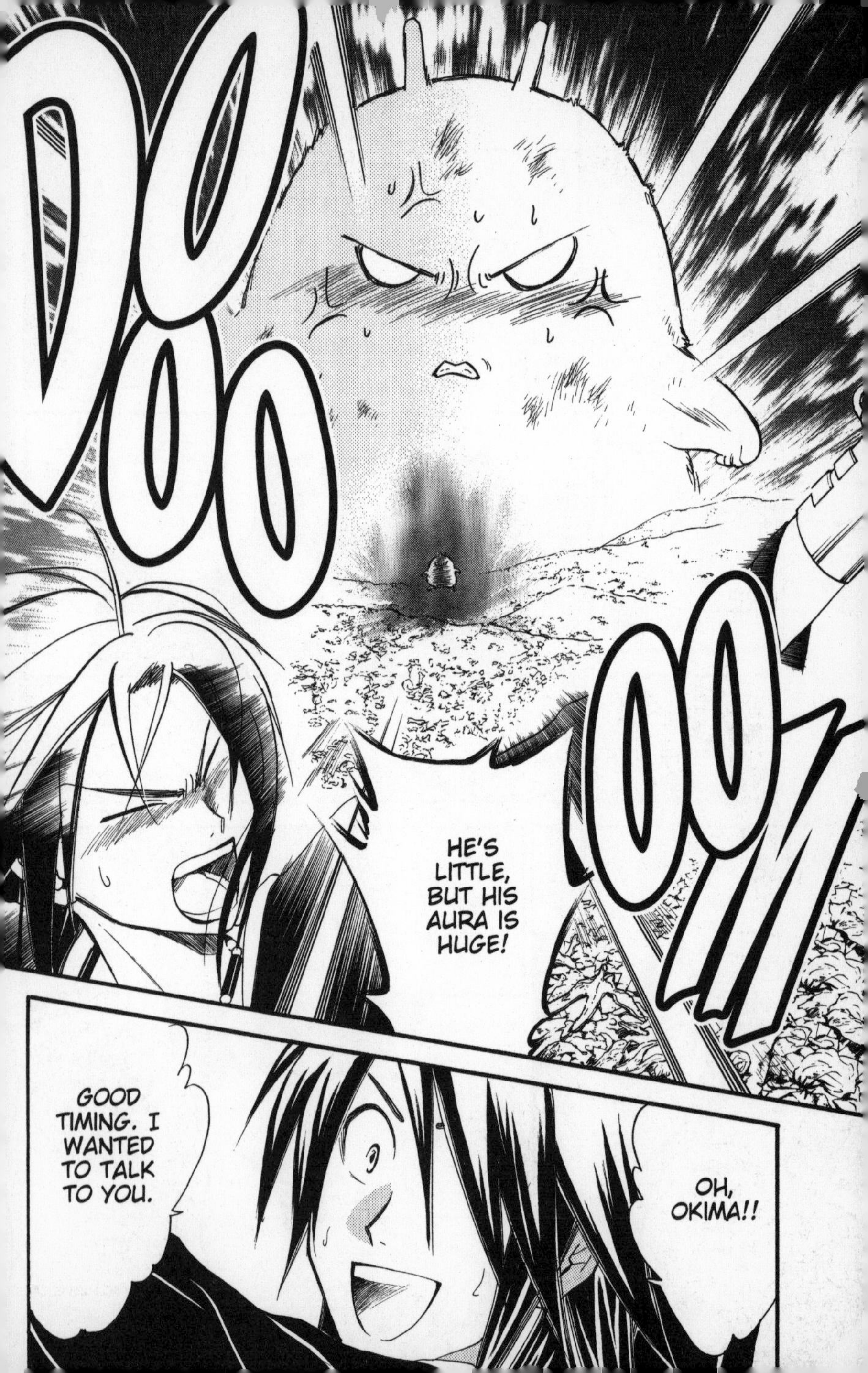
HE'S LITTLE, BUT HIS AURA IS HUGE!
OH, OKIMA!!
GOOD TIMING. I WANTED TO TALK TO YOU.

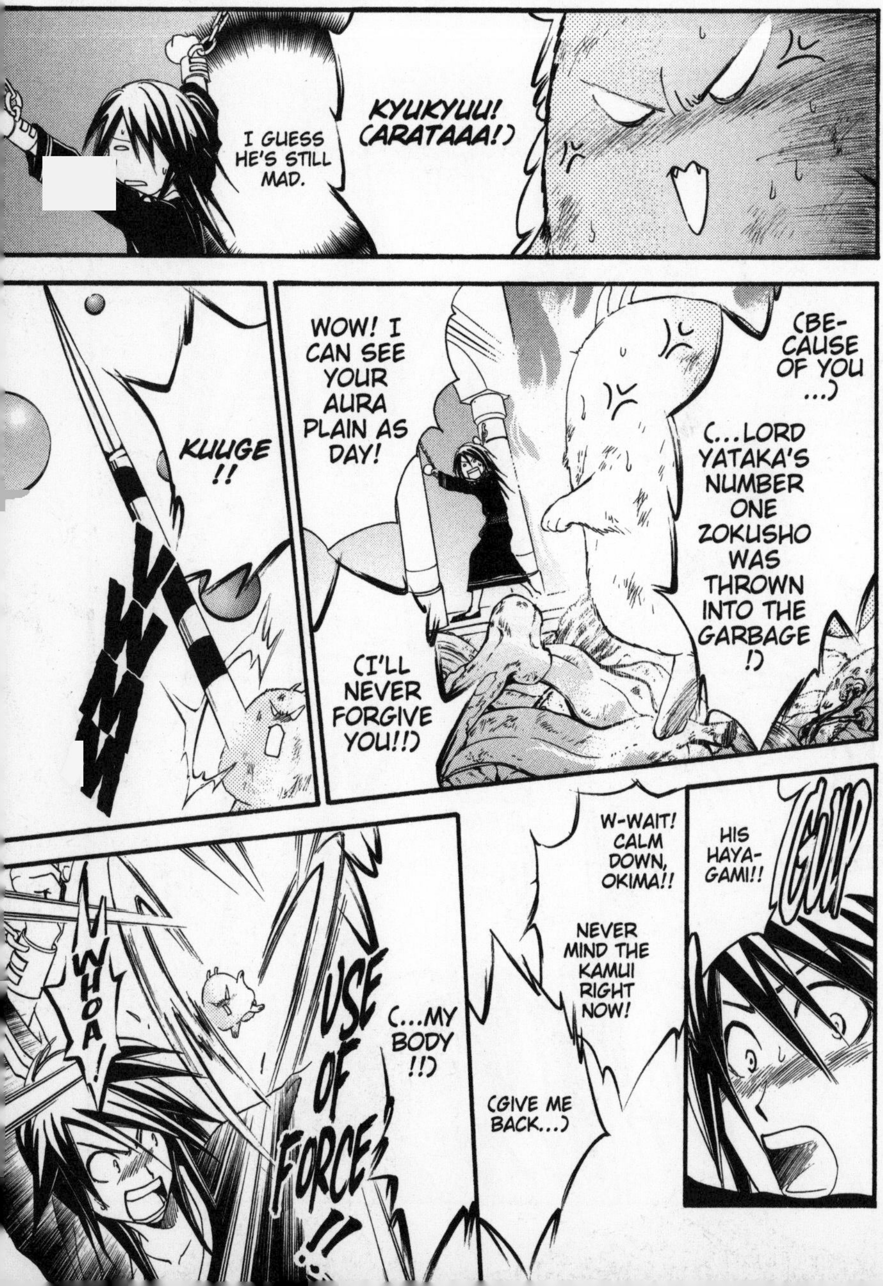
KYUKYUU! (ARATAAA!)
I GUESS HE'S STILL MAD.
(BE-CAUSE OF YOU ...)
(...LORD YATAKA'S NUMBER ONE ZOKUSHO WAS THROWN INTO THE GARBAGE!)
WOW! I CAN SEE YOUR AURA PLAIN AS DAY!
(I'LL NEVER FORGIVE YOU!!)
KUUGE!!
GULP
HIS HAYA-GAMI!!
W-WAIT! CALM DOWN, OKIMA!!
NEVER MIND THE KAMUI RIGHT NOW!
(GIVE ME BACK...)
(...MY BODY!!)
USE OF FORCE!!
WHOA!

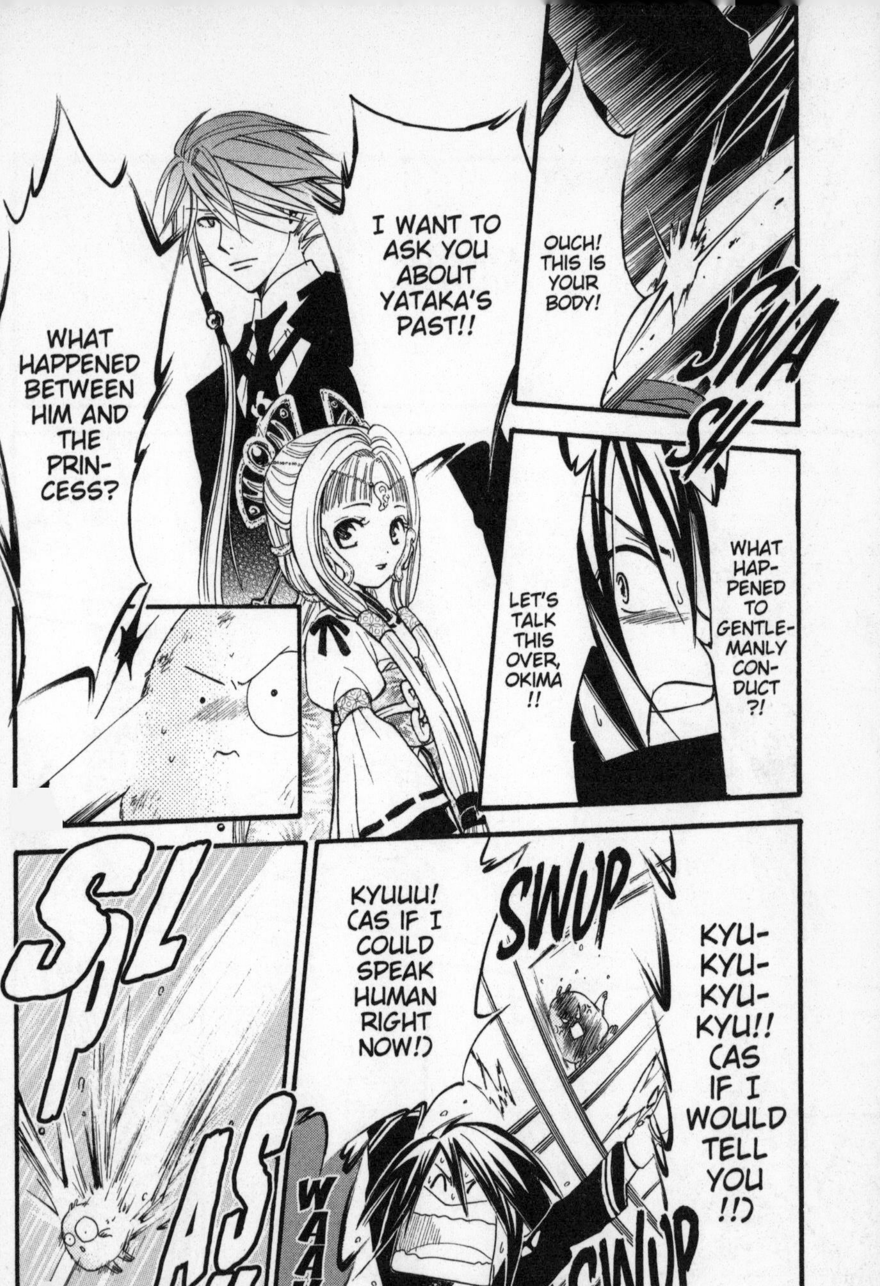
SMASH
OUCH! THIS IS YOUR BODY!
WHAT HAPPENED TO GENTLEMANLY CONDUCT?!
LET'S TALK THIS OVER, OKIMA!!
I WANT TO ASK YOU ABOUT YATAKA'S PAST!!
WHAT HAPPENED BETWEEN HIM AND THE PRINCESS?
SWUP
KYU-KYU-KYU-KYU!! (AS IF I WOULD TELL YOU!!)
KYUUU! (AS IF I COULD SPEAK HUMAN RIGHT NOW!)
WAAH!
SWUP
SPLASH

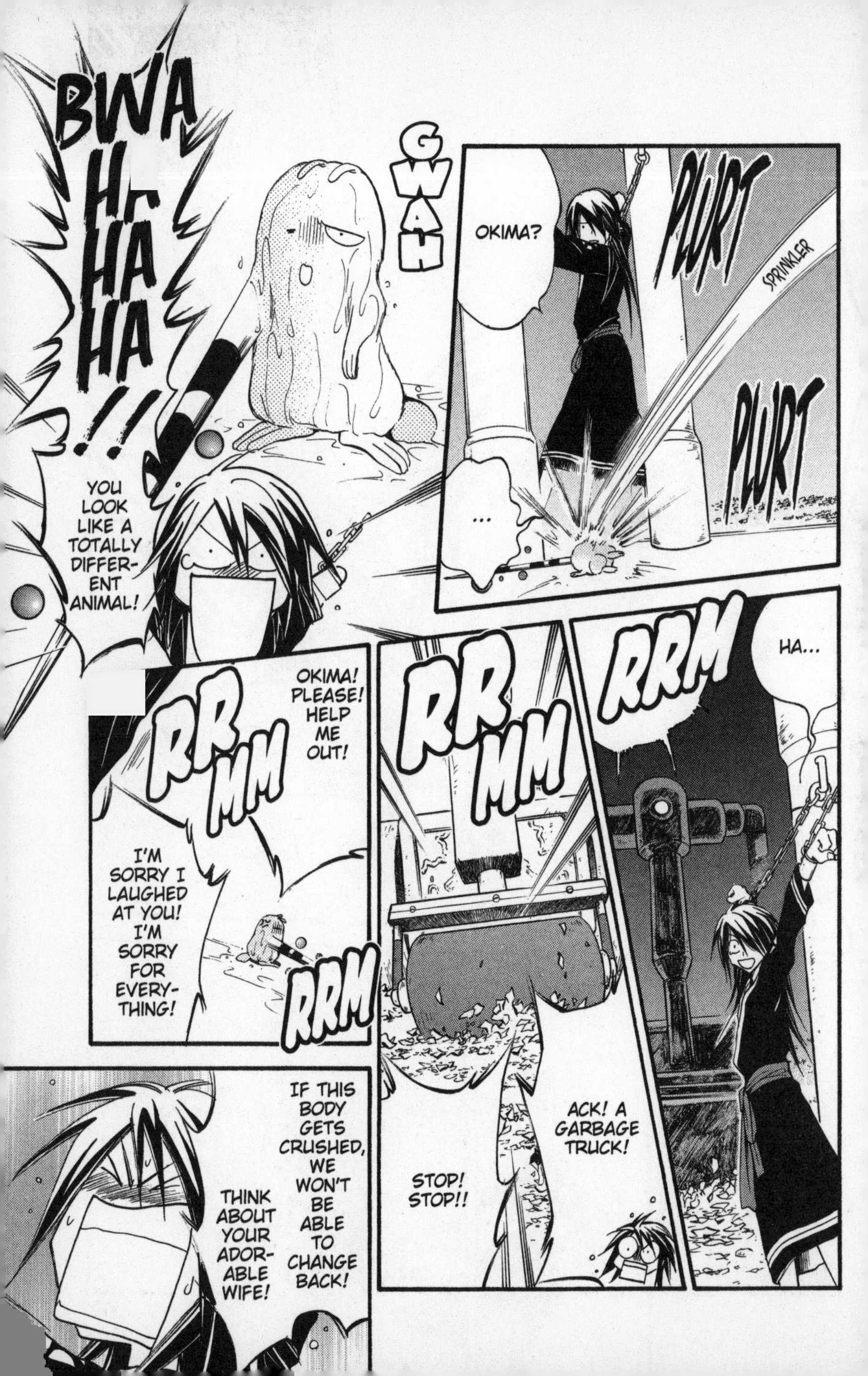
OKIMA?
PLURT
PLURT
SPRINKLER
...
GWAH
BWA HA HA HA HA!!!
YOU LOOK LIKE A TOTALLY DIFFER-ENT ANIMAL!
RRM
HA...
RRMM
RRMM
OKIMA! PLEASE! HELP ME OUT!
I'M SORRY I LAUGHED AT YOU! I'M SORRY FOR EVERY-THING!
RRM
ACK! A GARBAGE TRUCK!
STOP! STOP!!
IF THIS BODY GETS CRUSHED, WE WON'T BE ABLE TO CHANGE BACK!
THINK ABOUT YOUR ADOR-ABLE WIFE!

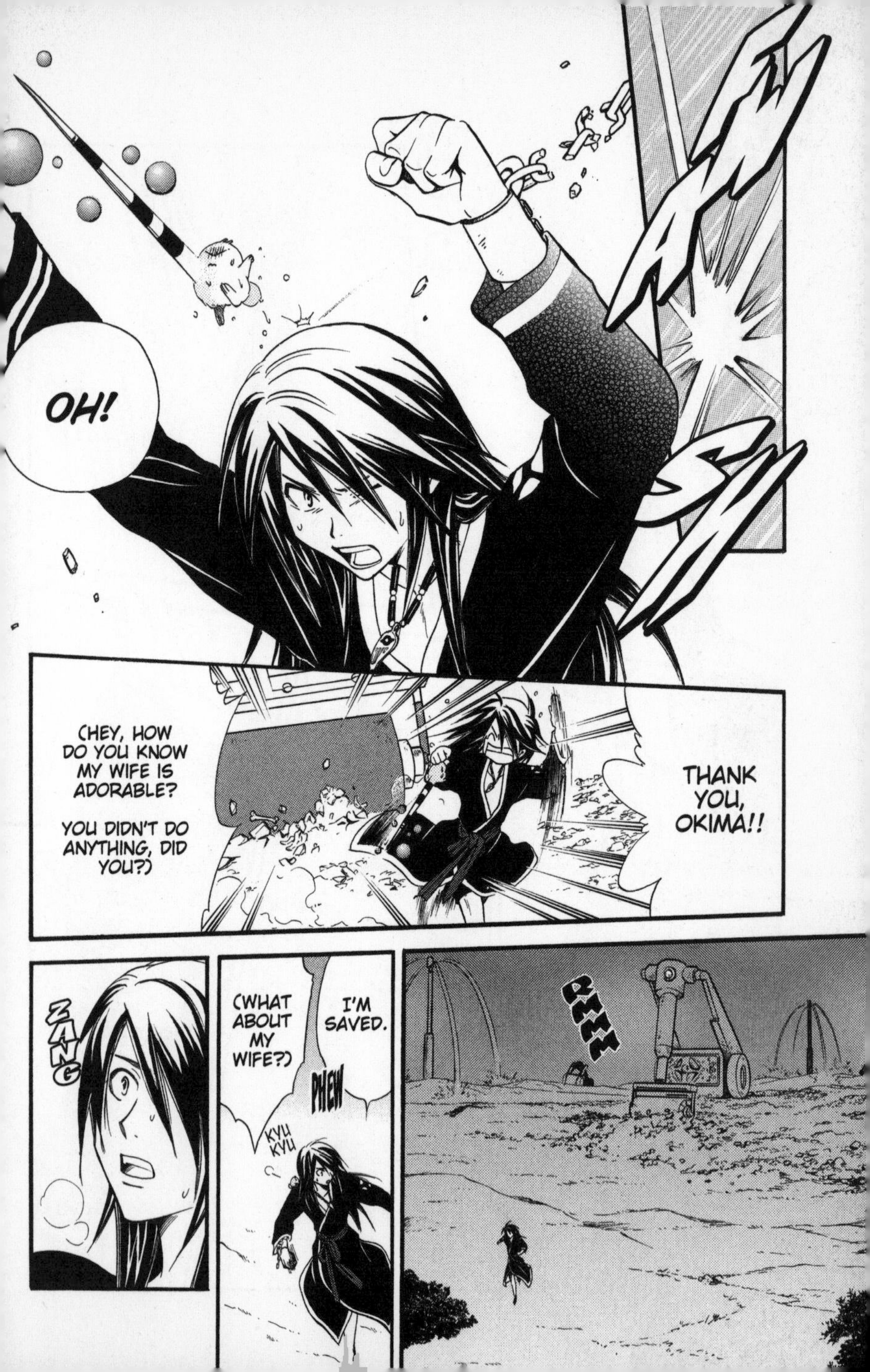
OH!
THANK YOU, OKIMA!!
(HEY, HOW DO YOU KNOW MY WIFE IS ADORABLE?
YOU DIDN'T DO ANYTHING, DID YOU?)
RMMM
I'M SAVED.
(WHAT ABOUT MY WIFE?)
PHEW
KYU KYU
ZANG

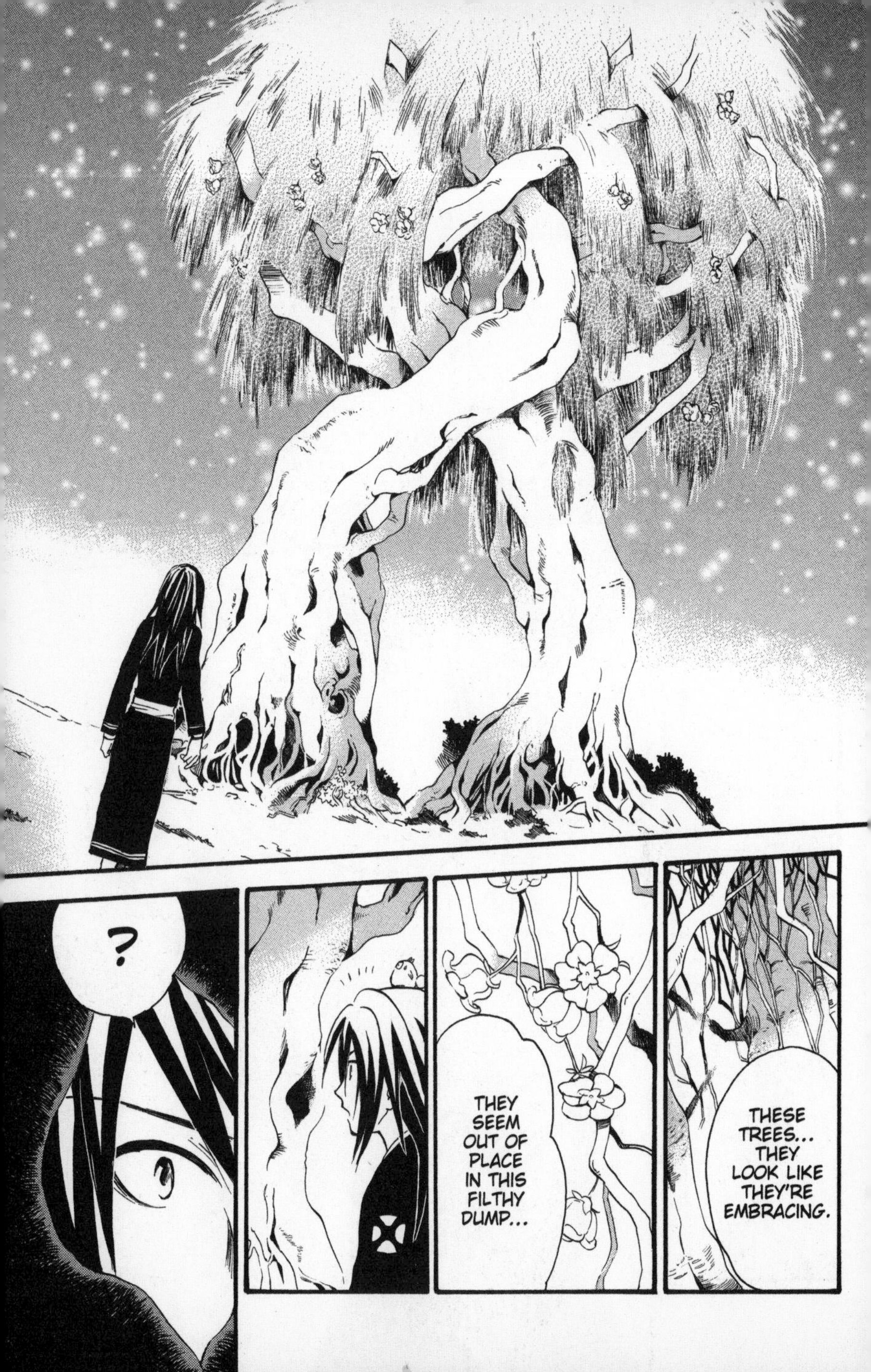
THESE TREES... THEY LOOK LIKE THEY'RE EMBRACING.
THEY SEEM OUT OF PLACE IN THIS FILTHY DUMP...
?

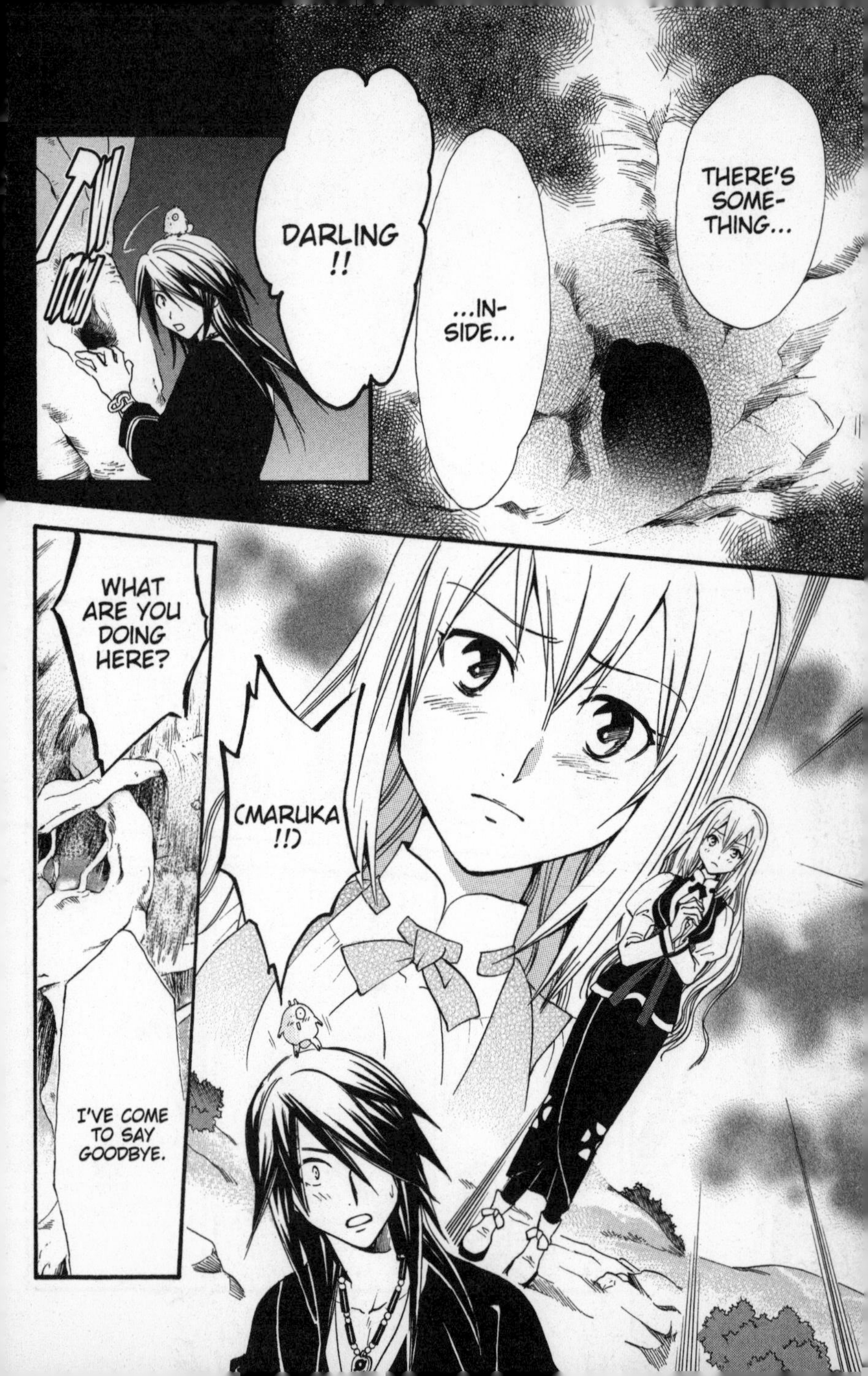
THERE'S SOME-THING...
...IN-SIDE...
DARLING!!
WHAT ARE YOU DOING HERE?
(MARUKA!!)
I'VE COME TO SAY GOODBYE.

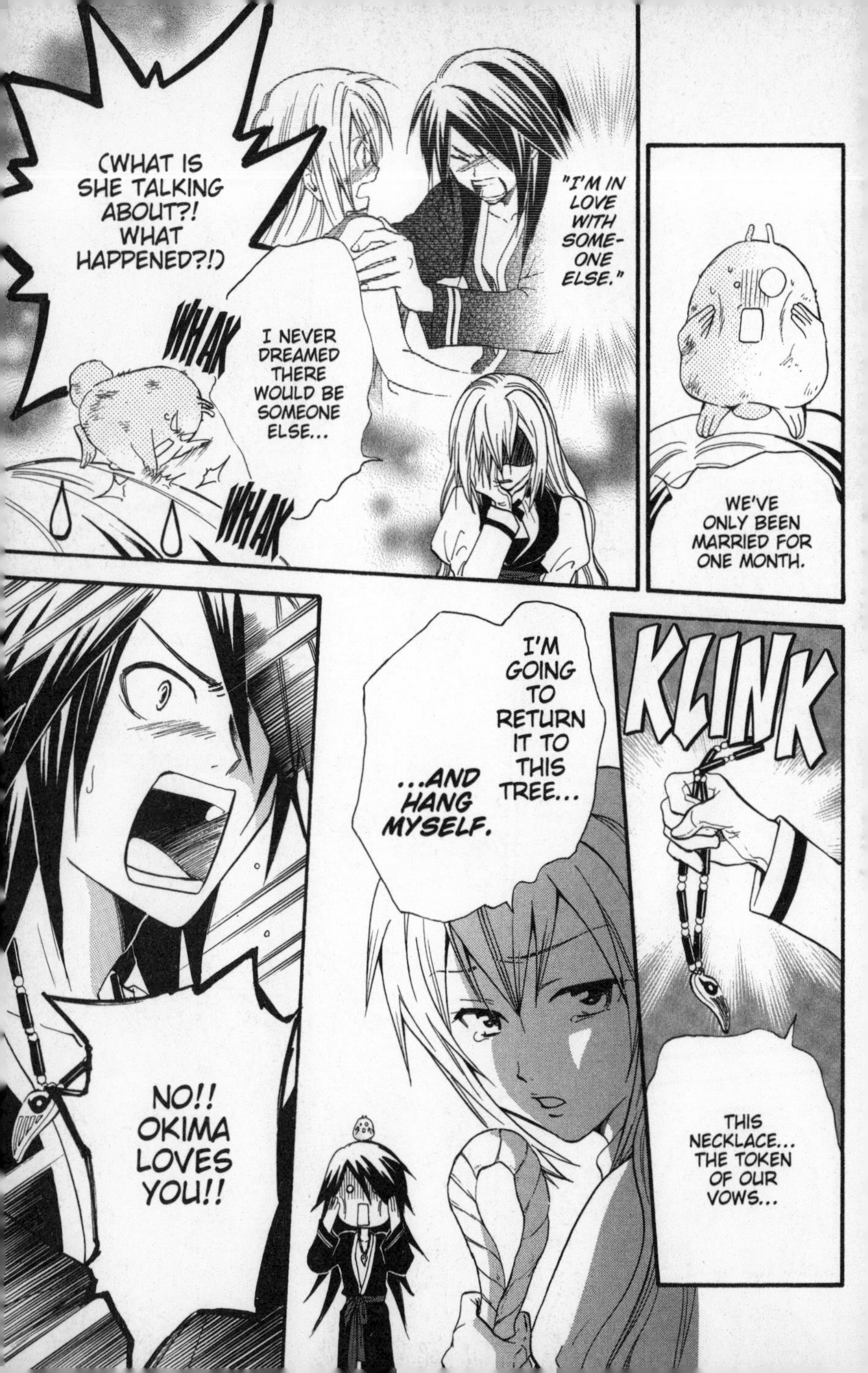
WE'VE ONLY BEEN MARRIED FOR ONE MONTH.
"I'M IN LOVE WITH SOME-ONE ELSE."
(WHAT IS SHE TALKING ABOUT?! WHAT HAPPENED?!)
I NEVER DREAMED THERE WOULD BE SOMEONE ELSE...
WHAK
WHAK
KLINK
THIS NECKLACE... THE TOKEN OF OUR VOWS...
I'M GOING TO RETURN IT TO THIS TREE...
...AND HANG MYSELF.
NO!! OKIMA LOVES YOU!!

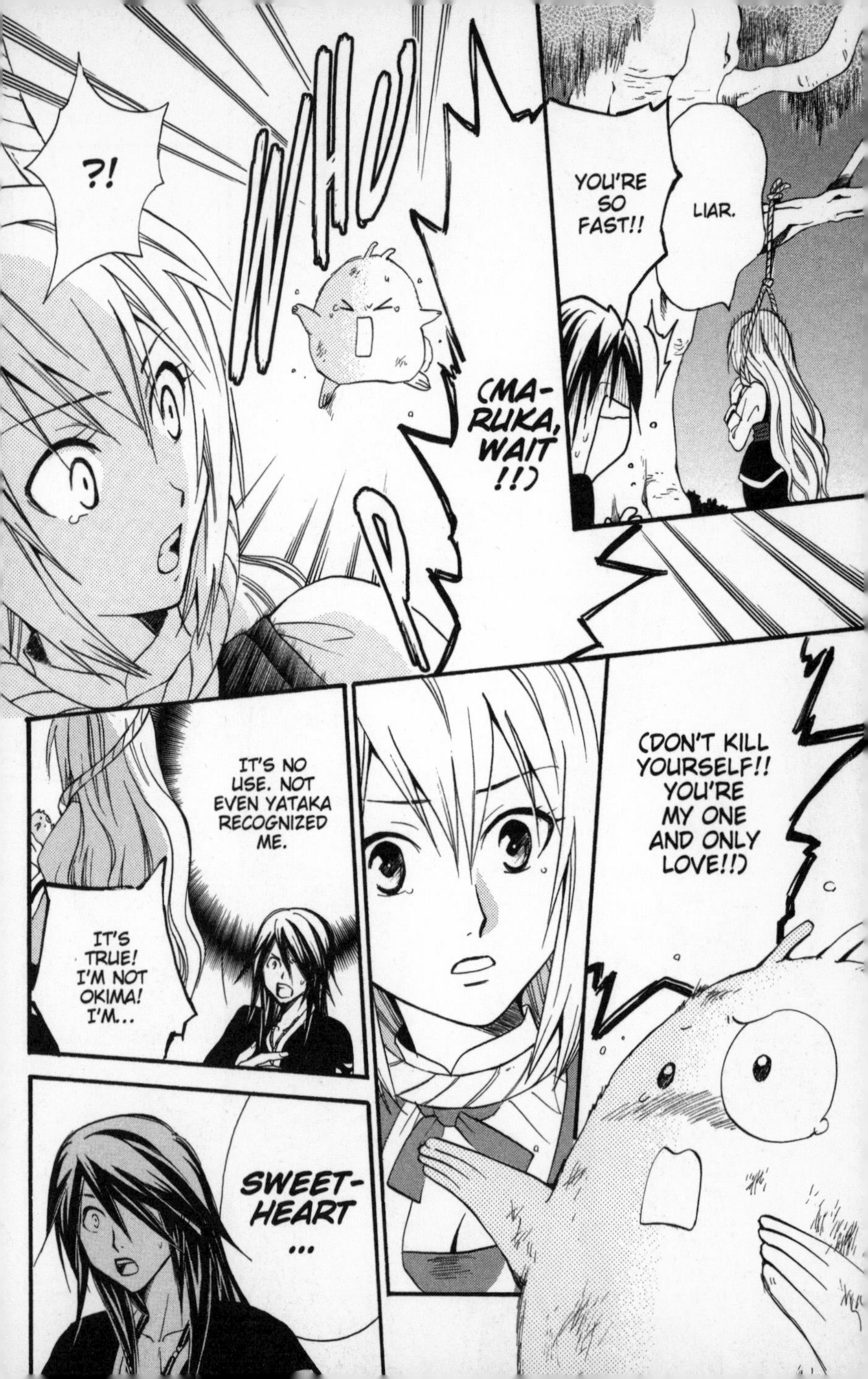
LIAR.
YOU'RE SO FAST!!
WHO!
(MA-RUKA, WAIT!!)
?!
(DON'T KILL YOURSELF!! YOU'RE MY ONE AND ONLY LOVE!!)
IT'S NO USE. NOT EVEN YATAKA RECOGNIZED ME.
IT'S TRUE! I'M NOT OKIMA! I'M...
SWEET-HEART ...

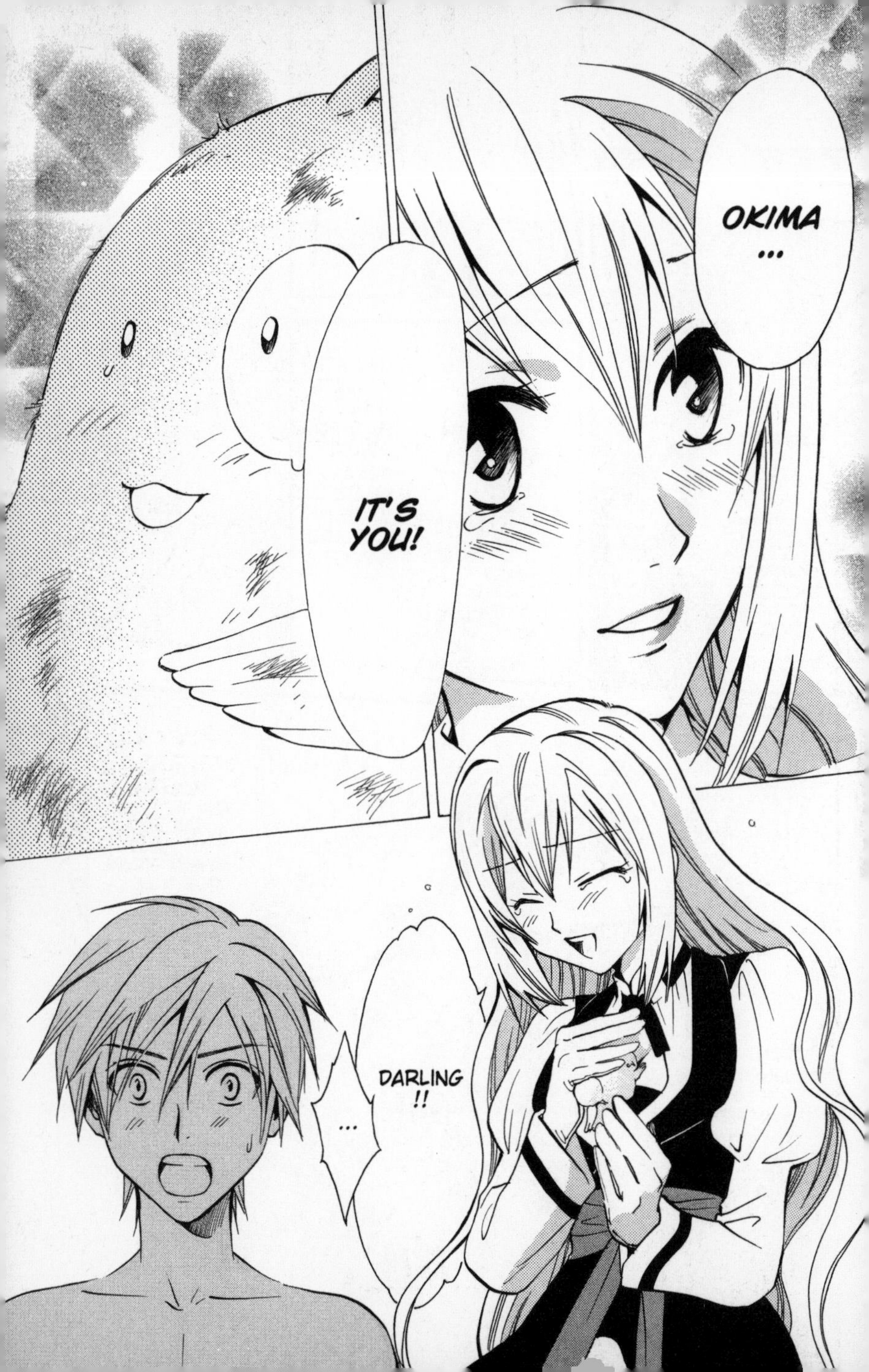
OKIMA ...
IT'S YOU!
DARLING !!
...

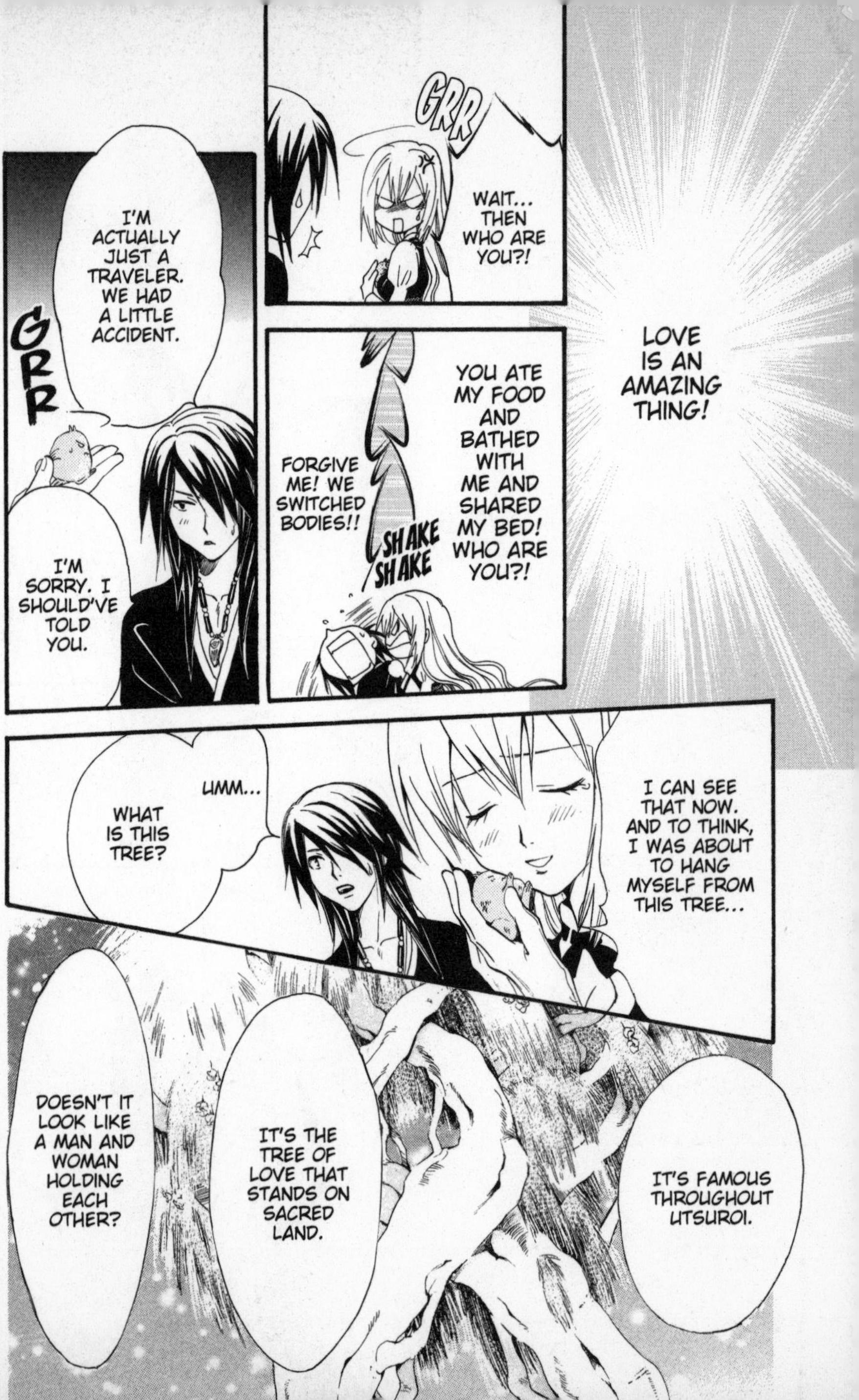
LOVE IS AN AMAZING THING!
GRR
WAIT... THEN WHO ARE YOU?!
YOU ATE MY FOOD AND BATHED WITH ME AND SHARED MY BED! WHO ARE YOU?!
FORGIVE ME! WE SWITCHED BODIES!!
SHAKE SHAKE
I'M ACTUALLY JUST A TRAVELER. WE HAD A LITTLE ACCIDENT.
GRR
I'M SORRY. I SHOULD'VE TOLD YOU.
I CAN SEE THAT NOW. AND TO THINK, I WAS ABOUT TO HANG MYSELF FROM THIS TREE...
UMM...
WHAT IS THIS TREE?
IT'S FAMOUS THROUGHOUT UTSUROI.
IT'S THE TREE OF LOVE THAT STANDS ON SACRED LAND.
DOESN'T IT LOOK LIKE A MAN AND WOMAN HOLDING EACH OTHER?

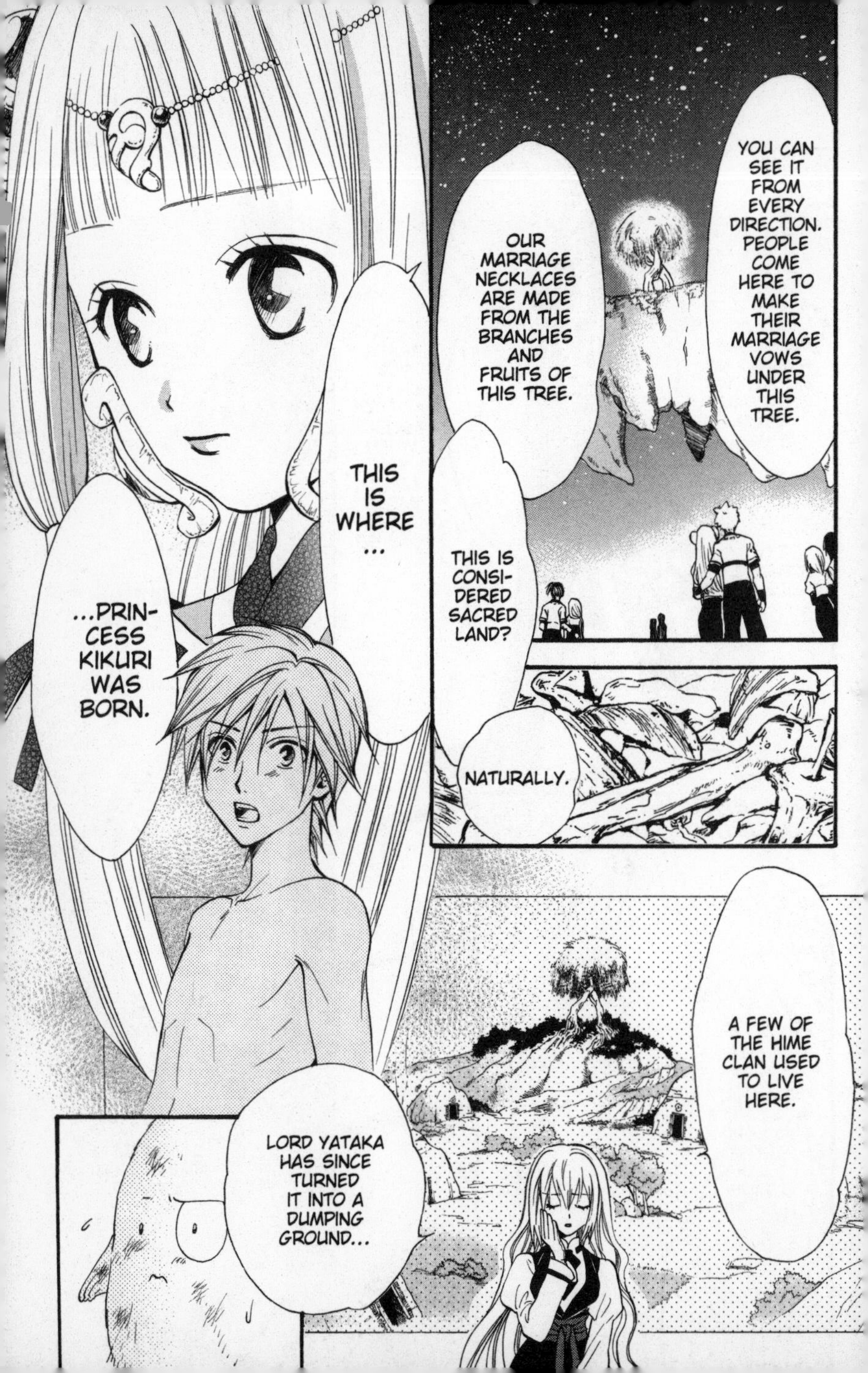
YOU CAN SEE IT FROM EVERY DIRECTION. PEOPLE COME HERE TO MAKE THEIR MARRIAGE VOWS UNDER THIS TREE.
OUR MARRIAGE NECKLACES ARE MADE FROM THE BRANCHES AND FRUITS OF THIS TREE.
THIS IS CONSI-DERED SACRED LAND?
NATURALLY.
THIS IS WHERE...
...PRIN-CESS KIKURI WAS BORN.
A FEW OF THE HIME CLAN USED TO LIVE HERE.
LORD YATAKA HAS SINCE TURNED IT INTO A DUMPING GROUND...

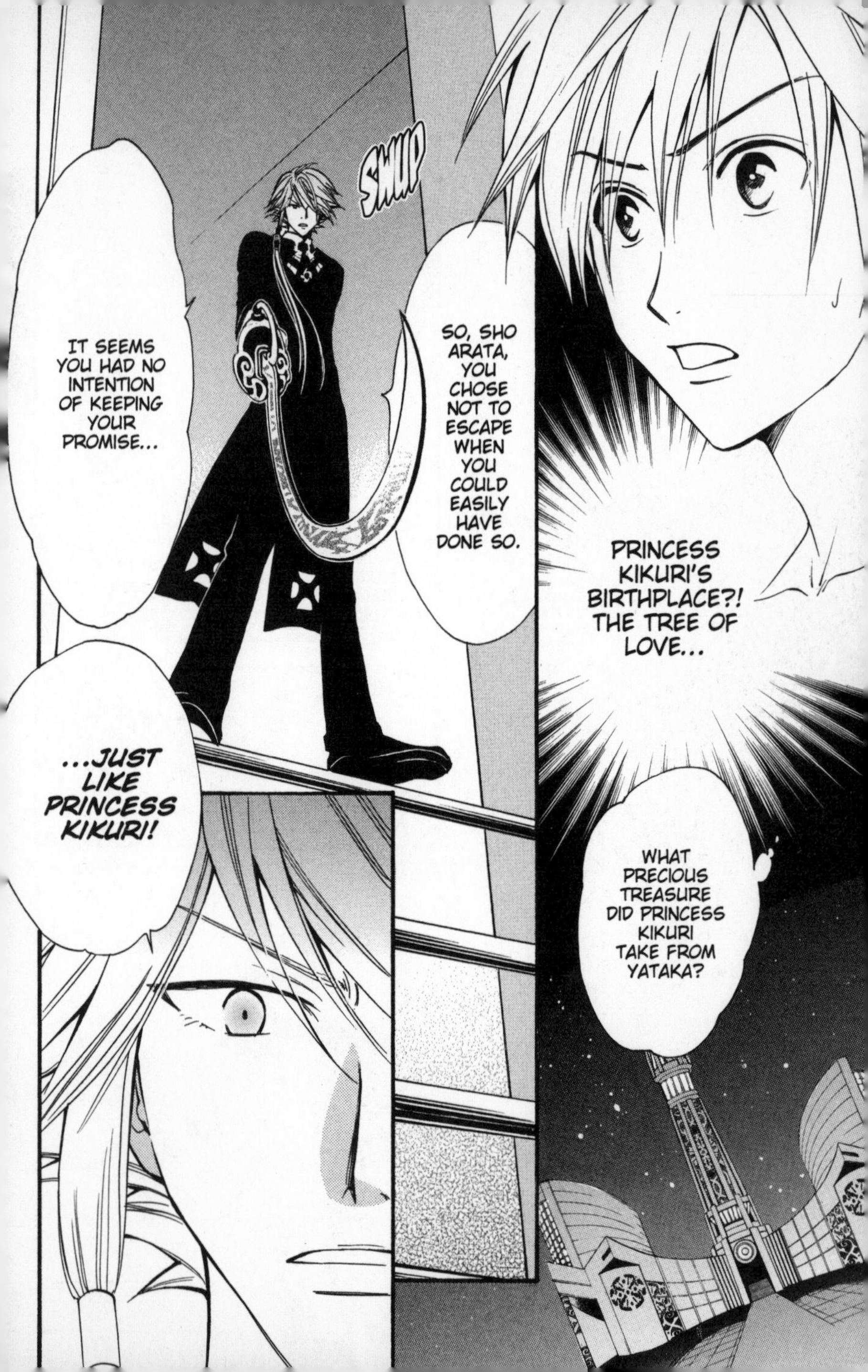
PRINCESS KIKURI'S BIRTHPLACE?! THE TREE OF LOVE...
WHAT PRECIOUS TREASURE DID PRINCESS KIKURI TAKE FROM YATAKA?
SWUP
SO, SHO ARATA, YOU CHOSE NOT TO ESCAPE WHEN YOU COULD EASILY HAVE DONE SO.
IT SEEMS YOU HAD NO INTENTION OF KEEPING YOUR PROMISE...
...JUST LIKE PRINCESS KIKURI!

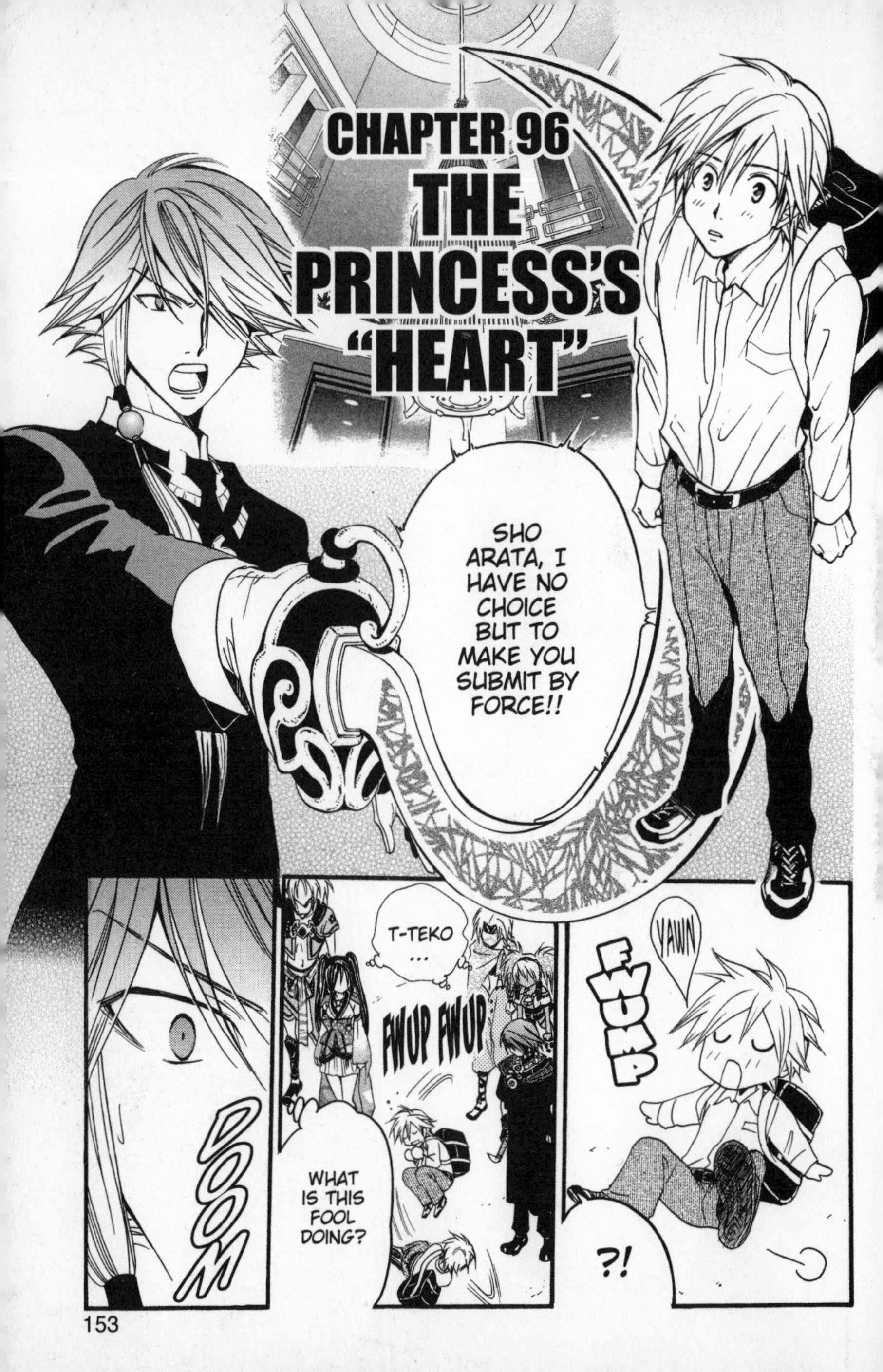
CHAPTER 96
THE PRINCESS'S "HEART"
SHO ARATA, I HAVE NO CHOICE BUT TO MAKE YOU SUBMIT BY FORCE!!
YAWN
FWUMP
?!
T-TEKO ...
FWUP FWUP
WHAT IS THIS FOOL DOING?
DOOM

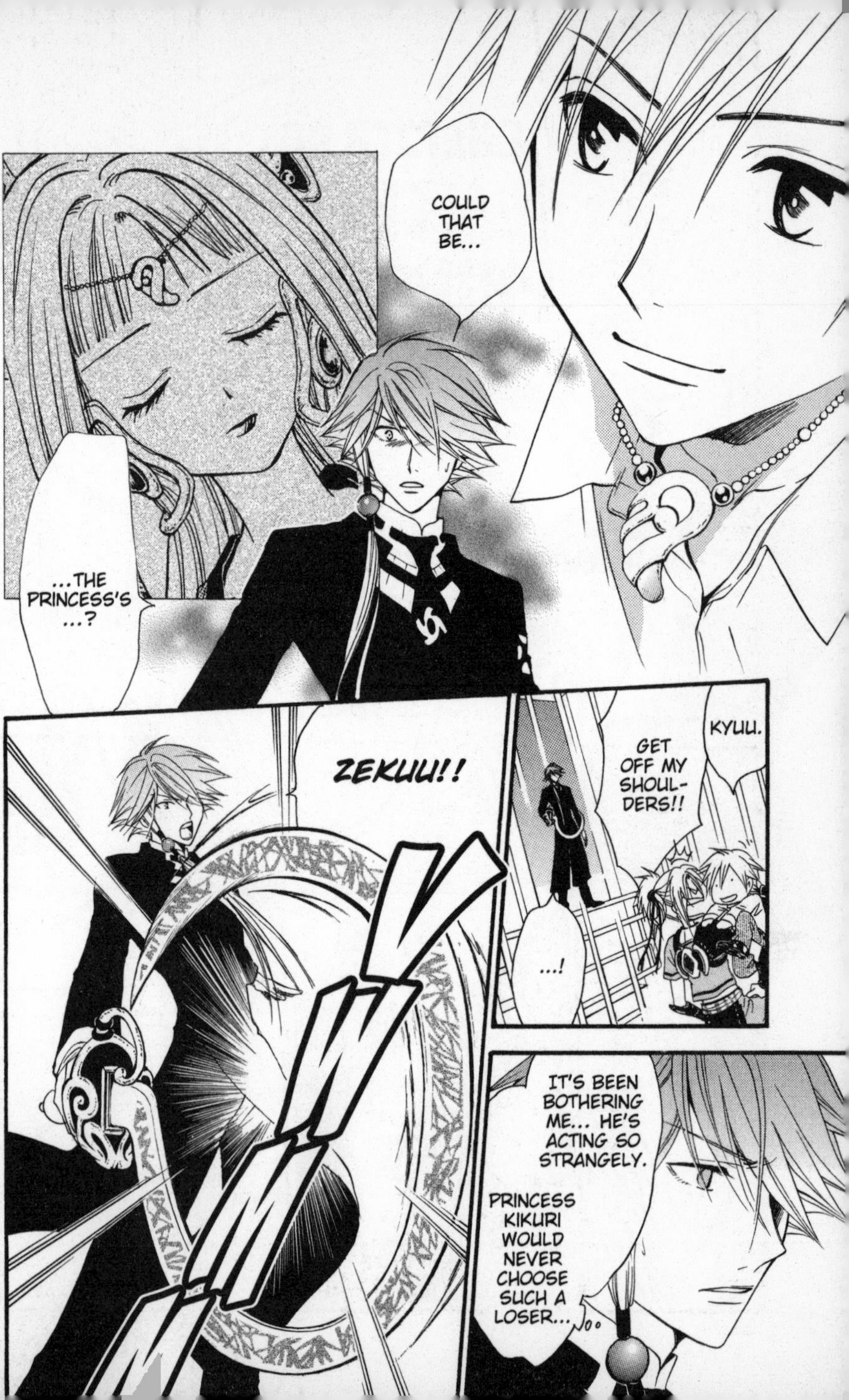
COULD THAT BE...
...THE PRINCESS'S ...?
KYUU.
GET OFF MY SHOULDERS!!
...!
IT'S BEEN BOTHERING ME... HE'S ACTING SO STRANGELY.
PRINCESS KIKURI WOULD NEVER CHOOSE SUCH A LOSER...
ZEKUU!!

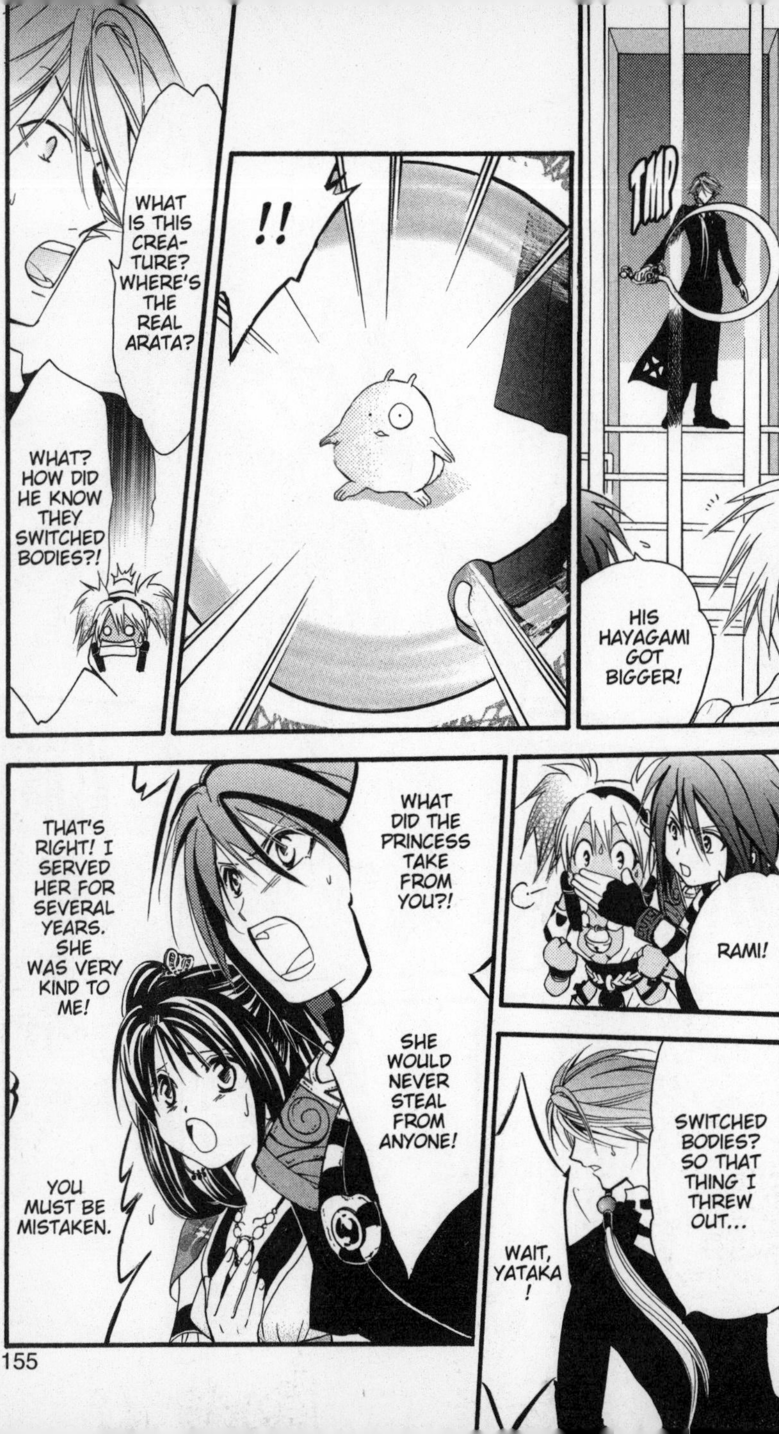
TMP
HIS HAYAGAMI GOT BIGGER!
!!
WHAT IS THIS CREA-TURE? WHERE'S THE REAL ARATA?
WHAT? HOW DID HE KNOW THEY SWITCHED BODIES?!
RAMI!
SWITCHED BODIES? SO THAT THING I THREW OUT...
WAIT, YATAKA!
WHAT DID THE PRINCESS TAKE FROM YOU?!
THAT'S RIGHT! I SERVED HER FOR SEVERAL YEARS. SHE WAS VERY KIND TO ME!
SHE WOULD NEVER STEAL FROM ANYONE!
YOU MUST BE MISTAKEN.

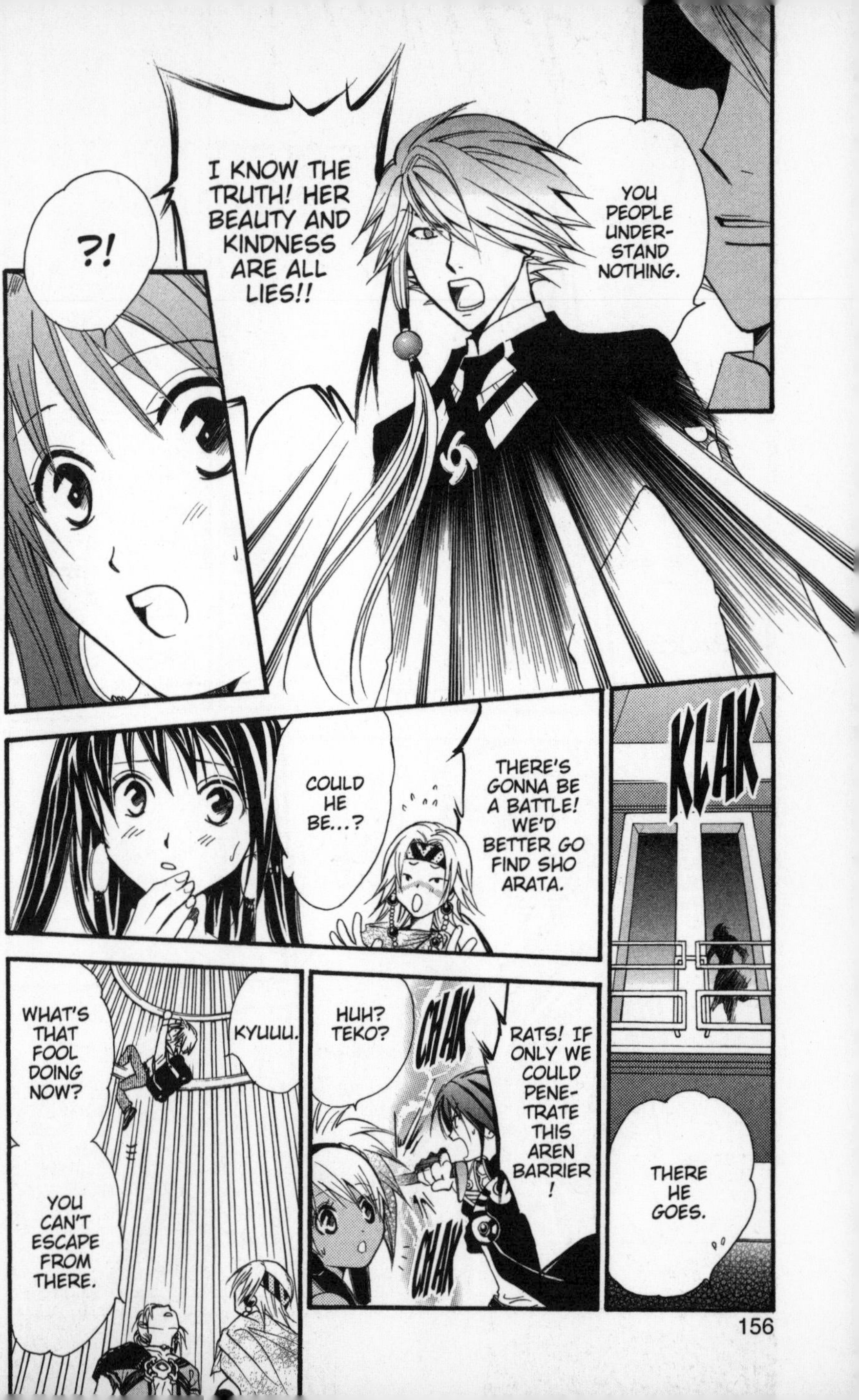
YOU PEOPLE UNDER-STAND NOTHING.
I KNOW THE TRUTH! HER BEAUTY AND KINDNESS ARE ALL LIES!!
?!
KLAK
THERE HE GOES.
THERE'S GONNA BE A BATTLE! WE'D BETTER GO FIND SHO ARATA.
COULD HE BE...?
RATS! IF ONLY WE COULD PENE-TRATE THIS AREN BARRIER!
CHAK
CHAK
HUH? TEKO?
KYUUU.
WHAT'S THAT FOOL DOING NOW?
YOU CAN'T ESCAPE FROM THERE.

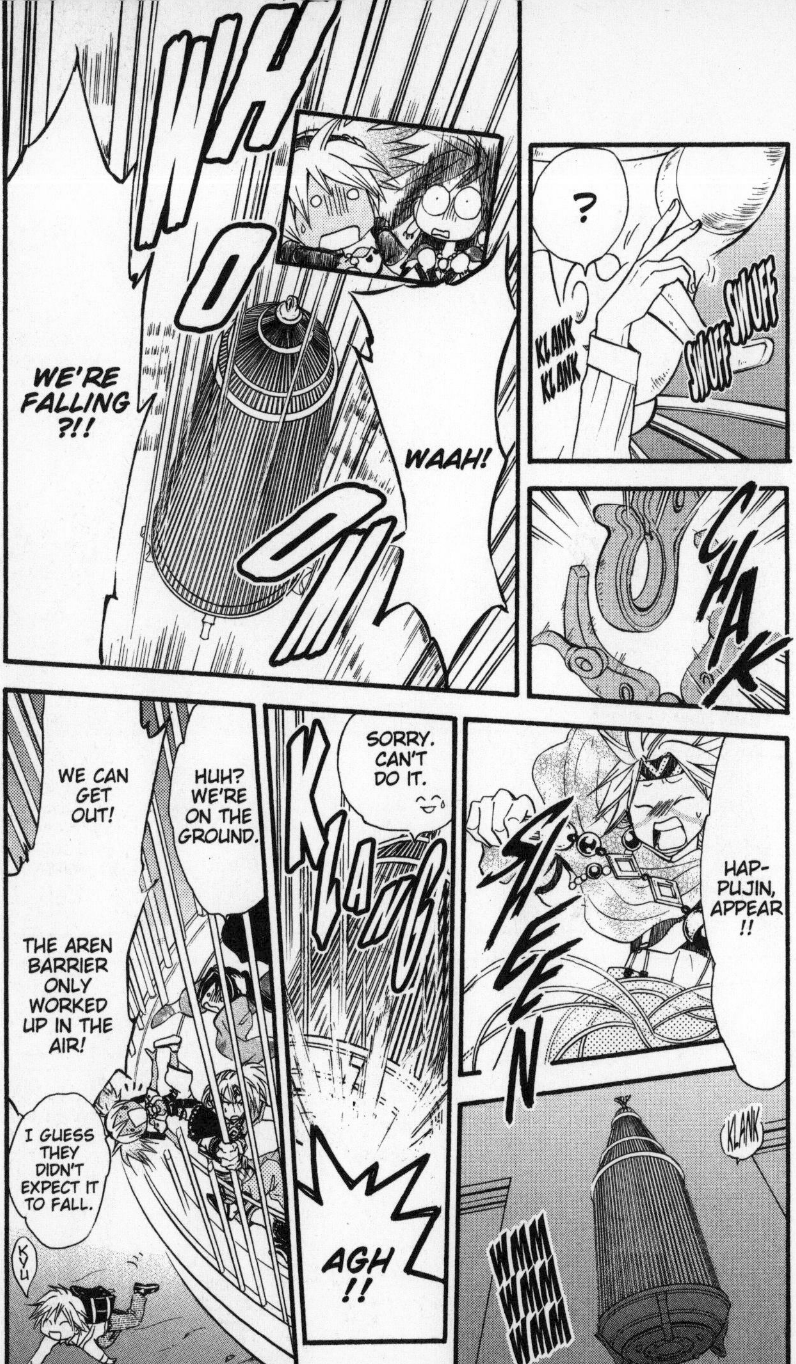
?
KLANK KLANK
SWUFF SWUFF
CHAK
WE'RE FALLING ?!!
WAAH!
HAP-PUJIN, APPEAR !!
KLANK
WMMM WMMM WMMM
SORRY. CAN'T DO IT.
AGH !!
HUH? WE'RE ON THE GROUND.
WE CAN GET OUT!
THE AREN BARRIER ONLY WORKED UP IN THE AIR!
I GUESS THEY DIDN'T EXPECT IT TO FALL.
KYU

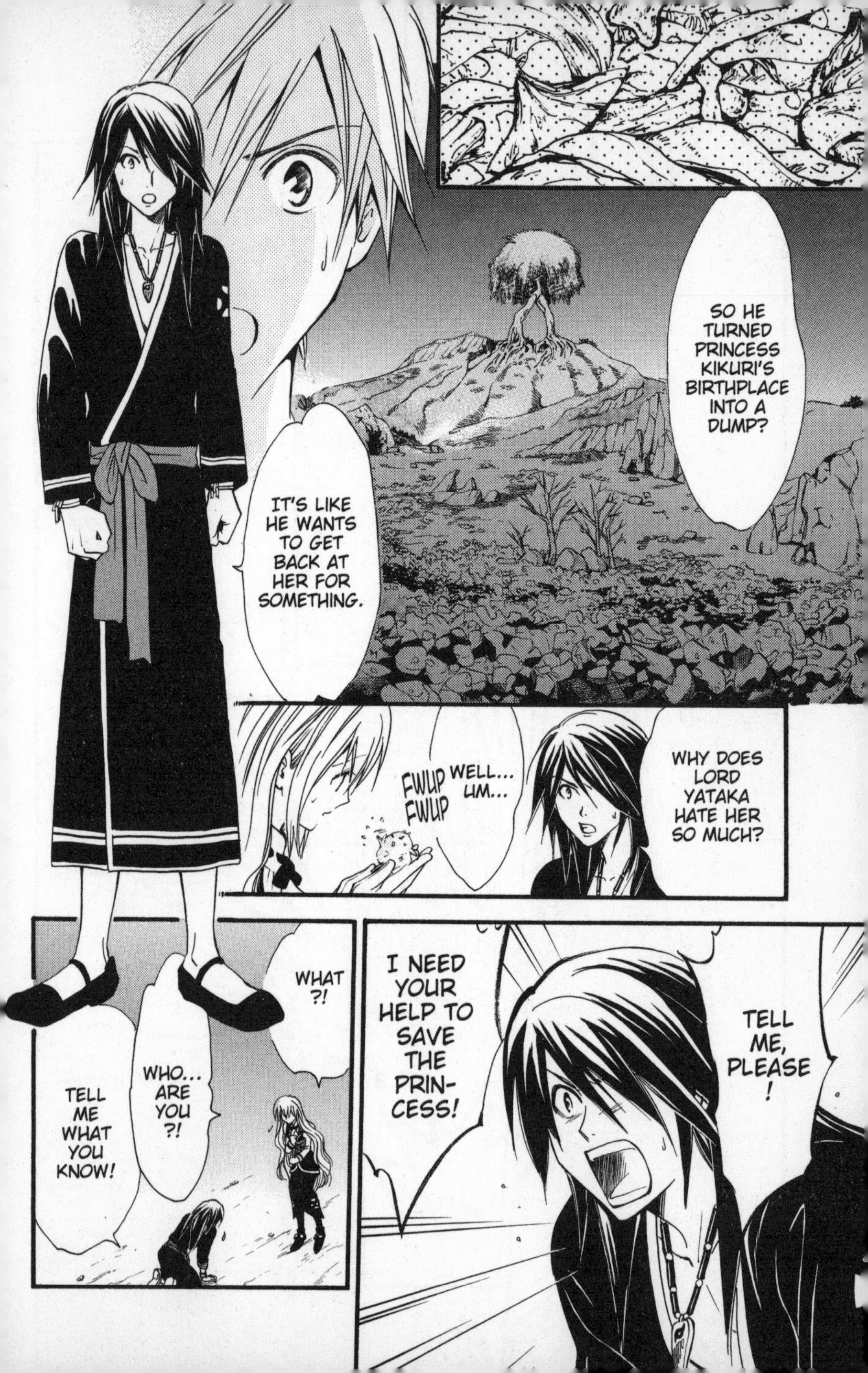
SO HE TURNED PRINCESS KIKURI'S BIRTHPLACE INTO A DUMP?
IT'S LIKE HE WANTS TO GET BACK AT HER FOR SOMETHING.
WHY DOES LORD YATAKA HATE HER SO MUCH?
WELL... UM...
FWUP FWUP
TELL ME, PLEASE!
I NEED YOUR HELP TO SAVE THE PRIN-CESS!
WHAT?!
WHO... ARE YOU?!
TELL ME WHAT YOU KNOW!

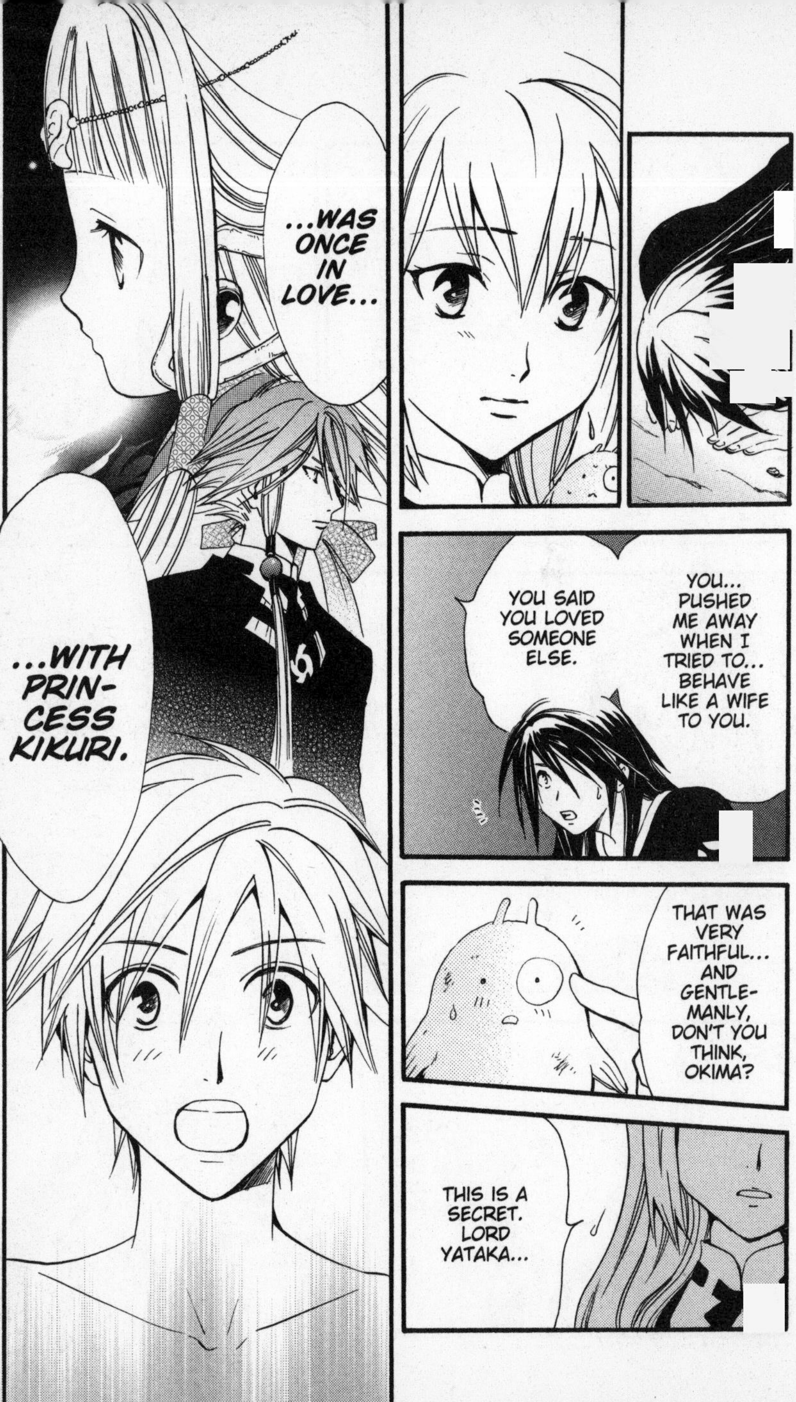
YOU... PUSHED ME AWAY WHEN I TRIED TO... BEHAVE LIKE A WIFE TO YOU.
YOU SAID YOU LOVED SOMEONE ELSE.
THAT WAS VERY FAITHFUL... AND GENTLE-MANLY, DON'T YOU THINK, OKIMA?
THIS IS A SECRET. LORD YATAKA...
...WAS ONCE IN LOVE...
...WITH PRIN-CESS KIKURI.

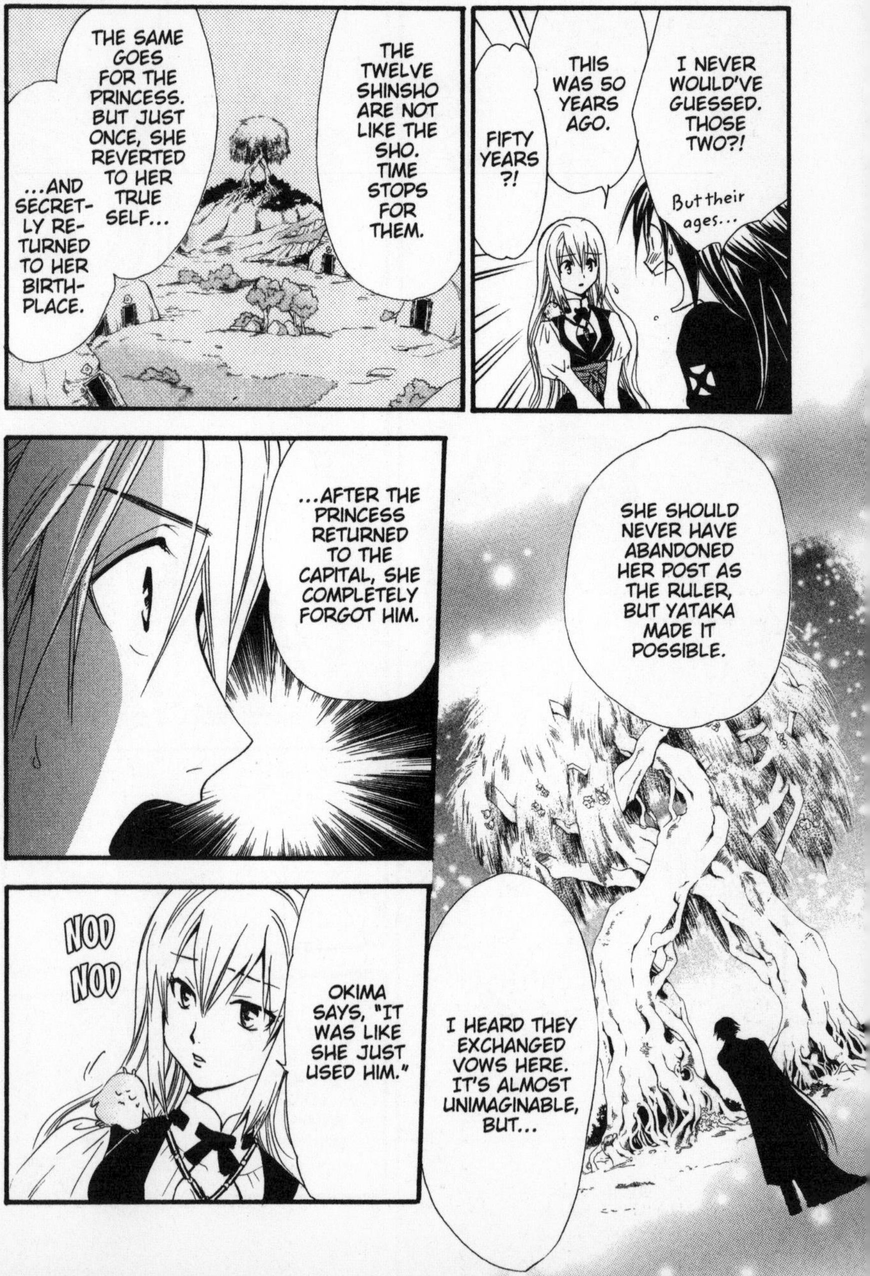
I NEVER WOULD'VE GUESSED. THOSE TWO?!
But their ages...
THIS WAS 50 YEARS AGO.
FIFTY YEARS?!
THE TWELVE SHINSHO ARE NOT LIKE THE SHO. TIME STOPS FOR THEM.
THE SAME GOES FOR THE PRINCESS. BUT JUST ONCE, SHE REVERTED TO HER TRUE SELF...
...AND SECRETLY RETURNED TO HER BIRTHPLACE.
SHE SHOULD NEVER HAVE ABANDONED HER POST AS THE RULER, BUT YATAKA MADE IT POSSIBLE.
I HEARD THEY EXCHANGED VOWS HERE. IT'S ALMOST UNIMAGINABLE, BUT...
...AFTER THE PRINCESS RETURNED TO THE CAPITAL, SHE COMPLETELY FORGOT HIM.
OKIMA SAYS, "IT WAS LIKE SHE JUST USED HIM."
NOD NOD

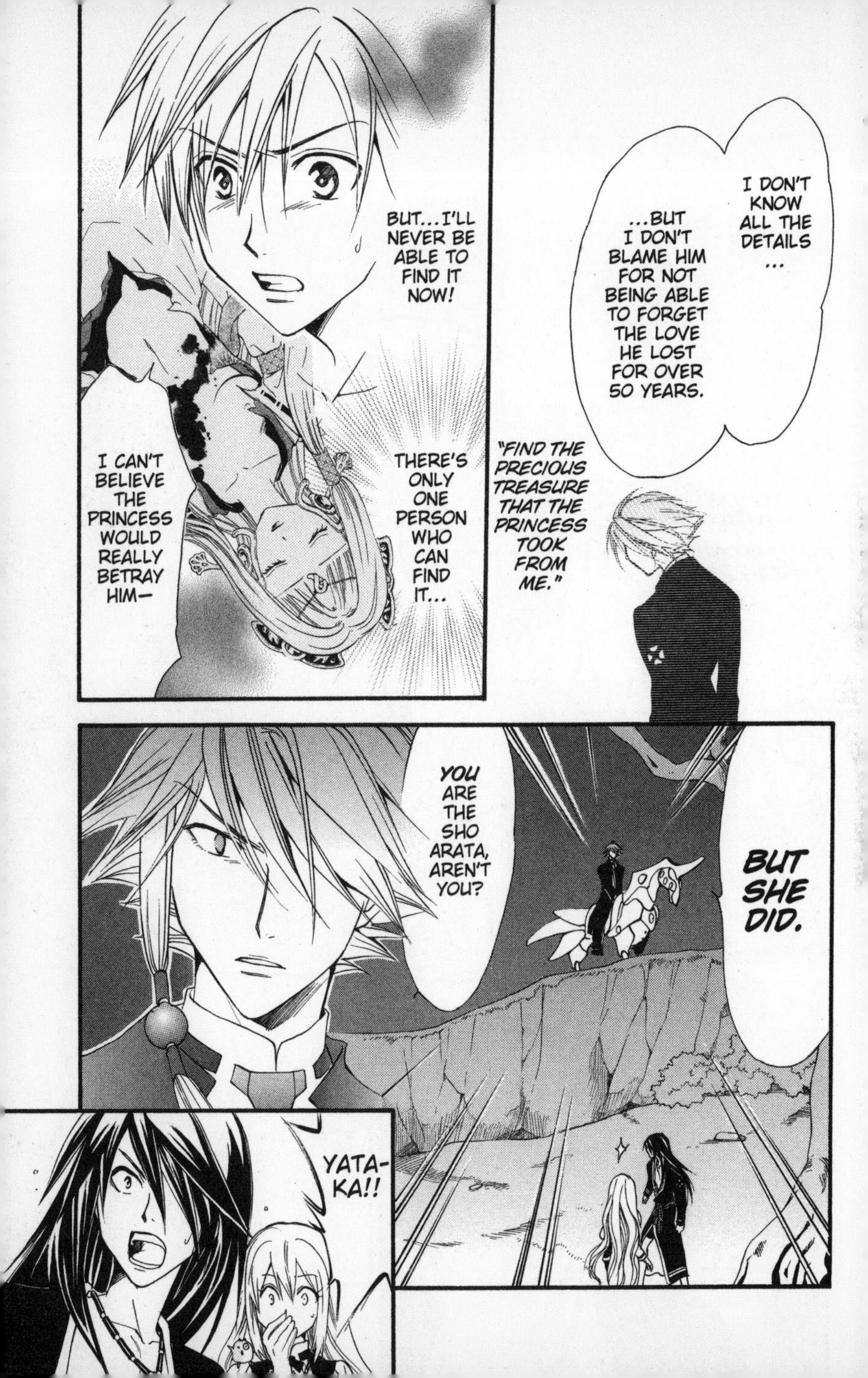
I DON'T KNOW ALL THE DETAILS...
...BUT I DON'T BLAME HIM FOR NOT BEING ABLE TO FORGET THE LOVE HE LOST FOR OVER 50 YEARS.
"FIND THE PRECIOUS TREASURE THAT THE PRINCESS TOOK FROM ME."
BUT...I'LL NEVER BE ABLE TO FIND IT NOW!
THERE'S ONLY ONE PERSON WHO CAN FIND IT...
I CAN'T BELIEVE THE PRINCESS WOULD REALLY BETRAY HIM—
BUT SHE DID.
YOU ARE THE SHO ARATA, AREN'T YOU?
YATA-KA!!

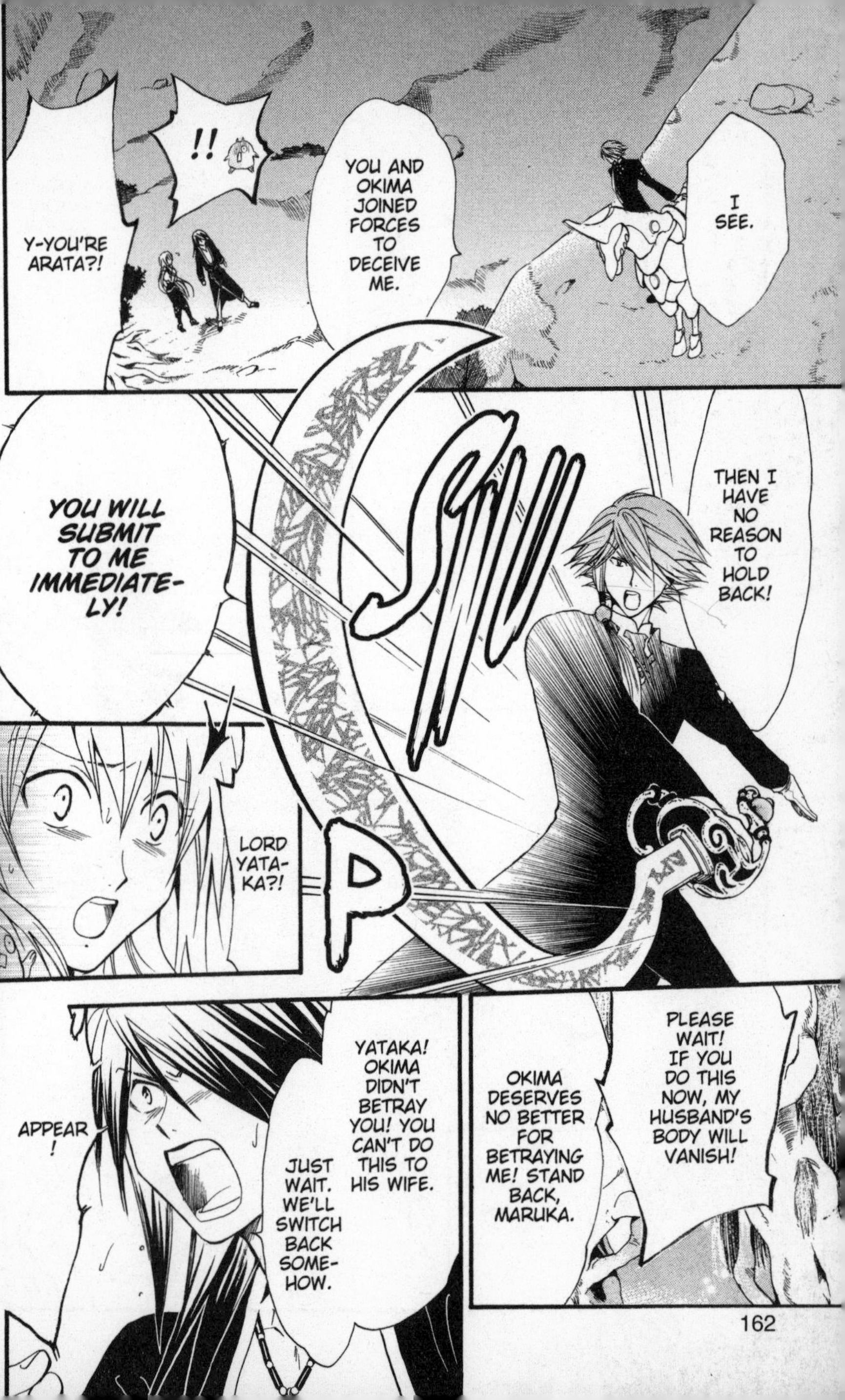
I SEE.
YOU AND OKIMA JOINED FORCES TO DECEIVE ME.
!!
Y-YOU'RE ARATA?!
THEN I HAVE NO REASON TO HOLD BACK!
YOU WILL SUBMIT TO ME IMMEDIATE-LY!
LORD YATAKA?!
PLEASE WAIT! IF YOU DO THIS NOW, MY HUSBAND'S BODY WILL VANISH!
OKIMA DESERVES NO BETTER FOR BETRAYING ME! STAND BACK, MARUKA.
YATAKA! OKIMA DIDN'T BETRAY YOU! YOU CAN'T DO THIS TO HIS WIFE.
JUST WAIT. WE'LL SWITCH BACK SOMEHOW.
APPEAR!

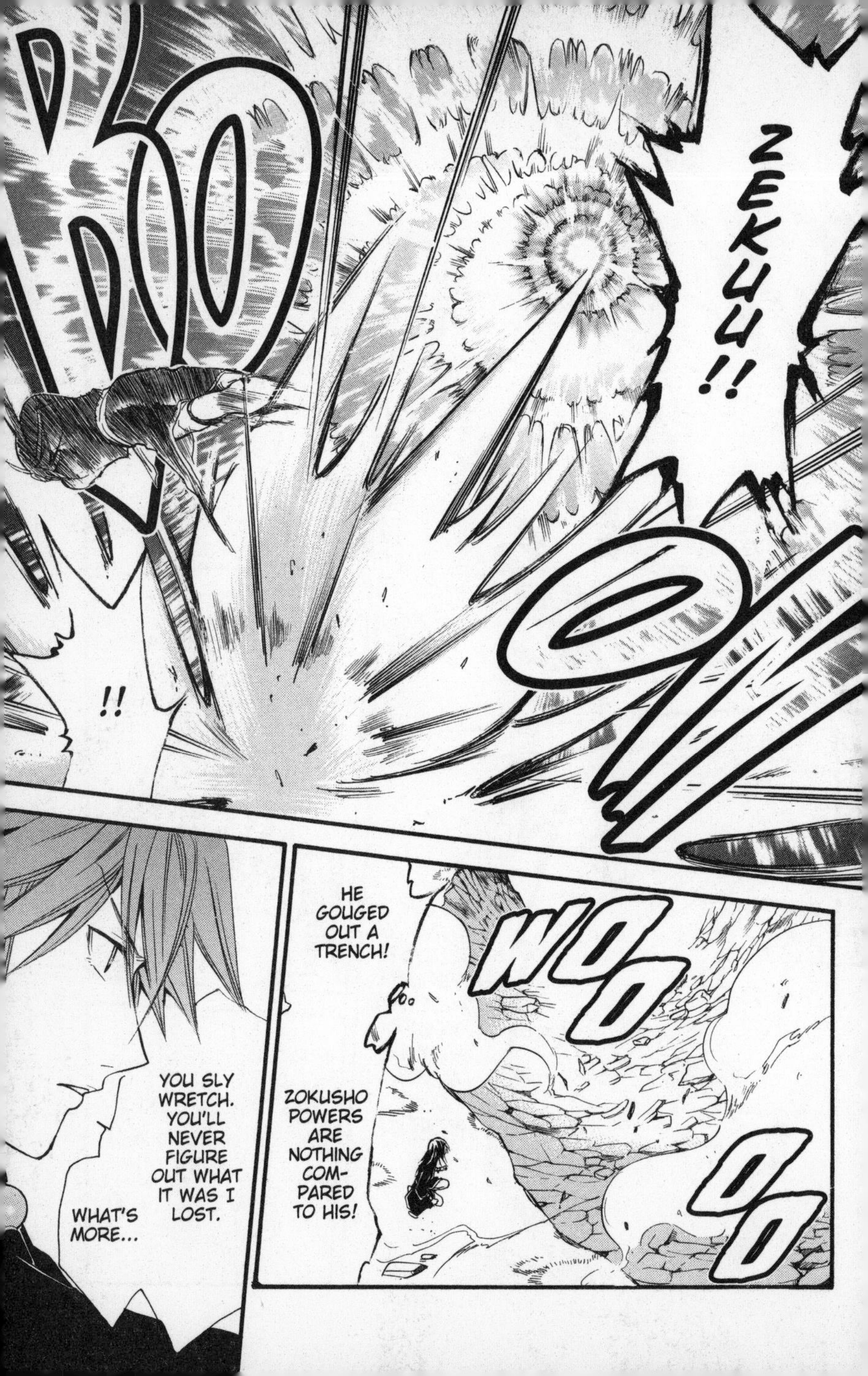
ZEKUUU!!
!!
HE GOUGED OUT A TRENCH!
ZOKUSHO POWERS ARE NOTHING COM-PARED TO HIS!
YOU SLY WRETCH. YOU'LL NEVER FIGURE OUT WHAT IT WAS I LOST.
WHAT'S MORE...

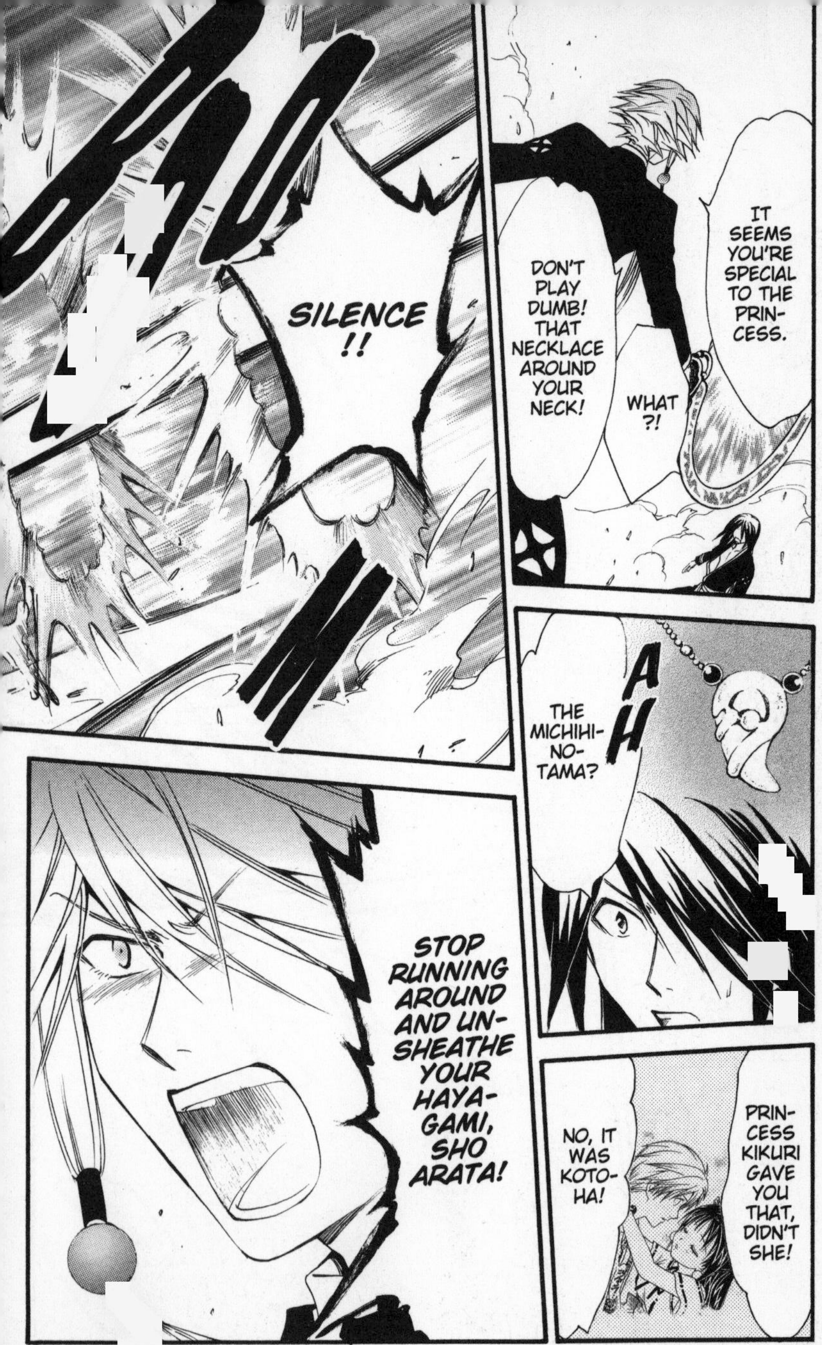
IT SEEMS YOU'RE SPECIAL TO THE PRIN-CESS.
WHAT?!
DON'T PLAY DUMB! THAT NECKLACE AROUND YOUR NECK!
AH
THE MICHIHI-NO-TAMA?
PRIN-CESS KIKURI GAVE YOU THAT, DIDN'T SHE!
NO, IT WAS KOTO-HA!
SILENCE!!
STOP RUNNING AROUND AND UN-SHEATHE YOUR HAYA-GAMI, SHO ARATA!

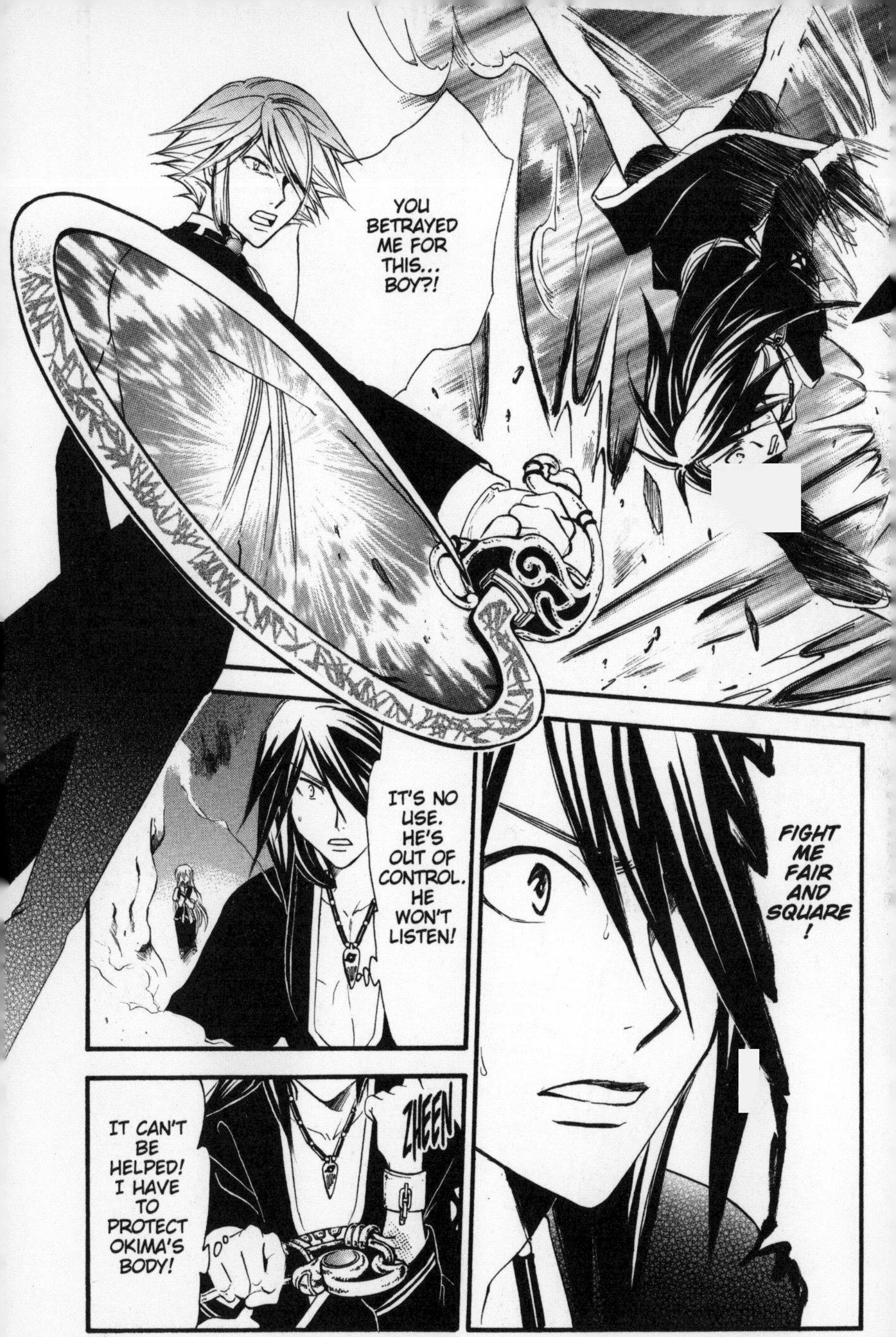
YOU BETRAYED ME FOR THIS... BOY?!
FIGHT ME FAIR AND SQUARE!
IT'S NO USE. HE'S OUT OF CONTROL. HE WON'T LISTEN!
ZHEEN
IT CAN'T BE HELPED! I HAVE TO PROTECT OKIMA'S BODY!

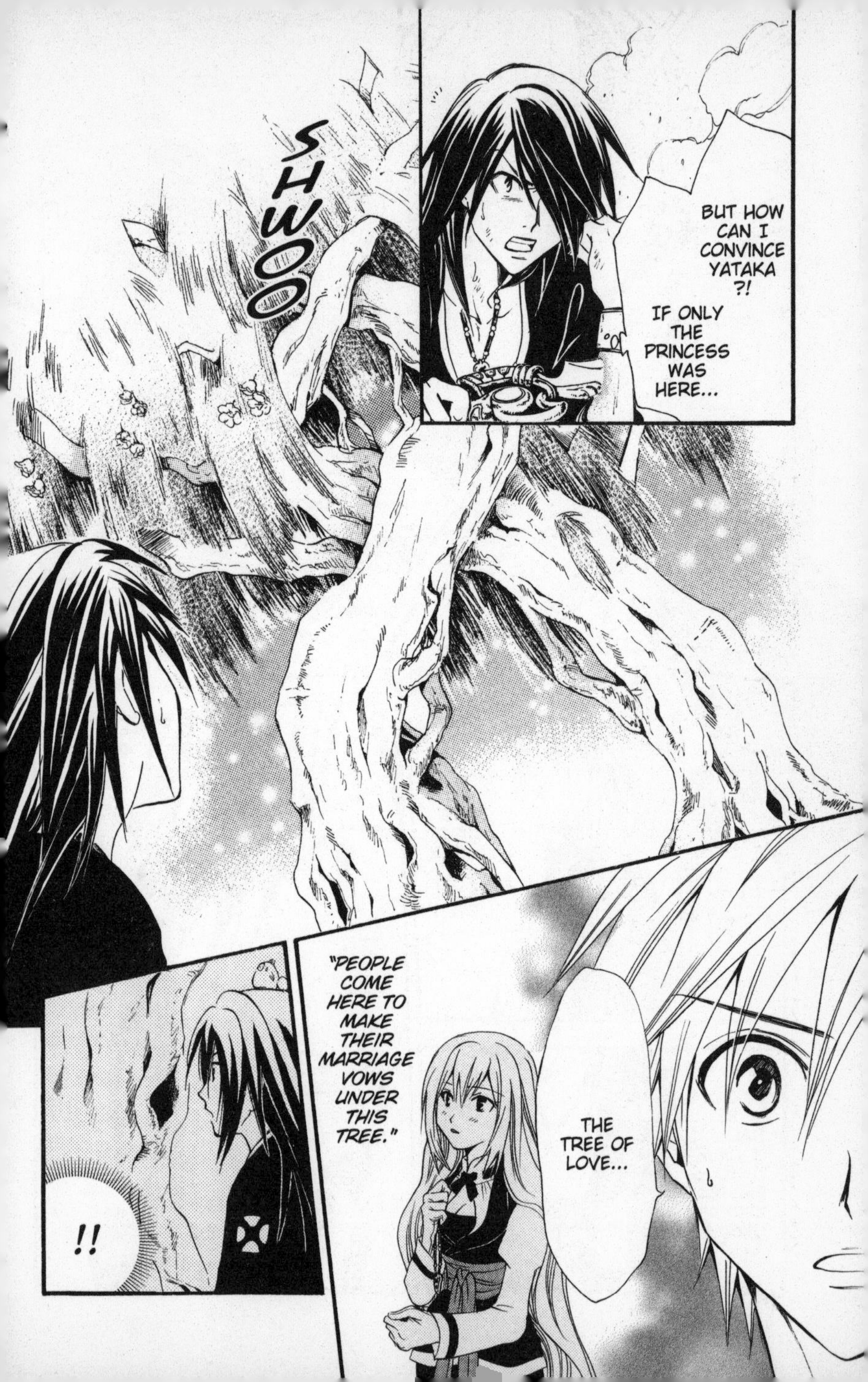
BUT HOW CAN I CONVINCE YATAKA ?!
IF ONLY THE PRINCESS WAS HERE...
SHWOO
THE TREE OF LOVE...
"PEOPLE COME HERE TO MAKE THEIR MARRIAGE VOWS UNDER THIS TREE."
!!

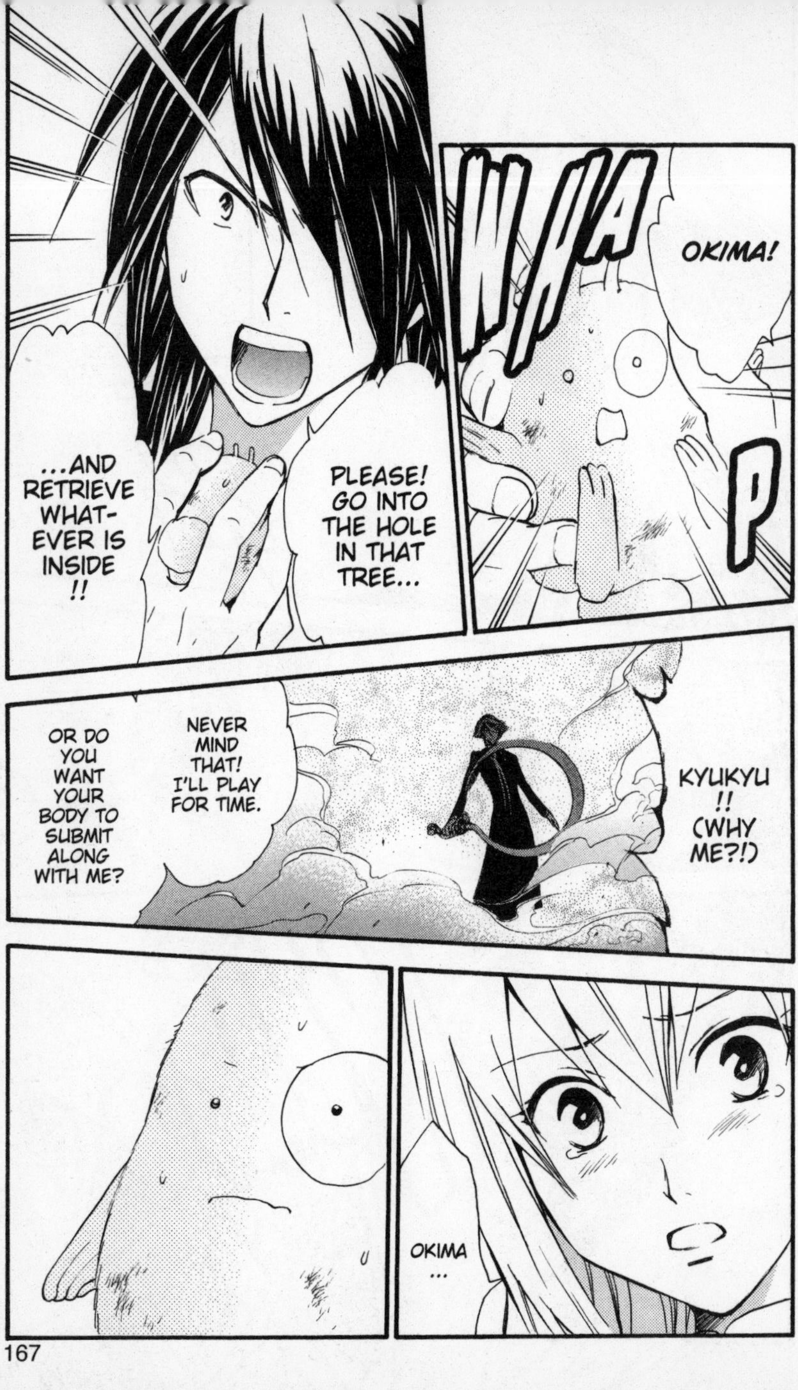
WHAP
OKIMA!
PLEASE! GO INTO THE HOLE IN THAT TREE...
...AND RETRIEVE WHAT-EVER IS INSIDE!!
KYUKYU!! (WHY ME?!)
NEVER MIND THAT! I'LL PLAY FOR TIME.
OR DO YOU WANT YOUR BODY TO SUBMIT ALONG WITH ME?
OKIMA...

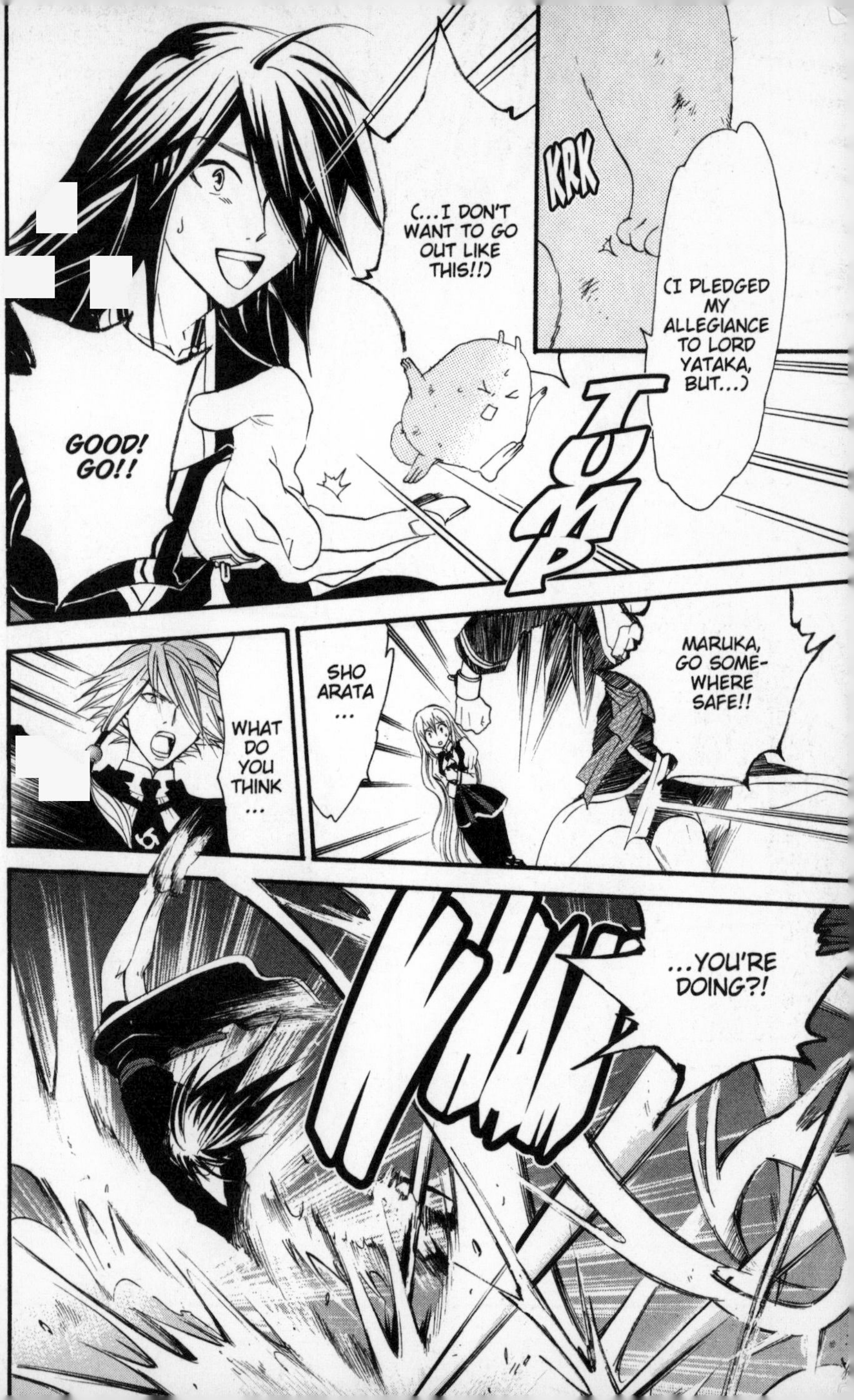
KRK
(I PLEDGED MY ALLEGIANCE TO LORD YATAKA, BUT...)
(...I DON'T WANT TO GO OUT LIKE THIS!!)
JUMP
GOOD! GO!!
MARUKA, GO SOME-WHERE SAFE!!
SHO ARATA ...
WHAT DO YOU THINK ...
...YOU'RE DOING?!

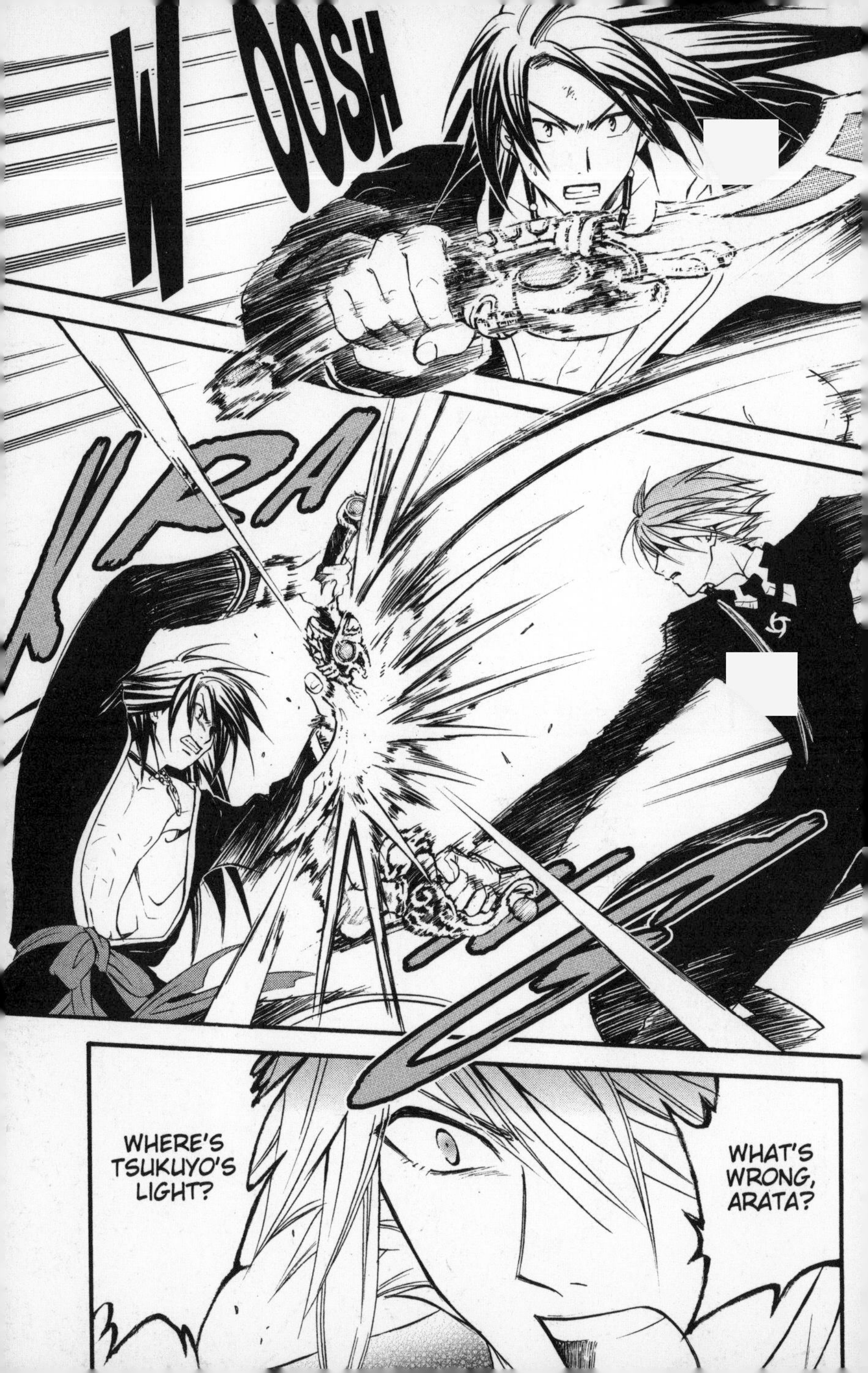
W OOSH
WHAT'S WRONG, ARATA?
WHERE'S TSUKUYO'S LIGHT?

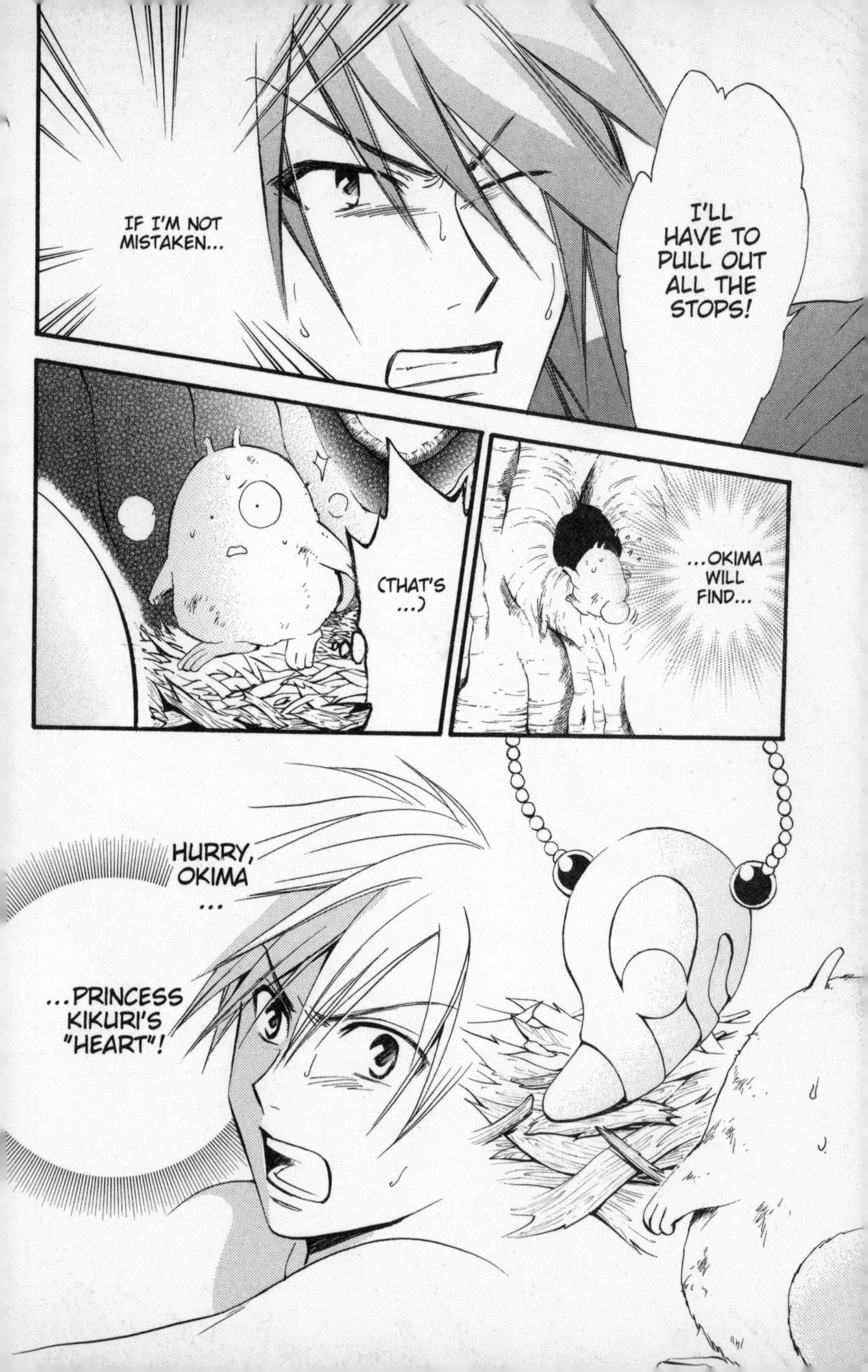
I'LL HAVE TO PULL OUT ALL THE STOPS!
IF I'M NOT MISTAKEN...
...OKIMA WILL FIND...
(THAT'S ...)
HURRY, OKIMA ...
...PRINCESS KIKURI'S "HEART"!

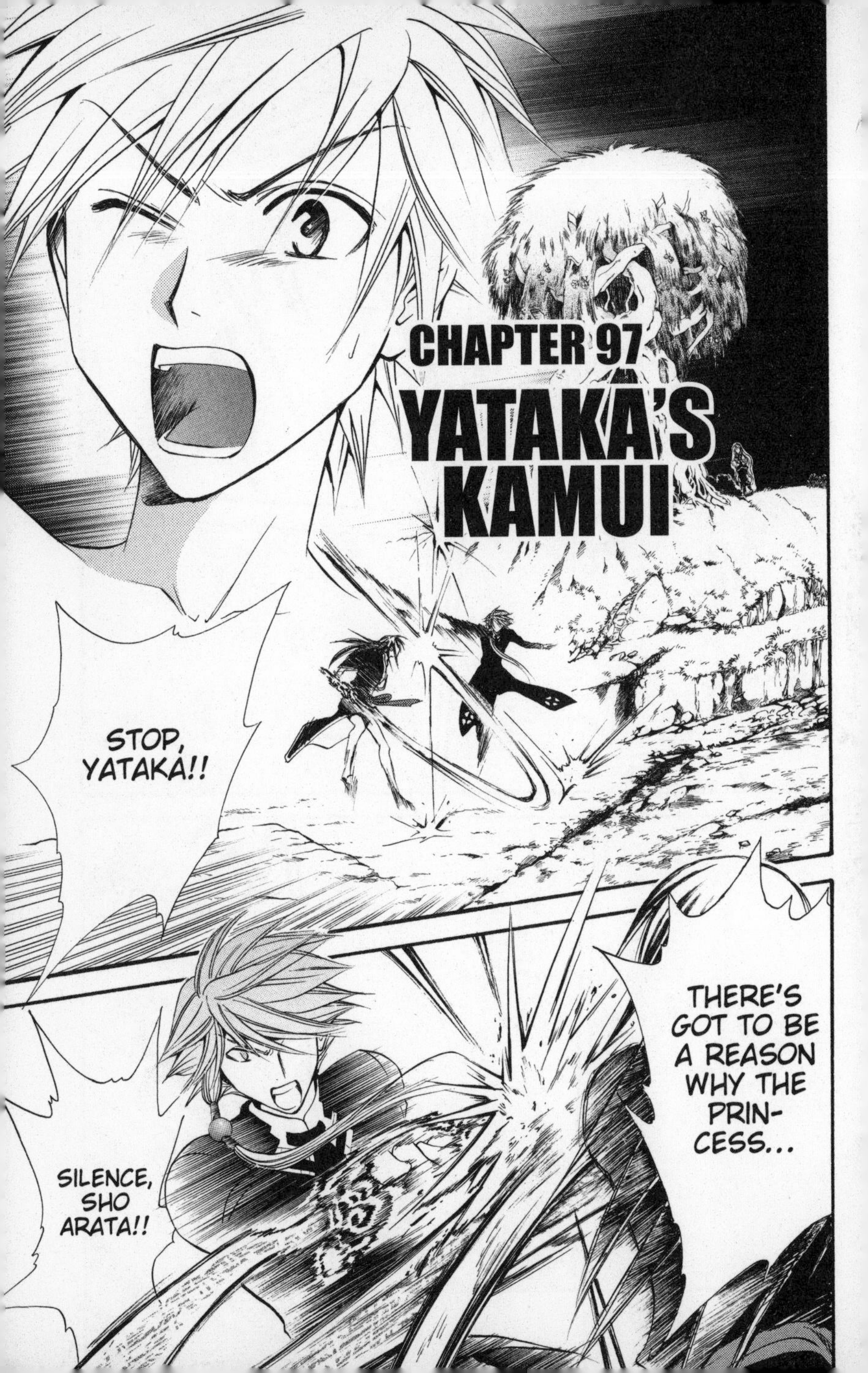
CHAPTER 97
YATAKA'S KAMUI
STOP, YATAKA!!
THERE'S GOT TO BE A REASON WHY THE PRIN-CESS...
SILENCE, SHO ARATA!!

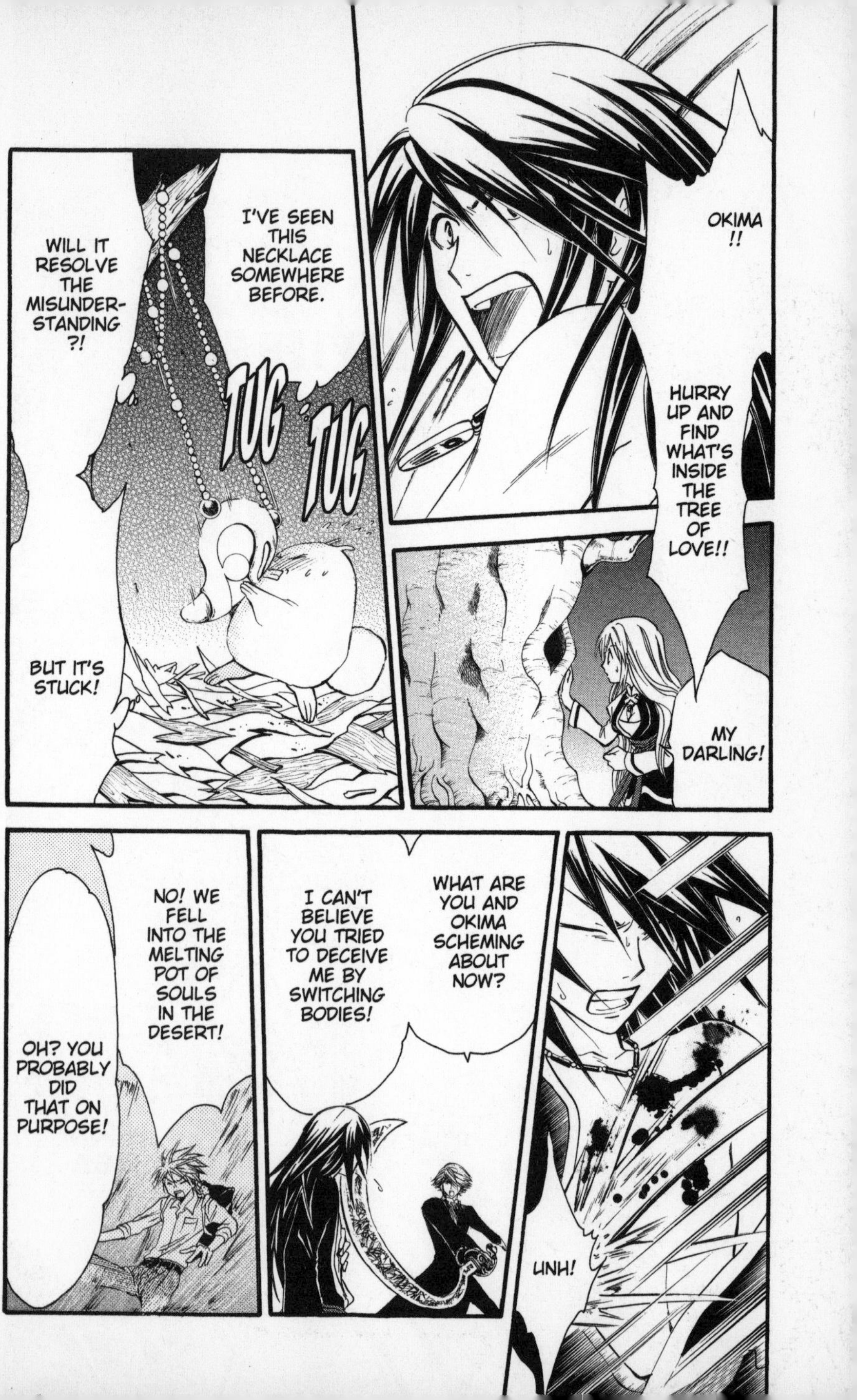
OKIMA!!
HURRY UP AND FIND WHAT'S INSIDE THE TREE OF LOVE!!
MY DARLING!
I'VE SEEN THIS NECKLACE SOMEWHERE BEFORE.
WILL IT RESOLVE THE MISUNDERSTANDING?!
TUG TUG
BUT IT'S STUCK!
UNH!
WHAT ARE YOU AND OKIMA SCHEMING ABOUT NOW?
I CAN'T BELIEVE YOU TRIED TO DECEIVE ME BY SWITCHING BODIES!
NO! WE FELL INTO THE MELTING POT OF SOULS IN THE DESERT!
OH? YOU PROBABLY DID THAT ON PURPOSE!

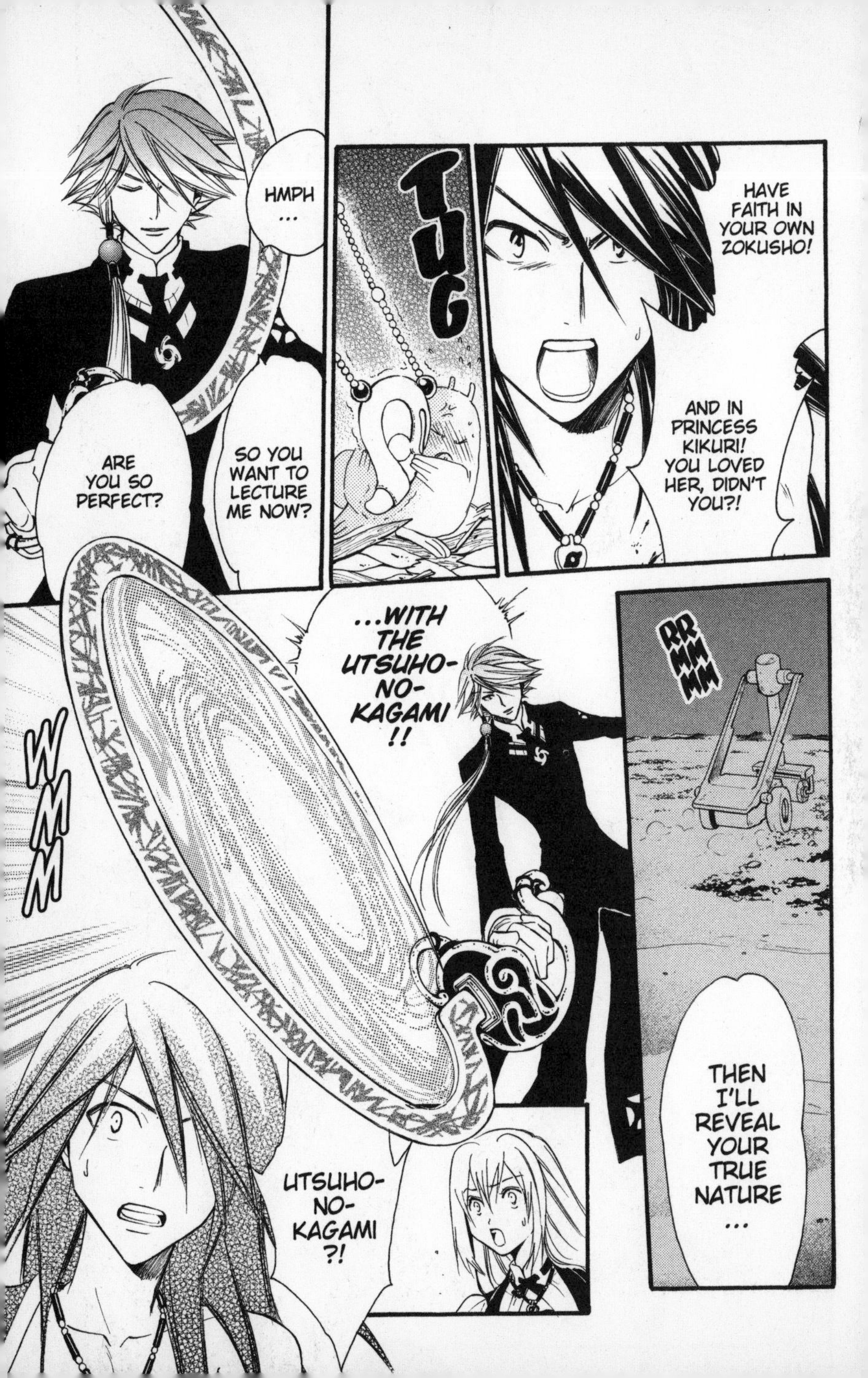
HAVE FAITH IN YOUR OWN ZOKUSHO!
AND IN PRINCESS KIKURI! YOU LOVED HER, DIDN'T YOU?!
TUG
HMPH ...
SO YOU WANT TO LECTURE ME NOW?
ARE YOU SO PERFECT?
RRMMMMMM
THEN I'LL REVEAL YOUR TRUE NATURE ...
...WITH THE UTSUHO-NO-KAGAMI!!
WMMM
UTSUHO-NO-KAGAMI?!

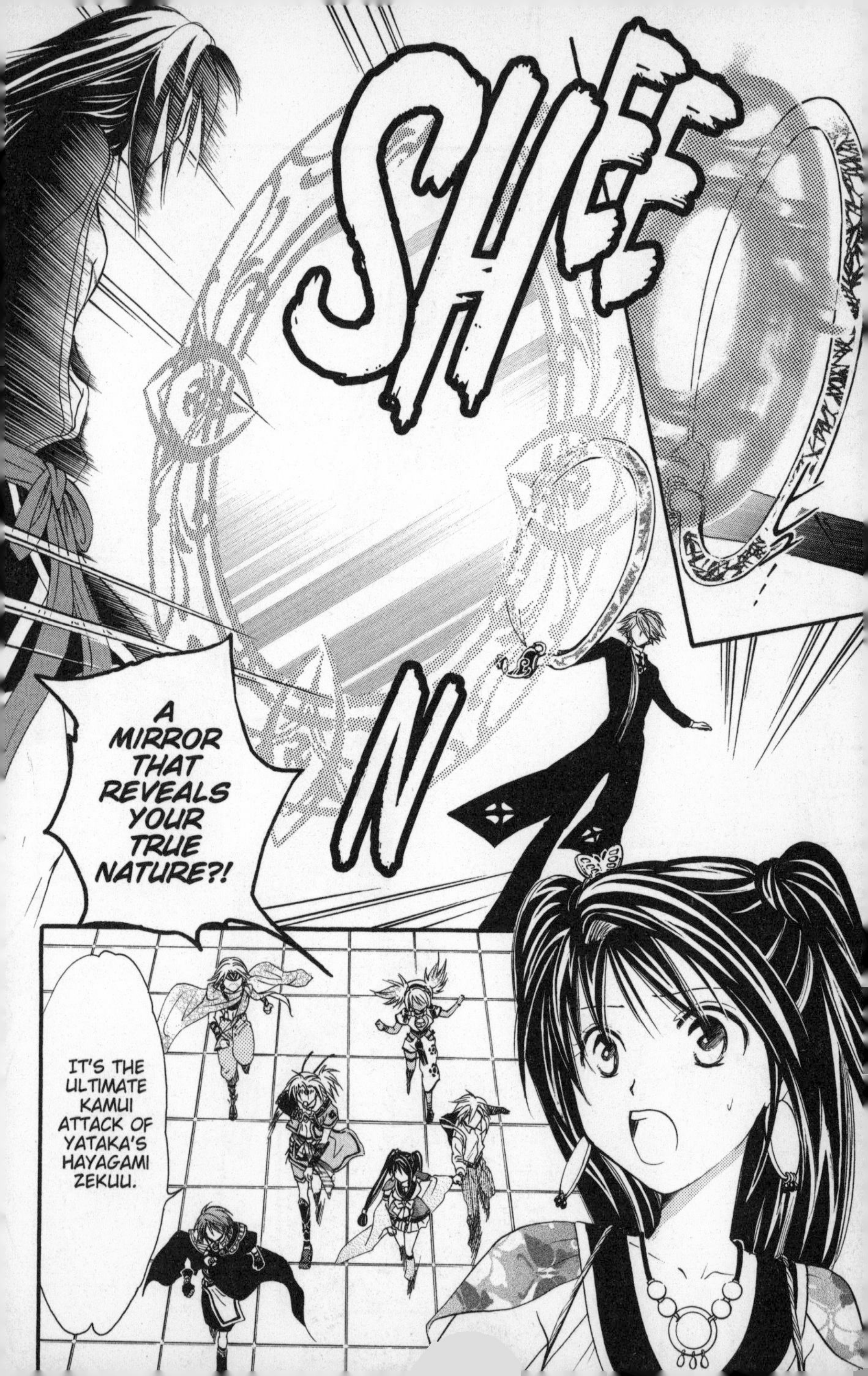
SHEEN
A MIRROR THAT REVEALS YOUR TRUE NATURE?!
IT'S THE ULTIMATE KAMUI ATTACK OF YATAKA'S HAYAGAMI ZEKUU.

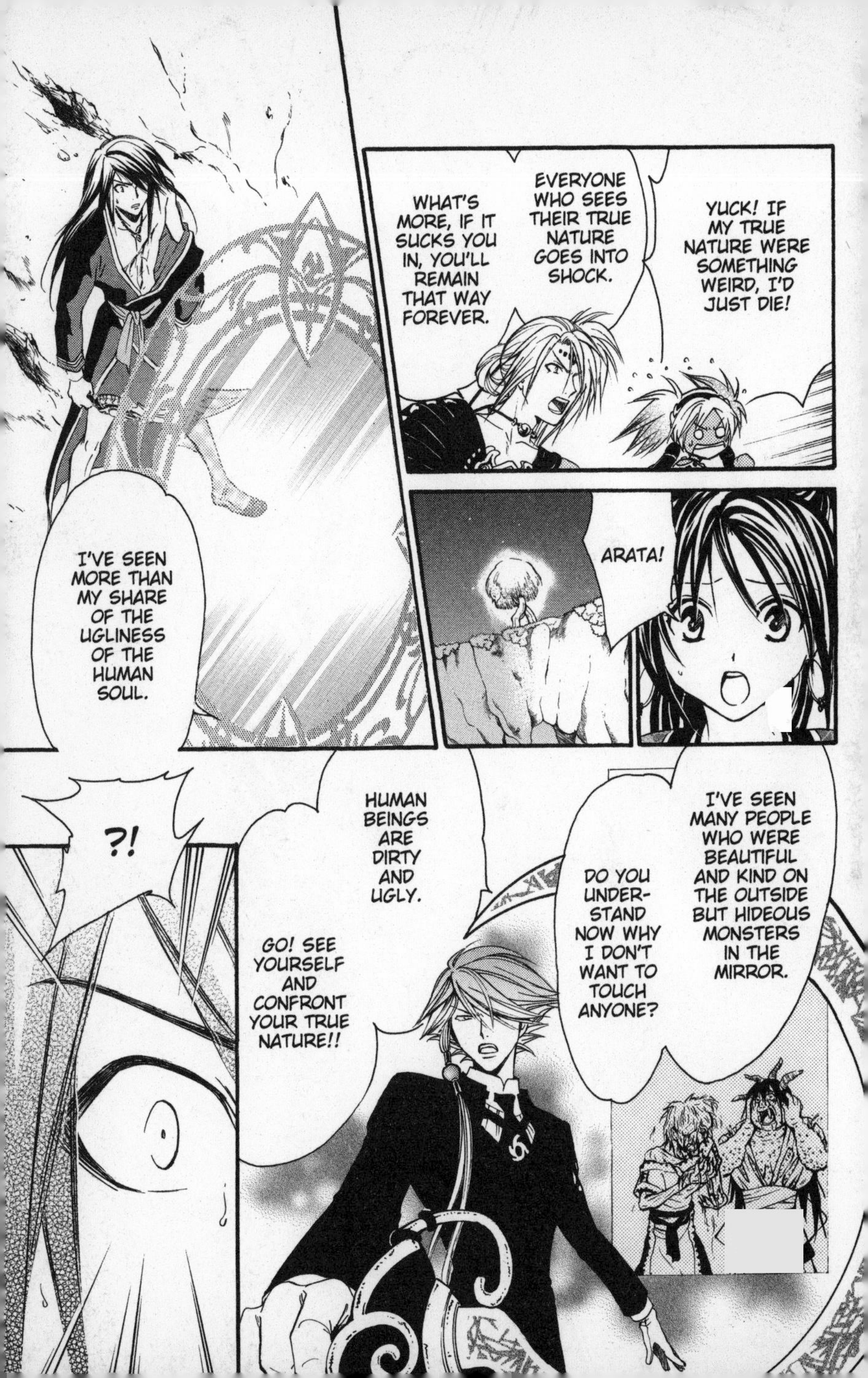

YUCK! IF MY TRUE NATURE WERE SOMETHING WEIRD, I'D JUST DIE!
EVERYONE WHO SEES THEIR TRUE NATURE GOES INTO SHOCK.
WHAT'S MORE, IF IT SUCKS YOU IN, YOU'LL REMAIN THAT WAY FOREVER.
ARATA!
I'VE SEEN MORE THAN MY SHARE OF THE UGLINESS OF THE HUMAN SOUL.
I'VE SEEN MANY PEOPLE WHO WERE BEAUTIFUL AND KIND ON THE OUTSIDE BUT HIDEOUS MONSTERS IN THE MIRROR.
DO YOU UNDER-STAND NOW WHY I DON'T WANT TO TOUCH ANYONE?
HUMAN BEINGS ARE DIRTY AND UGLY.
GO! SEE YOURSELF AND CONFRONT YOUR TRUE NATURE!!
?!

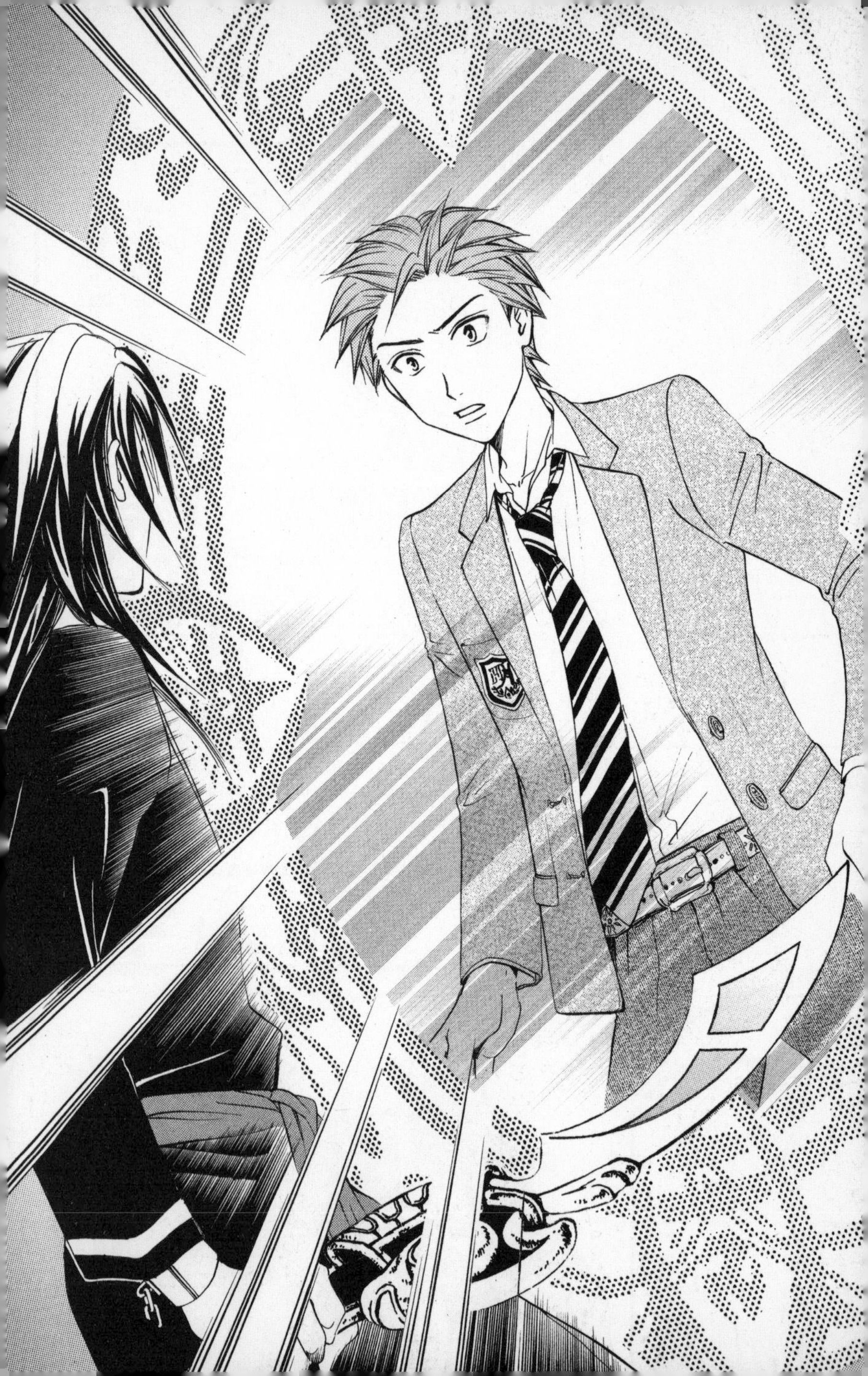

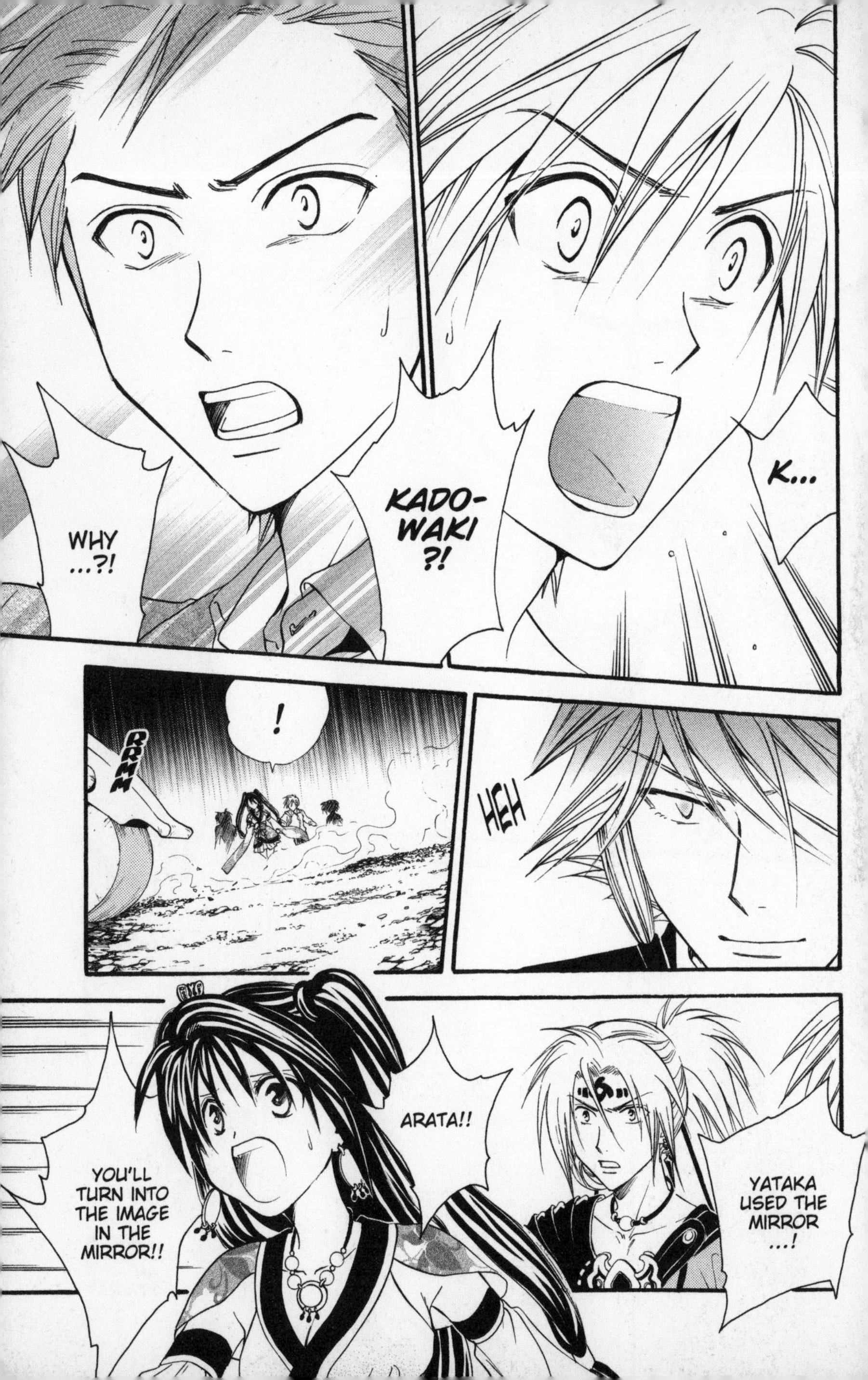
K...
KADO-WAKI?!
WHY ...?!
HEH
!
RRMM
YATAKA USED THE MIRROR ...!
ARATA!!
YOU'LL TURN INTO THE IMAGE IN THE MIRROR!!

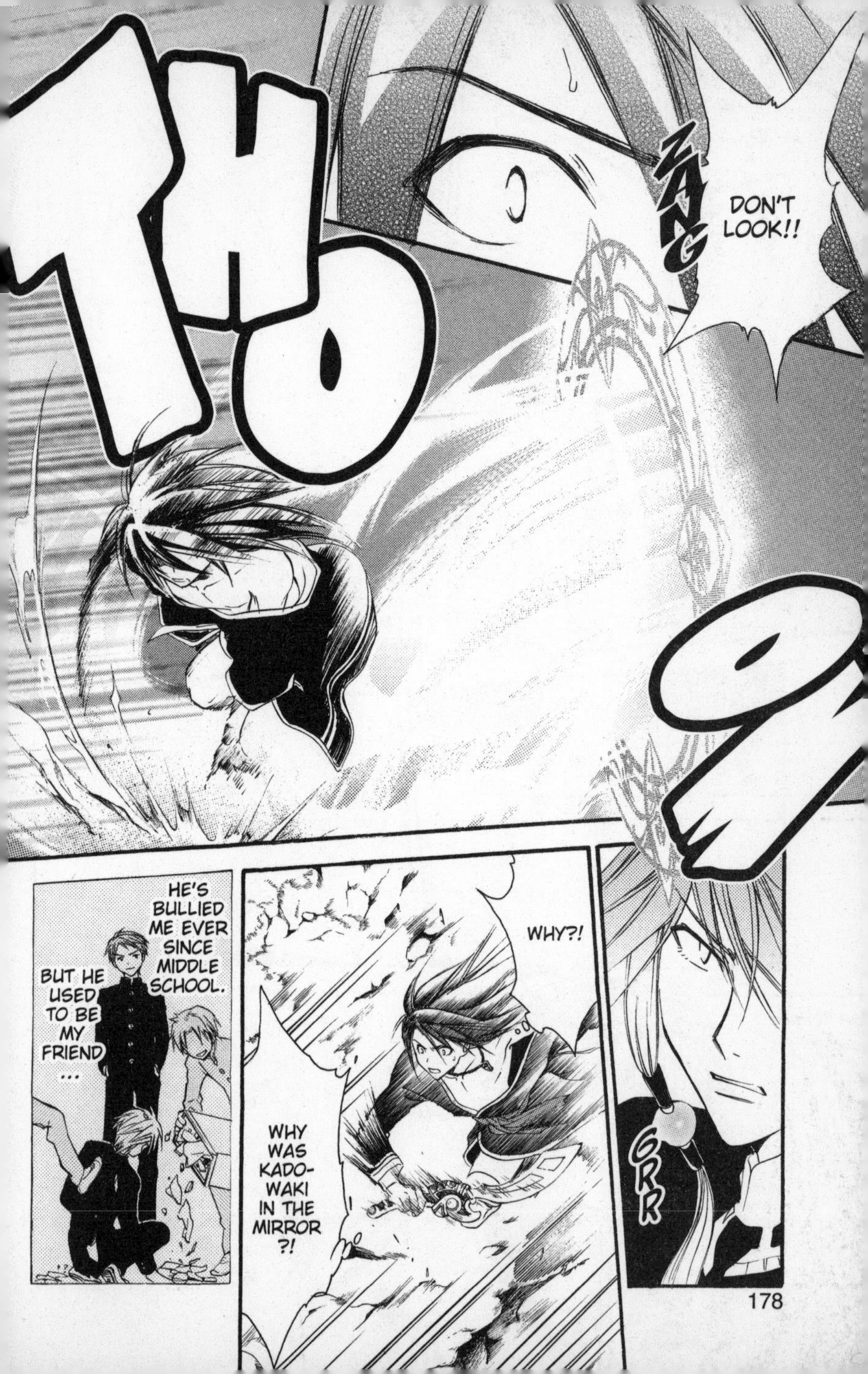
DON'T LOOK!!
ZANG
GRR
WHY?!
WHY WAS KADO-WAKI IN THE MIRROR?!
HE'S BULLIED ME EVER SINCE MIDDLE SCHOOL.
BUT HE USED TO BE MY FRIEND...

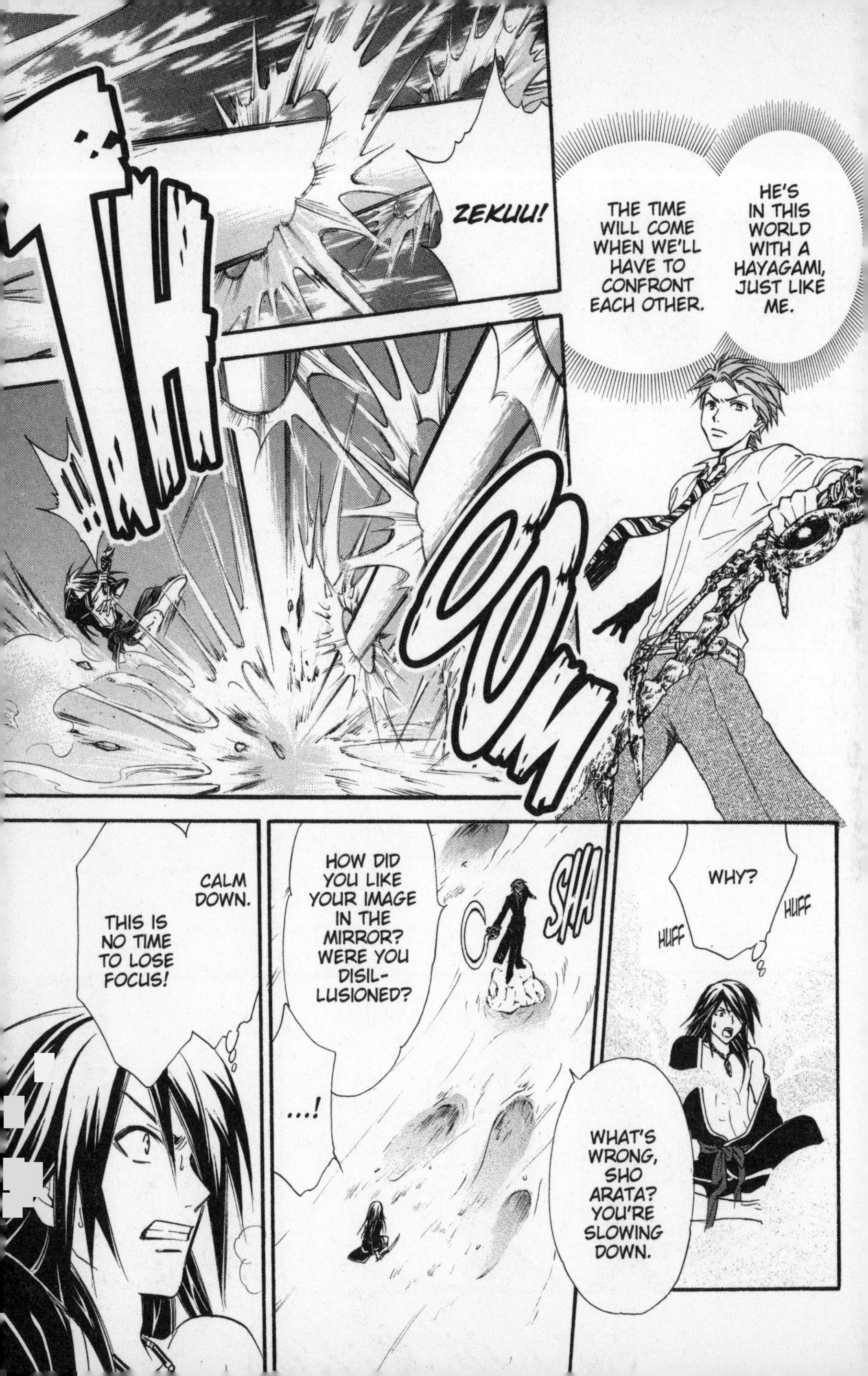
HE'S IN THIS WORLD WITH A HAYAGAMI, JUST LIKE ME.
THE TIME WILL COME WHEN WE'LL HAVE TO CONFRONT EACH OTHER.
ZEKUU!
!!
WHY?
HUFF
HUFF
WHAT'S WRONG, SHO ARATA? YOU'RE SLOWING DOWN.
SHA
HOW DID YOU LIKE YOUR IMAGE IN THE MIRROR? WERE YOU DISIL-LUSIONED?
...!
CALM DOWN.
THIS IS NO TIME TO LOSE FOCUS!

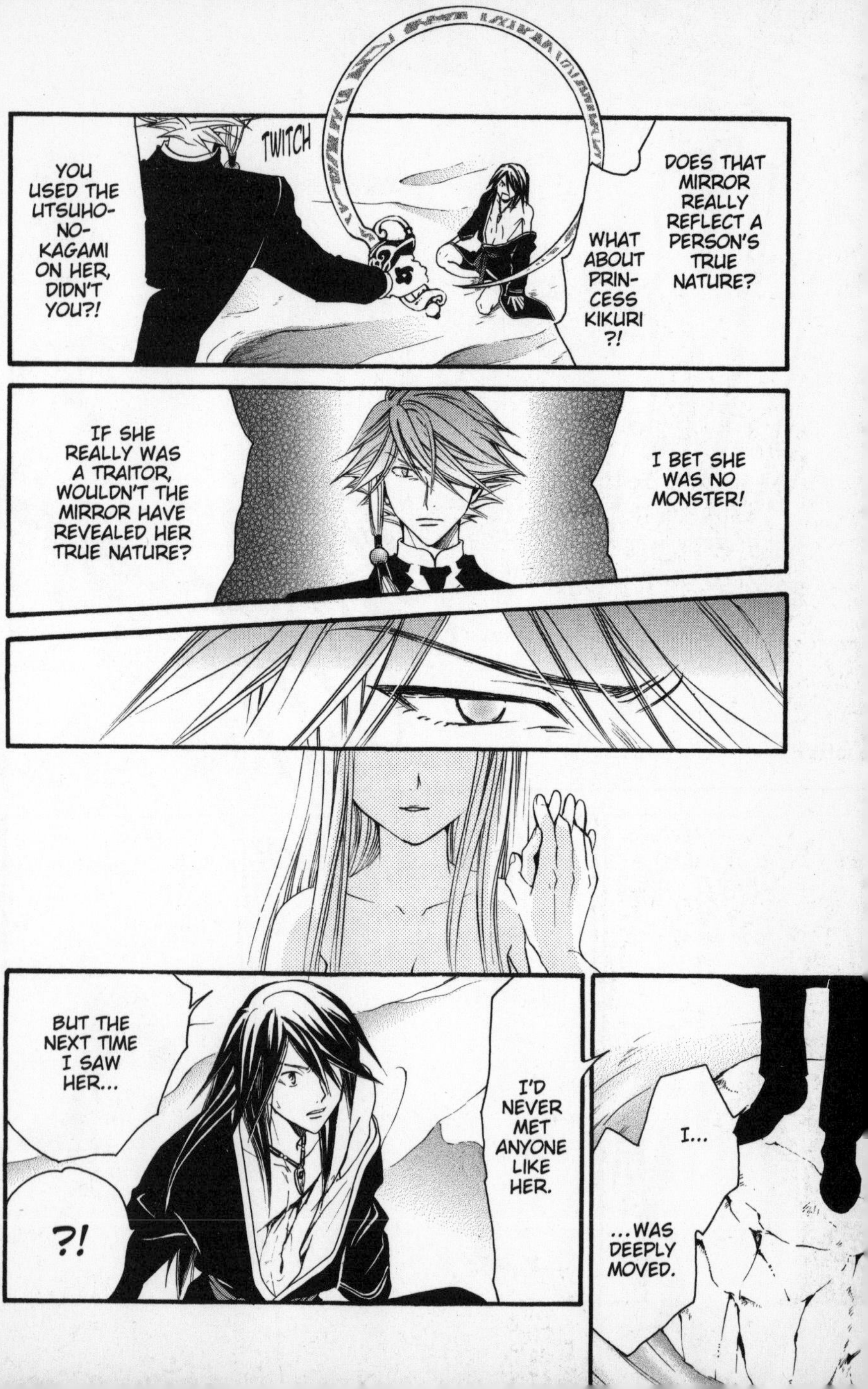
DOES THAT MIRROR REALLY REFLECT A PERSON'S TRUE NATURE?
WHAT ABOUT PRINCESS KIKURI?!
TWITCH
YOU USED THE UTSUHO-NO-KAGAMI ON HER, DIDN'T YOU?!
I BET SHE WAS NO MONSTER!
IF SHE REALLY WAS A TRAITOR, WOULDN'T THE MIRROR HAVE REVEALED HER TRUE NATURE?
I...
...WAS DEEPLY MOVED.
I'D NEVER MET ANYONE LIKE HER.
BUT THE NEXT TIME I SAW HER...
?!

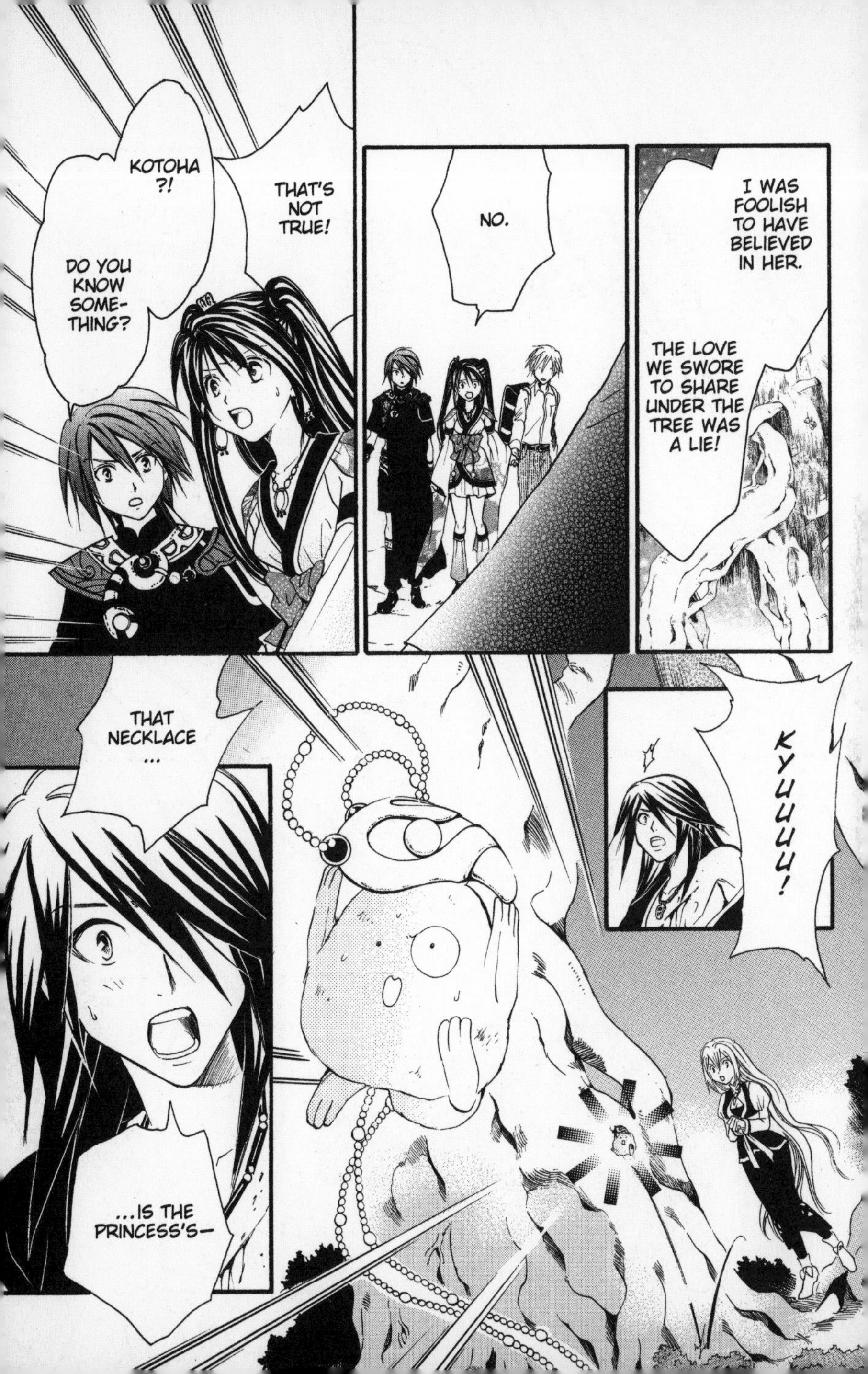
I WAS FOOLISH TO HAVE BELIEVED IN HER.
THE LOVE WE SWORE TO SHARE UNDER THE TREE WAS A LIE!
NO.
THAT'S NOT TRUE!
KOTOHA ?!
DO YOU KNOW SOME-THING?
KYUUUU!
THAT NECKLACE ...
...IS THE PRINCESS'S—

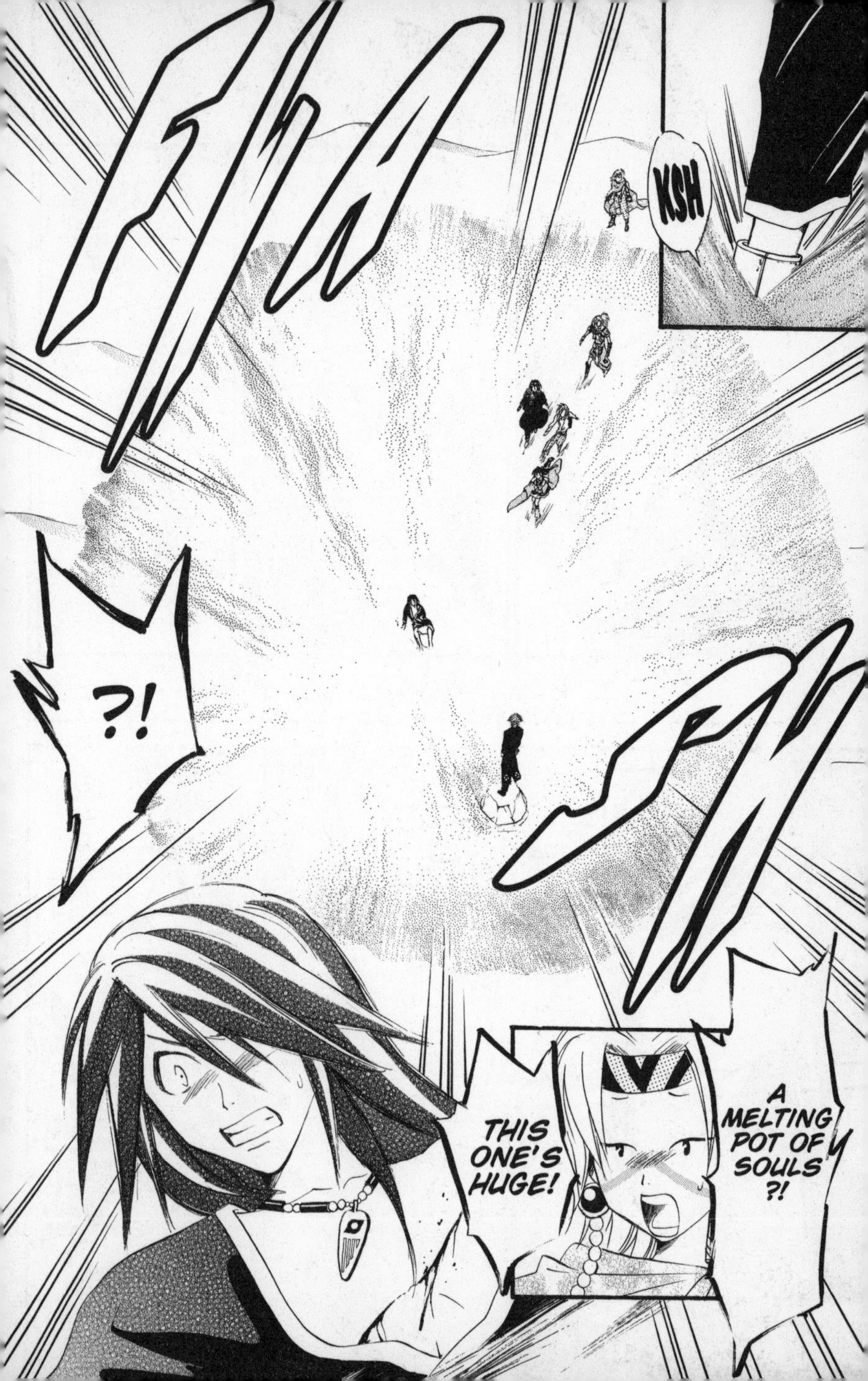
KSH
?!
A MELTING POT OF SOULS?!
THIS ONE'S HUGE!

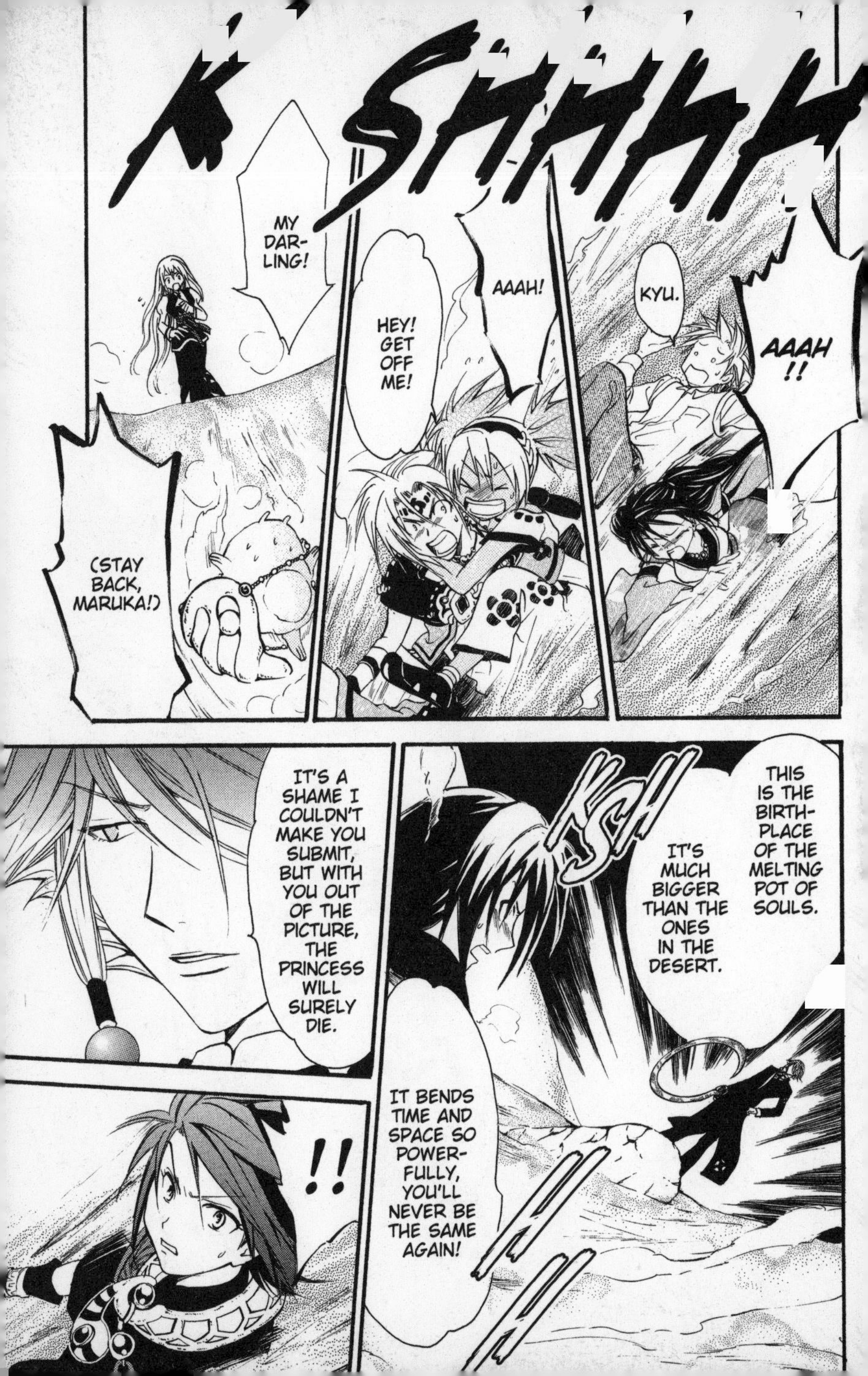
K SHHHH
KYU.
AAAH!!
AAAH!
HEY! GET OFF ME!
MY DARLING!
(STAY BACK, MARUKA!)
THIS IS THE BIRTHPLACE OF THE MELTING POT OF SOULS.
KSH
IT'S MUCH BIGGER THAN THE ONES IN THE DESERT.
IT BENDS TIME AND SPACE SO POWERFULLY, YOU'LL NEVER BE THE SAME AGAIN!
IT'S A SHAME I COULDN'T MAKE YOU SUBMIT, BUT WITH YOU OUT OF THE PICTURE, THE PRINCESS WILL SURELY DIE.
!!

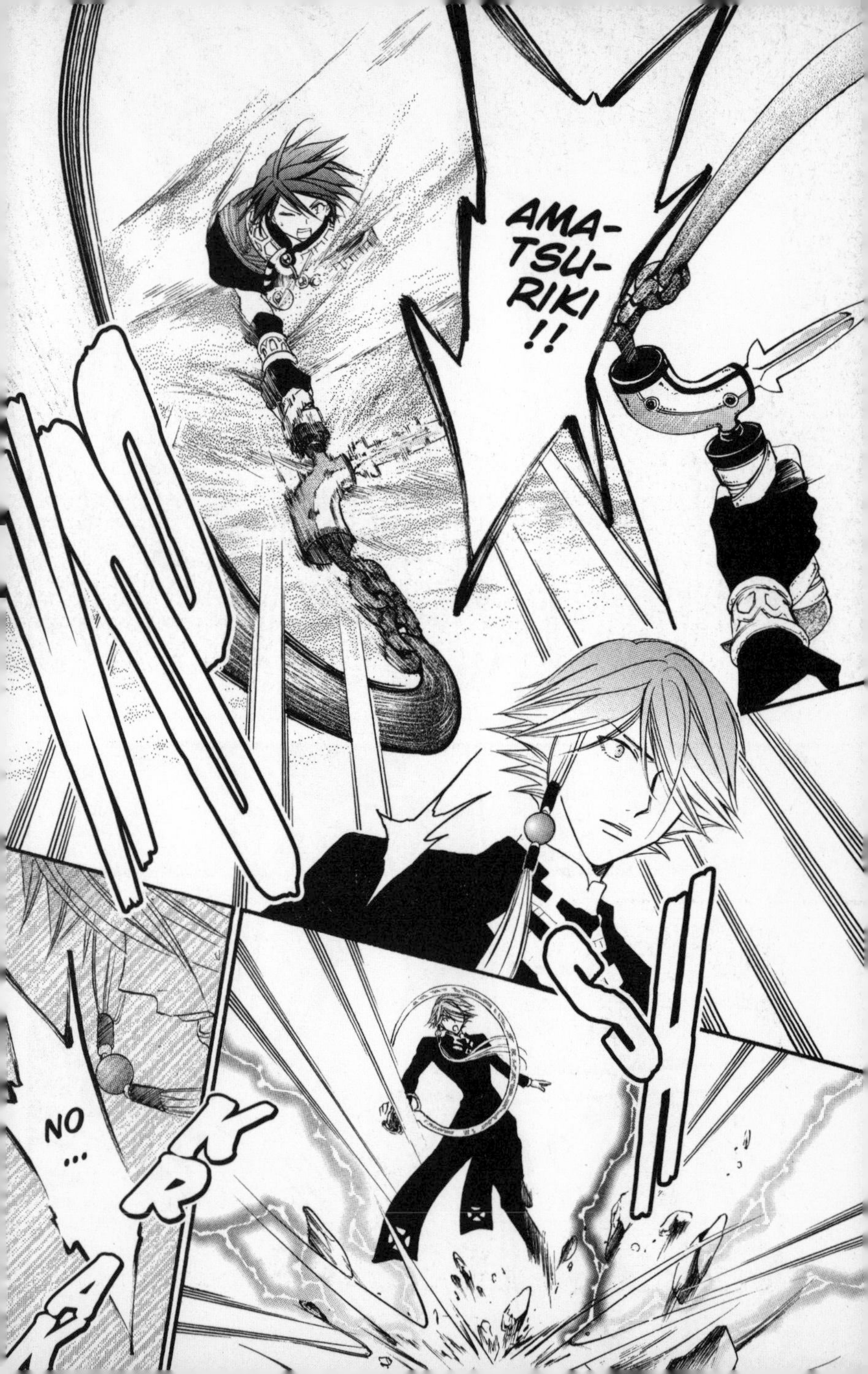
AMA-TSU-RIKI!!
NO ...

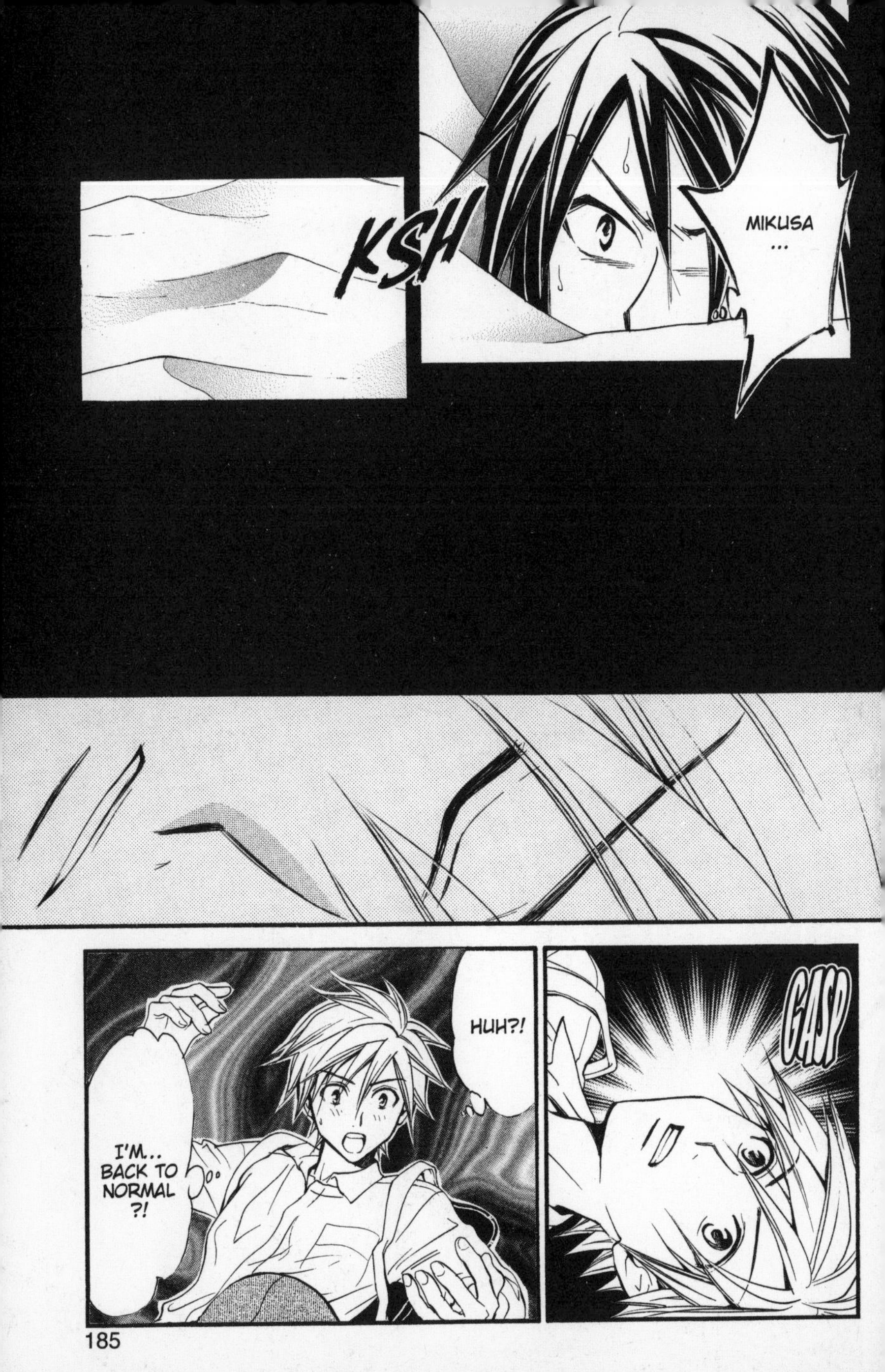
MIKUSA ...
KSH
GASP
HUH?!
I'M... BACK TO NORMAL ?!

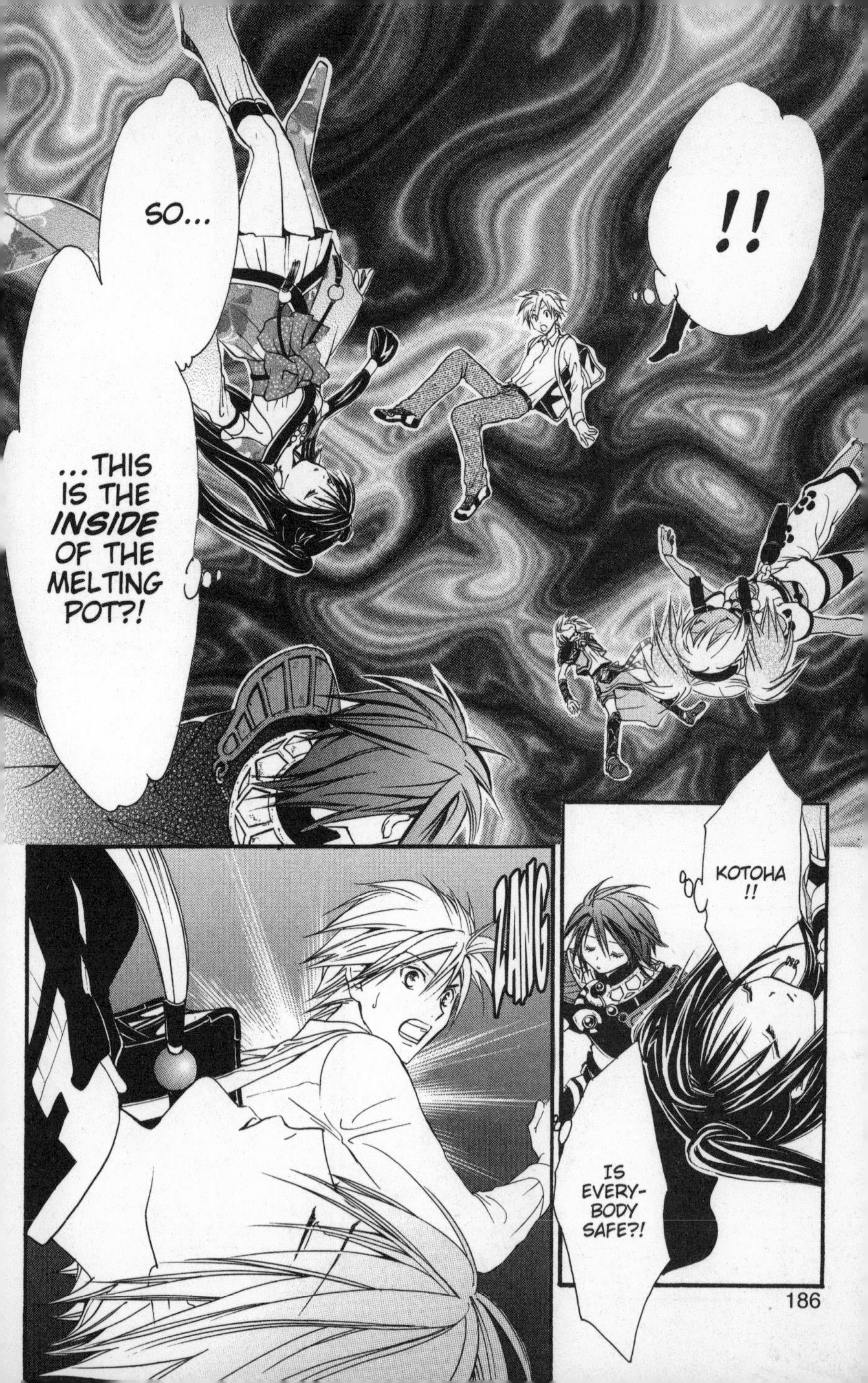
!!
SO...
...THIS IS THE *INSIDE* OF THE MELTING POT?!
KOTOHA !!
IS EVERY-BODY SAFE?!
ZANG

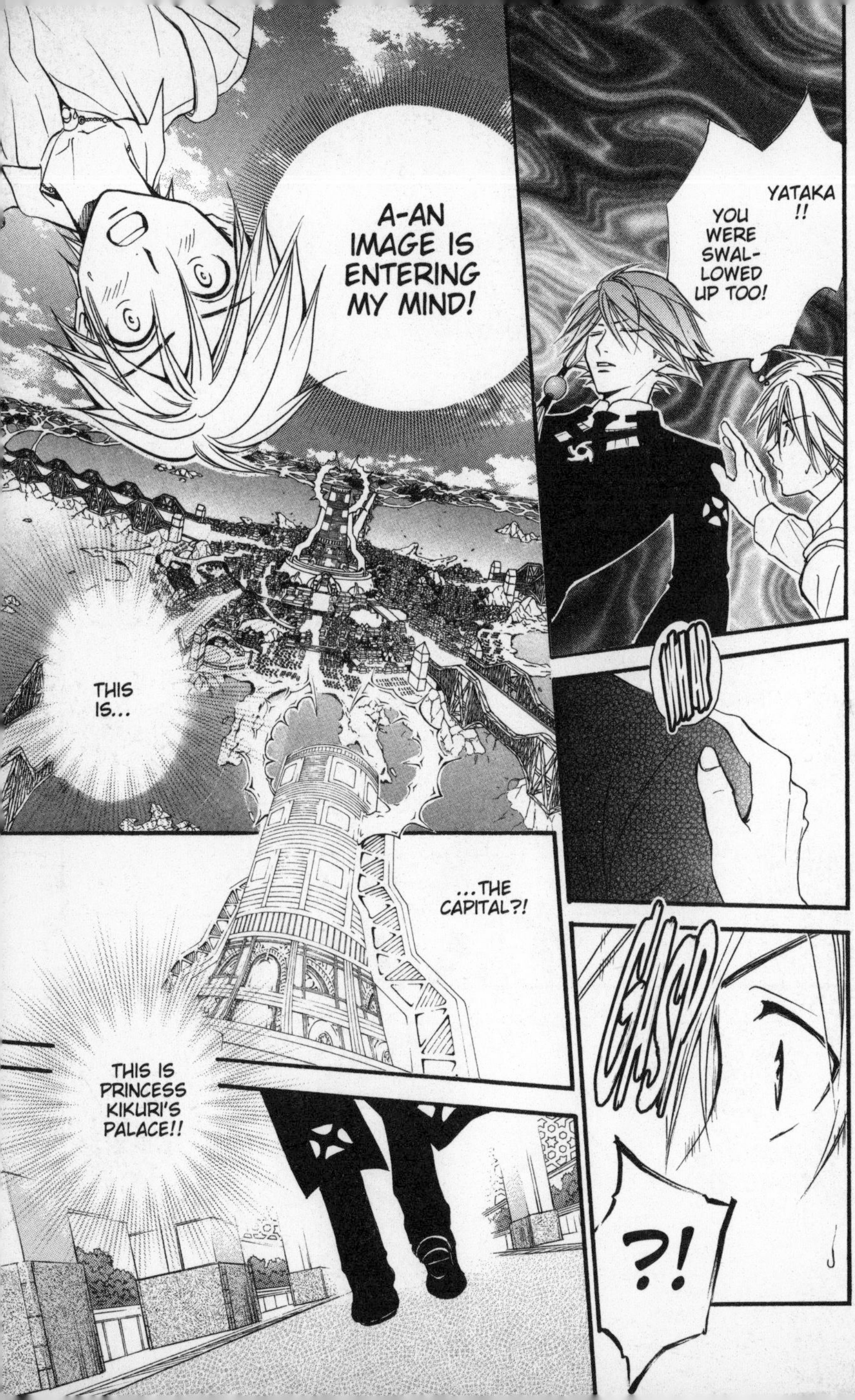
YATAKA !!
YOU WERE SWAL-LOWED UP TOO!
A-AN IMAGE IS ENTERING MY MIND!
THIS IS...
WHAP
...THE CAPITAL?!
GASP
?!
THIS IS PRINCESS KIKURI'S PALACE!!

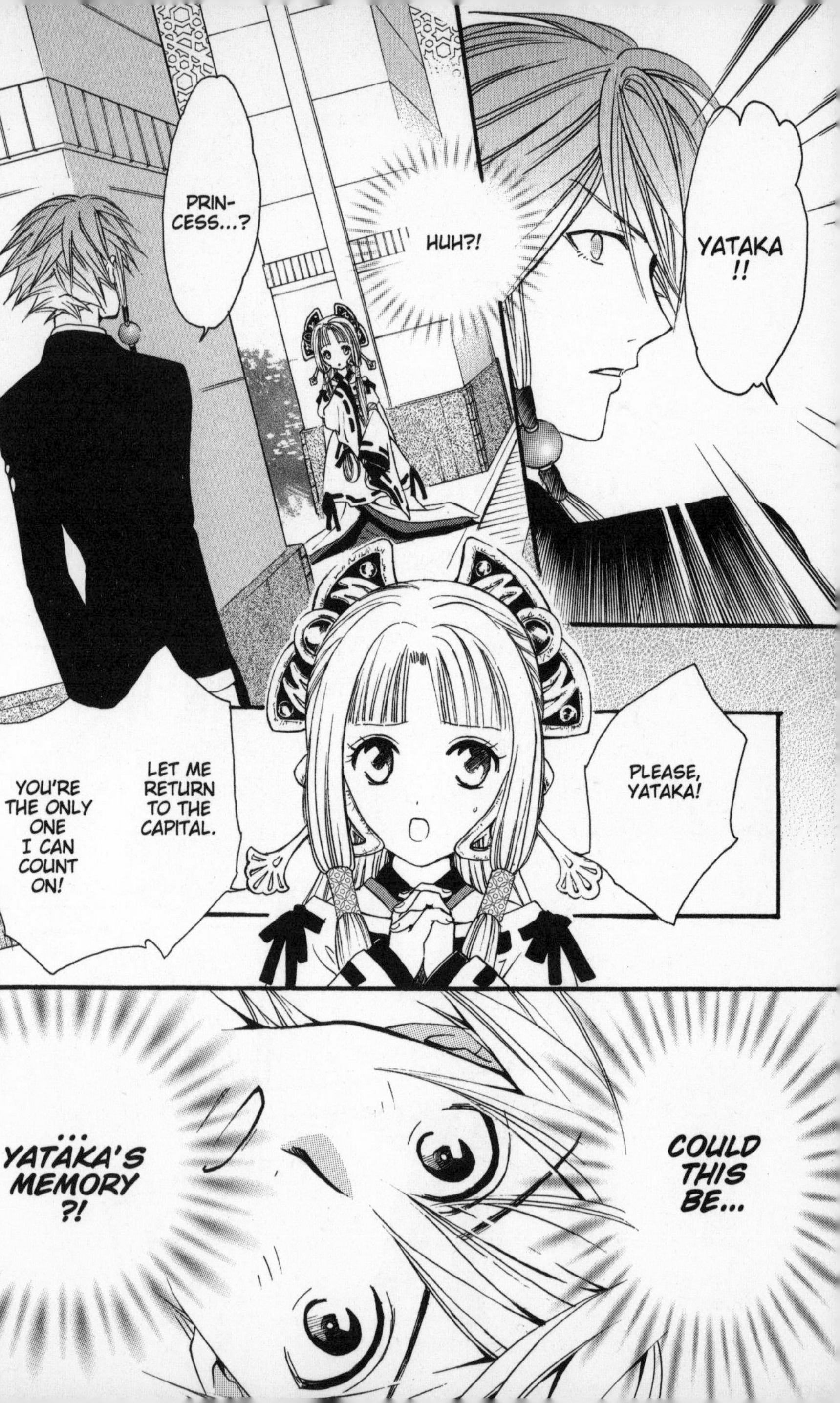
YATAKA !!
HUH?!
PRIN-CESS...?
PLEASE, YATAKA!
LET ME RETURN TO THE CAPITAL.
YOU'RE THE ONLY ONE I CAN COUNT ON!
COULD THIS BE...
...YATAKA'S MEMORY ?!

MIYABI GOT THE SAME NUMBER OF POINTS AS AKACHI IN THE AUTOGRAPHED SHIKISHI CONTEST! SHE WASN'T INCLUDED IN THE SPECIALLY COMMISSIONED WORK THIS TIME. SO MY ASSISTANT DREW THIS SHORT COMIC INSTEAD!!

BONUS ARAKAN INSTITUTE

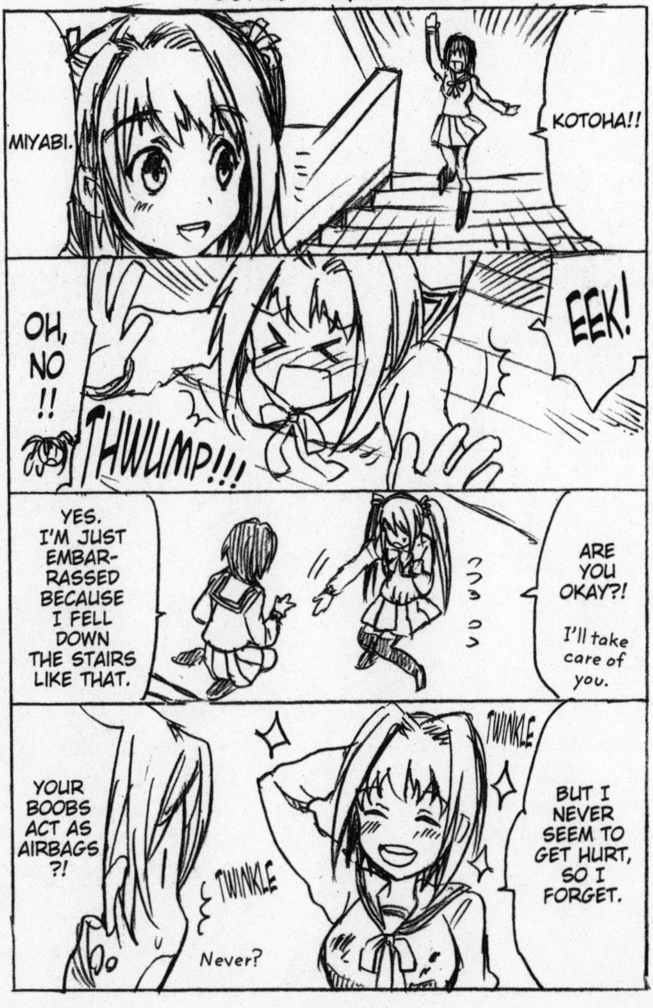
KOTOHA!!
MIYABI.
EEK!
THWUMP!!!
OH, NO!!
ARE YOU OKAY?!
I'll take care of you.
YES. I'M JUST EMBARRASSED BECAUSE I FELL DOWN THE STAIRS LIKE THAT.
TWINKLE
BUT I NEVER SEEM TO GET HURT, SO I FORGET.
TWINKLE
YOUR BOOBS ACT AS AIRBAGS?!
Never?

SEE YOU IN VOLUME 11!!

Thanks to everyone who submitted entries for our autographed shikishi contest in volume 8!

I enjoyed reading your affectionate comments about the various characters!! This time, we have a special consolation prize for those who didn't win—a reprint of a specially commissioned original work featuring the top ten characters! (^o^) This will increase your chances of becoming a winner!! For those of you thinking, "For sure, this time!" send in your entries! This is a one-time specially commissioned work. (←Take note of this!!) A rare commodity! And the reason I am behind in my work, but never mind!! (;▼;) We'll be sure to hold another autographed shikishi drawing soon!!

–Yuu Watase

*Applications for this drawing were accepted March 18–June 30, 2011.

AUTHOR BIO

Born March 5 in Osaka, Yuu Watase debuted in the *Shôjo Comic* manga anthology in 1989. She won the 43rd Shogakukan Manga Award with *Ceres: Celestial Legend*. One of her most famous works is *Fushigi Yûgi*, a series that has inspired the prequel *Fushigi Yûgi: Genbu Kaiden*. In 2008, *Arata: The Legend* started serialization in *Shonen Sunday*.

Arata THE LEGEND

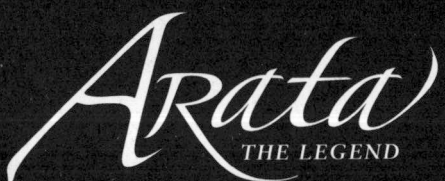

ARATA: THE LEGEND

Volume 10

Shonen Sunday Edition

Story and Art by YUU WATASE

Original Japanese edition "ARATAKANGATARI"
published by SHOGAKUKAN Inc.

English Adaptation: Lance Caselman
Translation: JN Productions
Touch-up Art & Lettering: Rina Mapa
Design: Ronnie Casson
Editor: Amy Yu

Printed in the U.S.A.

Published by VIZ Media, LLC
P.O. Box 77010
San Francisco, CA 94107

10 9 8 7 6 5 4 3 2 1
First printing, June 2012

RATED T FOR TEEN

PARENTAL ADVISORY
ARATA: THE LEGEND is rated T for Teen and is recommended for ages 13 and up. This volume contains fantasy violence.

ratings.viz.com

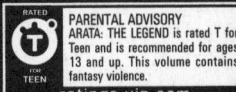

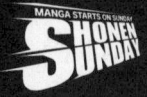

www.viz.com

MANGA STARTS ON SUNDAY

WWW.SHONENSUNDAY.COM

Five Leaves
Complete Series Premium Edition

This beautiful box set features the complete two-volume, twelve-episode DVD set of the acclaimed anime series and features the original Japanese audio with English subtitles, as well as a sturdy slipcase and full-color hardcover art book.

House of Five Leaves Complete Series Premium Edition comes with a hardcover art book (full-color, 30+ pages), featuring character information, episode guides, artwork, behind-the-scenes storyboards, draft designs, concept art, and even a glossary of terms for insight on the culture of feudal Japan.

House of Five Leaves
Complete Series Premium Edition
12 episodes • approx. 274 minutes • color
Bonus Content:
Clean Opening and Ending, Japanese Trailer

For more information, visit
NISAmerica.com

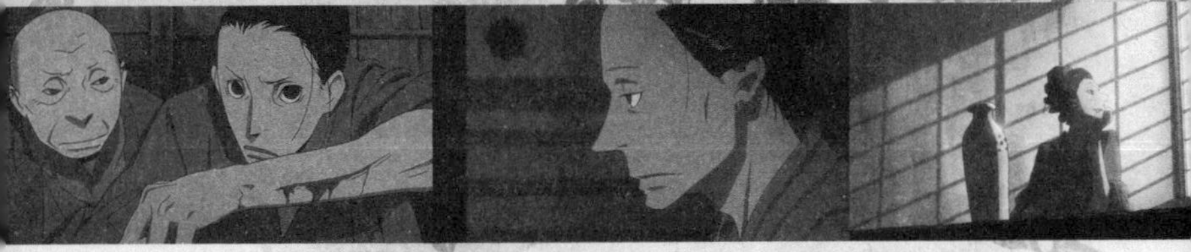

House of

from groundbreaking manga creator

Natsume Ono!

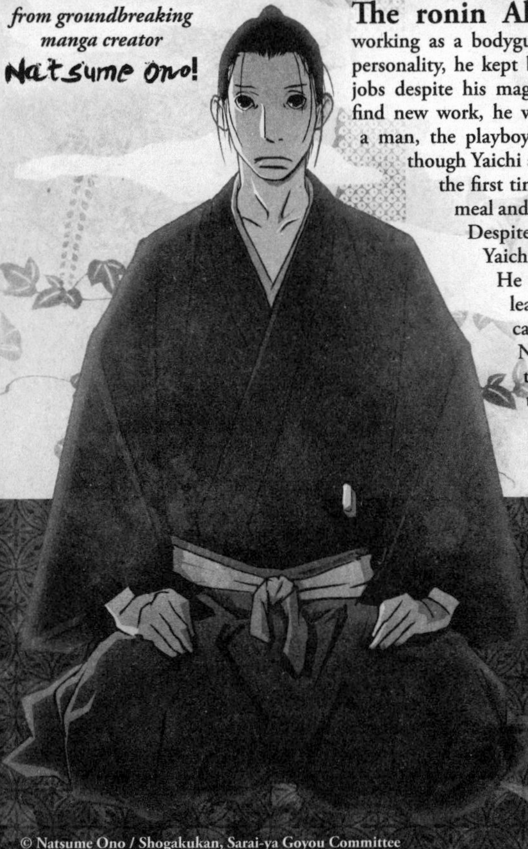

The ronin Akitsu Masanosuke was working as a bodyguard in Edo, but due to his shy personality, he kept being let go from his bodyguard jobs despite his magnificent sword skills. Unable to find new work, he wanders around town and meets a man, the playboy who calls himself Yaichi. Even though Yaichi and Masanosuke had just met for the first time, Yaichi treats Masanosuke to a meal and offers to hire him as a bodyguard. Despite the mysteries that surround Yaichi, Masanosuke takes the job. He soon finds out that Yaichi is the leader of a group of kidnappers who call themselves the "Five Leaves." Now Masanosuke is faced with the dilemma of whether to join the Five Leaves and share in the profits of kidnapping, or to resist becoming a criminal.

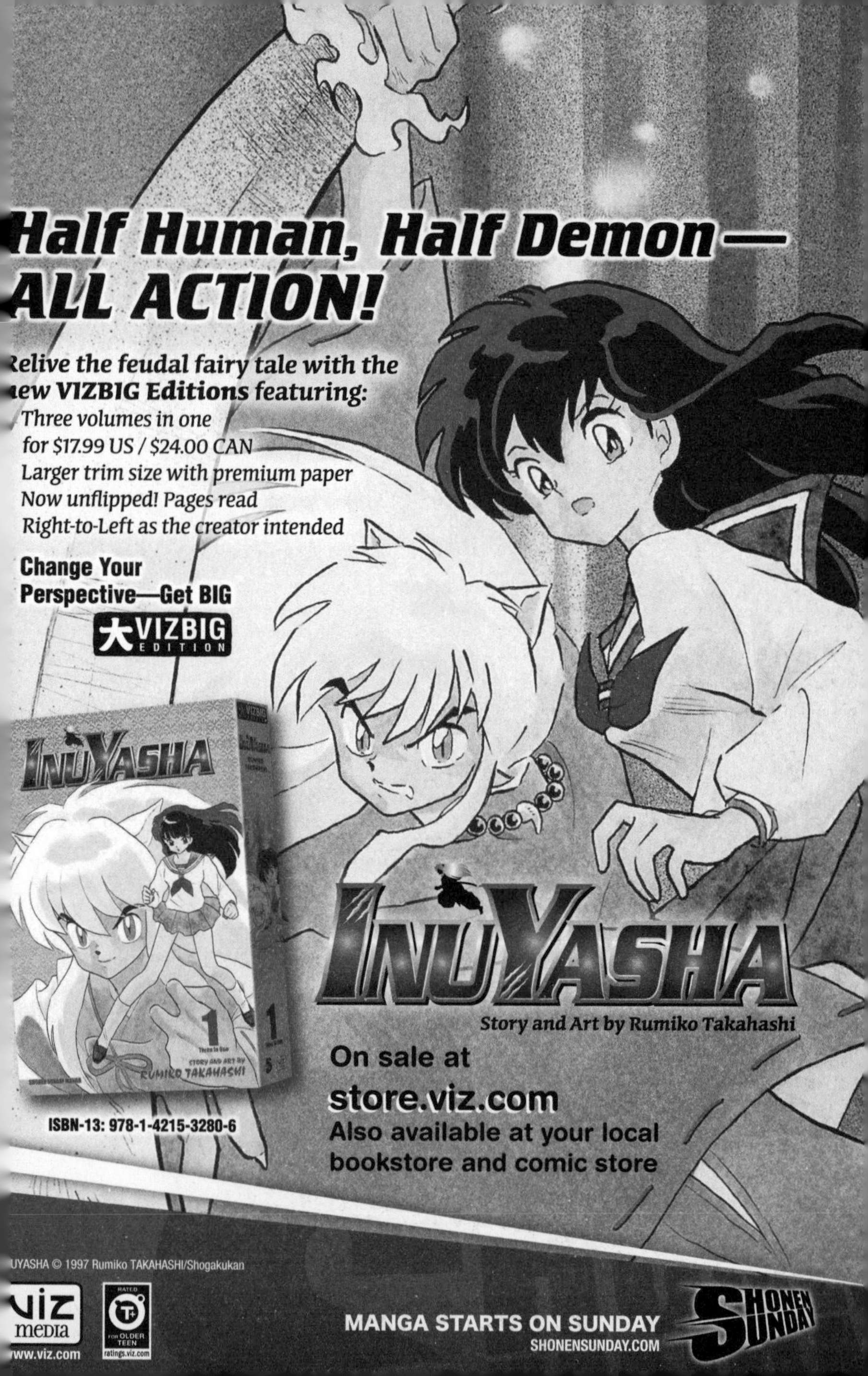
Half Human, Half Demon—
ALL ACTION!
Relive the feudal fairy tale with the new VIZBIG Editions featuring:
Three volumes in one for $17.99 US / $24.00 CAN
Larger trim size with premium paper
Now unflipped! Pages read Right-to-Left as the creator intended
Change Your Perspective—Get BIG
大 VIZBIG EDITION
INUYASHA
VIZBIG
1
Three in One
STORY AND ART BY RUMIKO TAKAHASHI
SHONEN SUNDAY MANGA
ISBN-13: 978-1-4215-3280-6
INUYASHA
Story and Art by Rumiko Takahashi
On sale at
store.viz.com
Also available at your local bookstore and comic store
UYASHA © 1997 Rumiko TAKAHASHI/Shogakukan
viz media
ww.viz.com
RATED T+ FOR OLDER TEEN
ratings.viz.com
MANGA STARTS ON SUNDAY
SHONENSUNDAY.COM
SHONEN SUNDAY

STUDENTS BY DAY,
DEMON-FIGHTERS BY NIGHT!

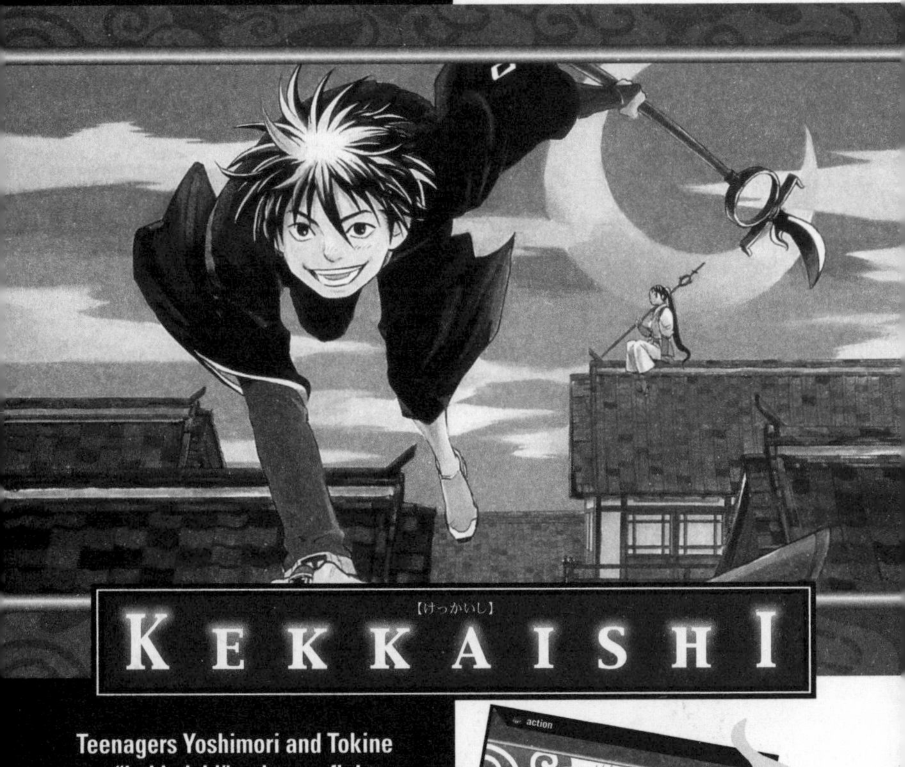

KEKKAISHI

Teenagers Yoshimori and Tokine are "kekkaishi"—demon-fighters that battle bad beings side-by-side almost every night. They also quarrel with each other, but their biggest fight is the one between their families. Can Yoshimori and Tokine fight together long enough to end their families' ancient rivalry and save the world?

Join this modern-day Romeo and Juliet adventure—graphic novels now available at *store.viz.com*!

ONLY $9.99!

viz media

www.viz.com
store.viz.com

© 2004 Yellow Tanabe/Shogakukan, Inc.

RIN-NE
Story and Art by Rumiko Takahashi
The latest series from the creator of
nuyasha and Ranma ½
Japan-North America
Simultaneous Manga Release!
SHONEN SUNDAY
RIN-NE
Story and Art by
RUMIKO TAKAHASHI
1
ead a FREE manga
review and order the
raphic novel at
tore.viz.com
lso available at your local
ookstore and comic store
VOL. 1 AVAILABLE NOW
SBN-13: 978-1-4215-3485-5
9.99 US | $12.99 CAN
KYOUKAI NO RINNE © 2009 Rumiko TAKAHASHI/Shogakukan
viz media
www.viz.com
RATED T+ FOR OLDER TEEN
ratings.viz.com
MANGA STARTS ON SUNDAY
SHONENSUNDAY.COM
SHONEN SUNDAY

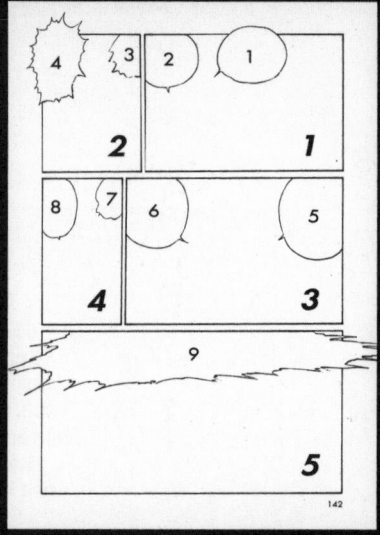

← Follow the action this way.

THIS IS THE LAST PAGE

Arata: The Legend has been printed in the original Japanese format in order to preserve the orientation of the original artwork.

Please turn it around and begin reading from right to left. Unlike English, Japanese is read right to left, so Japanese comics are read in reverse order from the way English comics are typically read. Have fun with it!